Only light can make a tree
and light can make a bone
Mother light gave birth to me
and light will take me home.

~ *Steven Foster*
1938-2003

"I didn't think it possible to make any day more interesting
than it is, but Cosmo Doogood does just that!"

~ *Bill Moyers*
Journalist, author,
executive editor of
Public Affairs Television

"This almanac makes me more alive,
more curious and bold. I love it."

~ *Coleman Barks*
Author, translator of
The Essential Rumi,
The Illuminated Rumi,
and other books

"If a book can be a celebration, then
Cosmo Doogood has thrown a great party."

~ *Paul Hawken*
Author, The Ecology of Commerce
and Natural Capitalism

"*Cosmo Doogood's Urban Almanac* is a delight to explore.
I recommend using it whenever you forget to
celebrate your life or want to go treasure hunting..."

~ *Gary Zukav*
Author of The Seat of the Soul,
The Dancing Wu Li Masters,
and other books.

"Quite simply, *Cosmo Doogood's Urban Almanac*
is a book of delights ... a compendium of joy."

~ *Terry Tempest Williams*
Author of Red *and* The Open
Space of Democracy

Cosmo Doogood's
URBAN ALMANAC
Celebrating Nature & Her Rhythms in the City

FOR THE YEAR

2005

MN

INCLUDES:
Secular and
Religious Festivals,
Important Birthdays
and Deathdays,
Rudolf Steiner's
Calendar of the Soul,
a Dream Journal,
Urban Survival
Strategies, Living
Urban Treasures,

Urban Sanctuaries:
Sacred Places and
Spaces in the City,
Urban Legends, Jokes,
Quotes, and Poems,
The Wisdom
of the Ages,
a Weather Journal,
AND
Pages and Pages of
Essential Miscellany

INCLUDING AN

EPHEMERIS

OF THE

MOTIONS of the SUN and MOON,

AND THE TRUE

Places and Aspects of the Planets

DISCARDED

FEATURING

A Daily Calendar and Ongoing...

A Field Guide to Urban Flora and Fauna,

&

Weather Predictions for the Entire United States,
for Twelve Months
(January 2005 – December 2005)

By **COSMO DOOGOOD** – PHILOM.
MINNEAPOLIS

PRINTED AND SOLD BY ERIC UTNE :: DESIGN: BOSSENOVA.COM

If the sun and moon should doubt
They'd immediately go out.
~*Wm. Blake*

THANKS TO:
Eli, Oliver, Sam, Leif and Cilla Utne;
Mark, Dana, and Aaron Bossen; Lizzie and Sally Coventry Holzapfel;
Emily Utne, Kathleen Melin, Elizabeth Larsen, Jim Lenfestey,
Will Winter, Linda Picone, Theresa Wolner, Sharon Grimes, Eric Larson,
Sarah Bell Haberman, Molly Gaines, Steven Foster & Meredith Little,
Gigi Coyle, Roger Milliken, Grant Abert, Josh Mailman, Richard Perl,
Tove Borgendale, Sharon Koukkari, Linda Bergh, Jennifer Fox,
John & Kerry Miller, Chris & Signe Schaefer, Irene Cherchuck,
Norman Davidson, Dennis Klocek, Christopher Bamford, David Lukas,
Robert Bly, Brian Baxter, Gary Snyder, Laure-Anne Bosselaar, John Fuller,
Brian Gray, Dave Aston, Henry Barnes, Claus Sproll, Marion Bornschlegel,
The Class of 2002, City of Lakes Waldorf School, Minneapolis, MN,
Mark Finser, Arthur Zajonc, Gene Gollogly, Jean Yeager, Cornelius Pietzner,
Craig & Patricia Neal, the Mud Lake Men, Michio Kushi, Bob Schwartz,
Robert Gass, Doc Lew Childre, The Donuts, SVN, Dennis Dietzel,
Susan Lantz, Ed Funk, Peter Blom, Frances Kane, Regina Brenner,
Linnea Lilja, Dominique Leveuf, Ron Goldstein, Kim Knutson,
Rebecca Sterner, Jim Gilbert, Steven Diver, Sherry Wildfeuer,
Wolfgang Held, Michael Bader, Ben Kressel, Lori Turner,
All the folks at Utne magazine, past and present, including
Julie Ristau, Jay Walljasper, and Debbie Cullen and, especially on this project:
Judy Rudrud, Lisa Proctor, Chris Dodge, Dianne Talmage, Jeremy Wieland,
Tim Morgan, Maureen Patrick, and Kristin Brabec,
And most of all to Nina, whose faith and love light the Cosmos

Cover photo: "Chrysler Building with Moonrise," © The Image Bank
Logo woodcut by Nick Wroblewski

Cosmo Doogood's Urban Almanac:
Celebrating Nature & Her Rhythms in the City

www.cosmosurbanalmanac.com

Published by Cosmo's Urban Almanac
4025 Linden Hills Blvd.
Minneapolis, Minnesota 55410 USA

Founder, Cosmo Doogood
Editor, Eric Utne
Designer, Margaret Bossen
Managing Editor, Martha Coventry

Cosmo Doogood's Urban Almanac is neither a book nor a magazine – it's both!
Magazine retailers, please scan the UPC code on the front cover. ISSN 1552-4671
Booksellers, please scan the bar code on the back cover. ISBN 0-9761989-0-8
Printed on New Leaf Good News Offset paper
100% Recycled, 40% Post-Consumer Waste, Processed Chlorine Free
Printed and Bound in Canada

CONTENTS

COSMO'S **URBAN ALMANAC**

In the summer of 1996 human habitation on earth made a subtle, uncelebrated passage from being mostly rural to being mostly urban. More than half of all humans now live in cities. The natural habitat of our species, then, officially, is steel, pavement, street-lights, architecture, and enterprise ~ the hominid agenda. With all due respect for the wondrous ways people have invented to amuse themselves and one another on paved surfaces, I find that this exodus from the land makes me unspeakably sad. I think of children who will never know, intuitively, that a flower is a plant's way of making love, or what silence sounds like, or that trees breathe out what we breathe in… ✄

— *Barbara Kingsolver*, Small Wonder

COURTEOUS READER

Some years ago, under a scorching midday sun and chilly midnight skies, I fasted for four days in California's Inyo Mountains, high above Death Valley. Alone, with nothing but water, I spent my days hiking the rugged mountain terrain or seeking shade under piñon trees and giant cacti. At night I watched the constellations come alive and their mythic figures move gracefully across the starry heavens. I had conversations with a bristle cone pine and a desert jaybird, and I experienced the full moon, on my final night, as a living being.

One month later, while standing on the sidewalk on 48th Street between Lexington and Third Avenues in New York City, a gentle wind caressed my cheek, causing me to turn toward the breeze. As I did so, I caught a glimpse of the full moon above the Chrysler Building. Immediately I was back in raw nature. Standing there in the heart of Manhattan I realized then that we are always in nature, wherever we are.

Pilgrimages to wild places like Death Valley help us connect to nature, to be sure. But what would it take for us to reestablish that connection, right where we live, day-to-day, in the city? *Cosmo Doogood's Urban Almanac* is an ongoing quest to answer that question.

Cosmo Doogood's Urban Almanac began when I was teaching the 8th grade at an inner-city elementary school and studying the American Revolution. A major source of revolutionary ideas was none other than Benjamin Franklin, truly the most influential founding father of our country. Scientist, inventor, statesman, bon vivant, Franklin sowed the ideals of independence, hard work, and personal and collective advancement in every issue of his enormously popular *Poor Richard's Almanack*. He began publishing his annual collection of astronomical and astrological calculations, planting tables, weather predictions, parables, folk wisdom, and sage advice in 1733 and, next to the Bible, it soon became the most popular colonial reading matter.

Franklin began his almanac to help his fellow colonists, over 90 percent of whom were farmers, live and work with the rhythms of nature. Today, in the U.S., even though fewer than 3 percent of us are farmers, several almanacs are still published in great numbers. But nothing exists to help urban dwellers re-establish, maintain, and celebrate their connection to nature in the city. *Cosmo Doogood's Urban Almanac* is dedicated to fulfilling that need and to following Poor Richard's noble tradition.

So, how can we 21st-century urbanites reconnect with nature and her rhythms? By looking up, looking out, and looking in.

Poor Richard's
Almanack 1733
*Introductory Page from
www.gettysburg.edu*

LOOK UP

Whatever we give our attention to and become intimate with eventually becomes our "familiar." What we become interested in, we eventually come to care for. By looking up at the night sky, and becoming familiar with the movements of the constellations and the visible planets, the starry heavens begin to live in us. We come to know where the moon and stars will be even before we look.

The same is true for the weather. By noting each day's changing weather patterns, like the high and low temperatures of the previous 24 hours, the cloud formations, the amount of precipitation, and the wind direction, the weather begins to live in our imagination and we develop what previous generations called the "weather eye." *(See p.16)*

LOOK OUT

By looking out, at the arrival of the migrating songbirds, the blooming of indigenous flowers, the ripening of fruit trees, the turning colors of autumn leaves, and the first signs of winter's chill, and noting the differing times of their occurrence compared to previous years, we become more connected with the places where we dwell. We become inhabitants rather than just residents. Our dream life becomes filled with images of local colors and textures, creatures and terrain. Looking out, we become, in time, native to the place where we live.

Looking out also includes meeting and connecting with other human beings. Rudolf Steiner, the Austrian philosopher who founded the Waldorf School movement, told the story of traveling on a train with a young man who spent the entire journey telling Dr. Steiner how ready he was to have a real "spiritual experience" and wondering if and when he'd ever have one. As the train pulled into its final destination Dr. Steiner asked the young man, "Do you remember the conductor

WHEREVER YOU GO, GO WITH ALL YOUR HEART :: *CONFUCIUS*

who took your ticket? If you had looked into his eyes when he was standing before you, then you would have had a genuine spiritual experience."

Laurens van der Post, the great Dutch anthropologist, observed that the harshest punishment in traditional, tribal societies was not condemnation, nor banishment, nor even public flogging. It was shunning, i.e., treating the individual as if he or she didn't exist, was invisible, anonymous. In other words, treating them the way most of us treat each other every day in most American cities. No wonder the theme song to "Cheers" resonates — we all want "a place where everyone knows your name."

We dedicate the Urban Almanac to the revolutionary spirit of Benjamin Franklin

Cosmo Doogood's Urban Almanac provides many ways to contact and connect with other human beings in the city. Try using the contents of any left-hand calendar pages or Essential Miscellany as conversational gambits. "Do you know Gandhi's 'Seven Deadly Sins,' AA's 12 Steps, or how to unstick a stuck tongue?" We celebrate individuals and organizations working to build community and embody the spirit of the place where they live. Wherever possible we provide links and contact information, so you can reach out and connect with them.

LOOK IN

Our final suggestion for connecting with nature and her rhythms in the city is to look in. Become conscious of your body's rhythms and their relationship to the rhythms around you. Christopher Bamford's distillation of Rudolf Steiner's "Calendar of the Soul," into one-line homeopathic meditations on the soul mood for each week of the year, is woven throughout the calendar section of the almanac. We also offer traditional monthly virtues to contemplate and practices to help you plan, review, and integrate each day of the week. Finally, we give thoughts and tools to help you establish a rhythm to the hours of your day — not for time management purposes, but to help you transform your relationship to and experience of time. Remember, nature's way is "a movement and a rest." Balance your busy day, no matter how graceful and flowing, with plenty of rest. The real work happens at night anyway, during sleep, with the help of the angels.

Yours for a greener, kinder, and more rhythmic world,

Cosmo

Sky Phenomena:
Naked-eye Observation of the Night Sky

By Norman Davidson

When I was a student in the teacher training course at Emerson College in England, I used to walk about a mile across local farmland to and from class, morning and evening, and could not help coming under the influence of the sky as it changed its face through the seasons. I remember particularly noticing the Moon and wondering what lay behind the alterations in its shape and position. Before I looked up a book on the subject, I worked on the problem right there under the wide Sussex skies.

When with further studies I had grasped the laws and principles behind the movements of the stars, there grew in me a deep enthusiasm and desire to observe more. When I found the principles behind the Moon's changing appearance, I longed to experience it again and again, and each waxing crescent in the west was a special event. The Moon became more than a fetching image; it began to speak a seasonal language. Earlier concepts of the universe were based on this Earth-centered, naked-eye astronomy and it still is the source for our immediate experience.

I was 36 years old when I started *seeing* the Moon for the first time. The educated person today often knows little about the observable sky. In 1988 Matthew Schneps of the Harvard-Smithsonian Center for Astrophysics interviewed Harvard seniors, alumni, and faculty at the school's graduation ceremony. When asked why the Moon appeared in different shapes like crescent or half, most of them said (wrongly) that it was because of the Earth's shadow. Again, most were of the opinion that it was hotter in summer than in winter because the Sun was closer to the Earth in summer (wrong again), an idea not derived from observation and an unlikely mistake for even medieval graduates or professors to have made. Altogether, only about 10 percent of the people interviewed answered both questions correctly.

The magic of the night sky has to be experienced for oneself. We can begin to remedy our alienation from the stars by direct, naked-eye observation of the night sky. Let's start with the celestial sphere.

The Celestial Sphere

The impression received on standing under the sky on a clear night is that one is surrounded by a dome or hemisphere of stars. This is the beginning of all astronomy and the phenomenon to which astronomers of all kinds, ancient and modern, must refer back — it is the celestial given. The horizon forms a circle, with the observer at the center (*Figure 1*).

A further observation follows if one remains under the night sky for a length of time — that the stars move together. The whole hemisphere appears to turn above one's head. Close observation over a number of hours reveals that the hemisphere turns on a fixed point above the horizon (*Figure 2*).

This movement shows some stars rising above the horizon and others setting. The impression is thus given of the stars being on a sphere, half of which is hidden, with the observer at the center. The sphere turns on an axis through the fixed point (*Figure 3*).

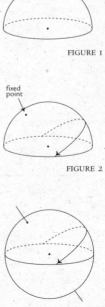

FIGURE I

fixed point

FIGURE 2

FIGURE 3

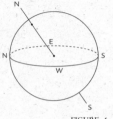

FIGURE 4

The fixed point is called the north celestial pole (seen by observers north of the Earth's equator), and the sphere's axis of rotation passes through it and down to an unseen south celestial pole. For the observer, the direction to the north celestial pole also indicates geographical, or true, north, from which the other cardinal directions are derived (*Figure 4*).

It can now be seen that, while some stars rise and set, others, toward the north, do not (*Figure 5*). The latter make circles above the horizon and are called circumpolar stars.

From our position in the center of the sphere, the horizon in any one direction appears level, and can be shown as a straight line. Looking toward the four cardinal points of the compass, the observer sees star movements as in *Figures 6, 7, 8,* and *9*.

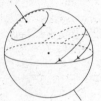

FIGURE 5

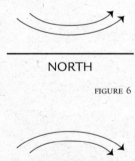

NORTH

FIGURE 6

EAST

FIGURE 7

SOUTH

FIGURE 8

WEST

FIGURE 9

The star movements are shown as parallel lines since the stars keep their same distances apart on the celestial sphere.

The Celestial Equator & Ecliptic

The Earth's equator, when projected out as a circle onto the celestial sphere, is called the celestial equator (*Figure 10*). The celestial equator's plane is at right angles to the axis line between the north and south celestial poles. All fixed stars on the sphere move parallel to the celestial equator. It cuts the horizon exactly east and west and from any one location on Earth it is a fixed, though imaginary, curve in space. Tilted at an angle of 23.44 degrees to the celestial equator is another imaginary circle called the ecliptic. This is the apparent path of the Sun through the constellations of the zodiac in one year.

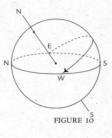

FIGURE 10

In the course of a day, the Sun, Moon, and planets move eastward to westward across the sky — virtually parallel to the celestial equator. Over longer periods (days, weeks, or months) Sun, Moon and planets have their own slow, individual movements in the opposite direction, west to east, through the band of the zodiac which has the ecliptic passing along it.

The Zodiac

Understanding the relationship of the 12 zodiacal constellations to the horizon and to the celestial equator is central to an understanding of observational astronomy. One can picture how some of these constellations lie above the celestial equator and some below (*Figure 11*). The constellations of the Fishes and the Virgin are on the equator, while the Bull is at the highest point above it and the Archer is furthest below. It must be emphasized that these names, translated from the Latin, relate to the visible star patterns in the sky and not to the signs of the zodiac (for example, the ones used by astrologers and designated as birth signs). The zodiac of signs and the zodiac of visible stars have shifted in relationship to each other over thousands of years, because of the slow movement of the celestial pole. This has caused the summer solstice point to move, on a conventional star map, from the constellation of Gemini (the Twins) to Taurus (The Bull) in 1989.

In one complete rotation round the celestial pole (i.e. one day) the zodiac can be seen to weave round the sky, sometimes standing high above the horizon, or low above it; sometimes cutting the horizon at the east/west points, or northeast/southwest, or southeast/northwest.

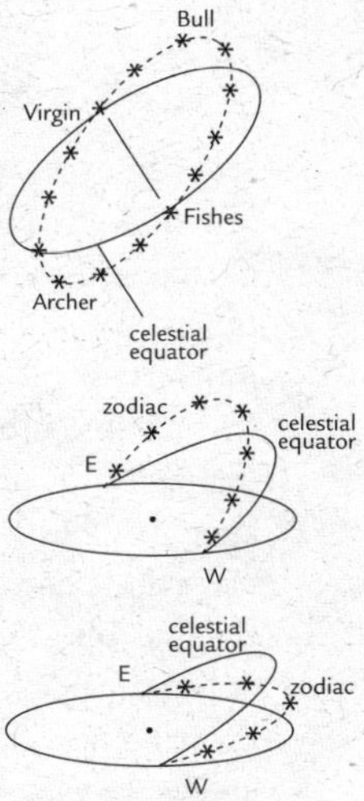

FIGURE 11

The Planets

To unaided vision, the planets look like stars. The two things which distinguish them are their movements and, usually, their brightness. There is a popular saying that stars twinkle and planets do not, which is mostly true. Twinkling occurs because differing densities and temperatures within the Earth's upper atmosphere cause light to refract at varying angles. A star is a point source of light and is easily affected by this, but a planet has a disc with a diameter and the trembling rays are less noticeable.

Planets can be divided into two groups: inferior ones, which are less distant from the Sun than from Earth, and superior ones, which are more distant from the Sun than from Earth. This particular difference in their positions gives them a completely dissimilar behavior as seen from Earth.

The inferior planets are Mercury and Venus. Seen from the Earth, they appear to oscillate to the left and right of the Sun and, in principle, can be represented as in *Figure 12*.

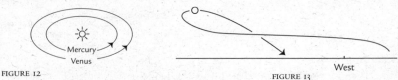

FIGURE 12

FIGURE 13

Venus moves further from the Sun and spends a longer time than Mercury does moving on its curve. It remains visible in the evening or morning sky for up to eight months.

Venus is the brightest of all the planets and at its evening appearance reaches "greatest brilliancy" toward the end of its path as it leaves the visible sky. At its morning appearance it is brightest soon after entering the sky. In 2005 Venus is an evening star from June to the end of the year. *Figure 13* shows how, from evening to evening just after sunset, she glides low above the western horizon. Toward the end of the year the planet lifts and loops backward

before becoming brightest around Christmas, then dives swiftly out of the evening sky by year's end. In January, 2007, Venus will return to the evening sky, but will step out a different dance which will take her on a high arc in the west.

The translation of an old Babylonian word for Mercury is "jumping." The planet appears in the sky about every two months, alternating between west and east, between evening and morning. It actually enters the sky seven times in the course of a calendar year, but seven curves are not completed within the 12 months.

The superior planets Mars, Jupiter, and Saturn present quite a different picture to the observer than do the inferior ones. The superior planets are not harnessed so closely to the Sun or to the evening and morning skies. They certainly appear in those places along with Venus and Mercury, but unlike them they pass completely out of the morning sky, back toward midnight and evening. In other words, in the morning they rise earlier and earlier, moving westward in relation to the Sun from day to day and week to week (*Figure 14*).

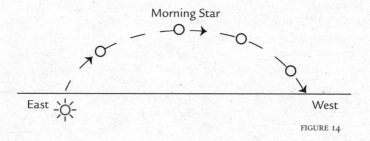

Morning Star

East　　　　　　　　　　　　West

FIGURE 14

STAR LIGHT, STAR BRIGHT

The apparent brightness of astronomical objects is expressed as "magnitude," a scale dating back more than two thousand years to the Greek astronomer Hipparchus, who decided that the brightest stars should be called "of the first magnitude," and that those stars only half as bright as magnitude 1 should be called "of the second magnitude," and so forth. The dimmest magnitude star that most people can see with the naked eye, on a clear night away from city lights, is magnitude 6. In what seems like a counterintuitive scale, the Sun, the brightest star, is a *minus* magnitude.

MAGNITUDE OF SOME COMMON ASTRONOMICAL OBJECTS

Sun	-26.8
Full moon	-12.7
Venus (at its brightest)	-4.1
Jupiter (at its brightest)	-3
Mars (at its brightest)	-2
Sirius (brightest star in sky)	-1.5
Arcturus, a bright star	0
Pointers, (at the end of the Big Dipper)	+2
Neptune	+8
Pluto	+14

— *Cosmo Doogood*

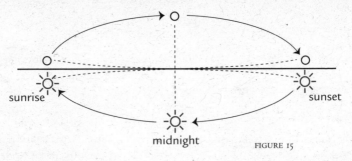

sunrise

sunset

midnight

FIGURE 15

This takes them beyond the limits of the curves of Venus and Mercury in the morning, and they can reach the midnight sky opposite the Sun. In fact, a superior planet is at its brightest when it sets at sunrise, and thus rises at sunset and is due south at midnight *(Figure 15)*. The planet in Figure 15 is said to be in "opposition" to the Sun.

When the superior planet rises at sunset, it fully enters the evening sky and continues its westward movement week by week, this time toward the Sun, until it becomes swallowed up in the light of sunset *(Figure 16)*.

Evening Star

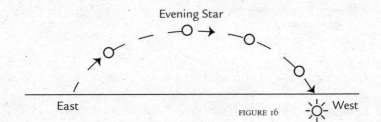

East

West

FIGURE 16

Mars spends about a year as an evening or morning star. Jupiter, which is further out in its orbit, is an evening or morning star for about 6 months. Saturn is further out still and shines in morning or evening for a little less time than does Jupiter.

For the observer under the night sky, Mars comes into opposition to the Sun about every 2 years and 7 weeks, at which time it is making a loop, taking about 2½ months to move backward (retrograde) in the loop against the stars. Jupiter makes a loop every year, spending about four months in retrograde motion. Saturn also makes a yearly loop, but spends longer in the retrograde part of it, about 4½ months. The farther out the planets are, the slower they move, and the smaller are their loops. This describes the situation for the watchful observer of any age, thousands of years ago or now. ✴

Norman Davidson writes, lectures and teaches at Sunbridge College in Spring Valley, New York. He is the author of Sky Phenomena: A Guide to Naked-eye Observation of the Stars *(Lindisfarne Press, Great Barrington, MA), and* Astronomy and the Imagination *(Penguin Books).*

For more information on naked-eye astronomy, see Acknowledgements, p. 328, and Resources, p. 328

LOOK OUT: 2005 SKY SUMMARY

This year early risers will be splendidly rewarded. The "inferior" planets (because they're closer to the sun than Earth), will be shining brightly. They will be joined by the waning crescent moon on January 8. Look to the southeast about an hour before dawn. Mars will be found to the right and above the trio.

MERCURY'S best evening displays occur around March 12 and July 9. Warm summer mornings around August 24 mean there are no excuses for not getting out of bed to catch a glimpse of the "jumping wanderer."

VENUS, brightest planet in the heavens, slips toward the rising sun as the year begins. It reappears in early June. Look for it low in the west just after sunset, sliding across the evening sky for the rest of the year.

MARS has a superiority complex this year, culminating in a flashy November 7 opposition. It begins the year near Antares (known to the Chinese as the "Fire Star"), then burns a path eastward until it reaches Taurus. On October 1 it goes retrograde. On December 10 it resumes direct motion.

JUPITER, bigger and more generous than the other planets (second only to Venus in brilliance), is a bit subdued this year. It begins a retrograde loop on February 2, reaches opposition in April, closes in on the sun at twilight in September, and disappears from view in October. Is it something we said?

SATURN, elder of the visible planets, takes nearly 29 1/2 years to go round the zodiac. This year it reaches opposition in mid-January, as it's still in the constellation Gemini. In April evenings just after sunset look for it high overhead, as Jupiter rises in the east. Saturn disappears into the sunset after June.

METEOR SHOWERS: Though the Quadrantids (peak January 3), and Geminids (December 13) are obscured by moonlight, the Perseids (August 11) and Draconids (October 8) should be spectacular this year.

ECLIPSES: A total, annular solar eclipse, visible in the Pacific Ocean, Central America, and northern South America, occurs at 20:35 UT on April 8. Partial views may be had in the southern US. There will be a penumbral lunar eclipse at 9:55 UT on April 24, an annular solar eclipse at 10:31 UT on October 3, and a partial lunar eclipse at 12:02 UT on October 17.

— *Cosmo Doogood*

LOOK UP: Weather

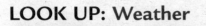

Developing the Weather Eye
How to Predict the Weather

Human interaction with the weather is as old as the hills. Those who spent a lot of time outdoors, like farmers and sailors, valued anyone who had the "weather eye" — the capacity to imagine future weather events in an exact way, based on very broad and subtle cues from the atmosphere.

To develop a good weather eye it was necessary to observe weather phenomena and climate patterns with one eye while dreaming into time with the other.

To make my forecasts I analyze daily weather data from satellites and the National Weather Service against a background of twenty-four years of geometric observations, linking climatic patterns across the U.S. with planetary motion. The rhythmic arising and fading of unusual weather is placed in a broader context of planetary movement so the large scale climatic patterns that are active behind unusual weather events can come into view. This geometrically complex work is then simplified into prognostications of likely weekly weather events.

Issues such as global warming take on a different perspective when seen against the time frames of planetary motion. As a result, climatic patterns such as El Nino and drought/flood cycles can be seen as rhythmic, living movements as well as abstract physical forces in the atmosphere.

Along with making reliable long-range forecasts, my goal is to provide you with the images and information you need to develop a weather eye. On the top of the right-hand pages of *Cosmo Doogood's Urban Almanac* are weather rhymes in the time-honored practice of the old weather almanacs. Some of the rhymes are accurate and some are simply silly. They are offered here to help ward off superstition and to awaken your soul to the sublimely poetic movements and the immense mysteries of the weather, which are truly only perceptible in the mind's eye.

~ *Doc Weather*

DOC WEATHER'S 2005
Pretty Good General Weather Forecast

> **Editor's Note:** *Doc Weather is a scientist, artist, and instructor at a California college. He has been studying and predicting the weather, using his own well-kept secret methods, for nearly 25 years. Two Chicago commodities traders have been using his long-range forecasts for years and swear they are more accurate, and profitable, than those of the National Weather Service or those other almanacs. Doc was reluctant to let us publish predictions that he'd have to make a year and a half in advance, knowing most people would compare them to the 5- and 10-day forecasts on the nightly news. But when we told him we'd call them "pretty good" predictions, he agreed. Let us know just how accurate he is.*

NATIONAL OVERVIEW:

This year we may finally see the return of El Nino as the western Pacific shows signs of an unusual warming. A warmth surge from the west that began in July and August of 2004 will continue into the Pacific near Hawaii through November 2004. In early December the buildup of warmth in the eastern Pacific will slacken. In the beginning of December the apparent waxing nature of the El Nino will subside for a few weeks.

In early **January** the surge will once again pick up and peak at midmonth then fade very slowly until mid February 2005 when the weak to moderate El Nino impulse will be over. As a result, the storm jet on the eastern Pacific will drop to the south late in 2004 and stay south through January 2005. This will bring ample rains to California, the Southwest, the Denver area, and the Gulf Coast at this time.

Look for good snows in Utah and the southern Rockies in January 2005.

In **February,** as the El Nino-like influence fades there will be a lull in the southern track. At this time watch for the northern tier states to see some fast moving Alberta Clippers, though large storms are not likely.

In mid-**March**, Mars enters a zone of influence that will bring strong weather changes to the Rockies in the second week and the Northern Plains and the Corn Belt in the third week. Watch for a strong storm center in Canada to bring cold and storms into the Great Lakes area and the Northeast after midmonth. A late March cold surge in the eastern third of the nation will bring tornado warnings to the Gulf states and cold into the East.

In early **April**, a solar eclipse will shift the action on the continent.

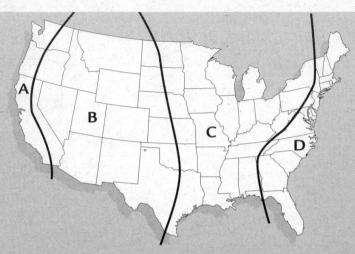

CLIMATIC REGIONS OF THE UNITED STATES
Doc Weather's Pretty Good "General Weather Forecast" considers the continental U.S. as a whole and focuses on the four major climatic regions: **A.** WEST COAST [Pacific/Maritime Zone] **B.** MOUNTAIN & HIGH PLAINS [Basin, Range and High Plains/Intermountain Zone] **C.** MID-CONTINENT [Corn Belt and Gulf States/Continental Zone] **D.** EAST COAST [Atlantic Seaboard Zone] Forecasts of each major climatic zone are further subdivided north and south when doing so is meaningful and appropriate.

This shift puts a disturbance zone over the climate gate in the Pacific Northwest (PNW). This gate controls the continental patterns. Look for storm centers to show up on both coasts as New England and the PNW are activated. A lunar eclipse in the third week completes the set and fixes the pattern for the next six months. Look for mild temperatures and settled conditions over most of the continent except for the Northeast. Expect storms and cold in the Midwest at month's end.

In early **May** watch for cool and wet conditions in most locations. At midmonth, drying and warming patterns will arise briefly in the mid-continent. In late May, cool and damp will return in most locations. **June** looks to be cool and damp with strong rains in mid continent at midmonth. Drier and warmer weather is in store for late June and early July, as wet shifts to dry west of the Mississippi. Look for an early **July** trough on the East Coast to continue the cool and wet conditions. Unsettled weather through July and **August** will dominate most locations east of the Mississippi with an active Midwest monsoon from the Gulf of Mexico. Look for unusual cold from Canada into the eastern third of the continent late in August.

September is likely to be close to normal in both temperatures and precipitation with no outstanding patterns. A pair of eclipses in **October** once again shifts the storm centers, as cooler and drier patterns dominate most of October, with moderate fronts moving across the Continent late in the month. Watch for a cold burst from Alberta to the Gulf Coast in the last week, signaling the beginning of winter for the Midwest. Strong cold into the heartland in the second week of November is paralleled by the first strong winter storms on the West Coast. The unsettled, cold and stormy pattern will continue in most locations through the last week of November.

A strong ridge on the West Coast in the first week of **December** will clear the skies and bring warmth on the coast but open the door to strong cold coming down from British Columbia into the continent. There will be mild temperatures and weak intermittent fronts in the second week. Christmas looks mild most places except for the Great Lakes as the end of the year ushers in a new pattern of storms with rain in northern latitudes just before the New Year. See the following pages for weather predictions for specific regions of the country. ☆

To learn more about developing the "weather eye" and how Doc Weather's planetary flux model works, go to www.docweather.com
>>
From Look at the Sky and Tell the Weather *by Eric Sloane, published by Dover Books.*

WEATHER SIGNS

Dew
A HEAVY DEW COLLECTS EARLY IN *FAIR* NIGHT AIR. NO DEW, *SIGN OF A RAIN.*

Leaves
WHITISH
SHOW THEIR *BACKS* WHEN NON-PREVAILING (STORM) WIND BLOWS THEM OVER.

Smoke
RISES SLOWER OR EVEN CURLS DOWNWARD WHEN PRE-STORM WINDS BLOW.

Birds
FLY HIGHER DURING THE HIGH PRESSURE AIR OF FAIR WEATHER SKIES.

Clouds
LOWER AS MOISTNESS OF A LOW PRESSURE AREA OF A STORM APPROACHES.

Insects
SWARM BEFORE A RAIN, CLING AND BITE MOST WHEN ATMOSPHERE IS MOIST

Odors
PREVIOUSLY CAPTIVE IN HIGH PRESSURE, FLOW OUT IN PRE-RAIN LOW PRESSURE.

Halos
OCCUR WHEN SUN OR MOON SHINE THROUGH ICE CLOUDS OF APPROACHING RAINSTORM.

WEST COAST / PACIFIC MARITIME

SUMMARY: January, moderate rains north, south; cool late. February, wet early, dry later. March, lamb then lion. Mid-April, wet PNW then mild, dry north / south. Mid-May, rains PNW; dry, south. June, unsettled north; dry late. July, hot south; unsettled, cool, north. Rains late August, early September, PNW; dry, south. September/ October, moderate wet N California. Mid-November, early December, strong storms then clear.

FORECAST

JAN. 2005 · 1: Storm jet to the south bringing good rains to PNW and N CA. 2nd to 4th. **2:** An El Nino-like pattern with a high in Alaska pushing the storm jet to the south on the West Coast bringing early week rain and storm to the PNW and N CA. **3:** Heavy rains in the PNW 15th to 18th. **4:** High into Alaska, wet into PNW and N CA, cold into Great Basin

FEB. 2005 · 1: Weak fronts to the north early in week. **2:** Jet stream to the south after 10th, rain PNW and N CA. **3:** Warmer with moderate to strong fronts from PNW south into central CA. **4:** Mild with fronts into PNW late in week.

MAR. 2005 · 1: Moderate fronts into the PNW. intermittent clouds and cool temps California. **2:** Mild and variable with moderate fronts north and south.Colder after the 12th. **3:** Blocking high over PNW early, dry and warmer to the south. Strong fronts into PNW 18th to 21st. **4:** High pressure pushing north early in the week and late. Clear and milder north and south on the coast.

APR. 2005 · 1: Dry, PNW and south early in the week. **2:** Strong storms into PNW 8th to 11th. **3:** Weak fronts to the north, dry and warmer to the south. **4:** Fronts into PNW starting on 21st, dry to south, but moist after 26th.

MAY 2005 · 1: Dry and warmer to south, shift to zonal flow in E Pac. **2:** Good rains north, weak rains south 12th to 14th. **3:** Colder with moderate rains PNW, dry and warm to the south. **4:** Dry and warmer PNW and CA, storm jet into Alaska.

JUNE 2005 · 1: Cool and unsettled PNW, hot and dry to south. **2:** Unsettled to the north after the 11th. **3:** Unsettled PNW and N CA late in week. **4:** Dry and warmer to the north. Dry and hot to the south.

JUL. 2005 · 1: Unsettled, PNW. Dry and warm to the south. **2:** Weak fronts PNW,10th and 11th, then dry, warm north and hot to south. **3:** Warm and dry north and south. **4:** Unsettled and cooler PNW, warm to the south.

AUG. 2005 · 1: Unsettled in the PNW early, weak to moderate rains later in the week. **2:** Weak fronts PNW, dry and temperate to the south. **3:** Unsettled to the north, dry and warmer to the south. **4:** Unsettled PNW, dry to the south.

SEP. 2005 · 1: Moderate rains late PNW, warm and dry to the south. **2:** Moderate fronts PNW and N CA early in the week. **3:** Weak to moderate fronts PNW and N CA, jet to the south. **4:** Clear and dry PNW and N CA. Jet to south, late.

OCT. 2005 · 1: Dry PNW, fronts to south at end of the week. **2:** Jet to south 12th and 13th. Cool and dry PNW. **3:** Cool with intermittent fronts PNW and N CA **4:** Fronts through PNW and N CA after 25th. High over Alberta.

NOV. 2005 · 1: Jet to south- weak fronts into PNW 2nd to 4th. **2:** Weak fronts early then strong high surge PNW, after 11th. **3:** Unsettled early, then moderate/good storms,PNW and N CA, 17th to 19th. **4:** Moderate/good fronts into PNW and N CA, 23rd to 25th.

DEC. 2005 · 1: High into Gulf of Alaska, moderate temps, north and south. **2:** Warmer with intermittent fronts PNW and N CA. **3:** Weak fronts, warmer, north and south. High builds late. **4:** High to north, weak fronts PNW, dry to south.

A

TO LEARN MORE ABOUT DOC WEATHER'S FORECASTS GO TO <WWW.DOCWEATHER.COM>

MOUNTAIN REGION / BASIN & RANGE

SUMMARY: Mostly snowy January, blizzard into February. Gradually milder into March then strong storms mid-month. April warm / dry; storms late. May warm / dry south, through June. July moderate rains midmonth, strong storm late. Settled September into October, dry / warm. Cool November, strong storms late. Early December strong, cold storm, late rains.

FORECAST

JAN. 2005 · 1: Stormy with snow from midweek. **2:** Look for an intensifying Alberta storm into Denver area. 11th and 12th. **3:** Mostly dry with possible fronts on the 17th and 18th. **4:** Cold wave with blizzard into High Plains 25th to 27th.

FEB. 2005 · 1: High Plains, Dry and Colder with winds. **2:** Moderate high south, possible fronts north. 10th to 13th **3:** A ridge to the south and Alberta clippers to the north, cold with light snows Dakotas to Michigan. **4:** Mild with maritime influences, storm jet horizontal across upper U.S.

MAR. 2005 · 1: Variable weather with fronts early and late in the week. **2:** Moderate high, Great Basin early, after 12th wet and wild storms into the Rockies. **3:** High pressure over Western states. Jet across northern tier, warmer and dry to the south. **4:** Watch our for a cold storm into western Plains 25th to 27th.

APR. 2005 · 1: Dry in the south, with weak to moderate fronts to the north. **2:** Moderate fronts to the north, dry and warmer to the south. **3:** Warmer in the south, intermittent fronts to the north. **4:** Storms in High Plains 25th to 28th.

MAY 2005 · 1: Dry to the north, warm and dry to the south. **2:** Jet into Alberta with fronts from the Dakotas to the Great Lakes midweek. **3:** Cool and dry to north early, then very unsettled MN to IL. **4:** Dry and warmer.

JUNE 2005 · 1: Dry and temperate to north. dry and hot to south. **2:** Cool, wet to the north, dry and clear to the south. **3:** Dry to north early then unsettled after 19th and 20th. **4:** Dry and warm to the south. Fronts to the north 24th and 25th.

JUL. 2005 · 1: Dry to the north, hot and dry to the south. **2:** Moderate to strong fronts with thunderstorms after the 10th in the Dakotas, WY. **3:** Moderate rains 15th and 16th, Minnesota to Kansas. **4:** Strong storms Dakotas to Kansas 21st to 24th.

AUG. 2005 · 1: Weak fronts early to the north, wet to south after the 5th. **2:** Thunderstorms Dakotas and south 12th to 14th. **3:** Unsettled early in the week, warmer and drier after the18th. **4:** Strong fronts from Alberta 21st to 25th and 29th to 31st.

SEP. 2005 · 1: Dry and warmer north and south. **2:** Weak to moderate fronts to the north. **3:** Cooler and unsettled early and late, to the north and south. **4:** Dry and warmer early in the week. Moderate fronts late.

OCT. 2005 · 1: Dry to north, possible storms in the Southwest. **2:** Dry and cool to north. **3:** Warmer and dry to south, weak fronts to north. **4:** High to north, 25th to 28th, warm to the south.

NOV. 2005 · 1: Wet and warm to south, clear and cool to north. **2:** Clear and cooler after the 11th. **3:** Unsettled to north early, then moderate/ good storms 18th to 20th. **4:** Moderate/good fronts to north 24th to 28th.

DEC. 2005 · 1: Strong cold and storms , Dakotas to Kansas, 2nd to 4th. **2:** Warmer with intermittent fronts to the north. **3:** Intermittent fronts, north and south, early then late. **4:** Storms with rains 26th to 28th.

MID-CONTINENT / CORN BELT & GULF

SUMMARY: January, rain/snow/cold; shifting to Alberta Clippers in February / storms late then mild into the middle of March, tornados late. April clear/mild/warming. May rains, early/late. Intermittent weekly June fronts into dry, early July. August, dry east / west Chicago. September, dry / west. October, dry / west; cold late. November, cold storms late into December then warm / wet /north with snow / rain Chicago at Christmas.

FORECAST

JAN. 2005 · 1: Rain and snow storms midweek then colder later in the week. **2:** Storm with rain and snow tracking from Kansas into Ohio. 12th and 13th **3:** Dry and warmer to the west with rain and cooler temps east near 17th and 18th. **4:** Strong cold after 25th, big storm central Corn Belt 27th to 28th.

FEB. 2005 · 1: Strong, fast storm running across the northern states. 3rd to 5th **2:** Stormy 11th to 14th snow eastern Corn Belt **3:** Moderate to strong storms with snows increasing towards the eastern Corn Belt. 17th to 20th **4:** Mild weather, storm jet to north.

MAR. 2005 · 1: Variable weather fronts midweek with scattered rains, moderate temperatures. **2:** Warm and dry to the south. Mild with thunderstorms, central, northern belt, cooler at week's end. **3:** Much cooler after midweek in the eastern belt. Look for intense late storms Great Lakes to New England. **4:** Strong cold storm 26th to 29th. Cold should drop far to south, watch for tornados in TX, OK, and KS.

APR. 2005 · 1: Temperate and clear, weak fronts to the north at midweek. **2:** Moderate fronts to the north, dry and cooler to the south. **3:** Warm and moist Gulf Coast, intermittent fronts central states. **4:** Storms north and central 27th to 29th.

MAY 2005 · 1: Moderate fronts central and eastern belt, beginning and end of week. **2:** End of week moderate rains north, good rains central belt. **3:** Dry and cooler central belt early, then unsettled conditions to the north and east. **4:** Warm early in week, then cooler with fronts to east, 27th and 28th.

JUNE 2005 · 1: Warm and wet to southeast, cold and dry to northeast. **2:** Widespread rains Kansas to Ohio Valley. **3:** Cool with fronts, east and north, after the 17th. **4:** Warm and wet , central and east 25th and 26th.

JUL. 2005 · 1: Dry to the north and west, moist to the east. **2:** Cool and dry to the north and SW, moderate fronts midweek. Warm and wet, central and east. **3:** Weak to moderate rains, north, central and eastern belt 17th to 19th. **4:** Cooler and wetter to the west, drier to central and east.

AUG. 2005 · 1: Warm and dry to the east, moderate rains 5th to 7th in the west. **2:** Thunderstorms Chicago to Ohio 12th and 14th. **3:** Weak fronts early then warmer and drier central and northeast. **4:** Strong cold front 26th to 30th in the west, moderate rains east.

SEP. 2005 · 1: Possible fronts to north 4th to 7th, dry west, central and east. **2:** Dry to the west. Moderate fronts central and eastern, early and late. **3:** Cooler with moderate fronts, wide coverage, early and late. **4:** Cooler with moderate fronts 23rd to 26th, Ohio Valley. Dry to west.

OCT. 2005 · 1: Cold and wet to the east, dry and mild to northwest. **2:** High and dry early, warmer west, cooler east. **3:** Dry and warmer to the west, cold to the east. **4:** Cold into Dakotas 27th to 29th, then into Gulf Coast, end of the week.

NOV. 2005 · 1: Late cold fronts MN to IL and south. **2:** Strong cold and clear late in the week, north and central belt. **3:** Storms to the north, western and central, 18th to 20th. **4:** Moderate/good fronts north and central belt, midweek to late.

DEC. 2005 · 1: Cold with strong snow storm Kansas to Ohio, 3rd to 5th. **2:** Warm and wet, eastern belt, late in the week. **3:** Alberta Clippers into Great Lakes late in the week. **4:** Storms with rain Great Lakes, Ohio Valley, 27th to 30th.

C

EAST COAST / ATLANTIC SEABOARD

SUMMARY: January, nor'easter late, also early February. Then cold / storms northeast, until last week. March storm track, Washington state to New York then colder to mid April. May storms Kentucky to New York through June. July cool/wet pattern north then warmer south. August, warm south/cool north with late rains. September, first snow last week/north. October/November cool unsettled / strong storm week 3 again early December.

FORECAST

JAN. 2005 · 1: Storms late in the week more to the south than to the north. **2:** A wet storm on the east coast at week's end from Wash. DC to NY. **3:** Good chance for a nor'easter from VA to NJ between the 16th and 19th **4:** Trough on the East coast, cold into Mid Atlantic states with snow late in week.

FEB. 2005 · 1: Nor'easter followed by cold 4th to 7th. **2:** Canadian trough with cold front late in week with rain and snow in the Mid Atlantic states and to the north. **3:** Cold midweek and later with storms late into mid Atlantic states and north into New England. **4:** Mild weather, fronts move off of the coast quickly.

MAR. 2005 · 1: Unsettled weather with weak fronts late in the week. **2:** Thunderstorms late in the week from Virginia to New York. **3:** Much cooler after midweek with intense storms. Possible strong nor'easter. **4:** Cold trough early in week , cold and stormy to the north, late in week.

APR. 2005 · 1: Cool to north, weak to moderate fronts VA to ME. **2:** Strong storm in New England 8th to 11th. **3:** Weak fronts to north, warm and moist to south. **4:** Strong low/ cooler in the mid Atlantic states, 25th to 29th.

MAY 2005 · 1: Cooler, moderate fronts 2nd and 3rd. stronger fronts 7th and 8th. **2:** Early and late, moderate to good rains, Northeast states. **3:** Good rains, cooler, late in week, KY to NY. **4:** Cooler on east coast, good rains KY to NY 29th and 30th.

JUNE 2005 · 1: Early cool and dry to north, gradually very wet KY to ME later. **2:** Trough brings cold and rain Wash. DC to ME. **3:** Cool with fronts, NJ to ME, 19th to 21st. **4:** Hot with fronts to mid Atlantic seaboard; the end of the week.

JUL. 2005 · 1: Cool and wet with east coast trough. **2:** Unsettled mid Atlantic states, early in week. Then clearing and warmer. **3:** Cool with moderate to good rains VA to NY late in week. **4:** Cooler and drier, possible fronts New England 25th to 28th.

AUG. 2005 · 1: Strong rains late in week mid Atlantic states. **2:** Clear and cool early, strong rains NE late in week **3:** Unsettled early, then cooler with fronts 19th to 21st. **4:** Cold front VA to ME, moderate to good rains 27th to 30th.

SEP. 2005 · 1: Possible weak rains late in week to the north. **2:** Cool with moderate to good late rains VA to NY. **3:** Unsettled and cooler midweek. **4:** Cooler, moderate fronts early, southeast. Possible snows NY to ME.

OCT. 2005 · 1: Strong fronts late in week, mid Atlantic states. **2:** Cold with moderate fronts late in the week, mid Atlantic states. **3:** Cold with moderate fronts 17th to 21st, mid Atlantic states. **4:** Cold with unsettled weather NJ and south.

NOV. 2005 · 1: Trough on East Coast, intermittent fronts early and late in the week. **2:** Unsettled early, then ridge forming with cooling to north, late. **3:** Moderate/good rains New England, late in the week. **4:** Cold with moderate/good fronts, early then late in the week.

DEC. 2005 · 1: Strong storm late in week, New England. **2:** Strong nor'easter mid Atlantic states, 11th to 13th. **3:** Warmer with intermittent fronts late in the week, to the north. **4:** Storms in New England, late in the week.

LOOK OUT: Phenology

The Art & Science of Phenology

By David Lukas

Phenology is the study of recurring natural phenomena. Whether you are a backyard gardener deciding when to plant seeds, or a scientist studying global climate change, you can contribute to our understanding of phenology.

Thoreau is probably the most famous phenologist. His copious journals are filled with observations on seasonal events, which he extended into commentary on philosophical and moral questions of the human spirit, suggesting just how deeply the quest to understand the natural world can go.

Ultimately the study of phenology is a personal story about your own relationship to nature. How do you connect with plants and animals? What is it that you notice or are curious about? The study of phenology is one of many ways to learn about your own spirit and love for life.

Included on the following pages are some suggestions of events to begin watching for. They are only a tiny fraction of the many countless possibilities. You may find that they don't work for your particular home region, but this is an invitation to amend these with your own observa-tions. Develop a calendar of natural events for your own neighborhood. These observations are limited only by your imagination, and you'll find that the more attention you pay to the natural world, the more connected you start feeling to Nature and her seasonal rhythms as they unfold around you.

The study of phenology is more important than ever. Detailed, repeated observations are an immensely valuable tool that will help us decide how to approach the challenges of global climate change. In Britain there is now a network of over 13,000 people reporting their phenological observations in an effort to monitor rapid changes to the environment, but such an effort has not been undertaken in North America. In this collective effort, there is no more important place to understand than your own backyard and neighborhood. ✍

(**Editor's Note:** *Cosmo hopes to help launch a phenology network in North America. Visit our web site www.cosmosurbanalmanac.com for further announcements and information.*)

David Lukas is a full-time naturalist, instructor and author of Wild Birds of California, *and other books.*

PHENOLOGY: CHECKLIST

DATE OBSERVED **SPRING**

_____ Look for restless flights of geese & ducks.

_____ Fields green up with new grass shoots.

_____ Flies on the side of the house on a warm day.

_____ Hungry squirrels and chipmunks show up at bird feeders.

_____ Early forest flowers bloom.

_____ Enthusiatic treefrogs trilling in neighborhood ponds.

_____ Sap moves in the trees.

_____ Long-forgotten flowers in the backyard.

_____ The weather turns briefly cold again.

_____ Ice disappears from lakes.

_____ Daylight savings begins.

_____ Fields are plowed.

_____ Newly arriving warblers sing.

_____ Apple trees flower.

_____ Butterflies fly on warm days.

_____ Spring in full bloom by late April.

DATE OBSERVED **SUMMER**

_____ Sun-warmed tomatoes fresh off the vine.

_____ Lots of berries for cobblers and pies.

_____ Days get longer.

_____ Turtles sunning on logs.

_____ Birds nesting or feeding young.

_____ Mosquitoes come out as the sun goes down.

_____ Nights filled with the hum of crickets.

_____ Thunderstorms billow up on hot days.

_____ Hurricane season starts!

_____ Salamanders retreat under damp logs.

_____ Young raccoons tag after their mothers.

_____ Tadpoles turn into tiny frogs.

_____ Bats dart in twilight skies.

_____ Kids search for monarch caterpillars.

_____ Dragonflies hunt over ponds.

_____ Hawks circle on thermals.

_____ Sandpipers show up again on mudflats.

FALL

_____ Leaves turn glorious colors.

_____ Flocks of small birds head south.

_____ Squirrels very actively making ready for winter.

_____ Hawks and eagles soar over high ridges.

_____ Time to rake fallen leaves.

_____ Pine cones start dropping seeds.

_____ Look for butterfly cocoons.

_____ Gulls on the beach hunker in the wind.

_____ Pumpkins are ready.

_____ Forests echo with the cries of elk.

_____ Antlered deer spar.

_____ Bears move into hibernation.

_____ First frost appears one morning.

_____ Snowbirds head for Florida.

_____ Ring-necked pheasants scurry across bare cornfields.

_____ Ice appears on small puddles.

WINTER

_____ Animal tracks in the snow.

_____ Ice-fishing season.

_____ Chickadees and finches flock to feeders.

_____ Morning mist hangs over open fields.

_____ Woodstove smoke lingers.

_____ Ducks gather in huge groups on open bays.

_____ Northern birds arrive after bad storms.

_____ Holly adds cheer to the season.

_____ Annual Christmas Bird Count.

_____ Squirrels sneak out for a quick bite.

_____ Birds already nesting in the far south.

_____ Great Horned Owls hooting on chilly nights.

_____ Days are very short now.

_____ Snow sounds squeaky on extremely cold nights.

_____ Full moon is especially bright.

PHENOLOGY: WEST COAST / PACIFIC MARITIME

JANUARY: Huddled flocks of thousands of ducks, geese, and other waterbirds wait out the storms in San Francisco Bay and in the marshy regions around Sacramento and Portland. Large numbers of bald eagles gather around these concentrations waiting for an easy meal as ducks fall prey to sickness and cold. Along the coast, gray whales undertake their famous migration to Baja California where they will spend the winter and have their calves. Great horned owls begin nesting around cities and farms and can be easily viewed in leafless trees. Iced-over ponds display flower-like patterns in the ice.

FEBRUARY: Tempted by a flush of warm false spring days, the first flowers make their appearance – red flowering currants along the coast, hazelnut and willow catkins in the forests, and odorous skunk cabbage in swamps of the north. Drawn forth by newly emerging flowers, Anna's hummingbirds in Los Angeles begin courting and nesting. Yellow-faced bumbles crawl forth to become the first conspicuous insect of the season as they buzz heavily from flower to flower in the Bay Area. Treefrogs fill the night with deafening choruses around Seattle. In bays along the coast, Pacific herring spawning runs attract thousands of predators like sea lions, gulls, and sea ducks.

MARCH: With spring just around the corner, migratory animals start moving in great numbers. Gray whales are northbound along the coast, males leading the way, followed by mothers with brand-new calves. Ducks and geese nervously bunch up then fly north in long V's stretching across the sky. Swallows make their long-awaited arrival at Mission San Juan Capistrano on March 19 (so the legend says). At every city park both native and introduced squirrels are making a ruckus with the wild chases that characterize their courtship. Rough-skinned newts are still breeding in some areas.

APRIL: Everything seems to unfold at once in April! First there are countless blooming flowers carpeting nearly every hillside and valley bottom. Lilies, monkeyflowers, violets, and many more flamboyant blossoms can be found. By mid month, warblers, vireos, and flycatchers that have spent winter in Mexico and Central America are arriving in full force around Portland. Look overhead for another show of the season's exuberant energy – there you will see hawks circling, tumbling, and calling excitedly in the thrill of their beautiful aerial courtship dances. A few common loons in full breeding plumage can still be seen along the coast, but most have already flown north to nest. Pacific treefrog tadpoles gather languidly at the shorelines of ponds.

MAY: At night, neighborhood skunks, opossums, and raccoons begin making regular rounds in San Diego, spurred by the need to find partners and breed. Many of them can be seen while crossing roads, so be extra careful while driving. Around woodlands and lawns, long-absent does reappear with their fragile spotted fawns in tow. Nearly every tree, shrub, or nest box is occupied by some form of nesting bird, from excitable chickadees to wispy swallows. Powerful spring winds off the ocean subside later in the month in the Bay Area, to be replaced by fog banks through the summer.

JUNE: Suburban lawns may show an extra bit of activity this month as young broad-footed moles leave their parents' burrows and strike forth in search of new homes. Visitors to the redwood region will be delighted by the impressive show of sweet-blooming rhododendrons. Rocks along the coast are absolutely covered in nesting seabirds this month – white gulls, black cormorants, and delightfully clownish puffins. Pods of killer whales may be seen in Puget Sound.

PHENOLOGY: WEST COAST / PACIFIC MARITIME

JULY: Super low tides along the coast make this a favorite month for visiting tidepools. In the interior valleys, acorns begin forming on oak trees, though they are scarcely noticeable yet. In the mountains, however, this is the season of outrageous alpine wildflower displays. Lupines, sky pilots, columbines, and many others create a tapestry of solid color in the famous mountain meadows of Mt. Hood, Mt. Rainier, and other Cascade peaks.

AUGUST: With grasslands golden brown and crackling dry, birds begin preparing for their migration south, starting with the gathering of massive swallow flocks in Willamette Valley and a steady trickle of shorebirds arriving from the north to feed at the muddy margins of lakes and ponds. Ripening in the lush warmth, this is the season to pick succulent blackberries for the tastiest cobblers and pies, if you can find a way to penetrate the prickly thickets. Around Seattle look for colorful, ripe madrone, Oregon grape, and kinnick-innick berries. Along the coast, sea lions disperse north and south from their breeding colonies, showing up in areas where they have been absent for months.

SEPTEMBER: No other sound announces the end of summer so dramatically as the eerie cries of bugling elk in mountain and coastal forests. Sounding part agony, and part fervent desire, this cry announces the beginning of fierce combat between males. Conifer trees across the region are fully laden with the weight of rusty brown seeds this month. Coastal waves may be tinged with red tide, a phenomenon that makes it temporarily unsafe to eat shellfish.

OCTOBER: Fall is now in full swing. Tinged red like incandescent flames, salmon surge upstream into the streams of their birth, fighting swift currents and leaping small waterfalls with an instinctive impulse that leaves the human imagination speechless. Squirrels everywhere

run hither and thither in search of newly fallen acorns to stash away for winter, stuffing their cheeks until they look utterly ridiculous, then making mad dashes to secret hiding places. Deciduous trees begin their graceful transitions from greens to yellows and reds. Swallows reputedly leave Mission San Juan Capistrano on October 23, the feast day of St. John (San Juan).

NOVEMBER: With the first full rains of the year soaking the forest litter, this is the season when lichens, mosses, and fungi awaken from their long dusty sleep. The addition of water allows lichens and mosses to begin photosynthesizing, giving them bright green or otherwise colorful surfaces. Fungi of diverse form begin to sprout from layers of needles and leaves on the forest floor. Sandhill cranes arrive from the north with loud bugling calls – standing five-feet tall they are most impressive birds.

DECEMBER: After a few more weeks of rain, things become wet enough that slugs and snails sally forth from their hiding places. Stroll outside on a wet night with a flashlight and you will be truly impressed by the great numbers and many types you can find. Rainfall reaches its peak in parts of the Pacific Northwest. Along the southern California coast, this is a time to find thousands of monarch butterflies in the restful sanctuary of old eucalyptus groves. Elsewhere, look for pieces of bull kelp washed up on beaches after powerful storms. Take time this month to sign up for a Christmas Bird Count – a 100-year tradition of counting birds for one day that is sponsored by the National Audubon Society. Look around for bird nests that have been hidden in leaves all summer long.

PHENOLOGY: MOUNTAIN REGION / BASIN & RANGE

JANUARY: Wherever the snow lies deepest, this is the season for finding animal tracks laying down their stories. You might find the signs where a coyote cautiously stalked a cottontail then made its final eager chase, or you might find the scuff marks of deer pawing down for old grass tufts. Around your house you're more likely to find evidence of the neighbor's cat on its nightly prowls, or the deep imprint of a great horned owl diving into the snow after a mouse. When visiting lakes and reservoirs, search barren treetops for wintering bald eagles; large numbers gather around Denver.

FEBRUARY: Under ice-covered lakes, hibernating animals are using up the oxygen in the water, sometimes resulting in a fish die-off. Common ravens begin their acrobatic courtship flights over the open landscape. Down in the southlands the changing seasons make their first appearance as spring cautiously unfurls in some desert areas. Courageous lizards sun themselves on rocks around Phoenix. Butterflies and spiders make an appearance. In a good year, fields of lupines and poppies line roadsides west of Tucson. Meanwhile, around Salt Lake City the immense flocks of ducks on Great Salt Lake are starting to get a little restless in preparation for their long journey north next month.

MARCH: Wander into the wooded hills of Texas this month and you are likely to hear the insistent gobbling of male wild turkeys calling from their lofty perches. By the end of the month, spring truly arrives in the desert as the sweet cooing of white-winged doves fills neighborhoods around San Antonio. To the north, cottonwoods, poplars, and willows erupt in lacy displays of flowering catkins even before setting leaves. In colder areas, American robins scan for worms on freshly thawed soil. Winter often makes a final hard showing this month with lengthy icy storms.

APRIL: Depending on the year and location, warming days equal spectacular runoff as snows melt on lower mountain slopes. Newly budding willow thickets along these waterways greet the first songbirds as they migrate north from Mexico and Central America. In the Reno area fantastic numbers of songbirds follow these moist slivers of green as they snake across the lonely desert. Around Albuquerque it's already getting warm enough that rattlesnakes start to emerge from their wintering dens to sun themselves on adjacent rocky slopes. Shorebirds move north in huge numbers, stopping to feed on mudflats around Great Salt Lake.

MAY: One of the year's favorite events around Tucson is the annual blooming of the mighty saguaro cacti. It's also a bonanza for pollinators, including large numbers of long-nosed bats that come out only at night. Migrating warblers are wrapping up their northbound migration and settling in to nest in northern areas like Missoula. Expect to see orange-crowned, yellow-rumped, and Wilson's warblers. Common raven eggs are already hatching. Red-winged blackbirds sing raucously around every marsh, and elk move upslope toward their summer feeding grounds.

JUNE: Every evening at dusk a million Mexican free-tailed bats issue from the mouth of the cave at Carlsbad Caverns National Park creating an awe-inspiring nightly ritual. Find smaller, though always impressive, flights at a cave in your own area. The high plains east of Denver are vibrant with birdsong this month, look for horned larks, several species of longspurs, mountain plovers, and many types of spar-

PHENOLOGY: MOUNTAIN REGION / BASIN & RANGE

rows, along with burrowing owls, prairie dogs, and ferruginous hawks. Coyote pups may be seen gamboling around the mouths of their dens. Calliope hummingbirds begin nesting in mountain meadows, as glacier lilies bloom through the edges of melting snowbanks.

JULY: On one of your sunset walks don't be surprised to run across a large hairy tarantula trotting alongside. In the dusk you may hear the plaintive nasal calls of common nighthawks looping back and forth in pursuit of flying insects. On a hot afternoon, the air may be filled with a veritable blizzard of fluffy white cottonwood seeds. Mountain meadows are at their peak flowering with gilias, penstemons, and asters brightening meadows in all colors of the rainbow. Bumbling young ground squirrels and chipmunks are abundant.

AUGUST: Along with the summer monsoon season in the desert Southwest come torrential daily downpours and new life for spadefoot toads that come out at night to breed around ephemeral pools. In the mountains outside Albuquerque the rains also nourish a spectacular late summer wildflower bloom that seems totally out of character with the otherwise scorching hot days. At one time this was also the month when the prairies would have rumbled with highly agitated male buffalos launching into full battle and stirring up great clouds of dust in preparation for mating. Tasty berries like huckleberries, raspberries, and currants are ripening.

SEPTEMBER: In the mountains of northern Utah, landlocked salmon known as kokanee leave the lakes they have inhabited all summer and move up into feeder streams to spawn. Looking like rainbow trout most of the year, spawning males take on a dramatic brilliant red and green coloration. Higher in the mountains, forests begin echoing with the haunting bugling calls of amorous bull elks. From Denver, many folks head into Rocky Mountain National Park for the most impressive elk-viewing opportunites. The high sharp ridges north

and west of Salt Lake City are world famous for attracting many thousands of migrating raptors this month. Sharp-eyed observers may notice the fine specks of golden eagles, red-tailed hawks, sharp-shinned hawks, and other species moving overhead. American robins begin gathering in large flocks and feeding on berry-laden plants.

OCTOBER: In a giant sweep through west Texas, more than a hundred million migrating monarch butterflies from across the eastern United States funnel southbound toward their Mexican wintering grounds. Numbers can reach as high as an estimated 300 butterflies per minute in some areas, literally filling the air like a firestorm of fierce orange autumn leaves. But the real fall colors belong to cottonwoods and aspens that line wet areas throughout the western mountain region. Drier slopes in the Southwest offer a harvest of piñon pine nuts this fall, a delicious food that humans have treasured for 10,000 years.

NOVEMBER: Pushed out of northern regions by the growing threat of winter, snow geese and sandhill cranes arrive on their wintering grounds throughout the Southwest. Most famous of all are the huge flocks that pass Albuquerque en route to Bosque del Apache National Wildlife Refuge. Along with the same movement rough-legged hawks from Canada arrive to begin feeding on voles in open fields. Elk descend from the mountains into their wintering grounds at lower elevations. Despite the cold, it is still possible to find roadrunners sunning themselves on rocky perches around Phoenix on any of the warmer days.

DECEMBER: Winter activity is best shown by the eager energy of male mule deer sharpening their antlers in preparation for battles in which the bucks fight for access to females. Deep snow and iced-over lakes settle in for the winter at higher elevations. Both bears and squirrels are ensconced in their warm dens. Steller's jays make a noisy appearance at backyard bird feeders, often chasing away hungry mountain chickadees or purple finches.

PHENOLOGY: MID-CONTINENT / CORN BELT & GULF

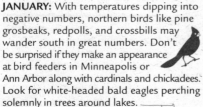

JANUARY: With temperatures dipping into negative numbers, northern birds like pine grosbeaks, redpolls, and crossbills may wander south in great numbers. Don't be surprised if they make an appearance at bird feeders in Minneapolis or Ann Arbor along with cardinals and chickadees. Look for white-headed bald eagles perching solemnly in trees around lakes. Now that the leaves have fallen, take a moment to appreciate the different textures of tree bark. Bull moose are dropping their antlers, while white-tailed deer tramp down the snow in areas where they gather.

FEBRUARY: Brief spells of sunshine give the snow an icy crust, and may draw out hardy butterflies like mourning cloaks around Cincinnati. Warm days make the buds on maples swell noticeably. Large flocks of robins begin to return to northern areas, while the first songs of cardinals, robins, and chickadees may be heard. Spring peepers and chorus frogs tentatively tune up their songs, which reach deafening peaks in March. American goldfinches molt in their first yellow spring feathers. Woodcocks begin their nocturnal, aerial courtship flights. Tom turkeys gobble loudly in distant woodland patches around Little Rock. Sportfishing enthusiasts know this is the season when largemouth bass around Dallas move into shallow waters to spawn.

MARCH: American and Fowler's toads join the nightly chorus of calling frogs. By day, the chorus is dominated by red-winged blackbirds that have taken up residence in every marshy patch. In the forests, there are a rash of early wildflowers like spring beauties and buttercups taking advantage of the abundant available sunshine before the forest trees leaf out. Some trees also flower at this time, look for dogwoods and buckeyes around Dallas. Once the ground begins to warm up look for the blue-bellied fence lizards courting with energetic bobs on fence posts. Overhead, broad-winged hawks undertake their long-distance migration back from South America. Snow-covered slopes near the Canadian border echo with the howls of wolves this month.

APRIL: Maple Sugar Making Month is the time when syrupy sap and sweet love begins to flow again. Flowers erupt into full splendor in every corner. Mightiest of all may be the vast carpets of bluebonnets that turn the Texas landscape into a piece of sky. The combination of warmth and rain draws out spring mushrooms like morels. Box turtles in search of mates may be seen crossing roads. Ruby-throated hummingbirds arrive like jewels on fire. The coastline south of Houston welcomes exhausted waves of songbirds that have just crossed the Gulf of Mexico from Central America. Northern regions start to see the break-up of ice but late killing frosts are still possible.

MAY: By now, deciduous forests are fully leafed out, creating a green-hued shade full of vibrant birdsong. Dozens of species of warblers, vireos, and tanagers defend territories and begin nesting this month. Moose and deer find secretive places to have their calves and fawns in northern Minnesota. The night air pulses with the strident songs of crickets and katydids under the occasional flashings of lightning bugs. Watch out, this is also the beginning of the chigger season. Wander the prairies in search of wildflowers with caution. Along the Gulf Coast the terns are nesting, six species in all.

JUNE: With forests in deep shade, flowers continue to bloom along the sunny edges. Look for penstemons and daisies outside

PHENOLOGY: MID-CONTINENT / CORN BELT & GULF

Chicago. Meanwhile, roadside milkweed flowers attract numerous butterflies. Berries from strawberries to gooseberries are ripening; act quickly if you want to taste one because animals are eagerly waiting for the harvest. In the north, this is the peak season for black flies and mosquitoes. Turtles come ashore to lay their eggs. White-tailed deer are growing new sets of antlers. On the shimmering sandy beaches of the Gulf Coast, flocks of black skimmers can be readily seen.

JULY: The sleepy month in midsummer can be a quiet drowsy time. Butterfly enthusiasts, however, do an annual 4th of July butterfly count because this is such a great time to see fritillaries, skippers, and swallowtails. In marshy areas of the north, this is the season to harvest blueberries. Moose escape into deeper waters to avoid the torment of flies and mosquitoes. Songbirds are wrapping up their nesting efforts, and many species are feeding squabbling fledglings. Likewise, young prairie dogs are easily viewed this month as they wander forth from their burrows and scramble playfully among dry grasses outside Kansas City.

AUGUST: Male ducks are nervous and dull-colored because they are undergoing a molt that leaves them temporarily flightless. Most retreat to the centers of ponds and shy away from your approach. The changing season is signaled by an influx of shorebirds arriving from their boreal breeding grounds. Migrating ruby-throated hummingbirds start to show up in numbers in places like St. Louis. Colorful warblers take on their drab fall plumage and feed earnestly in preparation for their journey south. In the woods outside Indianapolis look for signs that deer have begun rubbing the velvet off their antlers.

SEPTEMBER: Wherever there are mountains keep an eye out for the broad-winged hawk migration. While the most famous location to see the hawks is at Hawk Mountain in Pennsylvania, try the hills around Little Rock and other places. Forests are lively with the busy work of squirrels collecting ripening acorns and hickory nuts. Northerners savor the beginning of fall colors as aspens and other deciduous trees turn fiery red and orange. Wild rice ripens and is harvested by waterfowl. Loons gather into large flocks in preparation for their journey south. Up to 250,000 sandhill cranes can be seen in fields of the Texas panhandle.

OCTOBER: As cold creeps down from the north, the fiery band of fall colors retreats southward with the show, changing from aspens to maples, oaks, and ashes. Once the leaves turn and fall, and it becomes apparent that the songbirds have left as well, the effervescent northern cardinal becomes more apparent than ever. Juncos arrive from the north, and overhead anxious flocks of ducks and geese can be heard calling as they migrate in long formations. Crisp, sunny days can be the most beautiful of the entire year, though most people are outside raking leaves.

NOVEMBER: Newly bare trees reveal for the first time the year's crop of bird nests; you may be surprised how many there are. Cold weather drives eastern bluebirds to the warmer southern states. This is usually the time of the first snowfalls and enough accumulation that it's possible to ski or snowshoe. Lakes in the north start to ice over. White-tailed deer begin to court, but it's also the opening of the deer-hunting season. After a summer of being brown, snowshoe hares begin to turn white.

DECEMBER: During bouts of fierce cold, squirrels retreat into their cozy leafy nests high in the treetops. Animals everywhere, from mice to bears, are asleep in their cozy niches. Snows deepen, and ice on lakes starts to crack and boom as it shifts. Along the Gulf Coast, however, hundreds of thousands of birds enjoy milder weather. From New Orleans it's possible to see giant congregations of wintering ducks. In forested areas, look for freshly shed deer antlers.

PHENOLOGY: EAST COAST / ATLANTIC SEABOARD

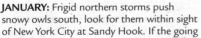

JANUARY: Frigid northern storms push snowy owls south, look for them within sight of New York City at Sandy Hook. If the going gets hard, deer may be reduced to nibbling on tree bark for nutrients. Grain fields can be filled with huge blackbird flocks looking for waste grain. Bald eagles huddle around icy feeding grounds at Chesapeake Bay, even as pairs in Florida are already starting to nest. Along the Atlantic coast, northern gannets can be observed in spectacular feeding dives. North of Tampa, manatees retreat to the warm waters of Crystal River. Near Jacksonville, shad move into shallow rivers to begin spawning.

FEBRUARY: A great season to find quiet and solitude on empty beaches, but an observant naturalist will note the growing signs of spring. Barred owls call whoo-cooks-for-you in the deep forest. Woodcocks are overhead at dusk sprinkling their twinkling courtship songs over the land-scape. A few cautious spring peepers announce the approaching symphony of frog song. Mourning Doves speak of love in their soft mournful calls. In valley bottoms the maples turn red with the first flush of budding flowers. In Florida the wood storks are already on the nest even as deep snows still grip the countryside of Burlington.

MARCH: Eastern screech owls begin courting in wooded Boston suburbs. Open ponds resound with the odd quacks of calling wood frogs and writhe with balls of mating spotted salamanders. Early spring violets and anemones bloom in Great Smoky Mountains National Park. Large flocks of American robins begin to wander north. A few courageous purple martins follow the line of melting snow north across the states. Groups of ducks and geese bunch up in restless preparation for migration.

Armadillos in Florida are out with their new babies in tow, and the largemouth bass fishing season opens.

APRIL: Spring's full splendor begins with shows of gorgeous bluebells outside Washington, D.C. Along the Blue Ridge Parkway, hillsides are splashed with the colors of blooming shad-bush, redbud, and dogwood. Poke around under leaves to find wild ginger flowers. Spring peepers and American toads fill nights with their raucous singing. Sunny days draw alligators out to sun themselves in southern marshes. Purple martins swoop back and forth in search of flying insects. Bluebirds guard boxes where they are building their nests. Great horned owls feed their downy youngsters, maybe even in the same trees where fox squirrels have their leafy nests.

MAY: Breeding horseshoe crabs carpet the beaches of Delaware Bay with the spring tide. Close to a million gulls and shorebirds gather to feed on crab eggs. Early in the month, migrating songbirds reach their peak numbers, many species promptly nesting. Trilliums bloom in forests outside Pittsburgh. Great Smoky Mountains National Park hosts so many wildflowers that people sometimes call it "Wildflower National Park." Deciduous trees like beech and maple fully leaf out, closing the forest in deep green shade. At night the calls of nighthawks and whippoor-wills ring out. After months of relative peace, mosquitoes in Florida emerge with a vengeance.

JUNE: In New England songbirds are at their peak nesting activity, while spotted fawns venture forth from the thickets where they were born. Laurels and rhododendrons bloom with fervent splendor in Shenandoah National Park. Along creeks, it would be hard to miss the hatches of aquatic insects, clouds

PHENOLOGY: EAST COAST / ATLANTIC SEABOARD

of mayflies may be especially prevalent. Barrier islands off the Carolina coast support colonies of nesting terns and skimmers. In the safety of trees nesting herons take up residence. Drawn by a mystery we can scarcely comprehend, loggerheads haul themselves onto beaches to lay their eggs by moonlight.

JULY: Time to harvest blueberries in northern Pennsylvania, though the deer flies will be biting as well. Freshwater turtles hatch from their eggs and scramble to the nearest pond. Lightning bugs fill the night with sparkling light shows. Already wrapping up their nesting season, barn swallows gather in large flocks. New England's coastal marshes hum with mosquitoes and marsh flies so there's lots of food for the birds. Thunderstorms and lightning roll across Florida. Young alligators appear in shallow waters of the same sloughs where the adults wait out the day's heat. The hot air drones with the shrill calling of cicadas.

AUGUST: Shorebirds from the Arctic arrive on beaches and mudflats. Forest greens transform into the yellows of late summer. Wild cherries and huckleberries ripen in Great Smoky Mountains National Park. Young opossums are on the prowl and may find your garbage can. In the scorching heat, vultures take advantage of rising thermals. Spiders throw out silken balloons and ride updrafts to new homes; look for their silvery strands floating past high lookouts. The first cool northwest winds trigger the beginning of hawk migration in the northern Appalachians. Along the Florida coastline, coral begin spawning.

SEPTEMBER: Tens of thousands of swallows migrate past Cape May. Peak hawk migration along mountain crests and the seashore, too. Monarch butterflies on the move. Late summer wildflowers like Queen Anne's lace and black-eyed Susans put on a good showing along roadsides. Spider webs are evident everywhere. The last purple martins wander south. Rainy days bring out mushrooms in great numbers. This is one of the months you can expect to find

bottlenosed dolphins moving through estuaries. Watch out, this is the peak season for hurricanes.

OCTOBER: Sharp-shinned hawks now dominate the river of migrating hawks. The final push of songbirds leaving the area may bunch up in coastal areas, making this a great time for birdwatchers. Fall colors abound—oaks, maples, hickories, and many others. Native brook trout begin spawning in the southern Appalachians. Acorns of the white oak ripen and are quickly eaten by black bears. Squirrels are in constant activity harvesting nuts. Robins flock to fruiting trees and bushes. Strong winds return to the Florida coast, and this is the time that southern bald eagles begin their courtship.

NOVEMBER: In the woodlands of New York, bucks have rubbed the velvet off their antlers and are ready to mate. Taking advantage of ice-free water, ducks and geese gather in large numbers, heading south only as ice begins to cover lakes. Raccoons and opossums may visit feeders at night to steal suet. Most deciduous leaves have fallen. Moths gather around porch lights at night until the first hard freeze. Witch hazel is in bloom. Winter preparations are finalized; most animals have either migrated south or moved underground. Sandhill cranes arrive on their southern wintering grounds around Okefenokee Swamp and Gainesville.

DECEMBER: Deep snows settle in across New England and higher ranges in the south. Waxwing flocks gather in berry bushes. Northern species like crossbills, hawk owls, or snowy owls may show up. Bird feeders become very active with chickadees, towhees, cardinals, and blue jays, plus many other hungry species. Leafy squirrel nests high in the trees are exposed among the bare branches. This is one of the few months in Florida that's relatively free of mosquitoes. Great time to walk the beaches in search of washed-up shells. Keep an eye out for flocks of wintering waterfowl and white pelicans. Roseate spoonbills are already nesting.

LOOK OUT: FIELD GUIDE – Urban Fauna

Pigeons
Flying Rats or Mythic Totems?

The humble pigeon, ubiquitous urban presence — with its mincing walk, bobbing head, and sweet coo-cooing — is actually the universally beloved dove, dressed down a bit. Or dressed up, depending on your taste for opalescent neck feathers and bright pink feet.

The common city pigeon's real name is rock dove, and the birds have been in America as long as the first foreign settlers. Staying around through both wilting summers and deep, dark winters, pigeons inspire with their hardiness. "On frigid February mornings, when most of us hunker down, pigeons take flight, their powerful wings flapping hard, producing body heat and their characteristic clapping sound," writes Laura Erickson, author of *For the Birds: An Uncommon Guide*. "Unlike songbirds, pigeons and doves have fleshy feet that are susceptible to frostbite, so they tuck their feet in against their lower belly when they fly. When roosting, they sit with their belly warming their feet; when walking about searching for food, they can literally freeze their toes off."

Along with their charm and dependability, pigeons — and their droppings — can also be a nuisance. Recently Paris, with its upwards of 80,000 pigeons, began constructing high-cost lofts to house 200 pigeons each. Workers will remove and destroy all but one of the 12 to 14 eggs pigeons lay each year so the adults will return to their new homes.

THERE ARE TWO TRAGEDIES IN LIFE. ONE IS TO LOSE YOUR HEART'S DESIRE – THE OTHER IS TO GAIN IT :: *GEORGE B. SHAW*

But pigeons help keep nature alive in the urban core, and, like us, their fellow inhabitants, they bring to the modern city an ancient lineage steeped in spirituality and symbolism. The dove or pigeon was Aphrodite's totem, the bird of passion, symbolically equivalent to female sexual anatomy; in India, the dove stands for lust. Roman iconography showed the human soul as a dove descending from Aphrodite (or Venus) to animate the human body. The soul returning to the Goddess after death was again envisioned as a dove. From this image, Christians copied the belief that the souls of saints became white doves that flew out of their mouths at the moment of death. In the Bible, the dove as Holy Ghost appears as St. John baptizes Jesus, coming down from the sky to transform his life.

The pigeon was Aphrodite's totem, the bird of *passion*

Despite their bad rep as flying rats, pigeons give simple pleasure to countless people on park benches all over the world. No matter what city you visit, the pigeon will be right there with you, reminding you to look around, strut your stuff, and stay the course.

~ *Martha Coventry*

>>
*Sidebar courtesy of Laura Erickson.
Originally published in the* Minneapolis Star Tribune, *February 4, 2004*

Columba livia
Columba is Latin for pigeon;
livia refers to the blue-gray color

IDENTIFICATION
What's the difference between a dove and a pigeon? There is none. When white doves are released at weddings and other celebrations, the birds are usually white pigeons. Pigeons can be any combination of reddish brown, black, white, or steel gray, and often have green or blue iridescent neck feathers that glitter in sunlight.

RANGE
Native to Africa, Asia, Europe and the Middle East. Found throughout North, Central and South America as an introduced species.

SEASON
Year-round resident.

NEST
The female builds from twigs that the male brings. Nests are well hidden, usually on covered building ledges and support structures under bridges, but sometimes on cliffs, where pigeons nested in their native range before civilization provided them with other options.

FOOD
Millet and other small seeds, bread, popcorn. Pigeons get plenty of food without handouts. In many neighborhoods, pigeons become nuisances when people feed them.

SOUND
Coos, easy for us to imitate. Also pigeons make a distinctive clapping sound with their wings when they take off in flight.

DISEASES
Pigeons are very clean birds and do not spread diseases. But as with any species, in confined spaces where droppings accumulate, disease organisms can multiply, causing problems for humans.

LOOK OUT: FIELD GUIDE – Urban Fauna

Rats!

"The largest one was close to two pounds and over a foot long, not including the tail—the size of a large California burrito." — *Robert Sullivan*, Rats

Rats. Just saying the word can make you shiver. Rats are nasty and powerful, they gnaw and sneak into cribs and spread death. They skitter along dark corners and leap at you when cornered. You poison them and the strongest live to breed a better offspring. All in all, rats can add up to one big nightmare come true.

But in all fairness, that's the reputation of the wild Norway rats of tenements, garbage heaps, and grain bins. The domesticated albino version is clever and clean, affectionate and sweet (though it still has that tail...).

Rats breed like, well, rats, with females, in a good food year, having a litter of up to 22 young each month. Although that adds up to a staggering amount of rats, they still don't outnumber people, contrary to popular belief. Conversely, when things go badly for rats and there aren't enough resources to go around, they set off on semi-suicidal mass migrations of millions, flowing over and through anything that stands in their way, even rivers, which may be the origin of the Pied Piper of Hamelin story.

The Western world's view of the rat differs greatly from the Eastern world's concept, where the rat is admired for its quick wits and its pack-rat ability to find precious and shiny objects and hold on to them. Both China and Japan consider the rat a symbol of good luck and wealth, though that doesn't stop them from trying to wipe them out. (A recent Beijing campaign laid down 300 tons of poison.)

In China and Japan, the rat is considered a symbol of good luck and wealth

If you were born in the year of Rat, according to the Chinese zodiac, you have a natural propensity for good taste, easy charm, and a funny and sharp sense of humor. You tend to be loyal and kind to your friends. A self-promoter and insatiably curious, the Rat stays on top of things and keeps his or her own life interesting.

The West is light years away from revering the rat in any way, but what is hard to deny is the rat's ability to find a home nearly anywhere, to feed itself, raise a family, and thrive in the harshest conditions and in the face of a world-wide extermination effort. If rats were people, we'd be filled with admiration.

~ *Martha Coventry*

Rattus Norvegicus

DESCRIPTION
Brownish gray above; grayish below. Scaly tail slightly less than half total length. Small eyes. Prominent ears.
Length: $12^{3}/_{8}$"–$18^{1}/_{8}$" (316–460 mm);
Tail: $4^{3}/_{4}$–$8^{1}/_{2}$" (122–215 mm).

BREEDING
Breeds year-round; like other rodents, sometimes mates within hours of giving birth; gestation 21–26 days; female may bear up to 12 litters per year of 2–22 young (usually about 5 litters of 7–11 young). Young born hairless and blind; open eyes at 2 weeks; are weaned at 3–4 weeks.

HABITAT
Cities, farms, and many types of human dwellings.

RANGE
Range Entire continental U.S.; Southern Canada and Pacific Coast north to Alaska.

DISCUSSION
The Norway rat is neither a native of Norway nor more common there than elsewhere. Probably originating in Central Asia, it arrived in North America about 1776 in boxes of grain brought by the Hessian troops hired by Britain to fight the American colonists. Loosely colonial, the Norway rat makes a network of interconnecting tunnels 2 to 3 inches (50-75 mm) across, up to 1 1/2 feet (450 mm) deep, and 6 feet (2 m) long. Such a network contains one or more chambers for nesting or feeding, one or more main entrances, and several escape exits.

Its vocalizations include squeaks, whistles, and chirps. The Norway rat is a good climber and swimmer. Omnivorous, it feeds on meat, insects, wild plants, seeds, and stored grain, contaminating with its droppings what it does not eat. It will kill chickens and eat their eggs. Food shortages and unfavorable climates sometimes limit this rat's reproductive potential, resulting in fewer and smaller litters. When food is abundant, females may produce a dozen litters in a year. At two years, females stop breeding and males' reproductive powers diminish. Snakes, owls, hawks, skunks, weasels, minks, and dogs are predators. The life span is about three years, but few Norway rats live that long.

>>
*Sidebar courtesy of
eNature (www.enature.com)*

LOOK OUT: FIELD GUIDE – Urban Fauna

Coyotes
Canis latrans (urbanicus)

"...in some areas of the literary Western world, Coyote is already taken for granted as a shorthand name for a particular figure which is out of Native American Indian lore but also in psychological terms refers to something in ourselves which is creative, unpredictable, contradictory: trickster human nature." — *Gary Snyder*

Coyote, *canis latrans*, is the most successful larger mammal in the hemisphere. Since European migration changed the ecology of the Americas by nearly extirpating wolves and cougars, their major natural enemies (after white people), coyotes have expanded their range relentlessly from coast to coast, Florida to the Arctic Circle. Just as the Indians of the West said they would.

Here comes Old Man Coyote, tras tras tras, walking through the tall grass, as told by California Indian storytellers. Coyote the trickster tricked the wary Gods to bring fire and light to earthly creatures, including humans, he named the animals, arranged the stars, got his head stuck in a buffalo skull, and juggled his eyes, losing one.

Long content to trot the deserts and mountains and Great Plains and, less eagerly, northern forests, Coyote got restless. He warily visited the suburbs — what a feast! — small yapping dogs and delicious house cats, not to mention tasty gardens and plentiful garbage. Well then, if the suburbs were so wonderful —

from Connecticut to the Hollywood Hills — then maybe the cities would be even better!

The jury is out on the wisdom of that decision, but Coyote is definitely in. Coyotes have been trapped along the lakefront park in downtown Chicago, hit by a car in downtown Minneapolis, and hunted down (with great difficulty) in Central Park, New York. Not to mention commonly sighted in the obvious lairs of Phoenix, Denver, and almost every square foot of Los Angeles and Santa Fe (where bears only deign to visit your garbage when the drought is bad).

PRONUNCIATION:
Both *ki-oat* (preferred in the Northwest and mountain states) and *ki-o-tee* preferred in the Spanish-inflected Southwest, are correct. Both derive from *coyotl* in Nahuatl, the language of the Aztecs.

Here's how coyotes succeed, in spite of intense, government-sponsored poison, bounties, fur trapping and other fruitless enterprises:
1) They are extremely wary.
2) They are extremely tricky.
3) They are extremely productive. Depending on conditions, females may have as many as 19 pups to replace those lost to predation, far fewer if population is stable.

~ *James P. Lenfestey,*
"The Urban Coyote"

Canis latrans, "barking dog"

IDENTIFICATION
Dog family, 23"-26" high, 4' long, prominent ears, slender snout, buff fur, and thick bushy tail with a black tip (said to be from sticking it into a fire guarded by fly gods to steal it for the people). Best runner among the canids, also a ready swimmer. Cagily teams up with other coyotes to trick other critters into becoming dinner. Sometimes impersonates people or other animals, usually to gain sex or food, rarely a library card.

DINING HABITS
Like you and me, an omnivore, Coyote will eat anything, from small mammals including yapping back yard dogs and prowling house cats, to fruits, nuts, winter carrion, and select garbage, very fond of watermelons, uncannily choosing only the ripe ones in your garden. Unlike you and me, Coyote is a careful eater, a wariness that helped him survive the poisons that nearly wiped out his major natural enemy, the wolf.

ACTIVITY
Mostly nocturnal, but day too, all year. May pair for life, or may not.

BREEDING
Late winter – April, 1-19 pups, often varying with environmental factors.

RANGE
Central Park to Hollywood, Miami Beach to Minneapolis.

FAVORITE SONG
At dawn, sunset, and throughout the night, a series of yips, yelps, howls, and yaps, usually to communicate with the group, who respond in chorus, annoying dogs who set to barking, entrancing humans who pause to listen.

LOOK OUT: LIFE IN THE CITY

The Myth of the City
A Search for Community
By Phillip Cousineau

Conversation, friendship, ideas, passion, and philosophy are notions one doesn't often associate with modern urban life. But in certain communities, the forces of design and culture invite us to contemplate the things that matter most in life.

The city, since Hamurabai's Babylon and Solomon's Jerusalem, looms large in the imagination as the place where the gap between the dream of community and the reality of isolation may be bridged. This has long been one of the great tasks of urban life, as attested to by the Roman adage, *"Magna civitas, magna solitudo"* (A great city, a great loneliness). The greatest of cities have been places that have embraced a mythic vision, a

This is the place where I live with family and friends and have conversations about things that move my soul. Conversations I cannot live without.

way of living that allows and encourages both community and privacy.

I have been driven to understand city life since leaving my hometown Detroit in my early 20s. When I left home I was embittered by memories of deadly riots, muggings, homicides, factory life, university days behind barbed wire, omnipresent fear, and the corrosive cynicism of most people I encountered around town. For years I wandered, from London to Jerusalem, Paris to Lisbon, Dublin to Manila, before finally settling in San Francisco, in hopes of finding a city that was as alive to me as Detroit was dead.

THE ORIGIN OF THE CITIES
Ten thousand years ago, ancient people began to settle together for the simple reason that it was easier to feed themselves that way. The first examples of cities have been found

Times Square in the pouring rain, 1959

amid the ruins of Ur and Babylon, sites encrusted with as much legend as history. Since then the chronicles of urban life are divided between the real and the fantastic, as men and women have dreamed of golden cities, hidden cities, invisible cities, ruined enchantments such as Pompeii, mystical realms like Shambhala, and labyrinthine worlds like Jorge Borges's Tlon, where "they seek neither truth nor likelihood; they seek astonishment."

"Famous cities have exhibited a persistence that transcends their geographical location, the quality of the climate, or their natural resources," writes Rene Dubus in *A God Within*. "Like the hallowed sites, they have remained true to their character despite changes in religious, economic, and political philosophies." These often ineffable qualities can be discerned while reading centuries-old descriptions of Paris, London, Venice, or Marrakesh, and realizing that the *genius loci*, the spirit of a place, defies time and challenges us to perceive them in a different way.

Anne Sofer wrote in the *London Times* in 1984, "Throughout history, from the vision of battlemented white towers on a distant hill as in Renaissance painting, to the glitter and raucous vulgarity of New York's Broadway in the 1930s — 'the city' has been an idea to quicken the pulse and lift the heart; it is a quality of excitement which London on a warm spring evening still abundantly has…"

THE DESIRE TO COMMUNE

Character, energy, heart, love, and one other vital ingredient. Arnold Toynbee emphasizes it when he writes, "What is essential is that the inhabitants of the city should be a genuine community."

The loamy roots of the word *community* lead us to the lost art of conversation. It derives from *commune*, which means "to converse intimately, exchange thoughts and feelings." The desire to commune is the core of the mystery of the city.

When T.S. Eliot's stranger in his long poem, "The Rock," asks what is the meaning of this or that city, do we respond, "To move money from bank to bank, wallet to wallet?" or "This is the place where I live with family and friends and have conversations about things that move my soul. Conversations I cannot live without."

"I have no money, no resources, no hopes," wrote Henry Miller while living in Paris. "I am the happiest man alive…."

I believe that this is what the noble cities throughout history have in common. They are places that are loved because of their continuity, their beauty, their intimacy. Cities become mythic when they transcend the perfunctory demands of the day and stand for something larger by encouraging timeless pursuits, something sacred.

"No other city lingers quite so tremendously in the memory," writes the maven of travel writers, Jan Morris. "When once you have entered the gates of Jerusalem, you are never quite the same person again." Is this not the quintessential description of the mythic city, the place that feels as if it has always existed, the place you never leave and never leaves you, the site that symbolizes the origins of all we deem sacred?

AND THEN, PARIS

"I have no money, no resources, no hopes," wrote Henry Miller while living in Paris. "I am the happiest man alive…"

Toynbee wrote in *Cities of Destiny*, "No one conscious of being part of Western civilization has, since the Middle Ages, ever been able to enter Paris wholly as a stranger. He comes conscious of a fundamental debt, and confident of recapturing an ancient inspiration. Even as a man in age may revisit a lover of his youth, or an exile after long wandering return to a second home."

This image of the second home is striking and illuminates for me the mystery of why Paris evokes more nostalgia than perhaps any city other than Jerusalem in all the world. Curiously enough, *nostalgia* refers to "the returns," the various attempts of the surviving Greek soldiers to return home after the Trojan War. What the word is telling us is that there is something deep in the Western soul that is always striving to find its home.

Japanese restaurant, San Francisco

Jazz in the street, Paris

"A city should be an organization of love," wrote Lewis Mumford in his 1938 classic, The Culture of Cities.

Perhaps the finest lesson I have learned from my time in far-flung places like Jerusalem, Dublin, Manila, and Paris is a new commitment of attachment to my own home ground. The beauty of the myth of great cities is that they teach us, like American Indians say, that every place is in the center of the world, including our own home. While mythic cities may inspire awe and devotion, the greatest of them all don't defeat us through spiritual or cultural intimidation, but remind us to take that devotion and attention home with us. ✂

Excerpted from Once and Future Myths

Phillip Cousineau leads tours and lectures on mythology, creativity and other subjects, and is the author of 17 books. For more information, see: www.philcousineau.net

LOOK OUT: LIFE IN THE CITY

The Joys of Walking
Solo, A Deux, En Masse
By Christopher Bamford

How many pairs of shoes did Dante wear out writing *The Divine Comedy*, wondered the Russian poet Osip Mandelstam. For Mandelstam, poetry and walking were so closely connected that he could not imagine Dante composing his great work other than on foot, walking the streets of Florence and the Italian towns and countryside of his exile.

In Japanese, the word for walk is the same word used for Buddhist practice

Mandelstam himself, like many poets and artists, knew that he had to move whenever he felt a poem or piece of prose "coming down." The experience would begin with a musical phrase, ringing insistently in his ear. At first, he would try to escape it, tossing his head, as though the phrase could be shaken out of his ear like a drop of water. Then, in a heightened state of excitement and anticipation, he would begin to move. He would start to walk, first inside his apartment, and then out into the streets, bending slightly forward, straining to catch this music from another source and translate it into words. Sometimes he would walk for 24 hours or more, crisscrossing St. Petersburg, stopping rapt in thought when the occasion demanded, until the inner voice — the daimon — ceased.

No one knew the importance of walking better than Henry David Thoreau, who, lamenting its loss, wrote in his inimitable way: "*I have met but with one or two persons in the course of my life who understood the art of Walking, that is, of taking walks, — who had a genius so to speak for sauntering; which word is beautifully derived "from idle people who roved about the country in the Middle Ages, and asked for charity, under the pretence of 'going a la Sainte Terre,' to the* Holy Land, *till the children exclaimed, 'there goes* a *Sainte-Terrer,'* — *'Saunterer,'* — a *Holy-Lander. They, who never go to the Holy Land in their walks, as they pretend, are indeed mere idlers and vagabonds; but they who do go there are saunterers, in the good sense, such as I mean. Some, however, would derive the word from* sans terre, *without land or home, which, therefore, in the good sense, will mean, having no particular home, but equally at home everywhere."*

Everywhere walking is the principle metaphor of the spiritual journey. In Japanese, for instance, the word for walk is the same word used for Buddhist practice: the practitioner is the walker, the path the walk walked. Rama Coomaraswamy tells the story of a blind man and a lame man set out for "the Holy City." They could make no progress until they joined forces, the lame man climbing on the back of the blind one and directing his footsteps.

The great Western thinkers have been great walkers. Hegel walked the *Philosophenweg* (the Philosopher's Way) named after him in Heidelberg, and Kant as an old man still shuffled down the *Philosophen-damm* (the Philosopher's Wall) in Königsberg. Kierkegaard endlessly paced and recorded his pacings through the streets of Copenhagen. Goethe dictated all his works on the hoof, walking back and forth in his garden.

Brenda Ueland in Minneapolis, 1939: "It is much better to walk alone — no cackle of voices at your elbow to jar the meditative silence of the morning."'

Centuries before, the Troubadours, nomadic, sauntering composers, walked (or rode) through Provence, creating the first civilization based upon love. Dante walked with Guido Cavalcanti and the other poets of the dolce stil nuovo; Ficino walked with his friends, who made up the Academy. Closer to our own time, the Wordsworths and Coleridge walked in the Lake District — and English Romanticism was born. Meanwhile, in London, "little" John Keats had his greatest insights — "negative capability," for instance — walking with his friend Dilke. In America, Emerson, Thoreau, Bronson Alcott, Margaret Fuller, Melville, Hawthorne, and Whitman all walked, many of them together, to create Transcendentalism. Rousseau, another great walker, when writing his *Reveries of a Solitary Walker*, would leave his cottage at dawn and return at nightfall, having walked all day, to write out a complete meditation, never needing to alter a word. He put it most succinctly: "I can only meditate when I am walking. When I stop I cease to think."

Rousseau, as always, was perhaps too extreme. Stopping, in fact, is as inherent to walking as absence is to friendship. Think of barefoot Socrates, cruising Athens and the quiet, sacred spots around it, in search of knowledge

NOTHING IS LESS IN OUR POWER THAN THE HEART, AND FAR FROM COMMANDING WE ARE FORCED TO OBEY IT :: *J. ROUSSEAU*

to be imparted and gained through conversation. From time to time he too, like Mandelstam, would be halted in his tracks by direct congress with the gods. Then he would stand, riveted to the ground, for hours on end, and those with him would simply have to wait.

In this practice of walking, Socrates was following a pattern well established by his rivals, the Sophists, who were famous wanderers and roving lecturers. Plato, likewise, with his Academy, walked and talked, stopping now and then to elicit geometric insights by drawing figures in the dirt. After Plato, Aristotle, when he set up his school, created a special colonnade or covered walk, called a peripatos, which gave the school its name: the Peripatetic (or walking) School.

To walk is to move one's body, soul, and spirit rhythmically and harmoniously through the world

Jesus was a great — perhaps the greatest — walker, moving constantly from one place to the next with his disciples and the women closest to him. He would teach (talk) as he walked, conversing on the dusty road with those about him, stopping when-

ever a crowd gathered and addressing them before moving on again.

To walk is to move one's body, soul, and spirit rhythmically and harmoniously through the world, all one's senses engaged in its variety, its beauty, truth, and goodness. The walker, in the high sense Thoreau alludes to, is in the world but not of it. One can do this alone, in solitude, or better together with others, either with a single, best friend or in a group. One never really walks alone. In either case, walking initiates one into a quasi-esoteric order: the order of friends, for walking and friendship go together "like a horse and carriage" as the old song puts it. A friend is the one with whom we walk the path. As Thoreau writes, "My companion and I, for sometimes I have a companion, take pleasure in fancying ourselves knights of a new, or rather an old, order — not equestrians or Chevaliers, not Ritters or riders, but Walkers, a still more ancient and honorable class I trust." ✦

Christopher Bamford is editor at SteinerBooks and Lindisfarne Books. He is the author of Voice of the Eagle: The Heart of Celtic Christianity *and* An Endless Trace: The Passionate Pursuit of Wisdom in the West. *Recently he edited and introduced* Start Now! The Spiritual Exercises of Rudolf Steiner.

LOOK OUT: LIFE IN THE CITY

Urban Eden
Grow delicious fruit, vegetables, and herbs in a really small space
By Adam and James Caplin

Every year, enough herbs, fruit, vegetables and salad leaves grow in James's garden for his family to have something homegrown in a meal almost every day, summer, spring and autumn. Even in winter there is often something to pick and eat. His garden isn't a vast vegetable plot, nor a kitchen garden. In fact it's a very small but luscious patch of jungle in the heart of the city. It is only 20 feet by 20 feet but there are runner beans twining through jasmine and wisteria, spinach growing beneath roses and great foaming pots of lettuce. James is not a professional gardener, nor is he someone with plenty of time on his hands. He lives a normal, stressed urban existence, with too much to do and too little time to do it.

In another part of the city, on a rooftop high above the traffic, Victoria plum trees thrive amongst tomatoes and nasturtiums. There are cherries and pears, and windowboxes filled with salads. Honeysuckle and viburnum scent the air. For the owner, this rooftop is a sanctuary as well as a source of delicious fresh food and constant beauty. These are Urban Edens. They are small town or city gardens, often surrounded by other gardens and houses, but as close to the Biblical picture of Paradise as you can get in this life.

Urban Eden gardening isn't, of course, anything new. In many ways, it's a return to an older sort of gardening, going right back to the Biblical idea of a Paradise before the fall. As it says in Genesis: "Then the Lord God planted a Garden in Eden, in the East, and there he put the man he had formed. He made all kinds of beautiful trees to grow there and produce good fruit." At some unknown but significant turning point food became so plentiful that to produce it yourself became a sign of poverty.

Creating a garden like this changes more than just the garden. With edibles growing and being used through the year, the impact of the seasons is felt more strongly and the natural rhythms of life are reinforced. When the sweet-corn seedlings go out, and there are a couple of rainy days, and they start to

Salads still juicy from the garden taste deliciously delicate and wonderfully strong at the same time

swell and shoot ahead, the drizzle comes as a positive boon. When the peaches are on the point of ripening, every sunny day has an extra resonance.

Urban Eden gardening is both exciting and satisfying. When something delicious comes from the garden, it's a triumphant feeling. You are, in a powerful and primitive way, making food. You are a provider. Fresh food always tastes better than store-bought food. Carrots lose flavour within hours of being picked; salads still juicy from the garden taste deliciously delicate and wonderfully strong at the same time. Soup cooked with dried rosemary is nowhere near as delicious as soup cooked with leaves just picked from a bush. The fact that it is your own rosemary, just plucked from the garden, adds to the pleasure.

Seed catalogues offer an extraordinary number of different varieties of vegetables, hundreds more than those typically grown commercially for their qualities of heavy and reliable cropping and long storage. Other varieties offer different advantages, each providing some peculiar delight. You can choose carrots that are short or long, round or tapered, big-rooted, small-rooted, early-cropping, late- cropping, dark orange, light yellow, sweet tasting, crisp, long-storing, disease-resistant...and so on, and on. The same is true for most vegetables — you only usually see red tomatoes in the shops, but you could grow yellow, orange, white, striped and even black ones, and in many different shapes and sizes.

When you grow your own it also makes you more aware of what is happening in the food chain. Much of the food we are now sold is either forced indoors, or imported from

EASIEST HERBS AND VEGETABLES FOR CONTAINERS

VEGETABLES	HERBS
French Beans	Small-leafed Basil
Runner Beans	Bay Leaves
Chard	Pot Marjoram
Cut-and-come-again Lettuces	Mint
Peppers	Myrtle
Potatoes	Oregano
Shallots	Rosemary
Sorrel	Thyme
Spinach	
Tomatoes	

abroad. You can only wonder what farmers have to do to get their fruit to look perfect and shiny enough for the supermarkets, as home grown specimens, grown without regular applications of pesticide and fungicide, are nowhere near so perfectly formed, and never as shiny.

When you have great-tasting food in the garden, cooking becomes easier. Garden-fresh vegetables are often so delicious that they are best served plain, rather than being "improved" with sauces and complex recipes. A good crop can help suggest an entire meal. With a superb crop of tiny French beans, the cook thinks about what will be delicious with the beans, rather than treating them as an accompaniment to a main dish. Urban Eden gardening can save you money, too. A salad from the garden, followed by a sorrel omelette made, of course, with home-picked sorrel, ending with a couple of your own ripe figs, tastes sublime, and costs hardly anything.

Gardening like this has other profound effects on the gardener. With a constant supply of ever-changing edible plants in the garden, it is tempting to go into the garden even more, if only to check on what is ready to pick and eat. Looking closely at plants, regularly, brings to one's

A well-designed urban garden requires as much, or as little, time as you want to give it.

attention all the other creatures that live in and amongst the plants, creatures that are all too often ignored. This includes birds and insects, slugs and snails. These creatures have a vital part to play and fascinating lives and habits. Once you get interested in them, they become less unnecessary pests or thieves than things with their own mysterious beauty.

Becoming aware of insect life and eating your own produce means it makes sense to be careful about what is sprayed on the garden. The less you spray, the more creatures will make their home there and eventually the balance will often tip against the pests, making it easier to maintain your garden without chemicals. An Urban Eden should hum with life, morning, noon, and night.

It is partly because of the interplay of all these elements that this way of gardening doesn't have to be time-consuming. Designed in the right way, an Urban Eden can thrive perfectly well if you don't have much time for it, and do better if you have more time for regular care.

Urban Eden gardening can also be quite a social activity. When there is a glut — even three runner bean plants, at the height of the season, can produce beans by the bagful — these can be shared with friends and neighbours. In return, you will probably receive something they have grown or cooked. Such exchange brings rewards of its own, reinforcing the sense of community that is such a vital part of urban life.

Garden-fresh vegetables are often so delicious that they are best served plain

A luscious garden in full swing is a delight for children. When they can go into the garden and pick their own fresh strawberries, even if there aren't many of them, it fires up an interest in plants, an appreciation which can be invaluable for an urban child. There are all sorts of wonderful lessons, from basic ones like the difference between ripe and unripe colours to the pleasure of nurturing, the miracle of planting their first seeds and having plants grow from them. Children love the process of picking food, and having it appear later on the table, transformed by cooking into something that they love to eat. The Urban Eden can be a place of magic for them.

But you don't even have to have a garden to grow something delicious in the middle of a city, as long as you have some access to the open air. When James lived in a flat with only a balcony, he grew a big terracotta pot full of new potatoes, and one glorious summer evening when entertaining some friends, tipped out the pot, scrubbed off the potatoes, and ate them there and then with butter and fresh garlic. Paradise, in the middle of the city. Welcome to the Urban Eden! ✒

ORNAMENTALS AND EDIBLES

It makes no sense for an Urban Eden gardener to distinguish plants into ornamental and edible categories. The division may have been useful once, but now it is just restrictive. In reality some edible plants are ornamental and some ornamental plants are edible; some supposedly edible plants are not really worth eating and some supposedly ornamental plants aren't particularly attractive.

The runner bean is a good example. It's a magnificent climber, with superb flowers, elegant fruit, and a striking leaf. If the beans weren't edible, more people might grow it in their back gardens! Ironically, it was first introduced into Europe as an ornamental. The Jerusalem artichoke *Helianthus tuberosus* is a relative of the sunflower, with a tall stem and striking yellow flowers; you get the added bonus of its edible tubers. The majestic artichoke *Cynara scolymus* can illuminate an area of border all by itself with its striking powdery green leaves and stunning flowerheads. But because they are thought of as edibles they are all too rarely grown in the ordinary back garden.

~ *Adam and James Caplin*

LOOK OUT: LIFE IN THE CITY

Foraging
Hunting for Urban Treasure
By Martha Coventry

Most city streets and back alleys are a veritable cornucopia of discarded or underappreciated treasures, if only you have the eyes to see them. For the modern day hunter-gatherer, foraging in the city is fun, it reconnects us to nature, and it gives us that rare taste of self-sufficiency that we can long for in our mostly comfortable urban lives.

Pick lilacs wherever and whenever you can to fill every vase in your house

Take a walk along residential city streets in the late winter and scope out the bundles of fruit-tree trimmings left on the curb. In Minneapolis, they need to be cut in fireplace lengths and tied with a string for the garbage haulers — perfect to tuck under your arm. Or, better yet, bring back your car and take away as much wood as you can. After several months kept dry, that throw-away wood will make a lovely fire and scent the surrounding air with sweet perfume.

As the snow finally melts and things start to green up, go into your unfertilized yard — or those of like-minded neighbors — and pick the first tender dandelion leaves before the plant starts to flower. Cut them off at the root crown so they hold together, wash and dry well, and toss them into a salad with other greens for their faintly acid taste. Or mix them with sizzling hot bits of salt pork like the French do, and dash them with vinegar.

A little later in the spring, towards late April or May, wild violets appear in almost every slightly untended yard and copse of wood. Pick them for the first bouquet of the year, or brush the petals with foamy egg white, sprinkle them all over with finely granulated sugar, and let stand until completely dry. Use them that night to lend a civilized purple beauty to a dish of vanilla ice cream or tapioca, a cheese cake or panna cotta.

And spring, too, is the time for one of the few things in life that are made for stealing – lilacs… fleeting, bountiful, joyously fragrant. The most honest of souls are known to carry little clippers in their purse or pocket, ready to nip flowers that are over-hanging sidewalks, or to scuttle into church parking lots in the evening to raid the bordering hedges. While driving in the country, you can spot lilac bushes growing tall and unkempt, the last remnants of a farm-stead long since gone. Pick lilacs wherever and whenever you can to fill every vase in your house.

Foraging isn't theft, it's public-spirited, civic-minded resourcefulness.

Raspberry bushes are difficult to maintain and many city gardeners simply give up after a few years, tired of figuring out the old canes from new and which ones to prune and when. Detour down the alleys in your neigh-borhood and you might see raspberry bushes run amok. You can grab a handful of berries here or there, but better even, knock on your neighbor's door and ask if you can pick them. If the answer is yes — as it probably will be — bring back a jar of homemade jam for a thank you.

Another berry goes completely unnoticed in the city for its goodness. It's the mulberry, the fruit that stains sidewalks purple in July and August and is viewed as pretty much of a nuisance. Look up next time you notice those telltale blotches under your feet and reach to pick a few berries. You'll find most are sweet and full of juice. Then eat or cook them the way you would their look-alike wild cousin, the blackberry.

Fall in most of the country is the last chance for urban foraging, but it happily offers up that most American fruit, the apple. Just the deadfall alone, picked up in a neighbor's yard, can be enough for several pies or jars of applesauce. And you'd be surprised how many varieties there can be in the city. Follow the raspberry rule, knock on the door and ask permission to gather the fruit that is obviously going to waste. Chances are you'll be invited to take all the apples you want and to come back to pick more. Follow the raspberry rule again and return with a freshly baked apple crisp. ✄

Foraging for the pleasures of hearth and home offers lots of opportunities all over the country. Send your ideas to ideas@cosmosurbanalmanac.com for next year's Cosmo Doogood's Urban Almanac. Happy foraging!

LOOK OUT: GREAT IDEAS

Ben Franklin Day

Forget Presidents Day:
Make a Holiday for Ben Franklin

By David Morris

Once upon a time, we celebrated two birthdays in the month of February: George Washington's and Abraham Lincoln's. One president founded a nation. The other kept it together. Now we celebrate a single Presidents Day and lump together all former chiefs of state, the noble and the criminal, the noteworthy and the nitwits. Let's dump this ridiculous collective birthday and instead use that day to honor the single greatest of all Americans — Benjamin Franklin!

No matter what your ideological persuasion, Ben Franklin is a role model. He was perhaps our greatest exemplar of individual initiative and yet he also devoted much of his life to public service.

Franklin's life was filled with individual accomplishment, "God helps those who help themselves," Franklin insisted. He was one of our most prolific inventors, a world-renowned scientist and perhaps the colonies' greatest entrepreneur. Yet he fervently believed that all innovation is a cooperative process. In 1744, he invented the smokeless fireplace, quickly dubbed the Franklin stove, but refused to patent it because "as we enjoy great Advantages from the Inventions of others, we should be glad of an Opportunity to serve others by any Invention of ours."

In 1750, Franklin published *Experiments and Observations on Electricity*. To a world fascinated and confounded by

THERE IS NO SECURITY ON THIS EARTH, THERE IS ONLY OPPORTUNITY :: *GEN. DOUGLAS MACARTHUR* the newly discovered force of electricity Franklin's clear explanations became a worldwide best seller. The book went into ten printings and was translated into four languages.

Cooperation and collective effort also marked his approach to social inventions. In 1727, at the age of 21, he created the Junto Club in Philadelphia. Members addressed social problems and proposed solutions. After a solution was devised, Franklin spread the word by discussing the solution in his newspaper. Then, again through his paper, he would invite the general public to an action-oriented meeting. This process led to the creation of Philadelphia's first fire department in 1736, and later, its street department and a plan for street lighting. In 1743, Franklin established the still extant American Philosophical Society, a sort of intercolonial Junto.

No matter what your ideological persuasion, Ben Franklin is a role model... He fervently believed that all innovation is a cooperative process

Franklin blended public spiritedness and private enterprise. By the 1730s, he was not only the public printer for Pennsylvania, but for Delaware, New Jersey, and Maryland. He helped establish printers in many colonies. Usually Franklin trained these printers and provided the investment capital for them to set themselves up in the printing business. Franklin received one third of the profits. In 1733, he published *Poor Richard's Almanack*. By 1748, the Almanac was selling 10,000 copies a year, enabling Franklin to retire and live comfortably off his investments and businesses for the rest of his long life.

Franklin's successes in the private sector did not turn him against the public sector. In 1753, he was appointed deputy postmaster general of the colonies. By 1761, the postal service was generating its first operating profit. When people complained about government taxes, he responded this way. Yes, taxes were a burden, but "we are taxed twice as much by our idleness, three times as much by our pride, and four times as much by our folly, and from these taxes the commissioners cannot deliver us."

In 1787, at age 81, Franklin was the oldest delegate to the Constitutional Convention and his presence lent credibility and legitimacy to that momentous occasion. That same year he became the president of the Pennsylvania Abolition Society, the oldest antislavery organization in the world. His last public act was to send to Congress a petition to end "the traffic in the persons of our fellowmen."

Ben Franklin died on April 17, 1790. If any American ever deserved a day of celebration it is Benjamin Franklin, the man the French economist Turgot, a contemporary of Franklin, described in these words, "He snatched the lightning from the skies and the scepter from the tyrants." ✍

LOOK IN: The Living Year

The Living Year &
The Alchemy of Time
Finding Our Feet on the Earth Again
By Christopher Bamford

All natural phenomena, from the smallest microorganisms to the galaxies, are rhythmic. We ourselves are rhythmic beings, from our breathing and heartbeat to the more hidden circulation of energies through our bodies. Rhythm seems to define life itself. Earlier human beings understood this and sought to embody a living sense of time based on the rhythmic workings of nature in all aspects of their lives. Today, however, we live cut off from these rhythms.

Five hundred years ago, Copernicus, Galileo, and Newton changed our world. We now live almost exclusively in space. Living time, once the great unifier, was reduced to linear, external, objective clock time: spatial, tape-measure time. We lost the sense of cyclical process and activity. We lost time's wholeness, in which everything is interconnected and recursive — each part connected to every other part.

ANCIENT TIME

Life for the ancients was guided by living time. The sky moved rhythmically over their heads in a great circle. It was alive. Day followed night, night followed day. Sun and moon rose and set, shifting from east to west across the horizon. The seasons turned. At night, the planets, stars, and galaxies wheeled through the darkness in graceful cyclical patterns. The Earth herself pulsed with life. Fecund and resonating, its cycles moved in cosmic harmony from seed to fruit to seed again.

Zodiacal Man

The human task was to bring body, soul, and mind into harmony with the heavens. This was the basis of religion, economy, government, and ordinary life. Even a person was not the "object" who stood before you, but a part of this holy, rhythmic time extending from before birth through life to death and beyond. The qualities of each month, day, hour, and even minute were recognized and acknowledged in the temples. There was a sense of unity – of the oneness of all life. Poetry, music, drama, and dance flourished, still connected to the cosmic sources of rhythm.

MEDIEVAL TIME

In the Middle Ages, spiritual life continued to be conceived in rhythmic terms. Monks and nuns organized their life of work and prayer rhythmically through the day, beginning with matins, and continuing through the canonical hours – lauds, prime, terce, sext, none, vespers, and compline – changing their form and content according to the seasons of the sacred year.

Ordinary life was also understood in terms of daily, monthly, and seasonal rhythms. Evolving from the monastic cycle, the most popular books of the Middle Ages were the Books of Hours, beautifully illuminated, portable guides, designed to be used by individuals who wished to live the year spiritually. Basically, these books were calendars, each month opening with a decorative miniature illustrating a typical activity or labor: January – feasting; February – sitting by the fire; March – pruning the vines; April – gardening; May – hawking or boating; June – haying; and so forth. Embedded within the calendar were the major liturgical feasts, different "offices" and prayer sequences, as well as the saints' days and other useful information such as the "zodiacal man" that depicts each zodiacal sign's rulership of different parts of the body.

THE RENAISSANCE

By the Renaissance, the old ways were declining. A last attempt to re-infuse civilization with a sense of living time was made by Marsilio Ficino, the creator of the Florentine Academy. Acting in congruence with the spiritual rhythms of time by the use of appropriate songs, prayers, fragrances, and even talismans – he claimed – would bring about health, love, and inspiration, as well as union with the gods. For a given historical moment, Ficino's impact was widespread. But in the short term, the rise of modern science, with its objectifying separation of human knowing from nature and the cosmos, was victorious. It remains for us, today, to recover living time in a new way. *Cosmo Doogood's Urban Almanac* begins to show us how to do it.

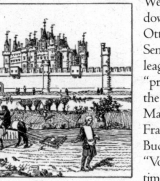

Medieval Time

THE LIVING YEAR

Inspired knowledge, coupled with precise observation of nature and the heavens, underlay the ancient understanding of living time. Today, to rebuild our connection to this living time, we must start as individuals from experience. If we pay attention to our experience, we will not only slowly free ourselves from the tyranny of clock time, but also begin to discover the mystery of rhythm and "real" time. Doing so, we will begin to give back to the stars what they once gave to us. Rather than being ruled by time and objectified schedules, we shall discover a new freedom.

SLOW LIVING

Usually, we think of time flowing from the past into the present, almost pushing us. But if we begin to practice as Cosmo advises, we can begin to rediscover time as a natural rhythm. We begin to slow down. This is what Otto Scharmer, Peter Senge, and their colleagues at MIT call "presencing." It's what the Institute of Heart Math calls "Freeze-Frame." It's what the Buddha called the "Void," in which linear time stops, suffering ends, and loving kindness blossoms. When we do this, we begin to act out of love – love for what is not yet; love for what we bring into being.

LOOKING IN

Cosmo advises us to "Look Up. Look Out. Look In." Looking up, we see the stars, the sky, the weather, the clouds and so on. Looking out, we see life spread out around us. Looking in is more complex. In one sense, it simply extends the sensitivity we develop for what is above and around us to what is within us. At this level, it means to take note of our impressions, moods, breathing rate, energy levels, and so on as they occur. We note these as they change though the day; also the mood of our colleagues, friends, family. We may also take note of our dreams; and of the moment of falling asleep and awakening. (Try asking a question at night, just before you sleep; in the morning, listen for the answer.) But there is more.

RUDOLF STEINER'S MEDITATIONS FOR THE LIVING YEAR

Rudolf Steiner has been called "the best-kept secret of the 20th century." He is known today, if at all, principally as the creator of Waldorf education and biodynamic agriculture, and as the inspiration for the Camphill movement for the care of the handicapped. But he was much more — a philosopher, a scientist, a radical social thinker, and, above all, a spiritual teacher. The heart of his work — which he called Anthroposophy — was to unite the human spirit with the spirit of the cosmos. Human beings, he felt, had become "cosmic hermits" and must again become "cosmic citizens." To help his students realize this, he gave many different kinds of meditations for living a spiritual year. In *Cosmo Doogood's Urban Almanac* this year, three of them — the calendar of the soul, the monthly virtues, and the

Book of Hours

eight-fold path — are reflected in the calendar pages.

THE CALENDAR OF THE SOUL

RIGHT ACTION PROCEEDS
FROM THE HEART
OF LOVE AND WORKS
(JANUARY 1-6)

The world is within us, as it is outside us. Rudolf Steiner's Calendar of the Soul verses allow us to inwardly follow the course of the year and, in so doing, cultivate different soul moods and capacities. Meditating on these verses, we align our own soul with the soul of the world. There are two basic movements of the natural world and they inspire our soul life. In the summer half of the year, as the Earth breathes out, (blossoms, comes alive) the soul lives in the power of the senses. During the winter months, when the Earth breathes in, (rests, gathers its powers for spring), by our own insight we can rise from the prison of our narrow view to become truly cosmic beings. The calendar section of the almanac presents one-line distillations or interpretations of the Calendar of the Soul. Look for them at very the top of every other right-hand page. *(See pages 65-300.)*

Courage

BECOMES THE POWER TO REDEEM
Challenges: envy, greed, timidity

MONTHLY VIRTUES

Besides the weekly Calendar of the Soul verses, Steiner also gives meditations for 12 monthly virtues (see the opening spread of each calendar month). Steiner believed that when one practices these virtues, new powers and capacities can arise to give deeper meaning and purpose to one's life. He also warns of the emotions that can derail this spiritual growth. In the above example from January, courage is the monthly virtue that, when practiced regularly and consciously, gives one the power and strength to redeem and make right. The challenges that are likely to arise when one practices the virtue of courage are envy, greed, and timidity. These challenges are sometimes not self-evident and often counter-intuitive. They come to make sense only after a period of actively working with the virtue.

A DAILY PRACTICE: THE BACKWARD REVIEW OR "RETROSPECT"

In the evening, before going to sleep, direct your thoughts from the present backward over the day's events. Create an image of your experiences, precisely and clearly, and then *look at* the events in the image. This is a practice of *viewing*, not remembering. Ask yourself what you can learn from your experiences.

continued, page 62

MERCURY MUST BE IN RETROGRADE

Three times a year, for a period of approximately 21 days, the planet Mercury appears to slow down and reverse direction. During Mercury's backward-moving cycles, astrologers advise their clients to go against the cultural grain by slowing down and delaying any kind of action. Mythologically, Mercury was considered the super-speedy messenger god—a kind of revved-up cosmic go-between. This makes Mercury, as some have pointed out, a fitting deity for our over-scheduled, time-stressed, era. Life sometimes stubbornly refuses to comply with our palm pilots or daytimers. Like Odysseus, "the man of twists and turns driven time and again off course," we are all running late, missing appointments, not making deadlines, forgetting birthdays—off course and late for life, yet still, somehow, sailing toward home. The popular lore that has grown up around Mercury retrograde may have re-emerged as a way to satisfy the modern-day need for more simplicity. So when Mercury goes into retrograde in the coming year (March 20 – April 12; July 23 – August 16; and November 14 – December 4), give yourself a break, pause for reflection, and take plentiful doses of slow, unstructured time.

Pythia Peay is the author of Mercury Retrograde: Its Myth and Meaning *(Tarcher/Putnam, 2004) www.pythiapeay.com*

THE EIGHTFOLD PATH

Rudolf Steiner created seven seals, which take their names from the sun, moon and the five visible planets (Saturn, Mercury, Mars, Jupiter and Venus). These seals correspond in their sequence to the days of the week: Saturn for Saturday, the Sun for Sunday, the Moon for Monday, Mercury for Tuesday Mars for Wednesday, Jupiter for Thursday, and Venus for Friday. This unfolding, metamorphosing sequence represents the evolutionary octave—the seven great planetary conditions or states—through which the Earth and humanity must pass. Steiner also adapted the Buddha's Eightfold Path for everyday use. The path was laid out by the Buddha as the way to free oneself from attachments and delusions. In the calendar section, we use Steiner's Planetary Seals to illustrate and complement seven of the Eightfold Path teachings. Right Meditation is not illustrated, but Steiner recommends that every sincere seeker develop some form of daily meditation practice.

RIGHT CONCEPTION

**SATURDAY: SATURN
RIGHT CONCEPTION.**
Think only meaningful thoughts. Learn to separate essential from inessential, truth from opinion. When listening to others, withhold all judgment.

RIGHT RESOLVE

**SUNDAY: SUN
RIGHT RESOLVE.**
Think through everything you do, then hold steadfastly to your decision.

RIGHT WORD

**MONDAY: MOON
RIGHT WORD.**
Speak only seriously, meaningfully. Never speak without a reason. Practice listening.

RIGHT DEED

**TUESDAY: MARS
RIGHT DEED.**
Be aware of the consequences of your actions. Make sure that no one is hurt by what you do.

RIGHT LIVELIHOOD

**WEDNESDAY:
MERCURY
RIGHT LIVELIHOOD.**
Be centered. Consider life as a means of inner work and act accordingly.

RIGHT ENDEAVOR

**THURSDAY: JUPITER
RIGHT ENDEAVOR.**
Know your limitations, but never leave undone what you can do. Be of service to others.

**FRIDAY: VENUS
RIGHT MEMORY.**
Learn as much as possible from your own life and that of others. Learn from your mistakes. Try to learn from everyone, even little children.

SUMMARY: RIGHT MEDITATION.
Periodically, take counsel with yourself, test your principles, weigh your duties, experience displeasure at your faults, strive harder toward the highest standards.

WORKING WITH THE DEAD

Rudolf Steiner gave many meditations and practices to help the living remain connected to those who have died. Each day we can remember some great human being who has gone before us, the fruits of whose life still live on among us. And we can remember in vivid pictures our own departed loved ones. We can read to them. We can become sensitive to their "gaze" in images and inspirations — thoughts that seem to come out of nowhere. We can ask them questions. As we go to sleep, we turn with a question, in deep, loving feeling, to the one who passed away. We carry the question into sleep. Awaking the next morning, we pay close attention to the first thing in our consciousness. The answer will be in our own voice, not that of the other.

Book of Hours

LOOK DOWN

Cosmo Doogood's Urban Almanac contains no section called "look down." Nevertheless, it is important to look down with gratitude — both outwardly, toward the ground we stand on, our unmoving Earth, and inwardly, physiologically toward our own organs, and psychologically toward our inner depths.

The key to all this is interest. Above all, develop an interest in what goes on within you and around you. Become passionate about it. Care. Start now! Welcome to the Living Year!

Christopher Bamford is editor at SteinerBooks and Lindisfarne Books. He is the author of Voice of the Eagle: The Heart of Celtic Christianity *and* An Endless Trace: The Passionate Pursuit of Wisdom in the West. *Recently he edited and introduced* Start Now! The Spiritual Exercises of Rudolf Steiner.

"*Thanks for a lovely weekend. Now you must come visit us in Washington Square.*"

Cosmo Doogood's

2005

CALENDAR

I will return on the wings of the clouds

CALENDAR KEY

Zodiacal Constellations

Symbol	Latin Name	English Name	Element
♈	Aries	Ram	Fire
♉	Taurus	Bull	Earth
♊	Gemini	Twins	Air
♋	Cancer	Crab	Water
♌	Leo	Lion	Fire
♍	Virgo	Virgin	Earth
♎	Libra	Scales	Air
♏	Scorpio	Scorpion	Water
♐	Sagittarius	Archer	Fire
♑	Capricorn	Goat	Earth
♒	Aquarius	Waterman	Air
♓	Pisces	Fishes	Water

Sun, Moon, and Planets

☉	Sun
☽	Moon
♁	Earth
☿	Mercury
♀	Venus
♂	Mars
♃	Jupiter
♄	Saturn
♅	Uranus
♆	Neptune
♇	Pluto

The Course of the Moon

●	New Moon
◑	First Quarter
○	Full Moon
◐	Last Quarter

Planetary Events

☍	Opposition	☌	Conjunction	△	Trine (120°)

A Note About Time

Central Standard Time (-6 hours from Universal Time [UT], formerly known as Greenwich Mean Time (GMT)), is used consistently throughout this Calendar. We have already compensated for Daylight Saving Time (-5 hours) from the first Sunday in April to the last Sunday in October. Rising and setting times for the Sun and Moon are for Minneapolis, Minnesota (longitude W93.3, latitude N45.0). Adjustments for other locations can be found at www.usno.navy.mil. Times for the phases of the Moon (full, quarter, and new) and other astronomical events are given in Universal Time (UT). Dates given for Islamic and Jewish holidays are for the evening on which the holiday begins, at sunset.

2005

January
S	M	T	W	T	F	S
						1
2	3	4	5	6	7	8
9	10	11	12	13	14	15
16	17	18	19	20	21	22
23	24	25	26	27	28	29
30	31					

February
S	M	T	W	T	F	S
		1	2	3	4	5
6	7	8	9	10	11	12
13	14	15	16	17	18	19
20	21	22	23	24	25	26
27	28					

March
S	M	T	W	T	F	S
		1	2	3	4	5
6	7	8	9	10	11	12
13	14	15	16	17	18	19
20	21	22	23	24	25	26
27	28	29	30	31		

April
S	M	T	W	T	F	S
					1	2
3	4	5	6	7	8	9
10	11	12	13	14	15	16
17	18	19	20	21	22	23
24	25	26	27	28	29	30

May
S	M	T	W	T	F	S
1	2	3	4	5	6	7
8	9	10	11	12	13	14
15	16	17	18	19	20	21
22	23	24	25	26	27	28
29	30	31				

June
S	M	T	W	T	F	S
			1	2	3	4
5	6	7	8	9	10	11
12	13	14	15	16	17	18
19	20	21	22	23	24	25
26	27	28	29	30		

July
S	M	T	W	T	F	S
					1	2
3	4	5	6	7	8	9
10	11	12	13	14	15	16
17	18	19	20	21	22	23
24	25	26	27	28	29	30
31						

August
S	M	T	W	T	F	S
	1	2	3	4	5	6
7	8	9	10	11	12	13
14	15	16	17	18	19	20
21	22	23	24	25	26	27
28	29	30	31			

September
S	M	T	W	T	F	S
				1	2	3
4	5	6	7	8	9	10
11	12	13	14	15	16	17
18	19	20	21	22	23	24
25	26	27	28	29	30	

October
S	M	T	W	T	F	S
						1
2	3	4	5	6	7	8
9	10	11	12	13	14	15
16	17	18	19	20	21	22
23	24	25	26	27	28	29
30	31					

November
S	M	T	W	T	F	S
		1	2	3	4	5
6	7	8	9	10	11	12
13	14	15	16	17	18	19
20	21	22	23	24	25	26
27	28	29	30			

December
S	M	T	W	T	F	S
				1	2	3
4	5	6	7	8	9	10
11	12	13	14	15	16	17
18	19	20	21	22	23	24
25	26	27	28	29	30	31

2004

January
S	M	T	W	T	F	S
				1	2	3
4	5	6	7	8	9	10
11	12	13	14	15	16	17
18	19	20	21	22	23	24
25	26	27	28	29	30	31

February
S	M	T	W	T	F	S
1	2	3	4	5	6	7
8	9	10	11	12	13	14
15	16	17	18	19	20	21
22	23	24	25	26	27	28
29						

March
S	M	T	W	T	F	S
	1	2	3	4	5	6
7	8	9	10	11	12	13
14	15	16	17	18	19	20
21	22	23	24	25	26	27
28	29	30	31			

April
S	M	T	W	T	F	S
				1	2	3
4	5	6	7	8	9	10
11	12	13	14	15	16	17
18	19	20	21	22	23	24
25	26	27	28	29	30	

May
S	M	T	W	T	F	S
						1
2	3	4	5	6	7	8
9	10	11	12	13	14	15
16	17	18	19	20	21	22
23	24	25	26	27	28	29
30	31					

June
S	M	T	W	T	F	S
		1	2	3	4	5
6	7	8	9	10	11	12
13	14	15	16	17	18	19
20	21	22	23	24	25	26
27	28	29	30			

July
S	M	T	W	T	F	S
				1	2	3
4	5	6	7	8	9	10
11	12	13	14	15	16	17
18	19	20	21	22	23	24
25	26	27	28	29	30	31

August
S	M	T	W	T	F	S
1	2	3	4	5	6	7
8	9	10	11	12	13	14
15	16	17	18	19	20	21
22	23	24	25	26	27	28
29	30	31				

September
S	M	T	W	T	F	S
			1	2	3	4
5	6	7	8	9	10	11
12	13	14	15	16	17	18
19	20	21	22	23	24	25
26	27	28	29	30		

October
S	M	T	W	T	F	S
					1	2
3	4	5	6	7	8	9
10	11	12	13	14	15	16
17	18	19	20	21	22	23
24	25	26	27	28	29	30
31						

November
S	M	T	W	T	F	S
	1	2	3	4	5	6
7	8	9	10	11	12	13
14	15	16	17	18	19	20
21	22	23	24	25	26	27
28	29	30				

December
S	M	T	W	T	F	S
			1	2	3	4
5	6	7	8	9	10	11
12	13	14	15	16	17	18
19	20	21	22	23	24	25
26	27	28	29	30	31	

2006

January
S	M	T	W	T	F	S
1	2	3	4	5	6	7
8	9	10	11	12	13	14
15	16	17	18	19	20	21
22	23	24	25	26	27	28
29	30	31				

February
S	M	T	W	T	F	S
			1	2	3	4
5	6	7	8	9	10	11
12	13	14	15	16	17	18
19	20	21	22	23	24	25
26	27	28				

March
S	M	T	W	T	F	S
			1	2	3	4
5	6	7	8	9	10	11
12	13	14	15	16	17	18
19	20	21	22	23	24	25
26	27	28	29	30	31	

April
S	M	T	W	T	F	S
						1
2	3	4	5	6	7	8
9	10	11	12	13	14	15
16	17	18	19	20	21	22
23	24	25	26	27	28	29
30						

May
S	M	T	W	T	F	S
	1	2	3	4	5	6
7	8	9	10	11	12	13
14	15	16	17	18	19	20
21	22	23	24	25	26	27
28	29	30	31			

June
S	M	T	W	T	F	S
				1	2	3
4	5	6	7	8	9	10
11	12	13	14	15	16	17
18	19	20	21	22	23	24
25	26	27	28	29	30	

July
S	M	T	W	T	F	S
						1
2	3	4	5	6	7	8
9	10	11	12	13	14	15
16	17	18	19	20	21	22
23	24	25	26	27	28	29
30	31					

August
S	M	T	W	T	F	S
		1	2	3	4	5
6	7	8	9	10	11	12
13	14	15	16	17	18	19
20	21	22	23	24	25	26
27	28	29	30	31		

September
S	M	T	W	T	F	S
					1	2
3	4	5	6	7	8	9
10	11	12	13	14	15	16
17	18	19	20	21	22	23
24	25	26	27	28	29	30

October
S	M	T	W	T	F	S
1	2	3	4	5	6	7
8	9	10	11	12	13	14
15	16	17	18	19	20	21
22	23	24	25	26	27	28
29	30	31				

November
S	M	T	W	T	F	S
			1	2	3	4
5	6	7	8	9	10	11
12	13	14	15	16	17	18
19	20	21	22	23	24	25
26	27	28	29	30		

December
S	M	T	W	T	F	S
					1	2
3	4	5	6	7	8	9
10	11	12	13	14	15	16
17	18	19	20	21	22	23
24	25	26	27	28	29	30
31						

IN ORDER TO CREATE THERE MUST BE A DYNAMIC FORCE, AND WHAT FORCE IS MORE POTENT THAN LOVE? :: *IGOR STRAVINSKY*

THE CALENDAR:
How to Use *Cosmo Doogoods' Urban Almanac*

The calendar pages are designed to be written on and used in a variety of ways — as an appointment calendar, a record of sky phenomena and the weather, a phenology notebook, a dream diary, or daily journal. Each day of the year has space for your thoughts and notes. Use them in whatever way suits you.

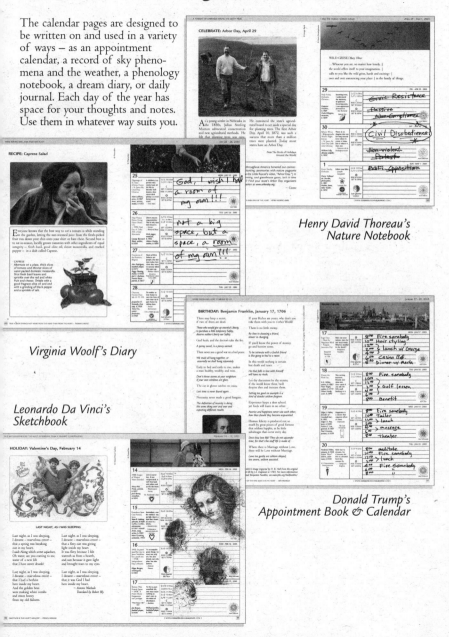

Henry David Thoreau's Nature Notebook

Virginia Woolf's Diary

Leonardo Da Vinci's Sketchbook

Donald Trump's Appointment Book & Calendar

COSMO DOOGOOD'S URBAN ALMANAC:
Left-Hand Pages

LIVING URBAN TREASURES
The Japanese people honor individuals who are masters of their traditional arts as "living national treasures." We honor individuals who embody the spirit of their city and give us a sense of community and place. This year's honorees include Studs Terkel, Jane Jacobs, Alice Waters, Louise Erdrich, and more...

URBAN SANCTUARIES
Where to go in your town for silence, repose, inspiration... like New York City's Cathedral of St. John the Divine, the Eloise Butler Wildflower Gardens in Minneapolis, and the Heavenly Pond in Los Angeles.

ESSENTIAL PLACES IN THE CITY
These are locations that embody the personality or character of a city, like Austin's Barton Springs public swimming hole, Denver's Tattered Cover Bookstore, or Miami's Domino Park.

URBAN SURVIVAL STRATEGIES
How to sneak into good seats, how to repurpose a fruitcake, how to unstick a stuck tongue, and more...

CIVILIZING IDEAS
Farmer's Markets, Citizens' Wisdom Councils, poetry slams, the dark sky movement, local currencies, and more...

Plus, the story behind various holidays, festivals, and celebrations; famous peoples' birthdays; historic events; proclamations; seasonal poems; songs; recipes; astronomical events—all chosen to deepen your sense of the living year.

GREEN CHRISTMAS, WHITE EASTER

CELEBRATE: Spring Equinox/Passover/Easter

Now the green blade riseth,
from the buried grain,
Wheat that in dark earth
many days has lain;
Love lives again,
that with the dead has been:
Love is come again,
like wheat that springeth green.
J.M.C. Crum

In contrast to the fall equinox celebration of Michaelmas, with its strong sense of self-awareness, individuation, and inner courage, the spring festivals emphasize union. Outwardly (in the northern hemisphere), the fertile Earth bursts with life, sending forth tender shoots and fragile blossoms. Insects are stirring, birds are nesting, and people are finding it very hard to stay indoors!

The procreation in nature is the physical aspect of a deeper spiritual message. As male and female must combine for new life to issue, so, within each of us, the union of masculine and feminine results in spontaneous, joyful creation. Yin and yang swim in

a circle of unity, the deepest of each containing the seed other. The message of spring i Difference is no cause for f but a priceless gift for world- a renewal.

Passover (April 23) and (March 27) follow the first ful after the spring equinox (Mar By combining the lunar cycle solar, they reemphasize the theme. United are moon and lamps of night and day. The dark and light births freedc hope. Like a chick bursting f shell, the Israelites escape bondage. As the deathly winter loosens, so the Son unites the heavens with the ea

For the Greeks, love ha levels, eros being only one time of the spring equinox, tion on all of love's aspects ders awe at the fullness of c reverence for the union of op that is the wellspring of all, cr
~ Jo

122 LOVE IS THE DIFFICULT REALIZATION THAT SOMETHING OTHER THAN ONE'S SELF IS REAL :: IRIS MURDOCH

The top of every left-hand page includes a weather aphorism or saying. The bottom of the page features a one-line quote about the heart, friendship, or love.

HOW TO USE THE CALENDAR:
Right-Hand Pages

THE ESSENTIAL CALENDAR OF THE SOUL, by Rudolf Steiner, translated, distilled, and "potentized" by Christopher Bamford into a one-line poem for each week. Use them to help you harmonize with the rhythms of the living year.

SEASONAL POEMS
By Rumi, Mary Oliver, Robert Frost, Thich Nhat Hanh, and others—52 poems that explore the soul mood of each week.

THE PLANETARY SEALS
Each day of the week is associated with a particular seal and a practice from the Eightfold Path of the Buddha.

THIS DAY IN HISTORY
Holidays, festivals, celebrations, birth dates and death dates, and noteworthy historic events—something to celebrate or remember for every day of the year.

QUOTES
Proverbs, famous sayings, and doggerel—timeless wit and wisdom, from the silly to the sublime.

THE NIGHT SKY
An ephemeris of conjunctions, oppositions and trines for all the planets of the solar system.

SUN AND MOON
Rising and setting times for the Sun and Moon, plus times of the full, quarter, and new Moon.

NG / Gerard Manley Hopkins

...ing is so beautiful as spring— | When weeds, in wheels, shoot long and
...and lush, | Thrush's eggs look little low heavens, and thrush |
...ugh the echoing timber does so rinse and wring |
...ar, it strikes like lightnings to hear him sing...

FRI - MAR 25 - 2005

God has no religion.
— Mahatma Gandhi

Good Friday (Christian) (Purim)

ANNUNCIATION (Christian)

RISE 6:06AM
SET 6:32PM

Full Moon 20:58UT

SAT - MAR 26 - 2005

Two roads diverged in a wood, and I took the one less traveled by. And that has made all the difference.
— Robert Frost

RISE 6:05AM
SET 6:34PM

SUN - MAR 27 - 2005

We choose our ... and sorrows long before we experience them.
— Kahlil Gibran

EASTER SUNDAY (Christian)

RISE 6:03AM
SET 6:35PM

Bartók composer, *b.1881*

GOOD FRIDAY (CHRISTIAN)
PURIM (JEWISH)

ANNUNCIATION (CHRISTIAN)

RISE 6:06AM
SET 6:32PM

Full Moon 20:58UT

26

"Make Up Your Own Holiday" Day
~ Khordadsal, Zoroastrian

Robert Frost poet, b.1874
Tennessee Williams, playwright, b.1911

Two roads diverged in a wood, and I — I took the one less traveled by, And that has made all the difference.
— Robert Frost

☽ ☌ ☿ 2:50AM
☽ ☌ ♃ 9:00AM
☽ △ ♆ 12:23PM

SET 6:29AM
RISE 7:42PM

RISE 6:05AM
SET 6:34PM

We choose our

SET

JANUARY

DEC 22- JAN 19

JAN 20- FEB 18

capricorn

aquarius

BIRTHSTONE
Garnet

FLOWER
Carnation

Courage

BECOMES THE POWER TO REDEEM

Challenges: envy, greed, timidity

Outside, it is cold, silvery, and suffused with a delicate milky haze. Gray hushed days follow each other, calling us to inner activity. Sitting by the fire or hurrying through the streets, our power of thinking grows. Filled with new ideas, we feel creative and courageous. Legend says "words spoken in winter go unheard until next summer." This is the message from Janus, the old Etruscan god of the doorway, after whom January was named. Janus stands between past and future, new and old. He has two faces. One looks back, the other forward. His third face is invisible. This is the face of eternity, the present moment: NOW. Warmth settles around our hearts. Summoned to great deeds of right action and selfless love, Janus bids us pass through his gate.

JANUARY IS:

HOBBY MONTH · HOT SOUP MONTH · OATMEAL MONTH · GLAUCOMA AWARENESS MONTH · FINANCIAL WELLNESS MONTH · NATIONAL BE-ON-PURPOSE MONTH RETAIL BAKERS MONTH · VOLUNTEER BLOOD DONOR MONTH · THANK-YOU MONTH RADON ACTION MONTH · MAIL-ORDER GARDENING MONTH · WALK YOUR PET MONTH BOOK BLITZ MONTH · EYE CARE MONTH · STAYING HEALTHY MONTH · BREAD MACHINE BAKING MONTH · GOURMET COFFEE MONTH · IMAGE IMPROVEMENT MONTH CREATIVITY MONTH · CANCER PREVENTION MONTH

Mercury, Venus and Mars are meeting before sunrise.

Mars

(Pluto)

Antares

Venus

Mercury

SCORPIO

SE   Jan 14, 7:00 a.m.

Jupiter

Spica

VIRGO

CROW

Jan 31, 7:00 a.m.   SW

STARS & PLANETS FOR JANUARY

All the planets are visible at some time this month. Seven conjunctions occur: Moon-Jupiter (4th), Moon-Mars (7th), Moon-Mercury (9th), Moon-Venus (9th), Mercury-Venus (14th), Moon-Saturn (24th), and Moon-Jupiter (31th), a veritable celebration of meetings. In the center of this incredible array of conjunctions is the movement of Mercury and Venus. The two planets are standing together from Christmas up to their conjunction on January 14th.

LOOK UP:

2   Earth at perihelion (closest to the Sun)

3   Quadrantid meteor shower peaks, view obscured by Moon

4   Moon near Jupiter

7   The waning Moon near Mars and Antares in the morning

8   The Moon, Mercury and Venus cluster in the southeast before dawn

10 New Moon, 12:03 UT

23 Saturn nearest to Earth and at opposition

25 Full Moon (Quiet Moon), 10:32 UT

LOOK OUT:

· Gray whales migrate to Baja California

· Wintering bald eagles gather near lakes and reservoirs in the Rockies

· In the Boundary Waters bull moose drop antlers

· Manatees retreat to Florida's Crystal River

JANUARY						
S	M	T	W	T	F	S
						1
2	3	4	5	6	7	8
9	10	11	12	13	14	15
16	17	18	19	20	21	22
23/30	24/31	25	26	27	28	29

People travel to wonder at the height of mountains, at the huge waves of the sea, at the long courses of rivers, at the vast compass of the ocean, at the circular motion of the stars; and they pass by themselves without wondering.

~ SAINT AUGUSTINE

Wishing · You · A
Happy · New · Year

THE GREAT MAN IS HE THAT DOES NOT LOSE HIS CHILD'S HEART :: *MENCIUS*

OUR STORY / *William Stafford*

Remind me again — together we | trace our strange journey, find | each
other, come on laughing. | Some time we'll cross where life | ends.
We'll both look back | as far as forever, that first day. | I'll touch you —
a new world then. | Stars will move a different way. | We'll both end.
We'll both begin. | Remind me again.

---

31   FRI · DEC 31 · 2004

First Night
Celebrations:
U.S. & CAN
~ Orange Bowl
Parade

*Henri Matisse,
Artist, b.1869*

**Learn from
yesterday, live
for today, hope
for tomorrow.**
— *Anon.*

NEW YEAR'S EVE

☾ SET 11:01AM
RISE 9:44PM

☼ RISE 7:51AM
SET 4:42PM

RIGHT MEMORY

---

1   SAT · JAN 1 · 2005

1899: Cuba
Liberation Day
~ Diet Reso-
lution Week
~ 1863:
Emancipation
Proclamation

NEW YEAR'S
DAY

*Frank Langella,
actor, b.1940
J.D. Salinger,
author, b.1919
Paul Revere,
revolutionary,
b.1735*

☽ ☌ ♅ 9:18AM

☾ SET 11:19AM
RISE 10:48PM

☼ RISE 7:51AM
SET 4:43PM

RIGHT CONCEPTION

---

2   SUN · JAN 2 · 2005

Kakizome: First
Writing/ Calli-
graphy Day,
Japan

*Isaac Asimov,
author, b.1920*

**What lies
behind us
and what lies
before us are
tiny matters
compared
to what lies
within us.**
— *Ralph W.
Emerson*

☾ SET 11:37AM
RISE 11:56PM

☼ RISE 7:51AM
SET 4:44PM

RIGHT RESOLVE

URBAN SANCTUARY:
Cathedral of St. John the Divine, New York City

Where else in America can you walk a labyrinth, bless your golden retriever (the first Sunday in October), and host a Medieval-themed birthday party for your child – all within reach of a subway? While the cornerstone for this eccentric Romanesque/Byzantine/Gothic revival cathedral was laid in 1892, St. John the Divine is still very much a work in progress; its ongoing construction is a reassuring constant in the now gentrified Morningside Heights neighborhood. The cathedral's stonecutters are chosen from the community and trained, much like apprentices in a medieval artisan society, in the art of masonry. For the less industrious pilgrim, those same granite and limestone walls keep the temperatures cool – a particularly satisfying feature during New York City's notoriously sweaty summers. From stained glass windows that look as though they were lifted straight from Notre Dame, to exhibitions of the most contemporary of contemporary art, St. John the Divine celebrates the creative spirit and is an active advocate for peace, social justice, and the environment. Resident peacocks preside over the Biblical Gardens, which burst with organically grown herbs, flowering plants, shrubs, and trees mentioned in the Bible. Never one to be pigeonholed into a clichéd version of the sacred, the Cathedral offers several different worship areas, including the Sports Bay, which celebrates over two dozen sports in its stained glass windows. Among the worthy pursuits: baseball, bowling, fishing, golf, figure skating, and, yes, auto racing.

The West Rose Window

~ *Elizabeth Larsen*

For more information on the Cathedral of St. John the Divine in New York City, see www.stjohndivine.org

A JOYFUL HEART IS THE INEVITABLE RESULT OF A HEART BURNING WITH LOVE :: *MOTHER TERESA*

NEW YORK CITY

3

MON · JAN 3 · 2005

Memento Mori Day (Latin : Remember, you die)

J.R.R. Tolkien, author, b.1892
Stephen Stills, musician, b.1945

Everything is a miracle. It is a miracle that one does not dissolve in one's bath like a lump of sugar.
— *Pablo Picasso*

☽ △ ♆ 12:39PM
♀ ♂ ♇ 5:33PM
☽ ♂ ♃ 7:23PM

☀
RISE 7:51AM
SET 4:45PM

Last Quarter
17:46UT

RIGHT WORD

4

TUE · JAN 4 · 2005

1893: Amnesty for Polygamists ~ Dimpled Chad Day

Isaac Newton, physicist, b.1643
Louis Braille, inventor, b.1809
Jacob Grimm, author, b.1785

Imagination is more important than knowledge. Knowledge is limited. Imagination encircles the world.
— *Albert Einstein*

EARTH AT
PERIHELION, 10PM

♀ ♂ ♇ 11:58PM

☾
RISE 1:05AM
SET 12:13PM

☀
RISE 7:51AM
SET 4:46PM

RIGHT DEED

5

WED · JAN 5 · 2005

Organize Your Home Day

Robert Duvall, actor, b.1931
Umberto Eco, author, b.1932
Alvin Ailey, dancer, b.1931
Walter Mondale, politician, b.1928

Wisdom begins in wonder.
— *Socrates*

TWELFTH NIGHT

The evening before Epiphany

☽ △ ♅ 1:16AM

☾
RISE 2:18AM
SET 12:35PM

☀
RISE 7:51AM
SET 4:47PM

RIGHT LIVELIHOOD

6

THU · JAN 6 · 2005

Carnivale Season begins (Jan 6 – Feb 24)

Carl Sandburg, poet, b.1878
Joan of Arc, saint, b.1412
Kahlil Gibran, poet, b.1883

THREE KINGS DAY

Fall seven times, stand up eight.
— *Japanese Proverb*

EPIPHANY OR
TWELFTH DAY

☽ △ ♄ 12:29PM

☾
RISE 3:36AM
SET 1:03PM

☀
RISE 7:51AM
SET 4:48PM

RIGHT ENDEAVOR

BIRTHDAY: Elvis Presley, January 8, 1935

LOVE ME TENDER
Love me tender,
Love me sweet,
Never let me go.
You have made my life complete,
And I love you so...

Lyrics by Vera Matson and Elvis Presley.
For more information about Elvis Presley,
see www.elvis.com

SNOW / *Philip Levine*

...It is as though the tears of all | the lost souls rose to heaven | and were
finally heard and blessed | with substance and the power of flight |
and given their choice chose then | to return to earth, to lay their | great
pale cheek against the burning | cheek of earth and say, There, there, child.

---

7   FRI · JAN 7 · 2005

Fasching Carnival
Begins (Munich)
~ Nanakusa: 7
medicinal plants
celebrated, Japan
~ Usokae:
Bullfinch Exchange
Festival, Japan

50 YEARS AGO
1955: Marian
Anderson becomes
1st black singer
to perform at
the Met

*Nicolas Cage,
actor, b.1964*

*Katie Couric,
TV host, b.1957*

☽ ☌ ♂ 9:36 PM

☾ RISE 4:58AM
SET 1:40PM

☀ RISE 7:51AM
SET 4:49PM

RIGHT MEMORY

---

8   SAT · JAN 8 · 2005

*Yvette Mimieux,
actor, b.1942
Stephen Hawking,
physicist, b.1942
David Bowie,
musician,
b.1947*

WOMEN'S OR
MIDWIFE'S DAY
(Greece)

EARTH'S
ROTATION
PROVED 1851

ELVIS PRESLEY'S
B-DAY: B.1935

☽ ☌ ♇ 11:05PM
☽ ☌ ☿ 7:49PM
☽ ☌ ♀ 9:02PM

☾ RISE 6:19AM
SET 2:31PM

☀ RISE 7:50AM
SET 4:50PM

RIGHT CONCEPTION

---

9   SUN · JAN 9 · 2005

1793: Aviation
in America
~ Martyrs' Day,
Panama
~ Feast of the
Black Nazarene,
Philippines

*Dave Matthews,
musician,
b.1967*

To accomplish
great things, we
must not only
act, but also
dream; not only
plan, but also
believe.
— Anatole France

*Joan Baez,
folksinger,
b.1941*

☾ RISE 7:32AM
SET 3:37PM

☀ RISE 7:50AM
SET 4:51PM

RIGHT RESOLVE

LIVING URBAN TREASURE: Virginia Beach's Pharrell Williams

People's energies are made of their souls," says Pharrell Williams.

Williams is best known as half of the extremely successful production duo the Neptunes — think Brittney Spears' "I'm a Slave 4 U," and Nelly's "Hot in Herre." Now, his band N.E.R.D. (Nothing Ever Really Dies), with longtime friend and co-producer Chad Hugo and Sheldon "Shay" Haley, is playing in cities around the world following the release of their second album, Fly or Die (March 2004).

Pharrell Williams' "Frontin'"

Williams' rise to fame began in 1991 when a music scout plucked him and Hugo from a talent show in sultry Virginia Beach, their hometown. Williams had marched in the school band, and been fired from

He's consistently silent on how he works; it's the place where sacred meets profane and Williams keeps the mystery.

McDonald's three times for being lazy. "I work very hard now," says Williams, "but I love what I do and that's different." Renown showered him in gold dust in the late 1990s when his rap-funk-pop-punk blend of music captured the airways. After producing and singing behind others, Williams came fully forward in the summer of 2003 with "Frontin'."

He promoted the covered up style — sideways cap, sagging oversize jeans, baggy sweatshirt — which lingers post millennium. But at 30, with a warm southern accent and the profile of a god, his essence shines through, powerful and clean. He doesn't drink or do drugs. "Everybody else can do what they want, but that stuff isn't for me," he says.

Williams calls on a spiritual energy in his music both as a writer-producer and performer-philosopher. He's consistently silent on how he works; it's the place where sacred meets profane and Williams keeps the mystery. Says Williams, "You don't want people to unzip you and see your gears... I think my music should speak more than me." As a band member, he has one outstanding rule: "Follow your spirit," Williams says, "If you stick with that, it won't matter when nine times out of ten your work doesn't go to number one."

~ *Kathleen Melin*

For more information on Pharrell Williams, see www.online-shrine.com/pharrell-williams

CENTRAL PARK, NYC

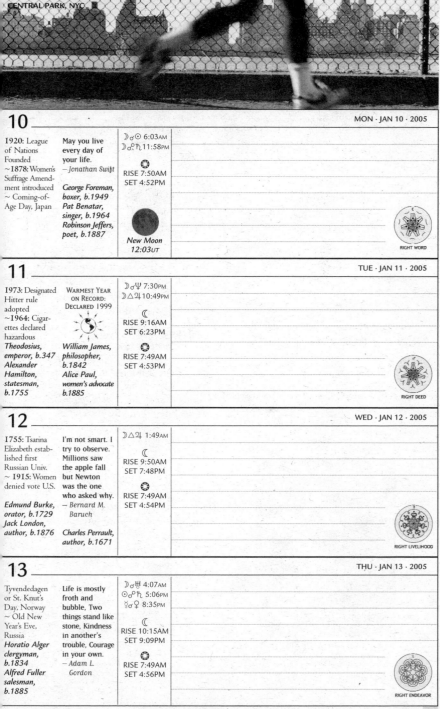

10 — MON · JAN 10 · 2005

1920: League of Nations Founded
~ 1878: Women's Suffrage Amendment introduced
~ Coming-of-Age Day, Japan

May you live every day of your life.
— Jonathan Swift

George Foreman, boxer, b.1949
Pat Benatar, singer, b.1964
Robinson Jeffers, poet, b.1887

☽☌☉ 6:03AM
☽☌♄ 11:58PM

☉
RISE 7:50AM
SET 4:52PM

New Moon 12:03UT

RIGHT WORD

11 — TUE · JAN 11 · 2005

1973: Designated Hitter rule adopted
~1964: Cigarettes declared hazardous
Theodosius, emperor, b.347
Alexander Hamilton, statesman, b.1755

WARMEST YEAR ON RECORD: DECLARED 1999

William James, philosopher, b.1842
Alice Paul, women's advocate b.1885

☽☌♆ 7:30PM
☽△♃ 10:49PM

☾
RISE 9:16AM
SET 6:23PM

☉
RISE 7:49AM
SET 4:53PM

RIGHT DEED

12 — WED · JAN 12 · 2005

1755: Tsarina Elizabeth established first Russian Univ.
~ 1915: Women denied vote U.S.

Edmund Burke, orator, b.1729
Jack London, author, b.1876

I'm not smart. I try to observe. Millions saw the apple fall but Newton was the one who asked why.
— Bernard M. Baruch

Charles Perrault, author, b.1671

☽△♃ 1:49AM

☾
RISE 9:50AM
SET 7:48PM

☉
RISE 7:49AM
SET 4:54PM

RIGHT LIVELIHOOD

13 — THU · JAN 13 · 2005

Tyvendedagen or St. Knut's Day, Norway
~ Old New Year's Eve, Russia

Horatio Alger clergyman, b.1834
Alfred Fuller salesman, b.1885

Life is mostly froth and bubble, Two things stand like stone, Kindness in another's trouble, Courage in your own.
— Adam L. Gordon

☽☌♅ 4:07AM
☉☍♄ 5:06PM
☿☌♀ 8:35PM

☾
RISE 10:15AM
SET 9:09PM

☉
RISE 7:49AM
SET 4:56PM

RIGHT ENDEAVOR

BIRTHDAY: Dr. Martin Luther King, Jr., January 15, 1929

In 1955, in Montgomery, Alabama, a black woman named Rosa Parks refused to give up her bus seat to a white passenger. She had defied segregation, which required blacks to sit in the rear of southern buses, and she was fined $14. The incident led to a boycott of the city's buses, and Martin Luther King, Jr., a minister who was born on January 15, 1929, was chosen to lead it. A year later the city's buses were integrated. King subsequently organized the Southern Christian Leadership Conference to promote civil rights and in 1964 won the Nobel Peace Prize. By the age of 39, when he was assassinated, he had inspired millions to share his dream of equality.

— The Book of Holidays Around the World

Even if I knew that tomorrow
the world would go to pieces,
I would still plant my apple tree.
— *MLK, Quoting Martin Luther*

*A nation that continues year after year
to spend more money on military defense than
on programs of social uplift is approaching
spiritual doom.*
— *The Trumpet of Conscience, 1967*

Our scientific power has outrun
our spiritual power. We have guided
missiles and misguided man.
— *Strength To Love, 1963*

*In the end, we will remember not the words
of our enemies, but the silence of our friends.*
— *The Trumpet of Conscience, 1967*

Freedom is never voluntarily given by
the oppressor; it must be demanded
by the oppressed.
— *Letter From Birmingham Jail, 4.16.1963*

Nonviolence means avoiding not only
external physical violence but also
internal violence of spirit. You not
only refuse to shoot a man, but you
refuse to hate him.   — *MLK*

*I said to my children, "I'm going to work
and do everything that I can do to see that
you get a good education. I don't ever want
you to forget that there are millions of God's
children who will not and cannot get a good
education, and I don't want you feeling that
you are better than they are. For you will
never be what you ought to be until they are
what they ought to be."*
— *MLK, 1.7.1968*

I submit that an individual who breaks a
law that conscience tells him is unjust,
and who willingly accepts the penalty of
imprisonment in order to arouse the
conscience of the community over its
injustice, is in reality expressing the
highest respect for law.
— *Letter From Birmingham Jail, 4.16.1963*

*It may be true that the law cannot make a man
love me, but it can keep him from lynching me,
and I think that's pretty important.*
— *MLK, Wall Street Journal, 11.13.62*

*For more information about
Martin Luther King, Jr.,
see www.thekingcenter.com*

Dr. Martin Luther King, Jr.

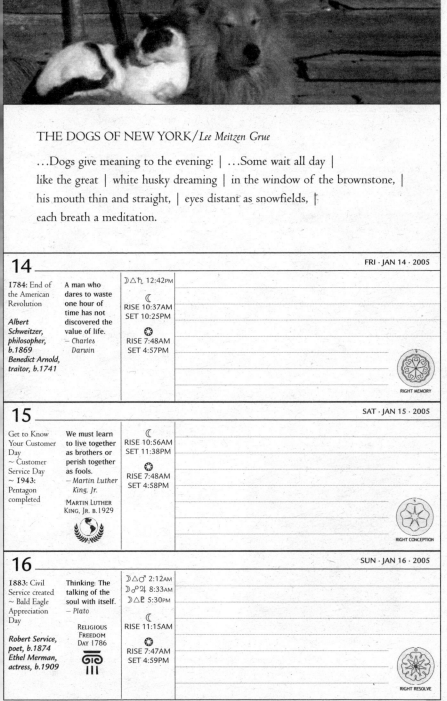

THE DOGS OF NEW YORK/*Lee Meitzen Grue*

…Dogs give meaning to the evening: | …Some wait all day |
like the great | white husky dreaming | in the window of the brownstone, |
his mouth thin and straight, | eyes distant as snowfields, |
each breath a meditation.

---

14 _____ FRI · JAN 14 · 2005

1784: End of the American Revolution

Albert Schweitzer, philosopher, b.1869

Benedict Arnold, traitor, b.1741

A man who dares to waste one hour of time has not discovered the value of life.
— *Charles Darwin*

☽△♄ 12:42PM

☾
RISE 10:37AM
SET 10:25PM

☀
RISE 7:48AM
SET 4:57PM

RIGHT MEMORY

---

15 _____ SAT · JAN 15 · 2005

Get to Know Your Customer Day
~ Customer Service Day
~ **1943:** Pentagon completed

We must learn to live together as brothers or perish together as fools.
— *Martin Luther King, Jr.*

MARTIN LUTHER KING, JR. B.1929

☾
RISE 10:56AM
SET 11:38PM

☀
RISE 7:48AM
SET 4:58PM

RIGHT CONCEPTION

---

16 _____ SUN · JAN 16 · 2005

1883: Civil Service created
~ Bald Eagle Appreciation Day

Robert Service, poet, b.1874
Ethel Merman, actress, b.1909

Thinking: The talking of the soul with itself.
— *Plato*

RELIGIOUS FREEDOM DAY 1786

☽△♂ 2:12AM
☽☍♃ 8:33AM
☽△♇ 5:30PM

☾
RISE 11:15AM

☀
RISE 7:47AM
SET 4:59PM

RIGHT RESOLVE

BIRTHDAY: Benjamin Franklin, January 17, 1706

Three may keep a secret,
if two of them are dead.

*Those who would give up essential Liberty,
to purchase a little temporary Safety,
deserve neither Liberty nor Safety.*

God heals, and the doctors take the fee.

A penny saved, is a penny earned.

There never was a good war or a bad peace.

*We must all hang together, or
assuredly we shall hang separately.*

Early to bed and early to rise, makes
a man healthy, wealthy, and wise.

*Don't throw stones at your neighbors
if your own windows are glass.*

The cat in gloves catches no mice.

Lost time is never found again.

Necessity never made a good bargain.

*The definition of insanity is doing
the same thing over and over and
expecting different results.*

If your Riches are yours, why don't you
take them with you to t'other World?

There is no little enemy.

*Be slow in choosing a friend,
slower in changing.*

If you'd know the power of money,
go and borrow some.

*To be intimate with a foolish friend
is like going to bed to a razor.*

In this world nothing is certain
but death and taxes.

*He that falls in love with himself
will have no rivals.*

Let thy discontent be thy secrets;
if the world know them 'twill
despise thee and increase them.

*Setting too good an example is a
kind of slander seldom forgiven.*

Experience keeps a dear school,
yet fools will learn in no other.

*Avarice and happiness never saw each other,
how then should they become acquainted.*

Human felicity is produced not so
much by great pieces of good fortune
that seldom happen, as by little
advantages that occur every day.

*Dost thou love life? Then do not squander
time; for that's the stuff life is made of.*

Where there is Marriage without Love,
there will be Love without Marriage.

*Laws too gentle are seldom obeyed;
too severe, seldom executed.*

Benjamin Franklin

*Benjamin Franklin's image engraved by H. B. Hall from the original
painted from life by J.A. Duplessis in 1783. For more information
about Benjamin Franklin, see www.pbs.org/benfranklin/*

PHILADELPHIA, PA

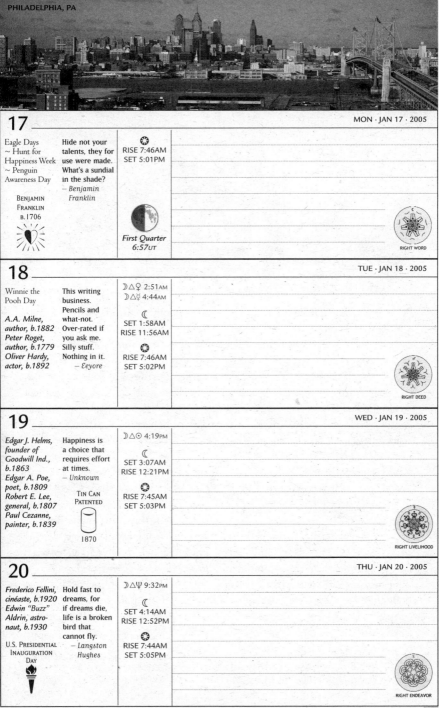

17 — MON · JAN 17 · 2005

Eagle Days
~ Hunt for
Happiness Week
~ Penguin
Awareness Day

BENJAMIN
FRANKLIN
B.1706

Hide not your
talents, they for
use were made.
What's a sundial
in the shade?
— *Benjamin
Franklin*

☉
RISE 7:46AM
SET 5:01PM

*First Quarter
6:57*UT

RIGHT WORD

18 — TUE · JAN 18 · 2005

Winnie the
Pooh Day

*A.A. Milne,
author, b.1882
Peter Roget,
author, b.1779
Oliver Hardy,
actor, b.1892*

This writing
business.
Pencils and
what-not.
Over-rated if
you ask me.
Silly stuff.
Nothing in it.
— *Eeyore*

☽△♀ 2:51AM
☽△☿ 4:44AM

☾
SET 1:58AM
RISE 11:56AM

☉
RISE 7:46AM
SET 5:02PM

RIGHT DEED

19 — WED · JAN 19 · 2005

*Edgar J. Helms,
founder of
Goodwill Ind.,
b.1863
Edgar A. Poe,
poet, b.1809
Robert E. Lee,
general, b.1807
Paul Cezanne,
painter, b.1839*

Happiness is
a choice that
requires effort
at times.
— *Unknown*

TIN CAN
PATENTED

1870

☽△☉ 4:19PM

☾
SET 3:07AM
RISE 12:21PM

☉
RISE 7:45AM
SET 5:03PM

RIGHT LIVELIHOOD

20 — THU · JAN 20 · 2005

*Frederico Fellini,
cinéaste, b.1920
Edwin "Buzz"
Aldrin, astro-
naut, b.1930*

U.S. PRESIDENTIAL
INAUGURATION
DAY

Hold fast to
dreams, for
if dreams die,
life is a broken
bird that
cannot fly.
— *Langston
Hughes*

☽△♆ 9:32PM

☾
SET 4:14AM
RISE 12:52PM

☉
RISE 7:44AM
SET 5:05PM

RIGHT ENDEAVOR

URBAN SANCTUARY:
American Moslem Society's Dearborn Mosque, Detroit

When the Islamic call to prayer reverberates through Dearborn's South End, the faithful gather at the American Moslem Society's Dearborn Mosque.

The call resonates over the working-class streets that for nearly a century have welcomed immigrants who sought work in the hulking and historic Ford Motor Company's Rouge plant, still an imposing and defining landmark.

Generations ago, the neighborhood teemed with people from throughout Europe. Even then, it was home to a small, but active Middle Eastern community. The mosque's first incarnation was built circa 1937, its primary members Sunni Muslims from Lebanon's Bekaa Valley.

Now, a modern three-story, nearly block-long mosque marks the intersection of Vernor and Dix and the neighborhood, which abuts Detroit's heavily Mexican southwest sector, is predominantly Middle Eastern. Almost every storefront has signs written in Arabic, as well as English.

The mosque's biggest services are on Friday, the most important day for believers to gather. Worshippers hail from Yemen, Lebanon, Iraq, Syria, and Palestine, and African-American Muslims also embrace Islam here. On that day, the streets are jammed with cars from throughout the Detroit area, but many people — men wearing prayer shawls and women covered in traditional gowns and scarves — emerge from neighborhood homes for the short walk to worship.

~ *Patricia Montemurri*

More information about the Detroit Mosque is available at www.bacon-ochs.mit.edu

OPEN YOUR HEART AND FORGIVE LIKE THE MASTER/

Rumi (translated by Coleman Barks)

Come, come, whoever you are, | wanderer, worshiper, lover of leaving. |
This is not a caravan of despair. | It doesn't matter that you've broken |
your vow a thousand times, still | come, and yet again, come.

---

21   FRI · JAN 21 · 2005

Eid-Al-Adha:
Feast of the
Sacrifice, Islam
~ 1915:
Kiwanis Intl.
Founded

ST. AGNES DAY

Roger Nash
Baldwin, founder
ACLU, b.1884

SQUIRREL
APPRECIATION
DAY!

Ethan Allen,
Revolutionary
War hero,
b.1738
Christian Dior
designer, b.1905

☽ ☌ ♂ 5:35ᴀᴍ
☽ △ ♃ 5:46ᴀᴍ
☽ ☍ ♇ 3:26ᴘᴍ

☾
SET 5:18AM
RISE 1:31PM

☉
RISE 7:43AM
SET 5:06PM

RIGHT MEMORY

---

22   SAT · JAN 22· 2005

Elfstedentocht:
11 Cities Skating
Race, Holland
~ 1973: Roe v.
Wade Decision

August
Strindberg,
composer,
b.1849
Lord Byron,
poet, b.1788

Fame is the
thirst of youth.
— George Gordon,
Lord Byron

George
Balanchine,
choreographer,
b.1904
Francis Bacon,
statesman,
b.1561

☽ △ ♅ 2:38ᴘᴍ

☾
SET 6:16AM
RISE 2:18PM

☉
RISE 7:43AM
SET 5:07PM

RIGHT CONCEPTION

---

23   SUN · JAN 23 · 2005

Babin Den:
Midwife or
Grandmother's
Day, Bulgaria
~ 1980: Carter
reinstates
Selective Service
registration

NATIONAL
HANDWRITING DAY

Edouard Manet,
painter, b.1832
Elizabeth Black-
well, 1st woman
MD, b.1849
John Hancock,
statesman,
b.1737

☽ ☌ ♀ 4:49ᴘᴍ
☽ ☍ ☿ 10:07ᴘᴍ

☾
SET 7:05AM
RISE 3:14PM

☉
RISE 7:42AM
SET 5:09PM

RIGHT RESOLVE

URBAN SURVIVAL STRATEGY:
How to Treat a Tongue Frozen to a Pole

1. Do not panic.

2. Do not pull the tongue from the pole. Pulling sharply will be very painful.

3. Move closer to the pole.

Get as close as possible without letting more of the tongue's surface area touch the pole.

4. Warm the pole with your hands.

A tongue will stick when the surface of the pole is very cold. The top few layers of the tongue will freeze when the

If your tongue is stuck to a pole, do not panic or pull it. Warm the pole with your hands until your tongue comes loose.

tongue touches the pole, causing bonding. Place your gloved hands on the area of the pole closest to the tongue. Hold them there for several minutes.

5. Take a test pull.

As the pole warms, the frozen area around the tongue should begin to thaw. Gently pull the tongue away from the pole. You may leave a layer or two of skin on the pole, which will be painful, but the tongue will quickly heal.

Alternative Method

Use warm water.

Pour water from a water bottle over the tongue and the pole. Do not use water that is cold, or it may freeze and exacerbate the problem.

Be Aware

o *Do not try to loosen your tongue with your own saliva:* Although saliva is relatively warm, the small amount you will be able to generate is likely to freeze on your tongue.

o If another person is present, have him or her pour warm (not hot) water over your tongue. This may be difficult to articulate while your tongue is stuck— pantomiming a glass of water poured over your tongue should do the trick.

From The Worst Case Scenario Survival Handbook

PRIVATE WAY
DANGEROUS PASSING

24 — MON · JAN 24 · 2005

Alacitas: honoring Ekeko, god of prosperity, Bolivia

Edith Wharton, author, b.1862

1ST CANNED BEER 1935

Don't be afraid to take a big step. You can't cross a chasm in two jumps.
— *David Lloyd George*

☽ ☌ ♄ 3:17AM

☽
SET 7:46AM
RISE 4:16PM

☉
RISE 7:41AM
SET 5:10PM

RIGHT WORD

25 — TUE · JAN 25 · 2005

Burns' Nights, Scotland, England, Newfoundland ~ Up-Helly-Aa, Scotland

W. Somerset Maugham, author, b.1874
Robert Burns, poet, b.1759
Virginia Woolf, author, b.1882

Oh wad some power the giftie gie us — To see ourselves as others see us.
— *Robert Burns*

MACINTOSH COMPUTER DEBUT 1984

☽ ☌ ☉ 4:32AM
☿ ☌ ♄ 12:04PM
☽ ☌ ♆ 10:59PM

☉
RISE 7:40AM
SET 5:12PM

Full Moon 10:32UT

RIGHT DEED

26 — WED · JAN 26 · 2005

1788: Australia Day: 1st British settlement
~1950: Republic Day, India

Angela Davis, activist, b.1944
Paul Newman, actor, b.1925

If you find it in your heart to care for somebody else, you will have succeeded.
— *Maya Angelou*

Douglas MacArthur, general, b.1880
Jules Feiffer, artist, b.1929

☽ △ ♂ 2:05PM
☽ △ ♃ 4:39PM

☽
SET 8:45AM
RISE 6:28PM

☉
RISE 7:39AM
SET 5:13PM

RIGHT LIVELIHOOD

27 — THU · JAN 27 · 2005

1973: Vietnam Peace Agreement signed

'Twas brillig, and the slithy toves Did gyre and gimble in the wabe; All mimsy were the borogroves, And the mome raths outgrabe.
— *Lewis Carroll*

Thomas Crapper, inventor, b. 1910
Mikhail Baryshnikov, dancer, b.1948
Wolfgang A. Mozart, composer, b.1756
Lewis Carroll, author, b.1832

♀ ☌ ♄ 2:52PM
☽ ☌ ♅ 3:38PM

☽
SET 9:06AM
RISE 7:35PM

☉
RISE 7:38AM
SET 5:14PM

RIGHT ENDEAVOR

CELEBRATION: St. Paul Winter Carnival, Jan. 28 – Feb. 6

1888: In 1888 the tallest building in St. Paul was made from 55,000 blocks of ice. Standing 130 feet at its highest point, the castle included a Sioux Indian village, skating rinks, toboggan run, and ski slide within the castle's 30-foot tall walls.

1937: The Carnival was revived on a large scale by a group of enthusiasts who sought to instill life in a city recovering from the Great Depression. Although simpler in design than its predecessors, the 1937 castle was the first to include an elevator.

1992: *"World's Largest Ice Castle!"* Like the first ice castle, this one was built to demonstrate to the world St. Paul's success and long-standing love of winter celebrations. The ice castle had 12 towers, the highest standing 150 feet tall. Built with more than 25,000 blocks of ice, it included a colorful rainbow lighting system and a sound system.

In 1885 a New York reporter wrote that St. Paul was "another Siberia, unfit for human habitation" in winter. Offended by this attack on their capital city, the St. Paul Chamber of Commerce decided to not only prove that St. Paul was habitable but that its citizens were very much alive during winter, the most dominant season. Thus was born the St. Paul Winter Carnival.

In 1886 King Boreas the First was crowned at the Winter Carnival. This festival also featured an ice castle, an elaborate creation made from Minnesota lake ice, which has evolved into an internationally recognized icon for St. Paul's festival.

~ *www.winter-carnival.com*

For more information about the Saint Paul Winter Carnival in St. Paul, Minnesota, see www.winter-carnival.com

I AM NOT I / *Juan Ramon Jimenez (translated by Robert Bly)*

I am not I | I am this one | walking beside me whom I do not see, | whom at times I manage to visit, | and whom at other times I forget; | who remains silent when I talk, | The one who forgives sweet, when I hate, | The one who takes a walk when I am indoors, | The one who will remain standing when I die.

---

28   FRI · JAN 28 · 2005

1986: Challenger Space Shuttle Explosion
~ St. Paul Winter Carnival Begins Jan 28 – Feb. 6
José Martí, writer, b.1853
Auguste & Jean-Felix Piccard, baloonists, b.1884

It is good to have an end to journey toward, but it is the journey that matters in the end.
— *Ursula K. Le Guin*

BUBBLE WRAP APPRECIATION DAY

♂ ☌ ♇ 11:47AM

☾ SET 9:25AM RISE 8:41PM

☉ RISE 7:37AM SET 5:16PM

RIGHT MEMORY

---

29   SAT · JAN 29· 2005

Thomas Paine, revolutionary, b.1737
Emmnauel Swedenborg, inventor/philosopher, b.1688
Anton Chekhov, writer, b.1860
W.C. Fields, actor, b.1880

NATIONAL PUZZLE DAY

Everything has been figured out, except how to live.
— *Jean-Paul Sartre*

☾ △ ♀ 6:09AM
☾ △ ☿ 3:07PM

☾ SET 9:42AM RISE 9:47PM

☉ RISE 7:36AM SET 5:17PM

RIGHT CONCEPTION

---

30   SUN · JAN 30 · 2005

Holiday of the Three Hierarchs, Greece
~1972: Bloody Sunday, N. Ireland
~ 1948: Mahatma Gandhi assassinated

NATIONAL INANE ANSWERING MACHINE MESSAGE DAY

Franklin D. Roosevelt, politician, b.1882

☾ △ ☉ 1:18PM
☾ △ ♆ 8:45PM

☾ SET 9:59AM RISE 10:55PM

☉ RISE 7:35AM SET 5:19PM

RIGHT RESOLVE

FEBRUARY

JAN 20- FEB 18

FEB 19- MAR 20

aquarius

pisces

BIRTHSTONE
Amethyst

FLOWER
Violet

Discretion
BECOMES MEDITATIVE STRENGTH
Challenges: indiscrimination

The days lengthen. The sun is still more red than gold. Yet the sky brightens when the clouds part and the rain (or snow) passes. The month opens with the Celtic festival of Imbolc, marking the lactation of the ewes, the flow of milk announcing the return of life: the joy of becoming. But spring is still far away. Patience and faith are called for.

Perhaps this is why the month takes its name from Februa, the Roman festival of Purification. To purify is to separate the gold from the dross, the good from the bad. It requires memory and the practice of discernment. Discernment is often symbolized by a sword, but there is something feminine about February. It is a gentle month, filled with feasts celebrating female figures like St. Brigit, the Virgin Mary, and the Virgin Goddess Artemis. They ask us to practice keeping silent, pondering all things in our hearts. Great strength, you may be sure, will come from such discretion.

FEBRUARY IS:

INT'L FRIENDSHIP MONTH · NAT'L CHERRY MONTH · NAT'L WILD BIRD FEEDING MONTH
RESPONSIBLE PET OWNERS MONTH · AMERICAN HISTORY MONTH · NAT'L HOBBY
MONTH · SOUP MONTH · EYE CARE MONTH · AMERICAN HEART MONTH · BLACK
HISTORY MONTH · CHILDREN'S DENTAL HEALTH MONTH · NAT'L EMBROIDERY MONTH
GRAPEFRUIT MONTH · SNACK FOOD MONTH · INT'L BOOST SELF-ESTEEM MONTH
EXPECT SUCCESS MONTH · LIBRARY LOVERS MONTH · MARFAN SYNDROME AWARENESS
MONTH · NAT'L WEDDINGS MONTH · N.C. SWEET POTATO MONTH

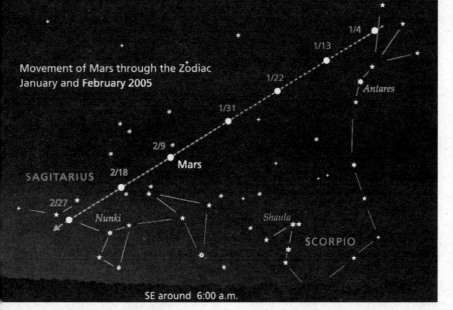

Movement of Mars through the Zodiac
January and February 2005

1/4
1/13
1/22
1/31
2/9
Mars
2/18
2/27

Antares

SAGITTARIUS

Nunki

Shaula

SCORPIO

SE around 6:00 a.m.

STARS & PLANETS FOR FEBRUARY

There is a nice conjunction of Mars, Venus and the waning crescent Moon on the morning of the 4th. Venus is probably no longer visible. Mars is passing through the bright field of Sagittarius's stars. Mercury is at superior conjunction, also not visible.

LOOK UP:

8   New Moon, 22:28 UT
14 Mercury passes behind the Sun
      (conjunction)
16 Waxing quarter Moon
24 Full Moon (Hunger Moon), 4:54 UT

LOOK OUT:

· Tree frogs fill the night with sound
  around Seattle

· Lupines and poppies line Tucson roadsides

· Brief sunshine spells give snow an icy crust
  across the Corn Belt

· Wood storks on the nest in Florida

FEBRUARY						
S	M	T	W	T	F	S
		1	2	3	4	5
6	7	8	9	10	11	12
13	14	15	16	17	18	19
20	21	22	23	24	25	26
27	28					

*Once the realization is accepted that even
between the closest human beings
infinite distances continue to exist, a
wonderful living side by side can grow up,
if they succeed in loving the distance
between them.*

~ RAINER MARIA RILKE

HOLIDAY: Groundhog's Day, February 2

SPRINGTIME SPLENDOR
(Tune = Love Me Tender)

Springtime splendor, springtime sweet,
how soon will it be?
If there's no shadow at your feet,
it may come suddenly
Springtime splendor, springtime true,
may be on its way
But if all the sky is blue,
winter's here to stay

© *1992 by Don Halley. All lyrics* © *Don Halley*

On February 2, feisty Punxsutawney Phil gets hauled out of his Pennsylvania home to see if he can see his shadow. If he does, then we'll have six more weeks of winter; if he doesn't, spring is on the way (in about six more weeks). The prognosticating tradition makes perfect sense, because anyone who's lived in the north knows that the clear, bright days of winter tend to be the coldest – and their brilliant sun casts the best shadows.

Groundhog's Day comes halfway between winter solstice (December 21) and the spring equinox (March 20), and like many traditions, its origin rests with life's basic needs – in this case, when will spring come so we can put seeds in the ground? In Europe, people long looked for signs of hibernating mammals coming out into the light to tell them warm weather was ahead. Immigrants brought that practice to America, and in the 1880's a group of friends in Punxsutawney, Pennsylvania, started going into the woods every February 2 to look for groundhogs – also known as woodchucks – to show them if winter was on its way out. By 1887, it was a full-fledged event.

The first days of February also mark several other ancient festivals and feast days, such as Candlemas and Imbolc, all having to do with light, fire, and the coming of spring.

For more information on Groundhog Day and Punxsutawney Phil, see www.groundhog.org

PITTSBURGH, PA

31 — MON · JAN 31 · 2005

1940: First Social Security check issued

Franz Schubert, composer, b.1797

Zane Grey, author, b.1872

EXPLORER 1 SPACE SATELLITE LAUNCHED 1958

Look at everything as though you were seeing it for the first time or the last time. Then your time on earth will be filled with glory.
— *Betty Smith*

☽ ☌ ♃ 4:08AM
☾ SET 10:17AM
☀ RISE 7:34AM SET 5:20PM

RIGHT WORD

1 — TUE · FEB 1 · 2005

St Brigid's Day, Ireland

Langston Hughes, poet/ author, b.1902

Clark Gable, actor, b.1901

BLACK HISTORY MONTH

Great spirits have always encountered violent opposition from mediocre minds.
— *Albert Einstein*

AMERICAN HEART MONTH

☽ △ ♅ 10:47AM
☾ RISE 12:05AM SET 10:37AM
☀ RISE 7:33AM SET 5:21PM

RIGHT DEED

2 — WED · FEB 2 · 2005

Imbolc: Wiccan Feast of Torches

W.H. Auden, poet, b.1907

James Joyce, author, b.1882

Ayn Rand, author, b.1905

A man of genius makes no mistakes.
— *James Joyce*

CANDLEMAS

GROUNDHOG DAY

☽ △ ♄ 4:56PM
☀ RISE 7:31AM SET 5:23PM

Last Quarter 7:27UT

RIGHT LIVELIHOOD

3 — THU · FEB 3 · 2005

150 YEARS AGO 1855: Wisc. Supreme Court declares U.S. Fugitive Slave Law unconstitutional

~ Setsubun: Bean-Throwing Festival, Japan

Gertrude Stein, writer, b.1874

A rose is a rose is a rose.
— *Gertrude Stein*

COLDEST N. AMER. TEMPERATURE

-81°F YUKON TERRITORIES, CAN. 1947

☉ ☌ ♆ 1:28PM
☾ RISE 02:36AM SET 11:33AM
☀ RISE 7:30AM SET 5:24PM

RIGHT ENDEAVOR

LIVING URBAN TREASURE: Toronto's Jane Jacobs

Jane Jacobs helped rescue our cities at a time when the trend called for razing whole neighborhoods, building expressways, and institutionalizing sprawl. She wrote her classic book, *The Death and Life of Great American Cities*, in 1961 to counter "the mad spree of deceptions and vandalism and waste that was called urban renewal." In the spring of 2004, at the age of 88, her latest book, *Dark Age Ahead*, appeared. Despite its title, Jacobs continues to believe in possibility. "Never underestimate the power of a city to regenerate," she says.

Jane Jacobs in Toronto

Jacobs described eminent domain as a "promiscuous use of power" that "invites corruption."

Born in Scranton, Pennsylvania, Jacobs spent her young adulthood in New York. After graduating from high school, she was loath to go on to college. (To this day, she refuses to accept honorary degrees.) Jacobs considered herself a writer, and earned money from freelance articles and other work until she finally landed at *Architectural Forum*.

When New York City threatened to destroy historic Washington Square in Greenwich Village and replace it with an expressway ramp, Jacobs got involved in a David and Goliath battle that represented her belief that humans, not institutions, are at the center of public thought. With her sons facing the draft in 1968, Jacobs and her family immigrated to Toronto, where she still makes her home.

In a 2001 symposium at Boston College, she said that expertise ungrounded in reality was the target of her first book and she described eminent domain as a "promiscuous use of power" that "invites corruption." Short blocks. Interspersed businesses and residences. High density. Diversity. Recognition of the street as the fundamental unit of the city. These are some of her antidotes to sprawl and its waste of land, energy, and time.

On October 29, 2002, she unveiled the Toronto Pedestrian Charter, the first of its kind in North America. It begins with a simple statement: "Walking is the most ancient and universal form of travel." It ends by saying that walking "creates opportunities for the informal social interaction that is one of the main attributes of a vibrant, livable city."

~ *Kathleen Melin*

For more information on Jane Jacobs, see www.janejacobs.com

ROAD SALT / *Louis Jenkins*

…Salt is not content just to eat the snow and ice. It starts in on your automobile. Rust spots develop, then holes where the salt has eaten through…You could repair those rust spots now, before the worst happens, but life is short. Who has time for that?

4
FRI · FEB 4 · 2005

◀ 1985: Torture abolished by the UN (signed but still not ratified by the U.S.)
~ 1948: Independence Day, Sri Lanka
~ Winterlude begins, Ottawa, CAN Feb 4–20

When you get to the end of your rope, tie a knot and hang on.
— *Franklin D. Roosevelt*

Charles Lindbergh, aviator, b.1902

☽ ☌ ♇ 10:28PM

☾
RISE 3:55AM
SET 12:15PM

☉
RISE 7:29AM
SET 5:26PM

RIGHT MEMORY

5
SAT · FEB 5 · 2005

Constitution Day, Mexico
~ 1993: Family Leave Bill Passed

◀ Hank Aaron, baseball player, b.1934
John Jeffries, physician/ meteorologist, b.1744

You will find as you look back upon your life that the moments when you have truly lived are the moments when you have done things in the spirit of love.
— *Henry Drummond*

☽ ☌ ♂ 7:07AM

☾
RISE 5:10AM
SET 01:12PM

☉
RISE 7:28AM
SET 5:27PM

RIGHT CONCEPTION

6
SUN · FEB 6 · 2005

◀ Homstrom: Burning of straw men on poles as symbol of winter's departure, Switzerland
~ Four Chaplains Sunday
~ Transfiguration, Christian

*Babe Ruth, baseball hero, b.1895
Bob Marley, reggae musician, b.1945
Aaron Burr, politician, b.1756*

PAY A COMPLIMENT DAY

☽ ☌ ♄ 7:47PM

☾
RISE 6:15AM
SET 2:24PM

☉
RISE 7:26AM
SET 5:29PM

RIGHT RESOLVE

CELEBRATE: Chinese New Year, February 9

Year of the Rooster (4703). The ancient Chinese calendar has 12 months based on the moon, six of them with 29 days and six with 30 days. An intercalary month is added every few years, so 7 out of 19 years have 13 months. The new year is celebrated in Chinese communities all over the world with a huge dragon – a symbol of good luck – leading noisy street processions.

The dragon is made of bamboo covered in paper or silk, and more than 50 people may support it underneath, making it weave and wind through the streets. Dancers, acrobats, clowns, and stilt walkers accompany the dragon, and fire-crackers scare away evil spirits. In Chinese homes, families hang red scrolls printed with wishes for good luck and prosperity, and children receive coins inside little red packets.

From The Book of Holidays Around the World. *For more information on Chinese New Year celebrations, see www.chinapage.com/newyear.html*

SAN FRANCISCO, CA

7
MON · FEB 7 · 2005

1974:
Independence
Day, Grenada

*Ashton Kutcher,
actor, b.1978
Chris Rock,
comedian,
b.1966
Charles Dickens,
author, b.1812*

The world is
so fast that
there are days
when the
person who
says it can't be
done is inter-
rupted by the
person who is
doing it.
— *Unknown*

☉△♃ 6:03AM
☽☌♀ 7:06PM

☾
RISE 7:05AM
SET 3:47PM

☀
RISE 7:25AM
SET 5:30PM

RIGHT WORD

8
TUE · FEB 8 · 2005

1910: Boy
Scouts of
America est.
~ Shrove Tues-
day, Christian
~ Nirvana Day,
Buddhist

*James Dean,
actor, b.1931
Jules Verne,
author, b.1828*

When I find
myself fading, I
close my eyes and
realize my friends
are my energy.
— *Unknown*

WARMEST YEAR
ON RECORD:
DECLARED 1999

☿☌♆ 4:10AM
☽☌♆ 8:32AM
☽☌☿ 9:04AM
☽△♃ 2:07AM
☽☌☉ 4:28PM

☀
RISE 7:24AM
SET 5:32PM

*New Moon
22:28UT*

RIGHT DEED

9
WED ·FEB 9 · 2005

Ash Wednesday:
Lent Begins,
Christian
*Alice Walker,
author, b.1944
Gypsy Rose Lee,
burlesque queen,
b.1914*

CHINESE
NEW YEAR

Courage is not the
absence of fear,
but rather the
judgment that
something else
is more impor-
tant than fear.
— *Ambrose
Redmoon*

☽☌♅ 5:27PM

☾
RISE 8:13AM
SET 6:39PM

☀
RISE 7:22AM
SET 5:33PM

RIGHT LIVELIHOOD

10
THU · FEB 10 · 2005

Hijra: Islamic
New Year

*Boris
Pasternak,
author, b.1890
Bertolt Brecht,
playwright,
b.1898*

Darkness can-
not drive out
darkness; only
light can do
that. Hate can-
not drive out
hate; only love
can do that.
— *Martin Luther
King, Jr.*

☿△♃ 4:43AM
☽△♄ 7:27PM

☾
RISE 8:37AM
SET 8:00PM

☀
RISE 7:21AM
SET 5:34PM

RIGHT ENDEAVOR

ESSENTIAL PLACE: Magazine Street, New Orleans

Magazine Street connects downtown New Orleans amd Audubon Park (above).

Other New Orleans streets are older, prettier, hipper, and destination spots at Mardi Gras. But the one that best encapsulates the city's jaunty charms is Magazine Street, a colorful six-mile stretch that curves along the Crescent City's lower edge, connecting downtown and the moss-draped oaks of Audubon Park. In between lies a mix of fancy boutiques and restaurants, homey neighborhood establishments, and enough seedy patches to preserve the street's character. "From the swanky to the funky to the outright junky" — this hasn't been picked up as a marketing slogan yet by the local merchants' association, but it fairly describes what lies behind Magazine's multicolored facades and creaking front doors. Rows of high-end shops are punctuated by the intermittent shotgun cottage, burglar-barred convenience store, or check-cashing joint. Antique dealers abound, from those with fussy displays and heart-stopping prices to musty caverns whose hodge-podges yield the occasional find.

On Magazine Street, you can buy a chandelier, an African mask, a dozen raw oysters, a haircut (upscale spa or striped-pole version), an Oriental rug, a costume, a cigar. And after a long day of poking through curios and finery, you can cool off the traditional New Orleans way: stopping at a snowball stand for a sphere of flavored shaved ice in a paper cup.

~ *Katy Read*

For more information on Magazine Street in New Orleans, see www.cityofNO.com

NEW ORLEANS, LA

THERE IS NO EASY ROAD TO FREEDOM/Nelson Mandela

There is no easy road to freedom… | None of us acting alone can achieve success. | We must therefore act together as a united people, | For reconciliation, for nation building, | For the birth of a new world.

---

11 — FRI ·FEB 11 · 2005

St. Bernadette of Lourdes, French
~ 1990: Nelson Mandela released from prison

THOMAS EDISON, INVENTOR, B.1847

We must use time wisely and forever realize that the time is always ripe to do right.
— *Nelson Mandela*

Jennifer Aniston, actress, b.1969

☾ RISE 8:58AM SET 9:17PM
☼ RISE 7:19AM SET 5:36PM

RIGHT MEMORY

---

12 — SAT · FEB 12 · 2005

1909: NAACP founded

John L Lewis, labor leader, b.1880
Charles Darwin, naturalist, b.1809
Abraham Lincoln, president, b.1809

People are just as happy as they make up their minds to be.
— *Abraham Lincoln*

DARWIN DAY

☾ ☌ ♇ ♃ 5:49PM
☾ RISE 9:17AM SET 10:31PM
☼ RISE 7:18AM SET 5:37PM

RIGHT CONCEPTION

---

13 — SUN · FEB 13 · 2005

1741: First magazine published in U.S.
~ Vasent Panchami, Hindu

Peter Gabriel, singer, b.1950
Grant Wood, painter, b.1892

Without change, something sleeps inside us, and seldom awakens. The sleeper must awaken.
— *Frank Herbert*

☾ △ ♇ 3:27AM
☾ △ ♂ 12:04AM
☾ RISE 9:36AM SET 11:43PM
☼ RISE 7:17AM SET 5:39PM

RIGHT RESOLVE

HOLIDAY: Valentine's Day, February 14

LAST NIGHT, AS I WAS SLEEPING

Last night, as I was sleeping,
I dreamt — marvelous error! —
that a spring was breaking
out in my heart.
I said: Along which secret aqueduct,
Oh water, are you coming to me,
water of a new life
that I have never drunk?

Last night, as I was sleeping,
I dreamt — marvelous error! —
that I had a beehive
here inside my heart.
And the golden bees
were making white combs
and sweet honey
from my old failures.

Last night, as I was sleeping,
I dreamt — marvelous error! —
that a fiery sun was giving
light inside my heart.
It was fiery because I felt
warmth as from a hearth,
and sun because it gave light
and brought tears to my eyes.

Last night, as I was sleeping,
I dreamt — marvelous error! —
that it was God I had
here inside my heart.

~ *Antonio Machado*
Translated by Robert Bly

14

1920: League of Women Voters founded

Mary Ann Prout, activist, b.1801
Jack Benny, comedian, b.1894

Love is never lost. If not reciprocated, it will flow back and soften and purify the heart.
— *Washington Irving*

ST. VALENTINE'S DAY

☽△♂ 12:04AM
☉♂☿ 4:50AM
♀♂♆ 6:47PM

☾
RISE 9:57AM

✴
RISE 7:15AM
SET 5:40PM

RIGHT WORD

15

Kamakura: Snow Cave Festival, Japan
Susan B. Anthony, advocate, b.1820
Gallileo Gallilei, astronomer, b.1564 Harold Arlen, song-writer, b.1905
Matt Groening, cartoonist, 1954

Somewhere, over the rainbow, way up high, there's a land that I heard of, once in a lullaby.
— *Harold Arlen*

LUPERCALIA: ROMAN FERTILITY FESTIVAL

☽△☉ 10:57PM

☾
SET 00:54AM
RISE 10:22AM

✴
RISE 7:14AM
SET 5:42PM

RIGHT DEED

16

1932: 1st patent issued for a tree: to James Markham for a peach tree
~ 1918: Independence Day, Lithuania

Edgar Bergen, ventriloquist, b.1903

To accomplish great things, we must not only act, but also dream; not only plan, but also believe.
— *Anatole France*

☽△☉ 10:57PM

✴
RISE 7:12AM
SET 5:43PM

First Quarter
00:16UT

RIGHT LIVELIHOOD

17

Bonten: Pole Festival, Japan
~ 1974: A Prairie Home Companion nat'l premiere

"WHO SHALL I BE?" DAY

Jim Brown, football player, b.1936

To live a pure unselfish life, one must count nothing as one's own in the midst of abundance.
— *Buddha*

Michael Jordan, basketball player, b.1963

♀△♃ 4:10AM
☽△♆ 6:12AM
☽△♃ 11:59AM
☽△♀ 12:56AM
☽♂♇ 11:23PM

☾
SET 3:10AM
RISE 11:27AM

✴
RISE 7:10AM
SET 5:44PM

RIGHT ENDEAVOR

ESSENTIAL PLACE: The Tattered Cover, Denver

Seems like everyone has heard of Denver's Tattered Cover bookstore. The main store at Cherry Creek is almost too popular, especially on cold weekend afternoons. Smaller and more intimate is the LoDo (Lower Downtown) location, occupying just two floors. But what two floors they are! The store is housed in the Morey Mercantile building, an 1896 red-brick warehouse built in the old post-and-lintel style with massive wooden columns spaced about 15 feet apart. On the first level, the original plank floors creak as you browse. The former loading docks are enclosed by glass so you can peruse history or travel books as you watch the snow fall. The store has the usual requisite coffee bar (with antique tables and chairs), along with a 2,000-title newsstand and all of the book sections you could want. On the second floor (carpeted, alas, for fire code reasons) there's a corner fireplace, and an events room (with its own fireplace) for book signings in the former executive offices of Morey Mercantile Co. Some of the windows are original, having survived more than a century, and look out over Denver's Union Station. The store so embodies the spirit of the city that former governor Roy Romer brought President Clinton here on a whim in 1996 so that he could buy some books (he bought three).

~ *Mark Barnhouse*

For more information on the Tattered Cover bookstore in Denver, see www.tatteredcover.com

MY SYMPHONY / *William Henry Channing*

To live content with small means, to seek elegance rather than luxury, and refinement rather than fashion, to be worthy, not respectable, and wealthy, not rich, to study hard, think quietly, talk gently, act frankly, to listen to stars and birds, babes and sages, with open heart, to bear all cheerfully, do all bravely, await occasions, hurry never — in a word, to let the spiritual, unbidden and unconscious, grow up through the common. This is to be my symphony.

---

18   FRI · FEB 18 · 2005

Kuomboka: River Festival, Zambia ~ Satisfied Staying Single Day

Yoko Ono, artist, b.1933 Milos Forman, filmmaker, b. 1932

It is not enough to have a good mind; the main thing is to use it well.
— René Descartes

PLANET PLUTO DISCOVERED 1930

☽△☉ 11:33PM
☽△☿ 7:56PM

☾ SET 4:10AM
RISE 12:12PM

✺ RISE 7:09AM
SET 5:46PM

RIGHT MEMORY

---

19   SAT · FEB 19 · 2005

Ashura, Islam ~ 1942: Japanese Internment began (lasted until 1945)

Nicolaus Copernicus, astronomer, b.1473

To me every hour of the light and dark is a miracle; Every cubic inch of space is a miracle.
— Walt Whitman

☽△♅ 12:11AM
☽☌♂ 5:27AM
☿☌♅ 11:44PM

☾ SET 5:03AM
RISE 1:05PM

✺ RISE 7:07AM
SET 5:47PM

RIGHT CONCEPTION

---

20   SUN · FEB 20 · 2005

Triodion, Orthodox Christian

Buffy Sainte-Marie, folksinger, b.1941 Ansel Adams, photographer, b.1902 Frederick Douglass, d.1895

Choose your friends by their character & your socks by their color. Choosing your socks by their character makes no sense, & choosing your friends by their color is unthinkable. — Unknown

☽☌♄ 6:06AM

☾ SET 5:46AM
RISE 2:06PM

✺ RISE 7:06AM
SET 5:49PM

RIGHT RESOLVE

CIVILIZING IDEA: Youth Speaks

When James Kass first set foot in a high school classroom to talk about poetry, he had no idea what was about to happen. Rather than the bored stares he expected, Kass was delighted to see the students come alive with interest. It was 1996, and he and some friends had just started an after-school writing program for teens called Youth Speaks based on the lofty notion that "the next generation can speak for itself," and that teaching kids to write poetry could help them find their voices and learn to think critically. "We wanted them to know that they could breathe in the world and breathe out poetry just as millions of others throughout the world and throughout history have done," Kass writes. "And that poetry was something that they were going to have to define for themselves." They also hoped to bring kids together from many different backgrounds, "diversifying the cultural dialogue." Eight years later, youth poetry is sweeping the nation, and Youth Speaks is leading the way. Thousands of teens have participated in its writing workshops, and the San Francisco-based nonprofit has chapters in New York and Seattle and has expanded beyond after-school programs, helping teachers integrate poetry into their classes, organizing poetry slams, and publishing chapbooks of poems by Youth Speaks students.

~ *Leif Utne*

*For more information on Youth Speaks,
see www.youthspeaks.org*

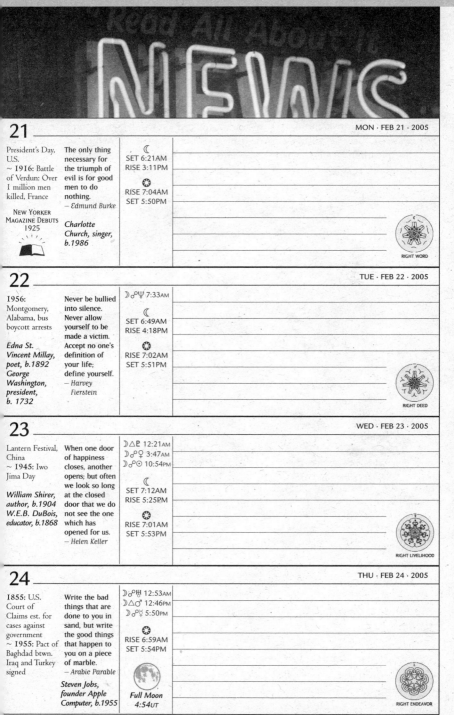

21

President's Day, U.S.
~ 1916: Battle of Verdun: Over 1 million men killed, France

NEW YORKER MAGAZINE DEBUTS 1925

The only thing necessary for the triumph of evil is for good men to do nothing.
— Edmund Burke

Charlotte Church, singer, b.1986

☾ SET 6:21AM
RISE 3:11PM

☀ RISE 7:04AM
SET 5:50PM

RIGHT WORD

22

1956: Montgomery, Alabama, bus boycott arrests

Edna St. Vincent Millay, poet, b.1892
George Washington, president, b. 1732

Never be bullied into silence. Never allow yourself to be made a victim. Accept no one's definition of your life; define yourself.
— Harvey Fierstein

☽ ♂♅ 7:33AM

☾ SET 6:49AM
RISE 4:18PM

☀ RISE 7:02AM
SET 5:51PM

RIGHT DEED

23

Lantern Festival, China
~ 1945: Iwo Jima Day

William Shirer, author, b.1904
W.E.B. DuBois, educator, b.1868

When one door of happiness closes, another opens; but often we look so long at the closed door that we do not see the one which has opened for us.
— Helen Keller

☽ △♇ 12:21AM
☽ ♂♀ 3:47AM
☽ ♂☉ 10:54PM

☾ SET 7:12AM
RISE 5:25PM

☀ RISE 7:01AM
SET 5:53PM

RIGHT LIVELIHOOD

24

1855: U.S. Court of Claims est. for cases against government
~ 1955: Pact of Baghdad btwn. Iraq and Turkey signed

Write the bad things that are done to you in sand, but write the good things that happen to you on a piece of marble.
— Arabic Parable

Steven Jobs, founder Apple Computer, b.1955

☽ ♂♅ 12:53AM
☽ △♂ 12:46PM
☽ ♂♇ 5:50PM

☀ RISE 6:59AM
SET 5:54PM

Full Moon
4:54UT

RIGHT ENDEAVOR

RECIPE: Buffalo Stew, as made by the Queen of Tarts

Once nearly 60 million buffalo (or bison) roamed the American plains, but the herds were decimated by white hunters toward the end of 19th century until only about 300 animals remained. The American herd is now more than 100,000 strong, thanks in large part to ranchers who are raising grass-fed buffalo for their meat, which is low in calories, low in bad saturated fat, and high in good fat or omega–3 fatty acids. It's also high in selenium, which may reduce the risk of cancer. Urban farmers' markets all over the country offer buffalo meat from local sources. Give it a try; you'll be helping to bring back an American treasure.

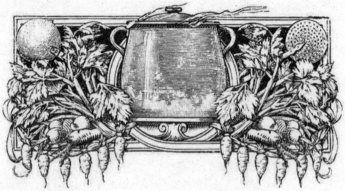

2½ to 3 lb. BUFFALO ROAST,
   cut into 1-inch cubes
1 lb. carrots, cut into 1-inch chunks
3 small turnips or parsnips,
   cut into large dice
2 large potatoes, cut into 1-inch chunks
4 small onions cut into quarters
8-10 garlic gloves, minced
3 cups water or broth
¾ c. dry red wine
1 15-oz. can tomato sauce

1 T. dijon mustard
2 tsp. honey
1 tsp. worcestershire sauce
1–2 tsp. balsamic vinegar
2 tsp. sea salt
2 tsp. freshly ground pepper
1 tsp. dried basil
1 tsp. dried thyme
1 tsp. celery seed

Preheat oven to 275°

Sear buffalo cubes over high heat in a dutch oven or large stock pot.

Remove from heat and add all cut vegetables. Combine with wine, water or broth, tomato sauce, worcestershire sauce, balsamic vinegar, honey and mustard.

Add to buffalo mixture. Add all herbs, salt and pepper. Stir to combine.

Place cover on pan and place in oven for 5 hours. No stirring or checking required. Remove from oven and dive right in. This recipe can also be made in a 300 degree oven and cooking time is reduced by one hour.

Great with red wine, a green salad, and baguettes!

SOMETIMES A MAN / *Rainer Maria Rilke (translated by Robert Bly)*

Sometimes a man stands up during supper and walks outdoors, and keeps on walking, because of a church that stands somewhere in the East. And his children say blessings on him as if he were dead.

And another man, who remains inside his own house, dies there, inside the dishes and in the glasses, so that his children have to go far out into the world toward that same church, which he forgot.

25

FRI · FEB 25 · 2005

75 YEARS AGO 1932: Immigrant A. Hitler gets German citizenship ~ 1964: Cassius Clay *(Muhammad Ali)* hvywt, champ **George Harrison, musician, b.1943 Auguste Renoir, painter, b.1841**

You are never given a wish without also being given the power to make it come true. You may have to work for it, however.
— *Richard Bach*

☉☌♅ 12:33AM

☾
SET 7:49AM
RISE 7:39PM

☀
RISE 6:57AM
SET 5:55PM

RIGHT MEMORY

26

SAT · FEB 26 · 2005

1848: Communist Manifesto published ~ 1919: Grand Canyon Natl. Park established

Victor Hugo, author, b.1802 "Buffalo Bill" Cody, frontiersman, b.1846

We are what we think. All that we are arises with our thoughts. With our thoughts, we make the world.
— *Buddha*

☾
SET 8:06AM
RISE 8:47PM

☀
RISE 6:56AM
SET 5:57PM

RIGHT CONCEPTION

27

SUN · FEB 27 · 2005

Ralph Nader, advocate, b.1934 Henry W. Longfellow, poet, b.1807 Rudolf Steiner, philosopher, educator, b.1861

The earth is but one country and mankind its citizens.
— *Baha'u'llah*

77TH ANNUAL ACADEMY AWARDS

☾△♆ 4:12AM
☾☌♃ 7:46AM
☿△♄ 3:51PM

☾
SET 8:23AM
RISE 9:56PM

☀
RISE 6:54AM
SET 5:58PM

RIGHT RESOLVE

MARCH

FEB 19 - MAR 20

pisces

BIRTHSTONE
Aquamarine

FLOWER
Tulip

MAR 21 - APR 19

aries

Inner Balance
BECOMES PROGRESS
Challenges: apathy, inertia, covetousness

*T*he days and nights approach each other in duration, balancing perfectly at the vernal equinox. Anything could happen. Despite the persistent winds and omnipresent mud (if you live in the country), promise is in the air. "The wind blows where it wants and you can hear the sound of it but you cannot tell where it is coming from and where it is going. So it is with those who are born of the spirit." March is the Martian month. We feel braced. Our great warrior's heart opens to the world in love. There's a warmth in the air. Nature begins her journey outward into beauty. Our senses awaken. Cosmic being flows into us. Winter's inwardness, its contraction, begins to turn inside out. Responding, we begin to flow outward, to expand.

"March is the month of expectation," wrote Emily Dickinson.

MARCH IS
AMERICAN RED CROSS MONTH · COLORECTAL CANCER AWARENESS MONTH · ETHICS MONTH · HELP SOMEONE SEE MONTH · HONOR SOCIETY MONTH · HUMORISTS ARE ARTISTS MONTH · MIRTH MONTH · IRISH-AMERICAN HERITAGE MONTH · INTERNATIONAL LISTENING MONTH · MENTAL RETARDATION AWARENESS MONTH · MUSIC IN OUR SCHOOLS MONTH · CHRONIC FATIGUE SYNDROME MONTH · COLLISION AWARENESS MONTH · EYE DONOR MONTH · FROZEN FOOD MONTH · KIDNEY MONTH · PREPARE YOUR HOME TO BE SOLD MONTH · TALK WITH YOUR TEEN ABOUT SEX MONTH · NATIONAL UMBRELLA MONTH · WOMEN'S HISTORY MONTH · OPTIMISM MONTH · PLAY-THE-RECORDER MONTH · POISON PREVENTION MONTH · YOUTH ART MONTH

Mercury's visibility curve and brightness

3/13

3/12

+

● Mercury

3/11

10°

3/14

3/6

3/20

2/28

7:15 p.m.   W

W

STARS & PLANETS FOR MARCH

The skittish Mercury is visible in the evening sky, especially on the 14th and 15th. Jupiter, the Moon and the star Spica are standing in a line on the 26th. The planets form a cross in the zodiac—Mercury, the Sun and Venus are in opposition to Jupiter and Mars and Saturn, forming a celestial right angle—an Easter configuration if ever there was one.

LOOK UP:

10 New Moon, 9:11 UT

11 The crescent Moon is in the vicinity of Mercury just after sunset

12 Mercury at greatest eastern elongation

19 Moon near Saturn

20 Spring Equinox

25 Full Moon (Crow Moon), 21:00 UT

29 Mercury moves between the Sun and Earth (inferior conjunction)

31 Venus moves behind the Sun (superior conjunction)

LOOK OUT:

· Swallows arrive in Capistrano, California

· Great Basin cottonwoods and willows erupt with lacy catkins

· Wolves howl along Canadian border

· Eastern screech owls begin courting

MARCH						
S	M	T	W	T	F	S
		1	2	3	4	5
6	7	8	9	10	11	12
13	14	15	16	17	18	19
20	21	22	23	24	25	26
27	28	29	30	31		

To be a philosopher is not merely to have subtle thoughts, nor even to found a school, but to so love wisdom as to live according to its dictates, a life of simplicity, independence, magnanimity, and trust.
~ HENRY DAVID THOREAU

BIRTHDAY: Dr. Seuss (Theodore Geisel), March 2, 1904

"...I know it is wet and the sun is not sunny. But we can have lots of good fun that is funny..."

The year 2004 was the Seuss-centennial, a word that looks and sounds nearly as marvelous as the characters Dr. Seuss thrilled us with for more than 60 years. Theodor ("Ted") Seuss Geisel was born on March 2, 1904, and the Seusscentennial celebrates the 100th anniversary of his birth.

And what a cause for celebration. During his career as an illustrator and writer of children's books, he filled the hearts and minds of generations of readers with joy, solace, and pure pleasure. His characters like Horton and Nerkle and Humpf-Humpf-a-Dumpfer stick around in our heads forever; the memory of their stories read to us by parents or grandparents, or enjoyed in wonderful solitude, mark our childhood innocence and delight.

In 1937, Dr. Seuss' first attempt at a child's book — *And to Think I Saw it on Mulberry Street* — met rejection after rejection. Finally, it was published and critics began to take notice. But it was when Houghton Mifflin and Random House challenged Geisl to write a reading primer that wasn't the usual boring, "See Dick run" kind of book, that he moved into our collective consciousness. His answer to that challenge was the *Cat in the Hat*.

Handsome, kind, and mischievous, Ted Geisel died on September 24,1991, and left us an entire universe of whimsical creatures dedicated to our happiness.

For more information on Dr. Seuss, see www.seussville.com

28 — MON · FEB 28 · 2005

Kalevala Day, Finland

Mary Lyon, Founder of Mt. Holyoke College, b.1797
Olaf Palme, Prime Minister of Sweden, assassinated 1986

You don't get harmony when everybody sings the same note.
— *Doug Floyd*

☽△♀ 11:08 AM
☽△♅ 7:08 PM

☾
SET 8:42AM
RISE 11:09PM

☀
RISE 6:52AM
SET 6:00PM

RIGHT WORD

1 — TUE · MAR 1 · 2005

50 YEARS AGO
1955: Israeli assault on Gaza kills 48
~ **1872:** Yellowstone Nat'l Park established
~ **1999:** UN Land Mine Ban
~ **1961:** Peace Corps established

You must do the things you think you cannot do.
— *Eleanor Roosevelt*

ICELAND: BEER DAY

Ralph Ellison, author, b.1914

☽△☉ 2:11AM
☽△♄ 8:04PM

☾
SET 9:05AM

☀
RISE 6:51AM
SET 6:01PM

RIGHT DEED

2 — WED · MAR 2 · 2005

1925: Highway numbers introduced
~ **1899:** Mount Ranier Nat'l Park established

Theodore Geisel "Dr. Seuss", author, b.1904

Fear less, hope more; Whine less, breathe more; Talk less, say more; Hate less, love more; And all good things are yours.
— *Swedish Proverb*

☽△☿ 4:25AM

☾
RISE 12:24AM
SET 9:33AM

☀
RISE 6:49AM
SET 6:02PM

RIGHT LIVELIHOOD

3 — THU · MAR 3 · 2005

200 YEARS AGO
1805: Louisiana /Missouri Territory formed

Alexander Graham Bell, inventor, b.1847

People only see what they are prepared to see.
— *Ralph Waldo Emerson*

ELVIS PRESLEY FIRST TV APPEARANCE 1955

☀
RISE 6:47AM
SET 6:04AM

Last Quarter 17:36UT

RIGHT ENDEAVOR

ESSENTIAL PLACE: Domino Park, Miami

Named after a famous Cuban Revolutionary who fought against Spanish oppression in the late 19th century, Maximo Gomez-Park – better known as Domino Park – is the liveliest meeting place in Miami's Little Havana. Here retirees and other men from the neighborhood keep Cuban culture alive by condemning the Castro regime while they slam down tiles and lay on the BS. (If you're a woman, or under the age of 65, don't even think about trying to get in on the fun.) Down the street on Calle Ocho, or Eighth Street, workers at the El Credito Cigar Factory rip, cut and roll tobacco leaves into *gigantes*, *supremos*, *panatelas*, and Churchills. Most of the workers learned their

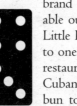

craft in the old country, which means that each cigar is painstakingly made by the same person. Aficionados rate the *La Gloria Cubana* brand among the finest available outside Cuba. Finish your Little Havana tour with a trip to one of the many shops and restaurants that offer fritas – Cuban hamburgers served on a bun topped with a tasty (and greasy) mound of shoestring potatoes. Wash it down with a Café Cubano or a Cuba Libre – basically a rum and coke with a generous splash of lime juice.

~ Elizabeth Larsen

*For more information on
Domino Park in Miami,
see icuban.com/3guys/domino.html*

MIAMI, FLORIDA

A RITUAL TO READ TO EACH OTHER / *William Stafford*

If you don't know the kind of person I am | and I don't know the kind of person you are | a pattern that others made may prevail in the world | and following the wrong god home we may miss our star… | the signals we give — yes, no, or maybe — | should be clear: the darkness around us is deep.

4
FRI · MAR 4 · 2005

World Day of Prayer, Interfaith

Knute Rockne, football legend, b.1888
Casimir Pulaski, Polish hero of US revolutionary war, b. 1747

It is one of the most beautiful compensations of life, that no man can sincerely try to help another without helping himself.
— *Ralph Waldo Emerson*

♀☌♅ 2:44AM
☽☌♇ 6:41AM

☽ RISE 2:56AM
SET 10:59AM

☉ RISE 6:45AM
SET 6:05PM

RIGHT MEMORY

5
SAT · MAR 5 · 2005

1770: Boston Massacre

Gerhardus Mercator, cartographer, b.1512
William Blackstone, first Boston settler, b.1595

From Stettin in the Baltic to Trieste in the Adriatic an iron curtain has descended across the continent.
—"Iron Curtain" speech: 1946 *Sir Winston Churchill*

☽ RISE 4:03AM
SET 12:03PM

☉ RISE 6:43AM
SET 6:06PM

RIGHT CONCEPTION

6
SUN · MAR 6 · 2005

1836: Fall of the Alamo

Elizabeth Barrett Browning, poet, b.1806
Gabriel Garcia Marquez, author, b.1928
Michelangelo, artist, b.1475

To the mind that is still, the whole universe surrenders.
— *Lao Tzu*

LEARN WHAT YOUR NAME MEANS DAY

☽☌♂ 12:46AM
☽☍♄ 2:28AM

☽ RISE 4:57AM
SET 1:20PM

☉ RISE 6:42AM
SET 6:08PM

RIGHT RESOLVE

URBAN SANCTUARY: Heavenly Pond, Los Angeles

The combination of the natural and the manmade at Heavenly Pond just makes sense for Los Angeles, where Commerce and Beauty somehow manage to co-exist.

Heavenly Pond sits in the Eastern Santa Monica Mountains where the man-made reservoirs in Franklin Canyon provided the water essential to Los Angeles' growth. The mountains, forest (no palm trees!), and lakes have been the backdrop for many of our favorite movies and television programs, including "Twin Peaks," and the opening of the "Andy Griffith Show." Just minutes from the bustle of Beverly Hills, Heavenly Pond is a secluded and yet accessible spot where volunteers devoted to healing touch come in fellowship, where Los Angeles parents introduce their children to the wilderness, and where anyone in search of a place to think and breathe can find succor. Leafy nooks where you can settle in with a book or a friend surround the pond, and fearless large fish swim so close to the surface you can almost touch them.

~ *Linda Picone*

*For a description and map
of Franklin Canyon, see
www.nps.gov/samo/maps/franklin.htm
Or read a quick history of the area at
www.jodavidsmeyer.com/combat/
personnel/franklin_history.html*

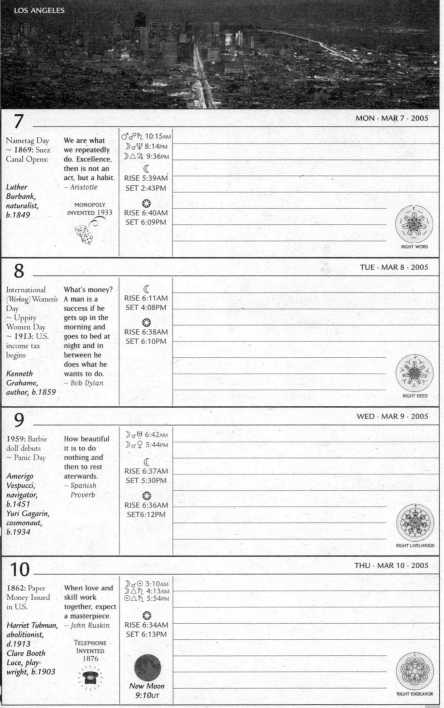

LOS ANGELES

7

Nametag Day
~ 1869: Suez
Canal Opens:

*Luther
Burbank,
naturalist,
b.1849*

We are what
we repeatedly
do. Excellence,
then is not an
act, but a habit.
— *Aristotle*

MONOPOLY
INVENTED 1933

♂☌♎♄ 10:15AM
☽☌♆ 8:14PM
☽△♃ 9:36PM

☾
RISE 5:39AM
SET 2:43PM

☀
RISE 6:40AM
SET 6:09PM

RIGHT WORD

8

International
(Working) Women's
Day
~ Uppity
Women Day
~ 1913: U.S.
income tax
begins

*Kenneth
Grahame,
author, b.1859*

What's money?
A man is a
success if he
gets up in the
morning and
goes to bed at
night and in
between he
does what he
wants to do.
— *Bob Dylan*

☾
RISE 6:11AM
SET 4:08PM

☀
RISE 6:38AM
SET 6:10PM

RIGHT DEED

9

1959: Barbie
doll debuts
~ Panic Day

*Amerigo
Vespucci,
navigator,
b.1451
Yuri Gagarin,
cosmonaut,
b.1934*

How beautiful
it is to do
nothing and
then to rest
afterwards.
— *Spanish
Proverb*

☽☌♅ 6:42AM
☽☌♀ 5:44PM

☾
RISE 6:37AM
SET 5:30PM

☀
RISE 6:36AM
SET6:12PM

RIGHT LIVELIHOOD

10

1862: Paper
Money Issued
in U.S.

*Harriet Tubman,
abolitionist,
d.1913
Clare Booth
Luce, play-
wright, b.1903*

When love and
skill work
together, expect
a masterpiece.
— *John Ruskin*

TELEPHONE
INVENTED
1876

☽☌☉ 3:10AM
☽△♄ 4:13AM
☉△♄ 5:54PM

☀
RISE 6:34AM
SET 6:13PM

New Moon
9:10UT

RIGHT ENDEAVOR

BIRTHDAY: Jack Kerouac, March 12, 1922

My manners, abominable at times, can be sweet. As I grew older I became a drunk. Why? Because I like ectasy of the mind. I'm a wretch. But I love, love.
— From *Satori in Paris*

...and everything is going to the beat. It's the beat generation, it be-at, it's the beat to keep, it's the beat of the heart, it's being beat and down in the world and like oldtime lowdown and like in ancient civilizations the slave boatmen rowing galleys to a beat and servants spinning pottery to a beat...

What is the feeling when you're driving away from people, and they recede on the plain till you see their specks dispersing? It's the too huge world vaulting us, and it's good-bye. But we lean forward to the next crazy adventure beneath the skies
— From *Motivation*

In a conversation with the writer John Clellon Holmes, Jack Kerouac coined the term "Beat Generation" to describe the "beatness" or "weariness" with the world of his post-war generation. As a young man, he crisscrossed the country, studying Buddhism, working at odd jobs, and staying with his friends Allen Ginsberg and William S. Burroughs. Eventually he wrote *On the Road*, the book that catapulted him into reluctant fame in 1957. Other books followed, including *The Dharma Bums* and *Big Sur*. By the time he died of alcoholism in 1969, Kerouac had left his mark on American literary history with his spontaneous prose style, and he continues to inspire legions of young people to live life on their own terms, to love intensely, and to risk everything.

...the only people for me are the mad ones, the ones who are mad to live, mad to talk, and to be saved, desirous of everything at the same time, the ones who never yawn or say a commonplace thing, but burn, burn, burn, like fabulous yellow roman candles exploding like spiders across the stars and in the middle you see the blue centerlight pop and everybody goes "Awww!"
— From *On the Road*

For more on Jack Kerouac, see
www.cmgworldwide.com/historic/kerouac/

FOR THE CHILDREN/*Gary Snyder*

In the next century | or the one after that | they say, |
are valleys, pastures. | We can meet there in peace | if we make it. |
To climb these coming crests | one word to you, to |
you and your children: | *Stay together* | *learn the flowers* | *go light.*

---

11   FRI · MAR 11 · 2005

1824: Bureau of Indian Affairs established
~ 1918: Start of Flu Pandemic

Lawrence Welk, bandleader, b.1903
Robert Paine, revolutionary, b.1731

You must be the change you wish to see in the world.
— *Mahatma Gandhi*

JOHNNY APPLESEED DAY

☽☌☿ 12:07PM

☾ RISE 7:18AM SET 8:05PM

☀ RISE 6:33AM SET 6:14PM

RIGHT MEMORY

---

12   SAT · MAR 12 · 2005

250 YEARS AGO
1755: 1st steam engine in U.S. installed, to pump water from a mine

Charlie "Bird" Parker, musician, d.1953

They always say that time changes things, but you actually have to change them yourself.
— *Andy Warhol*

Jack Kerouac, author, b.1922

☽☌♃ 12:35AM
☽△♇ 2:13PM

☾ RISE 7:38AM SET 9:20PM

☀ RISE 6:31AM SET 6:16PM

RIGHT CONCEPTION

---

13   SUN · MAR 13 · 2005

Good Samaritan Involvement Day
~ 1887: Earmuffs patented
L. Ron Hubbard, scientologist, b.1911
Abigail Fillmore created 1st White House library, b.1798

Without a struggle, there can be no progress.
— *Frederick Douglass*

PLANET URANUS DISCOVERED 1781

☾ RISE 7:58AM SET 10:34PM

☀ RISE 6:29AM SET 6:17PM

RIGHT RESOLVE

HOLIDAY: St. Patrick's Day, March 17

In the fourth century, Ireland's patron saint was sold into slavery. After six years as a cowherd he escaped to France, where he dreamed that the people of his country were summoning him back. On his return to Ireland he traveled widely, founding hundreds of churches and schools and convincing people to become Christians. He used the three-leaf shamrock to explain the Holy trinity — the idea that God the Father, Jesus the Son, and the Holy Spirit are one. On this day Irish people the world over celebrate by wearing a shamrock and, often, having a parade.

From The Book of Holidays Around the World

How to Dye a River Green

The Chicago River was turned green accidentally in 1962 when a group of plumbers used a fluorescent dye (later found to be harmful and banned by the EPA) to trace illegal pollutants. The accident gave someone the bright idea that this would be a good way to celebrate St. Patrick's Day. That same year, 100 pounds of vegetable dye was dumped into the Chicago River and it stayed green for a week. Nowadays, only 40 pounds of the harmless dye is used and the river stays green for several hours.

CHICAGO, ILLINOIS

14

Fallas de San
Jose, Spain

*Albert Einstein,
physicist,
b.1879*
*Casey Jones,
engineer,
b.1864*

The most
beautiful thing
we can
experience is
the mysterious.
— *Albert
Einstein*

♃ △ ♆ 1:46ᴀᴍ
♀ △ ♄ 6:11ᴘᴍ

☾
RISE 8:21AM
SET 11:47PM

✹
RISE 6:27AM
SET 6:18PM

RIGHT WORD

15

The Ides
of March
~ True
Confessions Day
~ National
Brutus Day
*Andrew Jackson,
7th U.S.
president,
b.1767*
*Julius Caesar,
d.44ʙᴄ*

Men at some
times are
masters of their
fates: The fault,
dear Brutus, is
not in our stars,
But in ourselves,
that we are
underlings.
— *William
Shakespeare*

☽ △ ♂ 12:10ᴀᴍ

☾
RISE 8:49AM

✹
RISE 6:25AM
SET 6:19PM

RIGHT DEED

16

Freedom of
Information Day
~ Natl.
Quilting Day
~ St. Urho's Day

*James Madison,
4th president,
b.1751*

Diamonds are
nothing more
than chunks of
coal that stuck
to their jobs.
— *Malcolm Forbes*

RETURN OF
THE CURLEWS,
UMATILLA, OR

☽ △ ♃ 3:12ᴘᴍ
☽ △ ♆ 3:56ᴘᴍ

☾
SET 12:56AM
RISE 9:23AM

✹
RISE 6:23AM
SET 6:21PM

RIGHT LIVELIHOOD

17

250 YEARS AGO
1755: Tran-
sylvania Land
Co. buys Ken-
tucky from a
Cherokee Chief
for $50,000
*Nat "King"
Cole, singer,
b.1919*
*Rudolf Nureyev,
dancer, b.1938*

Do what you
can, with what
you have,
where you are.
— *Theodore
Roosevelt*

ST. PATRICK'S DAY

☽ ☌ ♇ 7:43ᴀᴍ

✹
RISE 6:21AM
SET 6:22PM

*First Quarter
19:19ᴜᴛ*

RIGHT ENDEAVOR

PHENOLOGY: The Swallows Return to Capistrano, 3/19

MISSION SAN JUAN CAPISTRANO, SOUTHERN CALIFORNIA

When the swallows come back to Capistrano
That's the day you promised to come back to me
When you whispered, "Farewell," in Capistrano
Twas the day the swallows flew out to sea

"When The Swallows Come Back to Capistrano"
Written by Leon Rene; sung by the Ink Spots

The swallows that have come back each year for centuries to roost at the Mission San Juan Capistrano in San Juan, California, are cliff swallows. Winging their way north from Goya, Argentina, 6,000 miles away, they arrive around St. Joseph's Day on March 19, to be greeted by throngs of visitors, a parade, and a fiesta. Unfazed by their celebrity, they begin immediately to rebuild their mud nests on the ruins of the mission (its rebuilt Serra Chapel is the oldest building in California still in use) and throughout the valley. Towards the end of October, they will leave again, flying back to their winter home.

Though their great numbers have dwindled over the years because development in the Capistrano Valley has reduced the insect population, the swallows, driven by instinct and destiny, continue to connect us to the mystique and the comforting rhythm of migration.

For information on the Capistrano Swallows, see www.missionsjc.com/swallows.html and www.capovalley.com/swallows/

THE DESIDERATA/*Max Ehrmann*

You are a child of the universe no less than the trees and the stars;
you have a right to be here. And whether or not it is clear to you,
no doubt the universe is unfolding as it should.

---

18   FRI · MAR 18 · 2005

Canberra Day,
Australia
~ Flag Day,
Aruba
~ 1931: Electric
razor debuted
*Wilson Pickett,
singer, b.1941
Irene Cara,
singer, b.1959
John Updike,
author, b.1932*

Fear is the
main source
of superstition,
and one of the
main sources
of cruelty. To
conquer fear is
the beginning
of wisdom.
— *Bertrand
Russell*

☽△♅ 10:45AM

☾
SET 2:57AM
RISE 10:55AM

☀
RISE 6:20AM
SET 6:23PM

RIGHT MEMORY

---

19   SAT · MAR 19 · 2005

Natl. Day of
Oil, Iran

*Wyatt Earp,
gunslinger,
lawman,
b.1848
William
Jennings Bryan,
orator,
politician,
b.1860*

The journey is
the reward.
— *Tao Saying*

SWALLOWS
RETURN TO
SAN JUAN
CAPISTRANO,
YEARLY SINCE
1776

☽☌♄ 11:53AM

☾
SET 3:44AM
RISE 11:53PM

☀
RISE 6:18AM
SET 6:25PM

RIGHT CONCEPTION

---

20   SUN · MAR 20 · 2005

*Henrik Ibsen,
author, b.1828
Mitsumasa
Anno, author,
b.1926
Spike Lee, film-
maker, b.1957*

SPRING EQUINOX
12:33 (UT)

Spring is when
life's alive in
everything.
— *Christina
Rossetti*

PALM SUNDAY
(CHRISTIAN)

☽△♀ 1:18AM
☽☍♂ 6:59AM
☽△☉ 7:21AM

☾
SET 4:22AM
RISE 12:57PM

☀
RISE 6:16AM
SET 6:26PM

RIGHT RESOLVE

BIRTHDAY: William Morris, March 24, 1834

Founder of the Arts and Crafts movement, William Morris believed that simple objects crafted by hand were preferable to ornate mass-produced objects cheaply turned out by machine. He created elegant textile designs incorporating arabesques of plants, flowers, and birds, which found their inspiration in medieval tapestries and historical fabrics and relied on traditional methods, such as hand-block printing and vegetable dyeing.

From the exhibition "William Morris: The Reactionary Revolutionary"
at the Baltimore Museum of Art

Beauty, which is what is meant by art, using the word in its widest sense, is, I contend, no mere accident to human life, which people can take or leave as they choose, but a positive necessity of life. — *William Morris*

For more information on William Morris, see
www.morrissociety.org and also www.lbwf.gov.uk/wmg/about.htm

21

Noruz: New Day,
Zoroastrian
~ Nau-Roz:
New Year, Baha'i
~ Ostara, Wicca

*Johann
Sebastian Bach,
composer,
b.1685*

One's mind,
once stretched
by a new idea,
never regains
its original
dimensions.
— *Oliver Wendel
Holmes*

SELMA, ALABAMA
CIVIL RIGHTS
MARCH 1965

☽△☿ 11:15AM
☽☌♆ 4:48PM

☾
SET 4:52AM
RISE 2:04PM

☉
RISE 6:14AM
SET 6:27PM

RIGHT WORD

22

International
Day of the Seal,
since 1982

*George Benson,
singer, b.1943
Karl Malden,
actor, b.1914*

We never know
the worth of
water, 'til the
well is dry.
— *English Proverb*

UNITED NATIONS
WORLD DAY
FOR WATER

☽△♇ 8:20AM

☾
SET 5:16AM
RISE 3:11PM

☉
RISE 6:12AM
SET 6:28PM

RIGHT DEED

23

UN World
Meteorological
Day

*Akira
Kurosawa,
director,
b.1910*

I know not what
course others
may take, but as
for me, give me
liberty or give
me death.
— *Patrick Henry*

LIBERTY DAY
1775

☽☌♅ 11:17AM

☾
SET 5:37AM
RISE 4:19PM

☉
RISE 6:10AM
SET 6:30PM

RIGHT LIVELIHOOD

24

Maundy
Thursday,
Christian
~ 1989: Exxon
Valdez Oil Spill

*William Morris,
poet, b.1834
Harry Houdini,
magician,
b.1874*

The most
effective kind
of education
is that a child
should play
amongst lovely
things.
— *Plato*

☾
SET 5:55AM
RISE 5:26PM

☉
RISE 6:08AM
SET 6:31PM

RIGHT ENDEAVOR

CELEBRATE: Spring Equinox/Passover/Easter

Now the green blade riseth,
from the buried grain,
Wheat that in dark earth
many days has lain;
Love lives again,
that with the dead has been:
Love is come again,
like wheat that springeth green.

J.M.C. Crum

In contrast to the fall equinox celebration of Michaelmas, with its strong sense of self-awareness, individuation, and inner courage, the spring festivals emphasize union. Outwardly (in the northern hemisphere), the fertile Earth bursts with life, sending forth tender shoots and fragile blossoms. Insects are stirring, birds are nesting, and people are finding it very hard to stay indoors!

The procreation in nature is the physical aspect of a deeper spiritual message. As male and female must combine for new life to issue, so, within each of us, the union of masculine and feminine results in spontaneous, joyful creation. Yin and yang swim in a circle of unity, the deepest essence of each containing the seed of the other. The message of spring is peace: Difference is no cause for fighting, but a priceless gift for world- and self-renewal.

Passover (April 23) and Easter (March 27) follow the first full moon after the spring equinox (March 20). By combining the lunar cycle with the solar, they reemphasize the season's theme. United are moon and sun, the lamps of night and day. The tryst of dark and light births freedom and hope. Like a chick bursting from its shell, the Israelites escape from bondage. As the deathly grip of winter loosens, so the Son of Man unites the heavens with the earth.

For the Greeks, love had many levels, eros being only one. At the time of the spring equinox, meditation on all of love's aspects engenders awe at the fullness of creation, reverence for the union of opposites that is the wellspring of all creativity.

~ John Miller

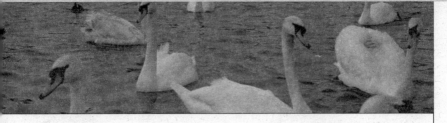

SPRING/*Gerard Manley Hopkins*

Nothing is so beautiful as spring— | When weeds, in wheels, shoot long and
lovely and lush, | Thrush's eggs look little low heavens, and thrush |
Through the echoing timber does so rinse and wring |
The ear, it strikes like lightnings to hear him sing....

---

25   FRI · MAR 25 · 2005

Old New Year's Day, was on this date until 1751
~ Magha Pujá Day, Buddhist

Béla Bartók composer, b.1881

God has no religion.
— *Mahatma Gandhi*

GOOD FRIDAY (CHRISTIAN)
PURIM (JEWISH)
ANNUNCIATION (CHRISTIAN)

☽△♂ 11:47AM
☽☌♀ 12:12PM
☽☌☉ 2:58PM

✺
RISE 6:06AM
SET 6:32PM

Full Moon 20:58UT

RIGHT MEMORY

---

26   SAT · MAR 26 · 2005

"Make Up Your Own Holiday" Day
~ Khordadsal, Zoroastrian

Robert Frost poet, b.1874
Tennessee Williams, playwright, b.1911

Two roads diverged in a wood, and I— I took the one less traveled by, And that has made all the difference.
— *Robert Frost*

☽☌♀♀ 2:50AM
☽☌♃ 9:00AM
☽△♆ 12:23PM

☾
SET 6:29AM
RISE 7:42PM

✺
RISE 6:05AM
SET 6:34PM

RIGHT CONCEPTION

---

27   SUN · MAR 27 · 2005

Cherry Blossom Festival begins, U.S.

Wilhelm Roentgen, scientist, b.1845
Sarah Vaughan, singer, b.1924
Mariah Carey, singer, b.1970

We choose our joys and sorrows long before we experience them.
— *Kahlil Gibran*

EASTER SUNDAY (CHRISTIAN)

☾
SET 6:48AM
RISE 8:58PM

✺
RISE 6:03AM
SET 6:35PM

RIGHT RESOLVE

POEM: Call Me By My True Names

Don't say that I will depart tomorrow—
Even today I am still arriving.

Look deeply: every second I am arriving
To be a bud on a Spring branch,
To be a tiny bird, with still-fragile wings,
Learning to sing in my new nest,
To be a caterpillar in the heart of a
flower,
To be a jewel hiding itself in stone.

I still arrive, in order to laugh and
to cry,
To fear and to hope.
The rhythm of my heart is the birth
and death
Of all that is alive.

I am a mayfly metamorphosing
On the surface of the river.
And I am the bird
That swoops down to swallow the
mayfly.

I am a frog swimming happily
in the clear water of a pond.
And I am the grass-snake
That silently feeds itself on the frog.

I am the child in Uganda, all skin
and bones,
My legs as thin as bamboo sticks.
And I am the arms merchant
Selling deadly weapons to Uganda.

I am the twelve-year-old girl,
Refugee on a small boat,
Who throws herself into the ocean
After being raped by a sea pirate.
And I am the pirate

My heart not yet capable
Of seeing and loving.

I am a member of the politburo,
With plenty of power in my hands.
And I am the man who has to pay
His "debt of blood" to my people
Dying slowly in a forced-labor camp.

My joy is like Spring, so warm
It makes flowers bloom all over the
Earth.
My pain is like a river of tears,
So vast it fills the four oceans.

Please call me by my true names,
So I can hear all my cries and laughter
at once,
So I can see that my joy and pain
are one.

Please call me by my true names,
So I can wake up
And the door of my heart
Could be left open,
The door of compassion.

~ *Thich Nhat Hanh*

---

28   MON · MAR 28 · 2005

Teacher's Day,
Czech Republic

~ 1979: Three
Mile Island
nuclear accident

Dianne Wiest,
actress, b.1948

One of the
lessons of
history is that
nothing is often
a good thing
to do and
always a clever
thing to say.
— *Will Durant*

)△⽊ 3:47AM

☾
SET 7:09AM
RISE 10:14PM

☀
RISE 6:01AM
SET 6:36PM

RIGHT WORD

---

29   TUE · MAR 29 · 2005

Youth Day,
Taiwan

Eugene
McCarthy,
politician, b.1916
Sam Walton,
Wal-Mart
founder, b.1918
Pearl Bailey,
singer, b.1918

All human
beings should
try to learn
before they die
what they are
running from,
and to, and why.
— *James Thurber*

DOW-JONES
TOPS 10,000
FIRST TIME: 1999

)△♄ 1:06AM
☉☌☿ 10:11AM
☿☌♀ 2:29PM

☾
SET 7:36AM
RISE 11:31PM

☀
RISE 5:59AM
SET 6:37PM

RIGHT DEED

---

30   WED · MAR 30 · 2005

Sean O'Casey,
playwright,
b.1880
Vincent Van
Gogh, painter,
b.1853

The believer is
happy; the
doubter is wise.
— *Hungarian
Proverb*

PENCIL PATENTED
1858

)△☿ 8:24AM
)△♀ 11:22AM
)△☉ 11:34AM
☉☌♀ 9:30PM

☾
SET 8:10AM

☀
RISE 5:57AM
SET 6:39PM

RIGHT LIVELIHOOD

---

31   THU · MAR 31 · 2005

1959: Dalai
Lama flees Tibet

Rene Descartes,
philosopher,
b.1596
Cesar Chavez,
labor leader,
b.1927
Charlotte
Brontë, author,
b.1855

The greatest
minds are
capable of the
greatest vices as
well as of the
greatest virtues.
— *René Descartes*

EIFFEL TOWER
OPENS 1889

)☌♇ 12:24AM

☾
RISE 12:48AM
SET 8:55AM

☀
RISE 5:55AM
SET 6:40PM

RIGHT ENDEAVOR

APRIL

MAR 21 - APR 19

APR 20 - MAY 20

Υ
aries

$\Uptau$
taurus

BIRTHSTONE
Diamond

FLOWER
Sweet Pea

Devotion
BECOMES THE FORCE OF SACRIFICE
Challenges: malice, defenselessness

A pril is the month of golden Aphrodite (Etruscan apru), modest, gentle goddess of love and beauty. She is the spirit of youth in everything. We find ourselves drawn outdoors again, into the breeze-filled air sitting warmly on our senses. We ray out into the light, the sun-illumined world. There are wider dawns and deeper twilights. As nature stirs, new life germinates within us. Outside, "wild puffing of emerald trees and flame-filled bushes" (D.H. Lawrence); within, an awakening sense of self in seeing. The intensity of nature's splendor all but overwhelms us. Light – liquid, yellow, and caressing, is poured over everything. Surrendering to its embrace with spontaneous devotion, our hearts are at peace. We, too, are reborn. We sense our freedom to do the good, to know the true, and to love the beautiful. We feel one with the world.

APRIL IS

ALCOHOL AWARENESS MONTH · ANIMAL CRUELTY PREVENTION MONTH · CALIFORNIA EARTHQUAKE PREPAREDNESS MONTH · COUPLE APPRECIATION MONTH · FLORIDA TOMATO MONTH · HOLY HUMOR MONTH · AMATEUR RADIO MONTH · CUSTOMER LOYALTY MONTH · LEGACY MONTH · INTERNATIONAL TWIT AWARD MONTH KEEP AMERICA BEAUTIFUL MONTH · MONTH OF THE YOUNG CHILD · AUTISM AWARE-NESS MONTH · CHILD ABUSE PREVENTION MONTH · GRILLED CHEESE SANDWICH MONTH · LAWN AND GARDEN MONTH · PECAN MONTH · NATIONAL POETRY MONTH NATIONAL PREPARE TO BUY A HOME MONTH · SELF-PUBLISHING MONTH NAT'L SMILE MONTH · WOODWORKING MONTH · SCHOOL LIBRARY MEDIA MONTH STRAW HAT MONTH · WORLD HABITAT AWARENESS MONTH

April, 22nd 9:00 P.M.   South-East

5:00 A.M.   South-East

STARS & PLANETS FOR APRIL

Jupiter dominates the night sky. At the end of the month Venus is visible in the evening sky. There is an interesting contrast between the more internal, subdued, yellowish light of Saturn and the bright, radiant, blue-green light of Venus.

LOOK UP:

2 Jupiter at opposition, rising at sunset in the east

3 Jupiter nearest the Earth

8 New Moon, 20:33 UT
   Annular/total solar eclipse at 20:33 UT, visible south of a line from southern California to New Jersey shore

4 Jupiter at aphelion (farthest from Sun)

24 Full Moon (Seed Moon), 10:07 UT
    Penumbral lunar eclipse, greatest visibility from South Pacific, at 9:55 UT

26 Mercury at greatest western elongation

LOOK OUT:

- Hawks begin their aerial courtship dances
- In Albuquerque, rattlesnakes emerge from wintering dens
- Maple sap begins to rise around the Great Lakes
- Spring peepers sound off in the night

APRIL						
S	M	T	W	T	F	S
					1	2
3	4	5	6	7	8	9
10	11	12	13	14	15	16
17	18	19	20	21	22	23
24	25	26	27	28	29	30

The fact that astronomies change while the stars abide is a true analogy of every realm of human life and thought, religion not least of all.
No existent theology can be a final formulation of spiritual truth.
~ HARRY EMERSON FOSDICK

HOLIDAY: April Fools' Day, April 1

Lorem ipsum dolor sit amet, consectetuer adipiscing elit, sed diam nonummy nibh euismod tincidunt ut laoreet dolore magna aliquam erat volutpat. Ut wisi enim ad minim veniam, quis nostrud exerci tation ullamcorper suscipit lobortis nisl ut aliquip ex ea commodo consequat. Duis autem vel eum iriure dolor in hendrerit in vulputate velit esse molestie consequat, vel illum dolore eu feugiat nulla facilisis at vero eros et accumsan et iusto odio dignissim qui blandit praesent luptatum zzril delenit augue duis dolore te feugait nulla facilisi. Lorem ipsum dolor sit amet, consectetuer adipiscing elit, sed diam nonummy nibh euismod tincidunt ut laoreet dolore magna aliquam erat volutpat. Ut wisi enim ad minim veniam, quis nostrud exerci tation ullamcorper suscipit lobortis nisl ut aliquip ex ea commodo consequat. Duis autem vel eum iriure dolor.

Lorem ipsum dolor sit amet, consectetuer adipiscing elit, sed diam nonummy nibh euismod tincidunt ut laoreet dolore magna aliquam erat volutpat. Ut wisi enim ad minim veniam, quis nostrud exerci tation ullamcorper suscipit lobortis nisl ut aliquip ex ea commodo consequat. Duis autem vel eum iriure dolor in hendrerit in vulputate velit esse molestie consequat, vel illum dolore eu feugiat nulla facilisis at vero eros et accumsan et iusto odio dignissim qui blandit praesent luptatum zzril delenit augue duis dolore. Lorem ipsum dolor sit amet, consectetuer adipiscing elit, sed diam nonummy nibh euismod tincidunt ut laoreet dolore magna aliquam erat volutpat. Ut wisi enim.

Lorem ipsum dolor sit amet, consectetuer adipiscing elit, sed diam nonummy nibh euismod tincidunt ut laoreet dolore magna aliquam erat.

For more information on Lorem Ipsum, see page 325.

POEM #63/ *e.e. cummings*

…come quickly come | run run | with me now |
jump shout (laugh | dance cry | sing) for it's Spring….

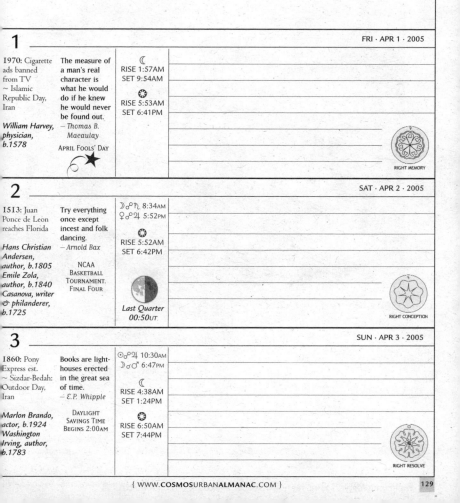

1

FRI · APR 1 · 2005

1970: Cigarette ads banned from TV
~ Islamic Republic Day, Iran

William Harvey, physician, b.1578

The measure of a man's real character is what he would do if he knew he would never be found out.
— *Thomas B. Macaulay*

APRIL FOOLS' DAY

☾ RISE 1:57AM SET 9:54AM

☼ RISE 5:53AM SET 6:41PM

RIGHT MEMORY

2

SAT · APR 2 · 2005

1513: Juan Ponce de Leon reaches Florida

Hans Christian Andersen, author, b.1805
Emile Zola, author, b.1840
Casanova, writer & philanderer, b.1725

Try everything once except incest and folk dancing.
— *Arnold Bax*

NCAA BASKETBALL TOURNAMENT. FINAL FOUR

☽☌♄ 8:34AM
♀☌♃ 5:52PM

☼ RISE 5:52AM SET 6:42PM

Last Quarter 00:50UT.

RIGHT CONCEPTION

3

SUN · APR 3 · 2005

1860: Pony Express est.
~ Sizdar-Bedah: Outdoor Day, Iran

Marlon Brando, actor, b.1924
Washington Irving, author, b.1783

Books are lighthouses erected in the great sea of time.
— *E.P. Whipple*

DAYLIGHT SAVINGS TIME BEGINS 2:00AM

☉☌♃ 10:30AM
☽☌♂ 6:47PM

☾ RISE 4:38AM SET 1:24PM

☼ RISE 6:50AM SET 7:44PM

RIGHT RESOLVE

BIRTHDAY: Billie Holiday, April 7, 1915

GOD BLESS THE CHILD
...Mama may have, papa may have
But God bless the child that's got his own
That's got his own...

Lyrics by Billie Holiday and Arthur Herzog.
For more information on Billie Holiday, see www.cmgww.com/music/holiday/

4
MON · APR 4 · 2005

50 YEARS AGO
1955: British Govt. signs treaty with Iraq ~ 1968: Martin Luther King, Jr. assassinated *Muddy Waters, singer, b.1915 Dorothea Dix, social reformer, b.1802*

It's a poor sort of memory that only works backward.
— *Lewis Carroll*

NCAA BASKETBALL FINALS (ST. LOUIS)

☽△♃ 12:48AM
☽☌♆ 6:04AM

☾ RISE 5:12AM
SET 2:46PM

☼ RISE 6:48AM
SET 7:45PM

RIGHT WORD

5
TUE · APR 5 · 2005

Tomb Sweeping Day, Taiwan

Gregory Peck, actor, b.1916 Bette Davis, actress, b.1908 Spencer Tracy, actor, b.1900 Booker T. Washington, educator, b.1856

Please subdue the anguish of your soul. Nobody is destined only to happiness or to pain. The wheel of life takes one up and down by turn.
— *Kalidasa*

☽☌♅ 6:44PM

☾ RISE 5:39AM
SET 4:07PM

☼ RISE 6:46AM
SET 7:46PM

RIGHT DEED

6
WED · APR 6 · 2005

50 YEARS AGO
1955: US nuclear test at Nevada Test Site ~ 1830: Mormon Church founded ~

Raphael, painter, b.1483 Ram Dass, author, b.1931

Things only have the value that we give them.
— *Molière*

FIRST MODERN OLYMPICS ATHENS GREECE

1896

☽△♄ 2:29PM

☾ RISE 6:01AM
SET 5:25PM

☼ RISE 6:44AM
SET 7:47PM

RIGHT LIVELIHOOD

7
THU · APR 7 · 2005

200 YEARS AGO
1805: Beethoven's Eroica premieres ~ 1994: Rwanda Massacres Remembrance Day *William Wordsworth, poet, b.1770 Billie Holiday, singer, b.1915*

An eye for an eye leaves everyone blind.
— *Mahatma Gandhi*

WORLD HEALTH DAY

W.H.O. FOUNDED 1948

☽☌☿ 11:07AM

☾ RISE 6:21AM
SET 6:41PM

☼ RISE 6:42AM
SET 7:49PM

RIGHT ENDEAVOR

ASTRONOMY: Total Solar Eclipse, April 8, 3:35pm CDT

You may have noticed that the full Moon rises as the Sun sets. The Earth stands in between the Sun and the Moon – but not exactly. Most of the Sun's rays pass by the Earth and hit the Moon, which reflects them down to us. (The rest disappear into space. Without a body to reflect it, light is invisible.) At new Moon, however, the Moon is between the Earth and the Sun. The Sun's rays bounce off the back of the Moon and into space. Since they don't reach us, the Moon is totally dark.

Like with the full Moon, a lunar eclipse only takes place when the Earth is between the Moon and the Sun. This time, the Earth lines up just so, preventing any sunlight from reaching the Moon. We can observe the Earth's disk (really a sphere) moving across the face of the Moon as it slowly blocks off the sunlight.

A solar eclipse can only take place at the new Moon, when the Moon comes exactly between the Sun and the Earth. The Moon is just the right size and distance from the Earth to obscure the Sun, even though the Sun is much, much bigger. (If the Sun were a grapefruit, the Moon would be a grain of sand and Earth a BB.) This is because the Moon is so close to Earth. Occasionally, an annular, or ring-shaped, eclipse will occur, with a halo of sunlight showing around the Moon.

Eclipses have long been regarded as ominous (sometimes accompanied by the strange behavior of animals). The Crucifixion has been dated to April 3, A.D. 33, when a lunar eclipse was visible from Jerusalem. Though now we understand why eclipses occur, their eerie fascination persists.

~ *John Miller*

For more information on eclipses and astronomy, see www.skyandtelescope.com

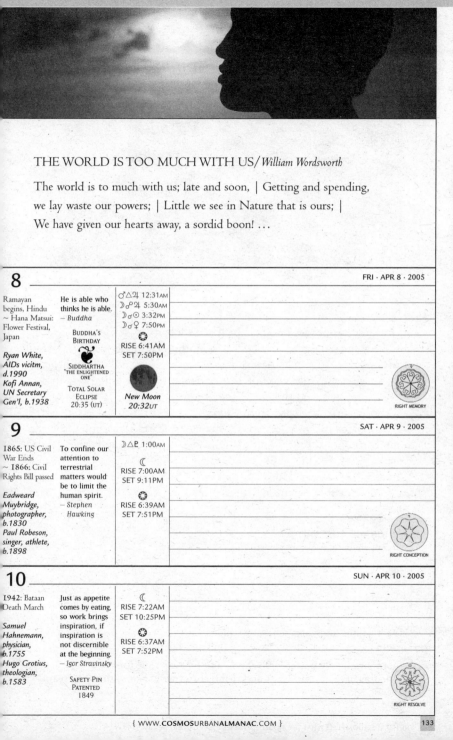

THE WORLD IS TOO MUCH WITH US/ *William Wordsworth*

The world is to much with us; late and soon, | Getting and spending,
we lay waste our powers; | Little we see in Nature that is ours; |
We have given our hearts away, a sordid boon! …

---

8   FRI · APR 8 · 2005

Ramayan
begins, Hindu
~ Hana Matsui:
Flower Festival,
Japan

*Ryan White,
AIDs vicitm,
d.1990
Kofi Annan,
UN Secretary
Gen'l, b.1938*

He is able who
thinks he is able.
— *Buddha*

BUDDHA'S
BIRTHDAY

SIDDHARTHA
"THE ENLIGHTENED
ONE"

TOTAL SOLAR
ECLIPSE
20:35 (UT)

♂△♃ 12:31AM
☽♂♃ 5:30AM
☽♂☉ 3:32PM
☽♂♀ 7:50PM

☼
RISE 6:41AM
SET 7:50PM

*New Moon
20:32UT*

RIGHT MEMORY

---

9   SAT · APR 9 · 2005

1865: US Civil
War Ends
~ 1866: Civil
Rights Bill passed

*Eadweard
Muybridge,
photographer,
b.1830
Paul Robeson,
singer, athlete,
b.1898*

To confine our
attention to
terrestrial
matters would
be to limit the
human spirit.
— *Stephen
Hawking*

☽△♇ 1:00AM

☾
RISE 7:00AM
SET 9:11PM

☼
RISE 6:39AM
SET 7:51PM

RIGHT CONCEPTION

---

10   SUN · APR 10 · 2005

1942: Bataan
Death March

*Samuel
Hahnemann,
physician,
b.1755
Hugo Grotius,
theologian,
b.1583*

Just as appetite
comes by eating,
so work brings
inspiration, if
inspiration is
not discernible
at the beginning.
— *Igor Stravinsky*

SAFETY PIN
PATENTED
1849

☾
RISE 7:22AM
SET 10:25PM

☼
RISE 6:37AM
SET 7:52PM

RIGHT RESOLVE

RECIPE: Rhubarb Custard

Rhubarb

Just when you think spring will never come, up through the hard winter soil pushes the shockingly red rhubarb, its scarlet knobs robed in bright green, tightly curled leaves. Within days it seems, a big, beautiful plant sits in your bare garden. Like a loyal friend, your rhubarb is back, with its yearly promise of puckery sauces, tart chutneys, endless crisps and pies, and rhubarb custards.

Rhubarb, originally from China, is the perfect urban plant, asking only a patch of fairly fertile, well-drained soil and some sun. Officially, it's best only through June, but in cool summers, and with careful harvesting of tender stalks, you can enjoy it all summer. One thing to remember: rhubarb leaves are poisonous because of their high oxalate content, so only eat the lovely red stems.

RHUBARB CUSTARD

3 cups rhubarb, stalks split lengthwise and diced
2 egg yolks
2 egg whites
¾ cup sugar
pinch of salt

1 ½ T. flour
1 ¾ cup scalded milk, cooled
¼ tsp. freshly grated nutmeg
(more to taste)

Beat whites and yolks separately. Blend sugar, salt, milk, flour, and nutmeg into yolks, then mix in the rhubarb. Fold in egg whites.

Turn into lightly buttered 9 x 9 pan and bake at 350° for about 45 minutes until custard is set and slightly browned. Serve with thick cream.

11

1945: Liberation of Buchenwald ~ Barbershop Quartet Day

Ellen Goodman, columnist, b.1948
Jane Matilda Bolin, 1st black female judge b.1908

A patriot must always be ready to defend his country against its government.
— Edward Abbey

CIVIL RIGHTS ACT SIGNED INTO LAW 1968

♀△♇ 4:05AM

☾
RISE 7:47AM
SET 11:38PM

☼
RISE 6:35AM
SET 7:54PM

RIGHT WORD

12

1934: "The Big Wind" 231mph Mt. Washington, NH ~ 1955: Polio vaccine announced
Franklin D. Roosevelt, d.1945
David Letterman, comic, b.1947

The future belongs to those who believe in the beauty of their dreams.
— Eleanor Roosevelt

FIRST MAN IN SPACE 1961

YURI GAGARIN USSR

☾
RISE 8:19AM

☼
RISE 6:33AM
SET 7:55PM

RIGHT DEED

13

1962: *Silent Spring* pub. by Rachel Carson ~ Baisakhi, Sikh
Thomas Jefferson, president, b.1743
Butch Cassidy, outlaw, b.1866
Al Green, singer, b.1946

Use what talent you possess: the woods would be very silent if no birds sang except those that sang best.
— Henry Van Dyke

☽△♂ 1:39AM
☽△♆ 1:58AM
♂♂♆ 7:11AM
☽♂♇ 4:03PM

☾
SET 12:46AM
RISE 8:57AM

☼
RISE 6:32AM
SET 7:56PM

RIGHT LIVELIHOOD

14

1865: A. Lincoln assassinated ~ 1890: OAS formed
Arnold Toynbee, historian, b.1889
Anne Sullivan, teacher, b.1866

All words are pegs to hang ideas on.
— Henry Ward Beecher

FIRST WEBSTER'S DICTIONARY 1828

☉△♇ 1:51AM
☽△♅ 10:40PM

☾
SET 1:47AM
RISE 9:45AM

☼
RISE 6:30AM
SET 7:58PM

RIGHT ENDEAVOR

CIVILIZING IDEAS: Time Dollars

Time Dollar celebration

In a society where capitalism can run amok, a new currency — "time dollars" — offers an appealing approach for exchanging life's commodities.

People earn time dollars by using their talents and resources to help others. It may be through activities like yard work, tutoring, cooking, or providing childcare or transportation. One hour of service equals one dollar earned, and individuals can use their time dollars to "buy" similar help when the need arises or for products or discounts from organizations participating in time dollar exchanges.

There are time dollar programs in more than 100 communities in about 30 states, as well as Japan and Great Britain. In Brooklyn, senior citizens who help other elders to remain self-sufficient can use time dollars for a 25 percent discount on their health insurance. And in Chicago, more than 1,000 elementary-school students have earned computers loaded with software by tutoring younger students. The computers cost 110 time dollars – 100 earned by the students and 10 by their parents.

Time dollars are, in essence, a social currency centered around civic engagement, and therein lies their lasting value. It's a universal arrangement — one dollar for every hour — and everyone's time is equally important.

~ *Rick Moore*

For more on time dollars, including how to get involved with a program in your neighborhood, see www.timedollar.org and www.accessfoundation.org.

NOTHING GOLD CAN STAY / *Robert Frost*

Nature's first green is gold, Her hardest hue to hold. |
Her early leaf's a flower; But only so an hour. |
Then leaf subsides to leaf. So Eden sank to grief, |
So dawn goes down to day. Nothing gold can stay.

15

FRI · APR 15 · 2005

1912: Sinking of the Titanic
~ **1955:** First McDonalds opens

Thomas Hart Benton, artist, b.1889
Bessie Smith, singer, b.1894

If the rich could hire someone else to die for them, the poor would make a wonderful living.
— *Jewish Proverb*

INCOME TAX DAY
$

☽ ☌ ♄ 10:02PM

☾ SET 2:38AM
RISE 10:41AM

✷ RISE 6:28AM
SET 7:59PM

RIGHT MEMORY

16

SAT · APR 16 · 2005

Lord's Evening Meal, Jehovah's Witness

Merce Cunningham, dancer, b.1919
Charlie Chaplin, actor, b.1889
Margarethe, Queen of Denmark, b.1940

The only difference between saints and sinners is that every saint has a past while every sinner has a future.
— *Oscar Wilde*

☽ △ ☿ 9:46PM

✷ RISE 6:26AM
SET 8:00PM

First Quarter
14:37UT

RIGHT CONCEPTION

17

SUN · APR 17 · 2005

75 YEARS AGO
1932: Haile Selassie ends slavery, Ethiopia
~ **1961:** Bay of Pigs invasion

Thornton Wilder, author, b.1897
J.P. Morgan, banker, b.1837

Do not dwell in the past, do not dream of the future, concentrate the mind on the present moment.
— *Buddha*

DOW JONES TOPS 3,000
FIRST TIME: 1991

☾ SET 3:53AM
RISE 12:48PM

✷ RISE 6:25AM
SET 8:01PM

RIGHT RESOLVE

ESSENTIAL PLACE: American Visionary Art Museum, Baltimore

The American Visionary Art Museum (AVAM) – the only museum in the United States that showcases self-taught, "visionary" art – sits on a shining strip of sand in front of the formerly industrial Baltimore Inner Harbor. The architecturally fantastic building, with its whimsical four-story high whirligig and winding central stairway, contains seven galleries filled with equally fantastic art. A café, a wildflower garden, and a whiskey warehouse turned sculpture gallery, complete the site, making the AVAM the pilgrimage destination of choice for devotees of the phantasmagorical .

The museum's collection is a painstaking assemblage of painstakingly assembled assemblages, like the 10-foot model of the Lusitania made entirely out of matchsticks.

The AVAM doesn't so much thumb its nose at the notion of "art," as carry on oblivious to the constraints of the conventional art world.

Along with the pieces on display, the AVAM offers an expansive idea of education. Each year, an exhibit strives to turn our thinking upside down around a familiar subject. In 2004, the museum attempted to dissolve the stereotypes of "young and creative, old and wise."

Whether you call it quirky, strange, bizarre, or utterly fascinating, visionary art is about listening to your own still voice within and this museum is devoted to "blowing on the embers" of that divine spark.

~ *Kathleen Melin*

For more information about the American Visionary Art Museum, see www.avam.org

BALTIMORE, MARYLAND

18
MON · APR 18 · 2005

Ramanavami, Hindu
~ Holocaust Day, Israel
~ 1775: Paul Revere's Midnight Ride
Albert Einstein, physicist, d.1955
Clarence Darrow, attorney, b.1857

The poet judges not as a judge judges but as the sun falling around a helpless thing.
— *Walt Whitman*

Conan O'Brien comedian b.1963

☽ ☌ ♅ ♄ 3:12AM
☽ ☌ ♂ 10:26AM
☽ △ ♇ 5:17PM

☾
SET 4:19AM
RISE 1:55PM

✵
RISE 6:23AM
SET 8:03PM

RIGHT WORD

19
TUE · APR 19 · 2005

75 YEARS AGO
1932: Herbert Hoover suggests 5-day work week
~ 1993: Branch Davidian Fire, Waco TX
Roger Sherman, statesman, b.1721
Kate Hudson, actress, b.1979

The important thing is not to stop questioning.
— *Albert Einstein*

1775 START OF AMERICAN REVOLUTION

BATTLE OF LEXINGTON & CONCORD

☽ △ ☉ 3:13AM
☽ △ ♀ 2:03PM
☽ ☌ ♅ 11:14PM

☾
SET 4:41AM
RISE 3:02PM

✵
RISE 6:21AM
SET 8:04PM

RIGHT DEED

20
WED · APR 20 · 2005

1999: Columbine High School tragedy

Carmen Electra, actress, b.1972
Luther Vandross, singer, b.1951
Jessica Lange, actress, b.1949

Everyone is kneaded out of the same dough but not baked in the same oven.
— *Yiddish Proverb*

☾
SET 5:00AM
RISE 4:09PM

✵
RISE 6:20AM
SET 8:05PM

RIGHT LIVELIHOOD

21
THU · APR 21 · 2005

Ridvan, Baha'i
~ Mawlid an Nabi, Islam
~ Kartini Day, Indonesia
Charlotte Brontë, author, b.1816
Friedrich Froebel, educator, b.1782

If you want rainbows, you have to put up with the rain.
— *Dolly Parton*

KINDERGARTEN DAY

ABC

1ST KINDERGARTEN EST. 1837

☾
SET 5:17AM
RISE 5:17PM

✵
RISE 6:18AM
SET 8:06PM

RIGHT ENDEAVOR

CELEBRATE: Earth Day, April 22

CELEBRATE EARTH DAY WITH A MOTHER EARTH DINNER

To give Earth Day the attention it deserves, bring people together to eat and talk. The food should be fresh, local, preferably organic, and delicious. But the real focus of the dinner is the earth – what she gives us and what we can give back to her. All Earth Dinners involve appreciation and consciousness-raising, but how you do those things is up to you to create and enjoy. What follows is a simple plan for an Earth Day Dinner, but visit www.earthdinner.org for more ideas and then develop your own traditions.

Build the dinner itself around each of the four elements – Earth (root vegetables, grains, mushrooms...), Air (herbs, asparagus, flowers...), Fire (roasted meats and veggies, hot peppers...), and Water (fruit, sorbets...). Pot lucks are great, and each person or family can talk about the food they chose, including where it came from, who grew or raised it, and how they prepared it.

Grace is important, or take time before the meal to go around and talk about one thing each person appreciates about life or about his or her favorite place on Earth.

During dinner, you can take turns offering food stories from your childhood, like how you came to love your favorite comfort food. You can talk about how you balance convenience with caring for the Earth or even the doubts you have about sacrosanct environmental practices. Above all, make the dinner reverent but light-hearted, full of joy and the pleasure of each other's company.

After dinner, get comfortable with dessert or another glass of wine and educate each other about such things as what makes good soil, how to truly feed the world's hungry, or the pros and cons of genetically modified food.

End the evening with individual resolutions, including one to get back together each year to celebrate this day and to keep plugging away as advocates for our island home.

For more information on giving an Earth Dinner, see www.earthdinner.org

ASPHODEL, THAT GREENY FLOWER / *William Carlos Williams*

…It is difficult | to get the news from poems |

yet men die miserably every day |

for lack | of what is found there.

---

22 — FRI · APR 22 · 2005

50 YEARS AGO **1955:** Congress orders all US coins bear the motto *"In God We Trust"* ~

Jack Nicholson, actor, b.1937
John Waters, filmmaker, b.1946

When nations grow old, the arts grow cold and commerce settles on every tree.
— *William Blake*

1970 EARTH DAY

☽ ☌ ♀ ☿ 1:04AM
☽ ☌ ♃ 12:06PM
☽ △ ♆ 10:43PM

☾
SET 5:34AM
RISE 6:27PM

☀
RISE 6:16AM
SET 8:08PM

RIGHT MEMORY

---

23 — SAT · APR 23 · 2005

Passover, lasts until 5/1, Jewish ~ St. George's Day, England
William Shakespeare, b.1564 d.1616
Miguel Cervantes, author, d.1616
Michael Moore, filmmaker, 1954

Be not afraid of greatness: some are born great, some achieve greatness, and some have greatness thrust upon them.
— *William Shakespeare*

☽ △ ♂ 11:46PM

☾
SET 5:52AM
RISE 7:40PM

☀
RISE 6:15AM
SET 8:09PM

RIGHT CONCEPTION

---

24 — SUN · APR 24 · 2005

Wesak: Buddha Day, Buddhist
Robert Penn Warren, 1st US poet laureate, b.1905
Shirley MacLaine, actress, b.1934

PENUMBRAL LUNAR ECLIPSE 09:55 (UT)

The hand is the cutting edge of the mind.
— *Jacob Bronowski*

ROBERT BAILEY THOMAS B.1766

FOUNDER OF "THE FARMER'S ALMANAC"

☽ ☌ ☉ 5:06AM
☽ △ ♅ 2:39PM
☽ ☌ ♀ 5:14PM

☀
RISE 6:13AM
SET 8:10PM

Full Moon 10:06UT

RIGHT RESOLVE

CIVILIZING IDEA: Community Gardens

Concrete and congestion are a fact of life in most American cities, but a new movement challenges their residents to reject that double curse and take back the land. The urban farming movement, born 25 years ago but recently gaining momentum, encourages city dwellers to view local spaces — be they cramped backyards or weedy vacant lots — as future sites for people to meet, grow food, and even achieve economic independence.

Denver Urban Gardens, a project that now extends to more than 70 sites throughout the metro, describes its philosophy: "participants assume responsibility to improve their community, initiate a sense of pride in their surroundings, and improve their nutritional status through healthy, fresh food."

Chicago's City Farm, located between Cabrini Green and the Gold Coast, transforms food trimmings gleaned from local restaurants into rich compost to nurture crops of tomatoes, potatoes, and greens that it sells at farmers' markets and to local chefs. In the process, City Farm gainfully employs local residents and provides a natural sanctuary where people most crave one.

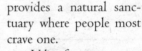

Urban farms are sprouting up nationwide, and along with their agricultural aims, many also offer educational programming and free public access to seeds, tools, and advice.

~ *Andi McDaniel*

For more information on urban farming or to find an urban farming project in your area, see:
Denver Urban Gardens: www.dug.org
Austin's Sustainable Food Center:
www.sustainablefoodcenter.org
Chicago's City Farm:
www.resourcecenterchicago.org
Portland's Growing Gardens:
www.growinggardens.org
Minneapolis' Youth Farm & Market Project
www.youthfarm.net

25 — MON · APR 25 · 2005

Anzac Day, Australia, New Zealand
~ 1915: Battle of Gallipoli

Meadowlark Lemon, athlete, b.1932
Ella Fitzgerald, singer, b.1917

Problems are only opportunities in work clothes.
— Henry Kaiser

FIRST LICENSE PLATES ISSUED 1901
① ② ③

TURN-OFF YOUR TV WEEK

☽△♄ 11:05AM

☾
SET 6:37AM
RISE 10:16PM

☉
RISE 6:11AM
SET 8:11PM

RIGHT WORD

26 — TUE · APR 26 · 2005

1986: Chernobyl nuclear reactor disaster ~
1937: Massacre, Guernica Spain

Frederick Law Olmstead, landscaper, b.1822
John James Audubon, artist, b.1785

Every problem has a gift for you in its hands.
— Richard Bach

RICHTER SCALE DAY

CHARLES RICHTER B.1900

☽△☿ 6:26PM

☾
SET 7:09AM
RISE 11:35PM

☉
RISE 6:10AM
SET 8:13PM

RIGHT DEED

27 — WED · APR 27 · 2005

1805: U.S. Marines attack Tripoli

Edward Gibbon, historian, b.1737
Ulysses Grant, general, b.1822
Ferdinand Magellan, explorer, b.1521

There are no mistakes, no coincidences. All events are blessings given to us to learn from.
— Elisabeth Kubler-Ross

Anouk Aimee, actress, b.1932

☽♂♇ 6:53PM
☿♂♃ 11:37AM

☾
SET 7:51AM

☉
RISE 6:08AM
SET 8:14PM

RIGHT LIVELIHOOD

28 — THU · APR 28 · 2005

1789: Mutiny on the Bounty
1945: Mussolini executed

Mifflin Gibbs, judge, b.1828
Jay Leno, comedian, b.1950
James Monroe, 5th president, b.1758

If you don't like something, change it. If you can't change it, change your attitude. Don't complain.
— Maya Angelou

☿♂♃ 10:37AM
☽△☉ 6:18PM

☾
RISE 12:48AM
SET 7:46AM

☉
RISE 6:07AM
SET 8:15PM

RIGHT ENDEAVOR

CELEBRATE: Arbor Day, April 29

As a young settler in Nebraska in the 1850s, Julius Sterling Morton advocated conservation and new agricultural methods. He felt that planting trees was especially important: More trees would provide not only beauty and lumber, but also serve as windbreaks on the prairie, and their roots would hold moisture in the soil. He convinced the state's agricultural board to set aside a special day for planting trees. The first Arbor Day, April 10, 1872, was such a success that more than a million trees were planted. Today most states have an Arbor Day.

From The Book of Holidays
Around the World

During the Depression, schoolchildren throughout America honored our connection to nature by accompanying tree-planting ceremonies with nature pageants featuring music, poetry, and dance. (See the Little Rascal's video, "Arbor Day.") In this era of shrinking forests, global warming, and greenhouse gases, isn't it time to revive the observance of Arbor Day? Find your state's Arbor Day organizers through the National Arbor Day Foundation at *www.arborday.org* .

~ *Cosmo*

WILD GEESE/*Mary Oliver*

...Whoever you are, no matter how lonely, |
the world offers itself to your imagination, |
calls to you like the wild geese, harsh and exciting– |
over and over announcing your place | in the family of things.

---

29   FRI · APR 29 · 2005

Holy Friday,
Orthodox
Christian

*Emperor
Hirohito,
b.1901
Duke Ellington,
musician,
b.1899*

Knowing trees,
I understand
the meaning
of patience.
Knowing grass,
I can appreciate
persistence.
— *Hal Borland*

ARBOR DAY

☽△♀ 8:59PM
☽☌♄ 5:00PM

☾
RISE 1:51AM
SET 9:55AM

☉
RISE 6:05AM
SET 8:16PM

RIGHT MEMORY

---

30   SAT · APR 30 · 2005

Beltane, Wicca
~Walpurgisnacht:
Witch's Night,
Europe
~ St. James the
Great Day, Orth-
odox Christian

*William Lilly,
almanac compiler,
b.1602*

There is no
disguise that can
for long conceal
love where it
exists or simu-
late it where it
does not.
— *Francois de la
Rochefoucauld*

☾
RISE 2:39AM
SET 11:13AM

☉
RISE 6:04AM
SET 7:18PM

RIGHT CONCEPTION

---

1   SUN · MAY 1 · 2005

Easter Sunday,
Orthodox

*Pierre Teilhard
de Chardin,
philosopher,
b.1881
Mother Jones,
labor leader,
b.1830*

Follow your bliss.
— *Joseph
Campbell*

MAY DAY

LABOUR DAY

WORLDWIDE
WORKER'S HOLIDAY

☽△♃ 12:57AM
☽☌♆ 12:27PM

☉
RISE 6:02AM
SET 8:19PM

*Last Quarter
6:24UT*

RIGHT RESOLVE

MAY

APR 20 - MAY 20

taurus

MAY 21- JUN 20

Ⅱ

gemini

BIRTHSTONE
Emerald

FLOWER
Lily

Equilibrium
BECOMES PROGRESS
Challenges: apathy, inertia, covetousness

*T*he soul expands into the cosmos. The sun is fully released from the bondage of winter. The shackles of our lower self seem to drop away. This is "the charming month of May," named for the Earth goddess Maia. Children dance around the Maypole. The Green Man, decked in bright, tender leaves, runs wildly through the woods. May I, Beltane, the Celtic festival of sacred fire, marks the opening of light and life. Thus spring turns toward summer. The Queen of the Fairies rides out on her white horse. Flowers everywhere reach for the heavens. Butterflies, hummingbirds return. In all this riot of life, growth, and color, we must strive for balance. With the equilibrium comes a certain dreaminess, but also increased intuitive powers. We feel prescient, no longer the captive of the brain. It is as if, in our soul-spiritual parts, we, too, can put forth shoots and leaves and flowers, returning to the heavens the life forces we have transformed through the winter.

MAY IS
ALLERGY/ASTHMA AWARENESS MONTH · BETTER HEARING & SPEECH MONTH · BREATHE EASY MONTH · CLEAN AIR MONTH · CREATIVE BEGINNINGS MONTH · FAMILY SUPPORT MONTH · FIBROMYALGIA AWARENESS MONTH · GET CAUGHT READING MONTH · BUSINESS IMAGE IMPROVEMENT MONTH · LAW ENFORCEMENT APPRECIATION MONTH · MELANOMA PREVENTION MONTH · BIKE MONTH · BOOK MONTH · EGG MONTH · GOOD CAR-KEEPING MONTH · HAMBURGER MONTH · MENTAL HEALTH MONTH · MOVING MONTH · PHYSICAL FITNESS MONTH · SALSA MONTH · WOMEN'S HEALTH CARE MONTH

WNW   May 9, 9:00 p.m.

W   May 13, 10:00 p.m.

STARS & PLANETS FOR MAY

Venus, Jupiter and Saturn are visible in the evening sky: Jupiter – southeast, Saturn – southwest, and Venus – northwest. On the 9th the waxing crescent Moon is in the neighborhood of Venus. At the end of May Venus stands between the horns of Taurus, the Bull.

LOOK UP:

  4 Eta Aquarid meteor shower peaks
  8 New Moon, 8:46 UT
23 Full Moon (Flower Moon), 20:19 UT

LOOK OUT:

· Long-absent does reappear with spotted fawns
· Mighty saguaro cacti bloom
· Chigger season begins.
· Breeding horseshoe crabs carpet Delaware Bay beaches

			MAY			
S	M	T	W	T	F	S
1	2	3	4	5	6	7
8	9	10	11	12	13	14
15	16	17	18	19	20	21
22	23	24	25	26	27	28
29	30	31				

I do not know what I may appear to the world; but to myself I seem to have been only like a boy playing on the seashore, and diverting myself now and then finding a smoother pebble or a prettier shell than ordinary, whilst the great ocean of truth lay all undiscovered before me.
~ ISAAC NEWTON

HOLIDAY: Cinco de Mayo, May 5

Mexican national holiday recognizing the anniversary of the Battle of Puebla in 1862, in which Mexican troops under General Ignacio Zaragoza, outnumbered three to one, defeated invading French forces of Napolean III. Anniversary is observed by Mexicans everywhere, with parades, festivals, dances, and speeches.

Portland, Oregon, sister city of Guadalajara, Mexico, celebrates Cinco de Mayo every year in Waterfront Park, with more than 300,000 people attending.

From Chase's 2004 Calendar of Events,

*For more information on
Cinco de Mayo, see
www.mexonline.com/cinco.htm*

2 — MON · MAY 2 · 2005

1932: Pearl S. Buck wins Pulitzer Prize ~ 1611: King James Bible published
Benjamin Spock, pediatrician, b.1903
Leonardo da Vinci, artist, d.1519

Beware the fury of the patient man.
— *John Dryden*

ROBERT'S RULES OF ORDER DAY
HENRY M. ROBERT B.1837
SIBLING APPRECIATION DAY

☽☌♂ 11:40AM
☾ RISE 3:44AM SET 1:53PM
☀ RISE 6:01AM SET 8:20PM

RIGHT WORD

3 — TUE · MAY 3 · 2005

Dia de la Cruz, Mexico ~ Nat'l Teacher Day
Pete Seeger, musician, b.1919
Niccolo Macchiavelli, statesman, b.1469
Golda Meir, prime minister, b.1898

With enough "ifs" we could put Paris in a bottle.
— *French Saying*

NAT'L PUBLIC RADIO 1ST NEWS BROADCAST 1971

☽☌♅ 2:56AM
☾ RISE 4:07AM SET 3:11PM
☀ RISE 5:59AM SET 8:21PM

RIGHT DEED

4 — WED · MAY 4 · 2005

1886: Haymarket Square riot
Horace Mann, educator, b.1796
Audrey Hepburn, actress, b.1929
George Will, columnist, b.1941

Everything that irritates us about others can lead us to an understanding of ourselves.
— *Carl Jung*

NAT'L WEATHER OBSERVER'S DAY

☽△♄ 12:41AM
☾ RISE 4:26AM SET 4:25PM
☀ RISE 5:58AM SET 8:23PM

RIGHT LIVELIHOOD

5 — THU · MAY 5 · 2005

Ascension Day, Christian ~ Children's Day, Japan
1904: Cy Young pitches a perfect game
Nellie Bly, journalist, b.1864
Karl Marx, communist, b.1818

The most wasted of all days is one without laughter.
— *e.e. cummings*

CINCO DE MAYO

☽☍♃ 7:47AM
☾ RISE 4:45AM SET 5:39PM
☀ RISE 5:56AM SET 8:24PM

RIGHT ENDEAVOR

PROCLAMATION: Mother's Peace Day, May 8

Arise, then, women of this day! Arise, all women who have hearts, whether your baptism be that of water or tears!

Say firmly: "We will not have great questions decided by irrelevant agencies. Our husbands shall not come to us, reeking with carnage, for caresses and applause. Our sons shall not be taken from us to unlearn all that we have taught them of charity, mercy and patience. We women of one country will be too tender of those of another country to allow our sons to be trained to injure theirs."

From the bosom of the devastated earth, a voice goes up with our own. It says, "Disarm, Disarm!"

The sword of murder is not the balance of justice. Blood does not wipe out dishonor, nor violence indicate possession. As men have often forsaken the plow and the anvil at the summons of war, let women now leave all that may be left of home for a great and earnest day of counsel. Let them meet first, as women, to bewail and commemorate the dead. Let them solemnly take counsel with each other as to the means whereby the great human family can live in peace, each bearing after his own time the sacred impress, not of Caesars but of God.

In the name of womanhood and of humanity, I earnestly ask that a general congress of women without limit of nationality may be appointed and held at some place deemed most convenient and at the earliest period consistent with its objects, to promote the alliance of the different nationalities, the amicable settlement of international questions, the great and general interests of peace.

~ Julia Ward Howe, 1870

Julia Ward Howe was born May 27, 1819, in New York City. A passionate defender of equal rights, she wrote the Battle Hymn of the Republic *and was the first woman elected to the American Academy of Arts and Letters. This proclamation marked the day Howe organized to encourage mothers worldwide to rally for peace. Let's take Mother's Day back from the commercial interests that have hijacked it and restore its meaning as a day to celebrate peace.*

CITY NAME

THE EARTH MOVERS / *Christopher Cokinos*

…right here, the birds | glow like tiny suns in the brush and branches: |
yellowthroat, goldfinch, Kentucky warbler, | feathers bright as goldenrod. |
I watch one yellowthroat | throw back its head, | throat quivering |
with song this May returning: | the song repeats, it drifts |
like wind-borne seed | over the stakes | ribboned with orange strips…

6
FRI · MAY 6 · 2005

1955: West Germany joins NATO
~ Ascension, Christian
~ 1527: Sack of Rome

Rabindranath Tagore, poet, b.1861

From error to error, one discovers the entire truth.
— *Sigmund Freud*

FOUNDER OF PSYCHOANALYSIS

SIGMUND FREUD B.1856

☽☌☿ 2:45AM
☽△♇ 8:22AM

☾
RISE 5:04AM
SET 6:52PM

☀
RISE 5:55AM
SET 8:25PM

RIGHT MEMORY

7
SAT · MAY 7 · 2005

50 YEARS AGO
1955: West European Union formed
~ 1824: Premiere of Beethoven's 9th Symphony

Pyotr Tchaikovsky, composer, b.1840

Live out of your imagination, not your history.
— *Stephen Covey*

KENTUCKY DERBY

☾
RISE 5:24AM
SET 8:06PM

☀
RISE 5:54AM
SET 8:26PM

RIGHT CONCEPTION

8
SUN · MAY 8 · 2005

1945: VE Day: Victory in Europe
~ Liberation Day, Slovakia
~ Victory Day, France
~ Helston Furry Dance, England
Robert Johnson, guitarist, b.1911
Antoine Lavoisier, chemist, b.1794

Nothing fixes a thing so intensely in the memory as the wish to forget it.
— *Michel de Montaigne*

MOTHER'S DAY

☽☌☉ 3:45AM
☿△♇ 7:01AM

☀
RISE 5:52AM
SET 8:27PM

New Moon
9:45AM

RIGHT RESOLVE

HOLIDAY: Limerick Day, May 12

Limerick Day is observed on the birthday of one of its champions, Edward Lear. The limerick, which dates from the early 18th century, has been described as the "only fixed verse form indigenous to the English language." It gained its greatest popularity following the publication of Edward Lear's *Book of Nonsense* (and its sequels).   *From* Chase's 2004 Calendar of Events

There was a Young Lady of Troy,
Whom several large flies did annoy;
Some she killed with a thump,
Some she drowned at the pump,
And some she took with her
to Troy.

There was an Old Man of the coast,
Who placidly sat on a post;
But when it was cold
He relinquished his hold
And called for some hot
buttered toast.

Limericks are short, humorous verses, often nonsensical and ribald. Made up of five lines, rhyming aabba, the dominant meter is anapestic, with two metrical feet in the third and fourth lines and three feet in the others. The form is said to originate from a song with the same verse construction, the refrain of which contains the place name, Limerick, Ireland. Edward Lear popularized limericks in his *Book of Nonsense* (1846).

Two more examples for your pleasure:

The profs of our great university
Display the most striking diversity:
Some wise and some foolish,
Some saintly, some ghoulish,
And some of the utmost perversity.
        ~*From* The Art of the Limerick
                by Cyril Bibby

One day F. Scott Fitzgerald in gloom,
Took a lesbian up to his room,
They spent all the night,
Deciding who had the right,
To do what and with which and
to whom.

        ~ *From the movie,* Getting Straight,
        screenplay by Robert Kaufman

For more information on Edward Lear, see
www.poets.org/poets/poets.cfm

9 — MON · MAY 9 · 2005

1945: Victory Day, Russia

John Brown, abolitionist, b.1800
Pancho Gonzales, athlete, b.1928

The instinct of a man is to pursue everything that flies from him, and to fly from all that pursue him.
— *Voltaire*

☽ ☌ ♀ 12:15AM
☽ △ ♃ 9:23PM

☾
RISE 6:17AM
SET 10:29PM

☉
RISE 5:51AM
SET 8:29PM

RIGHT WORD

10 — TUE · MAY 10 · 2005

1994: Nelson Mandela inauguration

T. Berry Brazleton, doctor, b.1918
Fred Astaire, dancer, b.1899

TRUST YOUR INTUITION DAY

It's a shallow life that doesn't give a person a few scars.
— *Garrison Keillor*

☽ △ ♆ 12:05PM

☾
RISE 6:52AM
SET 11:34PM

☉
RISE 5:50AM
SET 8:30PM

RIGHT DEED

11 — WED · MAY 11 · 2005

1862: Merrimac destroyed ~ National Windmill Day, Netherlands

Irving Berlin, lyricist, b.1888
Martha Graham, dancer, b.1894
Salvador Dali, artist, b.1904

The shoe that fits one person pinches another; there is no recipe for living that suits all cases.
— *Carl G. Jung*

☽ ☌ ♇ 12:35AM

☾
RISE 7:36AM
SET 12:30PM

☉
RISE 5:49AM
SET 8:31PM

RIGHT LIVELIHOOD

12 — THU · MAY 12 · 2005

Florence Nightingale, nurse, b.1820
Kate Hepburn, actress, b.1907
Tony Hawk, skateboarder, b.1969

LIMERICK DAY

EDWARD LEAR
b.1812

There was an old man with a beard ~ Who said "It is just as I feared!" ~ Two Owls and a Hen ~ Four Larks and a Wren ~ Have all built their nests in my beard."
— *Edward Lear*

☽ △ ♂ 4:28PM
☽ △ ♅ 8:46AM

☾
RISE 8:29AM
SET 12:16AM

☉
RISE 5:47AM
SET 8:32PM

RIGHT ENDEAVOR

BIRTHDAY: L. Frank Baum, May 15, 1856

We're off to see the Wizard,
The Wonderful Wizard of Oz.
You'll find he is a whiz of a Wiz!
If ever a Wiz! there was...

When L. (Lyman) Frank Baum wrote *The Wonderful Wizard of Oz* for children, it was not so much as a piece of fiction, but as a real tale they could lose themselves in. Born on May 15, 1856, Baum did many things until he joined illustrator Maxfield Parish in 1897 to create his first book, *Mother Goose in Prose*. In 1900, he wrote the instantly successful story of Dorothy and the Tin Man, Glinda and the Wicked Witch of the West, Toto and Aunt Em — characters now familiar to an astonishing number of people all over the world. Baum followed up with thirteen more books about Oz until his death in 1919.

Music by Harold Arlen, Lyrics by E.Y. Harburg, original story by L. Frank Baum. For more information on L. Frank Baum and the Wizard of Oz, see thewizardofoz.warnerbros.com/

ANOTHER SPRING ON OLMSTEAD STREET / *Len Roberts*

She's out there again with her five-cent | packets of seeds for green beans
and beets,… | not one of us | watching from the house dares to go out |
and touch her bare shoulder, not one of us | calls her name beneath the
streetlight's buzz | where she dreams and digs, where she buries |
time and again her white, white hands.

---

13   FRI · MAY 13 · 2005

Shavuot, Jewish

*Stevie Wonder,
singer, b.1950
Mary Wells,
singer, b.1943*

Keep away from
people who try
to belittle your
ambitions. Small
people always
do that, but the
really great make
you feel that
you, too, can
become great.
— *Mark Twain*

☽ ☌ ♄ 9:43AM

☾
SET 1:16AM
RISE 9:29AM

☉
RISE 5:46AM
SET 8:33PM

RIGHT MEMORY

---

14   SAT · MAY 14 · 2005

1607: Founding
of Jamestown, VA
~ Midnight
Sun, until July
30, Norway
*Cate Blanchett,
actress, b.1969
Thomas Gains-
borough, artist,
b.1727
Robert Owen,
scientist, b.1771*

We are, each of
us angels with
only one wing;
and we can only
fly by embracing
one another.
— *Luciano
de Crescenzo*

INTERNATIONAL
MIGRATORY BIRD
DAY

☾
SET 1:52AM
RISE 10:34AM

☉
RISE 5:45AM
SET 8:34PM

RIGHT CONCEPTION

---

15   SUN · MAY 15 · 2005

Pentecost,
Christian
~ Whitsunday,
Christian
~ Bay to
Breakers Race:
Largest footrace
in the world,
San Francisco
*Katharine Anne
Porter, author,
b.1890*

If the world
were a well-
tuned instrument
played in rhythm,
I would not
worship the
instrument but
him who made
it and played it.
— *Athenagoras*

*L. Frank Baum,
author, b.1856*

♂ ☌ ♅ 6:53AM
☽ △ ♇ 11:32PM

☾
SET 2:21AM
RISE 11:40AM

☉
RISE 5:44AM
SET 8:36PM

RIGHT RESOLVE

LIVING URBAN TREASURE: Chicago's Studs Terkel

Studs Terkel has been hanging around Americans for a long time; 92 years from the date of this writing. And for almost that same amount of time, he has been listening to these same Americans tell the stories of their lives.

Terkel is as famous for his unstoppable wit and energy as he is for his interviews. He started out as a radio performer in the 1930s and then, in 1949, began a short-lived television career. "Studs' Place," a weekly comedy that focused on the lives of working-class Americans in a Chicago restaurant, lasted from 1949 to 1950, when NBC cancelled it because network bosses decided that Terkel might be a communist.

Studs Terkel in Chicago

I still see that girl in the maroon smock who liked yellow daisies

Since then Terkel has interviewed the famous and the not-so-famous for WFMT, Chicago. Some of his interviews included philosopher Bertrand Russell, painter Jacob Lawrence, and dancer and choreographer Martha Graham. His interviews have always been deep, interesting, and extremely considerate of those he talks to. He lets people express their opinions without imposing his own judgments on the conversation.

Now in his nineties, Terkel is finally talking about his own life and work. Most recently he has published a book on death and dying. *Will the Circle be Unbroken?* contains interviews with an emergency medical technician, a social worker, an undertaker, and others about the spiritual and intellectual relationship that people have with the deaths of others, near and far, and with the idea of their own mortality. As he was beginning the book, Terkel's own wife, Ida, died at the age of eighty-seven. In an article for the *Atlantic Monthly*, he wrote "I still see that girl in the maroon smock who liked yellow daisies. Each week there is a fresh bunch of yellow daisies near the windowsill. On the sill is the urn containing her ashes. On occasion, either indignant or somewhat enthusiastic about something, I mumble toward it (her), 'Whaddya think of that, kid?'"

Terkel continues to write, travel, and speak throughout the country with all the energy, compassion, and wisdom with which he began his career. He is a true hero for the common man.

~ *Robert Birnbaum*

For more information on Studs Terkel, see
www.myhero.com/myhero/hero.asp

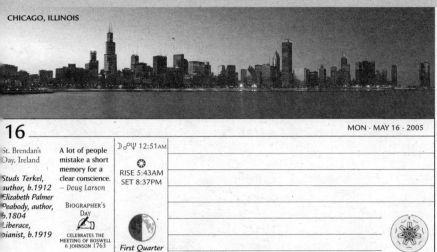

CHICAGO, ILLINOIS

16
MON · MAY 16 · 2005

St. Brendan's
Day, Ireland

Studs Terkel,
author, b.1912
Elizabeth Palmer
Peabody, author,
b.1804
Liberace,
pianist, b.1919

A lot of people
mistake a short
memory for a
clear conscience.
— Doug Larson

BIOGRAPHER'S
DAY

CELEBRATES THE
MEETING OF BOSWELL
& JOHNSON 1763

☽ ☌ ♇ 12:51AM

☀
RISE 5:43AM
SET 8:37PM

First Quarter
08:56PM

RIGHT WORD

17
TUE · MAY 17 · 2005

1954: School
segregation
banned, Brown
vs. Board of
Education
~ Constitution
Day, Norway
Mia Hamm,
soccer player,
b.1972
Edward Jenner,
doctor, b.1749

Many live in the
ivory tower called
reality; they
never venture
on the open
sea of thought.
— Francois
Gautier

☽ △ ☿ 5:43AM
☽ ☌ ♅ 9:31AM
☽ ☌ ♂ 12:36PM
♀ △ ♃ 3:34PM

☾
SET 3:03AM
RISE 1:53PM

☀
RISE 5:42AM
SET 8:38PM

RIGHT DEED

18
WED · MAY 18 · 2005

1980: Mt. St.
Helen's eruption

Meredith
Wilson,
composer,
b.1902
Pope John Paul
II, b.1920
Frank Capra,
filmmaker,
b.1897

The heart is
wiser than the
intellect.
— J.G. Holland

INTERNATIONAL
MUSEUM DAY

VISIT YOUR
RELATIVES DAY

☽ △ ☉ 8:00PM

☾
SET 3:21AM
RISE 2:59PM

☀
RISE 5:41AM
SET 8:39PM

RIGHT LIVELIHOOD

19
THU · MAY 19 · 2005

1936: Gone with
the Wind published
~ 1780: Dark
Day in New
England

Ho Chi Minh,
Vietnamese
pres. b.1890
Malcom X,
black civil rights
leader, b.1925

Do not pray
for tasks equal
to your powers;
pray for powers
equal to your
tasks.
— Phillips
Brooks

MAY RAY DAY

☽ ☌ ♃ 5:06PM
☽ △ ♀ 10:32PM

☾
SET 3:38AM
RISE 4:07PM

☀
RISE 5:40AM
SET 8:40PM

RIGHT ENDEAVOR

EVENT: International Jumping Frog Jubilee, May 20-22, 2005

Mark Twain's story, "The Celebrated Jumping Frog of Calaveras County," written in 1867, was among his most popular, but it wasn't until 1928 that local boosters of the town of Angels Camp, Calaveras County, California, decided to celebrate the paving of main street with the first Jumping Frog Jubilee. The winning frog jumped 3 feet 6 inches. Rosie the Ribeter set the current world's record in 1986 with a jump of 21 feet 5 3/4 inches. The cash prize for breaking that record is $5,000. The Jumping Frog Jubilee is held the 3rd weekend in May.

Well, Smiley kept the beast in a little lattice box, and he used to fetch him down town sometimes and lay for a bet. One day a feller, a stranger in the camp he was, come across him with his box, and says:

"What might it be that you've got in the box?"

And Smiley says, sorter indifferent like, "It might be a parrot, or it might be a canary, may be, but it ain't it's only just a frog."

And the feller took it, and looked at it careful, and turned it round this way and that, and says, "H'm so 'tis. Well, what's he good for?"

"Well," Smiley says, easy and careless, "He's good enough for one thing, I should judge he can outjump any frog in Calaveras County."

From The Celebrated Jumping Frog of Calaveras County and Other Sketches *(1867) by Mark Twain*

For more on the Calaveras County Fair and Jumping Frog Jubilee, see www.frogtown.org

MOON/*Billy Collins*

…tonight would be the night | to carry some tiny creature outside | and introduce him to the moon | And if your house has no child, | you can always gather into your arms, | the sleeping infant of yourself | …And while the wind ruffles the pear trees | in the corner of the orchard | and dark roses wave against a stone wall, | you can turn him on your shoulder | and walk in circles on the lawn, | drunk with the light…

---

20   FRI · MAY 20 · 2005

1927: First Trans-Atlantic flight, Lindbergh ~ 1932: Amelia Earhart Atlantic crossing
Henri Rousseau, painter, b.1844
Honore de Balzac, author, b.1799

I believe in the incomprehensibility of God.
— *Honore de Balzac*

NATIONAL BIKE TO WORK DAY

☽△♆ 8:24PM

☾ SET 3:55AM
RISE 5:18PM

☀ RISE 5:39AM
SET 8:41PM

RIGHT MEMORY

---

21   SAT · MAY 21 · 2005

1955: 1st Transcontinental solo flight ~ Intenational Jumping Frog Jubilee, Calif.
Al Franken, comedian, b.1951
Alexander Pope, poet, b.1688

A man should never be ashamed to own he has been in the wrong, which is but saying...that he is wiser today than he was yesterday.
— *Alexander Pope*

☾ SET 4:14AM
RISE 6:32PM

☀ RISE 5:38AM
SET 8:42PM

RIGHT CONCEPTION

---

22   SUN · MAY 22 · 2005

Trinity, Christian
Richard Wagner, composer, b.1813
Sir Arthur Conan Doyle, author, b.1859
Mary Cassatt, painter, b.1844

It is a capital mistake to theorize before one has data. Insensibly one begins to twist facts to suit theories, instead of theories to suit facts.
— *Arthur Conan Doyle*

☽△♅ 1:22AM
☽△♂ 9:59AM
☽☍♀ 3:14PM
☽△♄ 11:54PM

☾ SET 4:37AM
RISE 7:51PM

☀ RISE 5:37AM
SET 8:43PM

RIGHT RESOLVE

ORIGINS: The Transcendentalist Movement

HENRY DAVID THOREAU

MARGARET FULLER

RALPH WALDO EMERSON

The word is a misnomer. The divine presence (Emerson's "Over-Soul") that permeates the universe is not transcendent but extremely present (immanent), according to the philosophy of this remarkable constellation of souls. It is down to earth; it is of the earth.

The group's elder and mentor was Ralph Waldo Emerson. Profoundly well-read (Wordsworth, Goethe, the Upanishads, et al), he nonetheless urged self-reliance. Life, not books, should be one's teacher.

Henry David Thoreau was the doer to Emerson's thinker. Known for his two-year experiment with simple living at Walden Pond, Thoreau dressed as a working man (when he was not taking "fluvial excursions" along the rivers, unclad but for a hat to keep off the sun) and sought out conversation with simple folk. By contrast, he noted, "I doubt if Emerson could trundle a wheelbarrow through the streets." An ardent ecologist before the discipline existed, Thoreau worshipped daily at nature's altar. Yet he was hardly aloof from society or current political issues, preferring a night in jail to paying taxes to a government that justified slavery. His doctrine of *Civil Disobedience* inspired Tolstoy, Gandhi, and M.L. King.

But Margaret Fuller was the group's heart and soul. To Emerson, she wrote, "You are intellect. I am life!" A brilliant thinker herself, she directed much of her early passion to the advancement of women's rights. In Italy, at age 37, Fuller experienced the fullness of love (and motherhood!) for the first time, also joining with her lover Ossoli in the Italian Revolution. She thought her record of these experiences was her greatest written work, but could find no European publisher. So she and her family set sail to Boston, though Emerson had offered to serve as her American agent. In a gale, their ship ran aground on Fire Island, and all three were swept to their deaths. Thoreau searched for her body, but it was never found.

~ *John Miller*

For more information on the Transcendentalist Movement, see www.transcendentalists.com

23 — MON · MAY 23 · 2005

Declaration of the Bab, Baha'i ~ World Turtle Day

Friedrich Mesmer, hypnotist, b.1734 Margaret Fuller, journalist, b.1810

To love and be loved is to feel the sun from both sides.
— David Viscott

NY PUBLIC LIBRARY

FOUNDED 1895

☽☌☉ 3:18PM

❁ RISE 5:36AM SET 8:44PM

Full Moon 9:18PM

RIGHT WORD

24 — TUE · MAY 24 · 2005

Slavic Script & Bulgarian Culture Day ~ Buddha Day ~ Visakha Puja, Buddhist

Patti LaBelle, singer, b.1944 Bob Dylan, singer, b.1941

What you do speaks so loudly that I cannot hear what you say.
— Ralph Waldo Emerson

FIRST U.S. TELEGRAPH LINE OPENS 1844

♀△♆ 7:11AM
☽☌♀ 4:40PM

☾ SET 5:44AM RISE 10:31PM

❁ RISE 5:35AM SET 8:45PM

RIGHT DEED

25 — WED · MAY 25 · 2005

1963: African Freedom Day, Chad, Zambia

Raymond Carver, author, b.1938 Miles Davis, musician, b.1926 Ralph Waldo Emerson, author, b.1803

Tomorrow is a new day; you shall begin it serenely and with too high a spirit to be encumbered with your old nonsense.
— Ralph Waldo Emerson

☽☌♇ 1:52AM

☾ SET 6:35AM RISE 11:40PM

❁ RISE 5:34AM SET 8:46PM

RIGHT LIVELIHOOD

26 — THU · MAY 26 · 2005

1805: Napoleon crowned king of Italy ~ 1805: Lewis & Clark see Rocky Mtns ~ Corpus Christi, Christian

John Wayne, actor, b.1907 Sally Ride, astronaut, b.1951

The smallest bookstore still contains more ideas of worth than have been presented in the entire history of television.
— Andrew Ross

☾ SET 7:41AM

❁ RISE 5:34AM SET 8:47PM

RIGHT ENDEAVOR

BIRTHDAY: Isadora Duncan, May 27, 1878

My motto — sans limites.

*So long as little children are allowed
to suffer, there is no true love in this world.*

Art is not necessary at all. All that is
necessary to make this world a better
place to live in is to love — to love as
Christ loved, as Buddha loved.

*The dancer's body is simply the
luminous manifestation of the soul.*

It has taken me years of struggle,
hard work and research to learn to
make one simple gesture, and I know
enough about the art of writing to
realize that it would take as many years
of concentrated effort to write one
simple, beautiful sentence.

*What one has not experienced,
one will never understand in print.*

The finest inheritance you can give
to a child is to allow it to make its
own way, completely on its own feet.

*Any intelligent woman who reads the
marriage contract, and then goes into it,
deserves all the consequences.*

Perhaps he was a bit different
from other people, but what really
sympathetic person is not a little mad?

*The real American type can never be
a ballet dancer. The legs are too long, the
body too supple and the spirit too free for
this school of affected grace and toe walking.*

People don't live nowadays: they get
about ten percent out of life.

*The only dance masters I could have
were Jean-Jacques Rousseau,
Walt Whitman and Nietzsche.*

We may not all break the Ten
Commandments, but we are certainly
all capable of it. Within us lurks
the breaker of all laws, ready to spring
out at the first real opportunity.

*You were once wild here.
Don't let them tame you.*

Imagine then a dancer who, after
long study, prayer and inspiration, has
attained such a degree of understanding
that his body is simply the luminous
manifestation of his soul; whose body
dances in accordance with a music heard
inwardly, in an expression of something
out of another, profounder world.
This is the truly creative dancer;
natural but not imitative, speaking in
movement out of himself and out of
something greater than all selves.

Isadora Duncan

*For more information on Isadora Duncan,
see www.isadoraduncan.org*

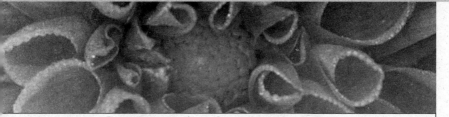

PEONIES/*Mary Oliver*

This morning the green fists of the peonies are getting ready | to break my heart | as the sun rises, | as the sun strokes them with his old, buttery fingers | …Do you also hurry, half-dressed and barefoot, into the garden, | and softly, and exclaiming of their dearness, | fill your arms with the white and pink flowers, | with their honeyed heaviness, their lush trembling, | their eagerness | to be wild and perfect for a moment, before they are | nothing, forever?

---

27   FRI · MAY 27 · 2005

1930: Scotch Tape patented

Hubert H. Humphrey, politician, b.1911
Isadora Duncan, dancer, b.1878
Rachel Carson, author, b.1907

The expert at anything was once a beginner.
— *Rutherford Hayes*

GOLDEN GATE BRIDGE OPENED
SAN FRANCISCO 1937

☽ ☌ ♄ 3:25AM
☽ △ ☿ 10:22AM
☽ △ ☉ 12:41AM

☾
RISE 12:35AM
SET 8:59AM

☀
RISE 5:33AM
SET 8:48PM

RIGHT MEMORY

---

28   SAT · MAY 28 · 2005

St. Bernard of Montjoux, France
~ 1892: Sierra Club founded

Rudolph Giuliani, NYC mayor, b.1944
Ian Fleming, author, b.1908

If you can imagine it, you can achieve it.
If you can dream it, you can become it.
— *William Arthur Ward*

☽ △ ♃ 4:02AM
☽ ☌ ♆ 6:15PM

☾
RISE 1:17AM
SET 10:21AM

☀
RISE 5:32AM
SET 8:49PM

RIGHT CONCEPTION

---

29   SUN · MAY 29 · 2005

Ascension of Baha'u'llah, Baha'i
~ 1453: Constantinople falls to the Turks

The basis of optimism is sheer terror.
— *Oscar Wilde*

Patrick Henry, patriot, b.1736
John F. Kennedy, 35th president, b.1917
G.K. Chesterton, author, b.1874

MT. EVEREST SUMMIT FIRST REACHED 1953

☽ △ ♀ 4:18AM
♀ ☌ ♇ 4:31AM

☾
RISE 1:48AM
SET 11:43AM

☀
RISE 5:31AM
SET 8:50PM

RIGHT RESOLVE

BIRTHDAY: Walt Whitman, May 31, 1819

Walt Whitman
1849

SONG OF MYSELF
I celebrate myself, and sing myself,
And what I assume you shall assume,
For every atom belonging to me as good belongs to you.
I loafe and invite my soul,
I lean and loafe at my ease observing a spear of summer grass...
~ *Walt Whitman*

From "Song of Myself" in Leaves of Grass

For more information on Walt Whitman, see www.whitmanarchive.org

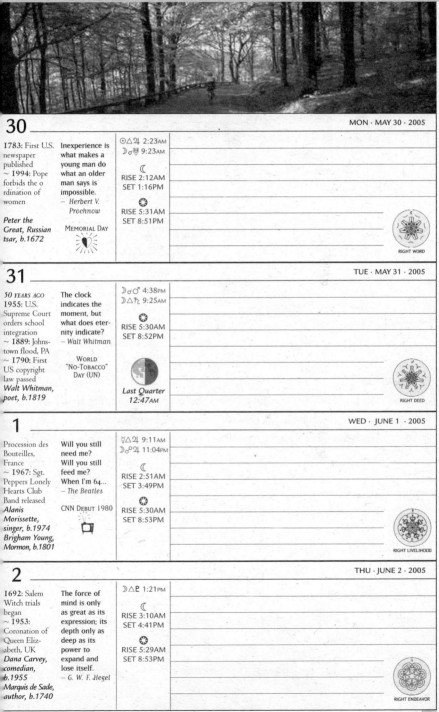

30 — MON · MAY 30 · 2005

1783: First U.S. newspaper published
~ 1994: Pope forbids the ordination of women

Peter the Great, Russian tsar, b.1672

Inexperience is what makes a young man do what an older man says is impossible.
— *Herbert V. Prochnow*

MEMORIAL DAY

⊙△♃ 2:23AM
☽♂♅ 9:23AM

☾
RISE 2:12AM
SET 1:16PM

✷
RISE 5:31AM
SET 8:51PM

RIGHT WORD

31 — TUE · MAY 31 · 2005

50 YEARS AGO
1955: U.S. Supreme Court orders school integration
~ 1889: Johnstown flood, PA
~ 1790: First US copyright law passed
Walt Whitman, poet, b.1819

The clock indicates the moment, but what does eternity indicate?
— *Walt Whitman*

WORLD "NO-TOBACCO" DAY (UN)

☽♂♂ 4:38PM
☽△♄ 9:25AM

✷
RISE 5:30AM
SET 8:52PM

Last Quarter
12:47AM

RIGHT DEED

1 — WED · JUNE 1 · 2005

Procession des Bouteilles, France
~ 1967: Sgt. Peppers Lonely Hearts Club Band released
Alanis Morissette, singer, b.1974
Brigham Young, Mormon, b.1801

Will you still need me? Will you still feed me? When I'm 64...
— *The Beatles*

CNN DEBUT 1980

☿△♃ 9:11AM
☽♂♃ 11:04PM

☾
RISE 2:51AM
SET 3:49PM

✷
RISE 5:30AM
SET 8:53PM

RIGHT LIVELIHOOD

2 — THU · JUNE 2 · 2005

1692: Salem Witch trials began
~ 1953: Coronation of Queen Elizabeth, UK
Dana Carvey, comedian, b.1955
Marquis de Sade, author, b.1740

The force of mind is only as great as its expression; its depth only as deep as its power to expand and lose itself.
— *G. W. F. Hegel*

☽△♇ 1:21PM

☾
RISE 3:10AM
SET 4:41PM

✷
RISE 5:29AM
SET 8:53PM

RIGHT ENDEAVOR

JUNE

MAY 21- JUN 20

gemini

JUN 21- JUL 22

cancer

BIRTHSTONE
Pearl

FLOWER
Rose

Perseverance
BECOMES FAITHFULNESS
*Challenges: unfaithfulness,
incapacitation*

*J*uno, who gives this month its name, walks in golden sandals in the heavy early morning dew. Life thrusts heavenward, the vegetation thickens, stands of trees become dense blocks of solid green. Dragonflies sweep over lakes warm enough to swim in; by night, fireflies emulate the stars. On perfect days, the light is so sweet and unthreatening that we lose ourselves in it without fear. Trusting ourselves to its warmth, we know to lose ourselves will be to find ourselves. We sense why some traditions speak of June as the "door of the year," the gateway to the inner realms of nature. From the heights Cosmic Intelligence streams down, irradiating the clouds and surrounding the landscape in golden glory. Nature is transfigured. Matter is spiritualized; spirit materialized.

JUNE IS:
ADOPT A SHELTER-CAT MONTH · CHILDREN'S AWARENESS MONTH · FIREWORKS SAFETY MONTH · GAY & LESBIAN PRIDE MONTH · INTERNAT'L MEN'S MONTH · PEOPLE SKILLS MONTH · PERENNIAL GARDENING MONTH · ACCORDION AWARENESS MONTH ROSE MONTH · REBUILD YOUR LIFE MONTH · STUDENT SAFETY MONTH VISION RESEARCH MONTH · BLESS-A-CHILD MONTH · DAIRY MONTH · SKIN CANCER AWARENESS MONTH · ENTREPRENEURS MARKETING MONTH · TURKEY LOVER'S MONTH

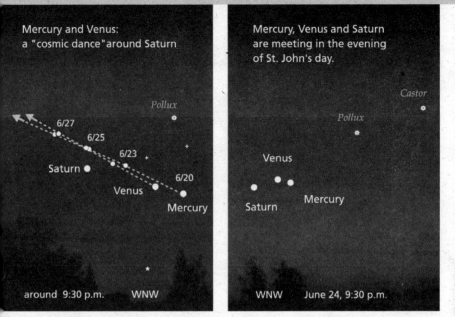

Mercury and Venus:
a "cosmic dance" around Saturn

Pollux

6/27
6/25
6/23
Saturn
6/20
Venus
Mercury

around 9:30 p.m.   WNW

Mercury, Venus and Saturn
are meeting in the evening
of St. John's day.

Castor

Pollux

Venus

Saturn   Mercury

WNW   June 24, 9:30 p.m.

STARS & PLANETS FOR JUNE

Watch how Venus, Saturn, and Mercury meet near Gemini's brightest stars Castor and Pollux, low in the western sky just after sundown, on the 21st. Watch how the conjunction shifts each night, like a dance. Before Saturn leaves the evening sky at the end of June it meets Venus in a nice conjunction on the 24th.

LOOK UP:

1 Mercury at superior conjunction

6 New Moon, 21:56 UT

21 Summer solstice, 6:45 UT
    Mercury, Venus, and Saturn cluster near Gemini's
    bright stars Castor and Pollux. Look low in the
    west-northwest just after sunset

22 Full Moon (Strawberry Moon), 4:15 UT

25 Venus and Saturn are low in the west-northwest
    just after sunset. Mercury is below and to the
    right of Venus

27 Mercury and Venus are close to each other

LOOK OUT:

· Rhododendrons blooming in the redwood region

· Mexican free-tailed bats burst forth nightly from
  a cave at Carlsbad Caverns National Park

· White-tailed deer growing new antlers

· Loggerhead turtles come ashore to lay eggs
  by moonlight

JUNE

S	M	T	W	T	F	S
			1	2	3	4
5	6	7	8	9	10	11
12	13	14	15	16	17	18
19	20	21	22	23	24	25
26	27	28	29	30		

The important thing is not to stop
questioning. Curiosity has its own reason
for existing. One cannot help but be in
awe when he contemplates the mysteries of
eternity, of life, of the marvelous structure
of reality. It is enough if one tries merely
to comprehend a little of this mystery
every day. Never lose a holy curiosity.

~ *ALBERT EINSTEIN*

URBAN SURVIVAL STRATEGY:
How to Get the Best Seats with Bleacher Tickets

Ever wonder how Jack Nicholson and Spike Lee get those great courtside seats at the Lakers and Knicks games? You don't think they pay full price, do you? "Moving" to better seats requires strategy, a cool head under pressure, and improvisational acting skill. Here are the basics for getting the perfect seat even if you're not Spike or Jack:

1. Wait until the game/event/ performance is about one quarter through. You don't want to take someone's seat who just got caught in traffic on their way over. Plus, you can use this time to scope out your options. You're looking for good location, quick access from the aisles, and extra spots you can scoot into if the real owner of the seats shows up.

2. Your chances are best when the security personnel are distracted by large groups, obnoxious audience members, or when they're moving down an aisle. (At sporting events, choose moments of pandemonium—home runs, touchdowns, baskets, etc.)

3. Walk confidently down to your seat of choice, visibly checking your ticket several times, as if you want to be sure you have the right one.

4. If you're asked to show your ticket, do not admit guilt. Spend a lot of time "looking" for it and keep asking the guard to stay because "you know you have it somewhere." Chat and joke while you look. They'll probably just take your word for it.

5. If your performance doesn't work, indignantly declare that you'll go find the lost ticket. Choose another section and begin again.

~ *Will Bellaimey*

Will Bellaimey, 16, has successfully moved to better seats in major league stadiums across North America.

WHY I NEED THE BIRDS / *Lisel Mueller*

When I hear them call | in the morning, before | I am quite awake, |
my bed is already traveling | the daily rainbow, | the arc toward evening; |
and the birds, following | their own discrete lives |
of hunger and watchfulness, | are with me all the way…

3
FRI · JUNE 3 · 2005

Sacred Heart of Jesus, Roman Catholic
~ 1972: First U.S. Woman Rabbi ordained

Ayatollah R. Khomeini, Iranian leader, d.1989

The sparrow is sorry for the peacock at the burden of his tail.
— *Rabindranath Tagore*

Jefferson Davis, confederate leader, b.1808

☉☌☿ 4:12AM
☾ RISE 3:29AM SET 5:53PM
✺ RISE 5:29AM SET 8:54PM

RIGHT MEMORY

4
SAT · JUNE 4 · 2005

1989: Tiananmen Square Massacre, China
~ 1942; Battle of Midway

*Dr. Ruth Westheimer, sex expert b.1928
Angelina Jolie, actress, b.1975*

Nothing is so strong as gentleness and nothing is so gentle as real strength.
— *Ralph W. Sockman*

♂△♄ 4:42PM
☾ RISE 3:51AM SET 7:05PM
✺ RISE 5:28AM SET 8:55PM

RIGHT CONCEPTION

5
SUN · JUNE 5 · 2005

1981: AIDS first noted
~ 1968: Robert F. Kennedy assassinated

*Bill Moyers, journalist, b.1934
Adam Smith, economist, b.1723*

Danger and delight grow on one stalk. — *English Proverb*

UN WORLD ENVIRONMENT DAY

John Maynard Keynes, economist, b.1883

☿△♆ 6:48PM
☾ RISE 4:18AM SET 8:15PM
✺ RISE 5:28AM SET 8:56PM

RIGHT RESOLVE

BIRTHDAY: Prince (Prince Roger Nelson), June 7, 1958

PURPLE RAIN
I never meant 2 cause U any sorrow
I never meant 2 cause U any pain...
I only wanted 2 see U laughing in the purple rain...

~ *Prince*

*For more information on Prince,
see www.prince.com*

6 — MON · JUNE 6 · 2005

50 YEARS AGO
1955: Rock Around the Clock hits #1
~ *1944:* **D-Day:** Allied forces land at Normandy
~ *1978:* Prop. 13: taxpayers revolt, Calif.

I regret that I have but one life to lose for my country.
— *Nathan Hale*

Nathan Hale, patriot, b.1755
Alexander Pushkin, author, b.1799

☽△♃ 2:43AM
☽☌☉ 4:55PM
☽△♆ 7:20PM

☼
RISE 5:27AM
SET 8:57PM

New Moon
21:55UT

RIGHT WORD

7 — TUE · JUNE 7 · 2005

50 YEARS AGO
1955: "$64,000 Question" TV premiere

Prince R Nelson, singer, b.1958
Louise Erdrich, author, b.1954
Paul Gauguin, painter, b.1848

One may have a blazing hearth in one's soul, and no one ever comes to sit by it.
— *Vincent van Gogh*

VCR INTRODUCED
1975

☽☌☿ 3:15AM
☽☌♇ 6:43AM
☿☌♇ 10:43PM
☉△♆ 11:52PM

☾
RISE 531AM
SET 10:21PM

☼
RISE 5:27AM
SET 8:57PM

RIGHT DEED

8 — WED · JUNE 8 · 2005

1783: Laki Volcano explosion, Iceland

Cochise, Apache leader, b.1874
Frank Lloyd Wright, architect, b.1867

Say oh wise man how you have come to such knowledge? Because I was never ashamed to confess my ignorance and ask others.
— *Johann Gottfried Von Herder*

☽☌♀ 7:34AM
☽△♅ 5:03PM

☾
RISE 6:21AM
SET 11:11PM

☼
RISE 5:27AM
SET 8:58PM

RIGHT LIVELIHOOD

9 — THU · JUNE 9 · 2005

Ascension, Orthodox Christian
~ *1898:* Hong Kong lease signed from Britain

Cole Porter, composer, b.1891
Donald Duck, cartoon, b.1934

Why does no one confess his sins? Because he is yet in them. It is for a man who has awoke from sleep to tell his dreams.
— *Lucius Annaeus Seneca*

☽☌♄ 10:40PM

☾
RISE 7:19AM
SET 11:50PM

☼
RISE 5:27AM
SET 8:58PM

RIGHT ENDEAVOR

FOUNDING: Alcoholics Anonymous, June 10, 1935

On this date in 1935, in Akron, Ohio, Dr. Robert Smith completed his first day of sobriety. Dr. Bob and William G. Wilson are considered to have founded Alcoholics Anonymous on that day.

From Chase's 2004 Calendar of Events

THE 12 STEPS TO RECOVERY

1. We admitted we were powerless over alcohol (or other affliction) – that our lives had become unmanageable.

2. We came to believe that a power greater than ourselves could restore us to sanity.

3. We made a decision to turn our will and our lives over to the care of God as we understood Him.

4. We made a searching and fearless moral inventory of ourselves.

5. We admitted to God, to ourselves, and to another human being the exact nature of our wrongs.

6. We were entirely ready to have God remove all these defects of character.

7. We humbly asked Him to remove our shortcomings.

8. We made a list of all persons we had harmed and became ready to make amends to them all.

9. We made direct amends to such people whenever possible, except when to do so would injure others.

10. We continued to take personal inventory and when we were wrong, promptly admitted it.

11. We sought through prayer and meditation to improve our conscious contact with God, as we understood Him, praying only for knowledge of His will for us and the power to carry that out.

12. Having had a spiritual awakening as the result of these steps, we tried to carry this message to alcoholics (those who still suffer), and practice these principles in all our affairs.

For more on the 12 Steps, see www.alcoholics-anonymous.org

THE GUEST HOUSE/ *Rumi (translated by Coleman Barks)*

This being human is a guest house. | Every morning a new arrival… |
…The dark thought, the shame, the malice, | meet them at the door
laughing, and invite them in. | Be grateful for whoever comes, because each
has been sent | as a guide from beyond.

---

10   FRI · JUNE 10 · 2005

1943: Ballpoint
Pen patented

Elizabeth
Hurley actress,
b.1965
Judy Garland
actress, b.1922
Maurice Sendak
artist, b.1928

We turn not
older with years,
but newer
every day.
— Emily
Dickinson

ALCOHOLICS
ANONYMOUS
FOUNDED 1935

☽ △ ♂ 5:18AM

☽
RISE 8:22AM

☼
RISE 5:26AM
SET 8:59PM

RIGHT MEMORY

---

11   SAT · JUNE 11 · 2005

King
Kamehameha
Day, Hawaii

Ben Jonson, play-
wright, b.1572
Jacques Cousteau,
undersea
explorer, b.1910
Richard Strauss,
composer,
b.1864

When you are
content to be
simply yourself
and don't com-
pare or compete,
everybody will
respect you.
— Lao-Tzu

☽ ☌ Ψ 7:00PM

☽
SET 12:22AM
RISE 9:28AM

☼
RISE 5:26AM
SET 9:00PM

RIGHT CONCEPTION

---

12   SUN · JUNE 12 · 2005

1939: Nat'l
Baseball Hall of
Fame opened

Anne Frank,
author, b.1929
George H.W.
Bush, 41st pres-
ident, b.1924
Johanna Spyri,
author, b.1827

Those who do
not remember
the past are
condemned to
repeat it.
— George
Santayana

♀ △ ♅ 5:41AM
☽ △ ♇ 6:40AM

☽
SET 12:47AM
RISE 10:34AM

☼
RISE 5:26AM
SET 9:00PM

RIGHT RESOLVE

BIRTHDAY: William Butler Yeats, June 13, 1865

THE LAKE ISLE OF INNISFREE

I will arise and go now, and go to Innisfree,
And a small cabin build there, of clay and wattles made:
Nine bean-rows will I have there, a hive for the honey-bee,
And live alone in the bee-loud glade.

And I shall have some peace there, for peace comes dropping slow,
Dropping from the veils of the morning to where the cricket sings;
There midnight's all a glimmer, and noon a purple glow,
And evening full of the linnet's wings.

I will arise and go now, for always night and day
I hear lake water lapping with low sounds by the shore;
While I stand on the roadway, or on the pavements grey,
I hear it in the deep heart's core.

~ *William Butler Yeats*

For more information on William Butler Yeats, see www.poets.org/exh/wbyea/

13

Shavuot, Jewish
~ 1963: Medgar
Evars assassi-
nated
~ 1966:
"Miranda"
rights established

*William Butler
Yeats, poet,
b.1865*

A poem is never
finished, only
abandoned.
— Paul Valéry

☽☌♅ 6:00PM
☉☌♇ 10:15PM

☾
SET 1:07AM
RISE 11:39AM

☀
RISE 5:26AM
SET 9:01PM

RIGHT WORD

14

Royal Ascot
horse races,
England
~ 1951: Univac
Computer
unveiled

*Margaret
Bourke White,
photographer,
b.1904*

May you live
every day of
your life.
— Jonathan Swift

FLAG DAY

*Harriet Beecher
Stowe, author,
b.1811*

☾
SET 1:25AM
RISE 12:44PM

☀
RISE 5:26AM
SET 9:01PM

RIGHT DEED

15

Corpus Christi,
Roman Catholic
~ 1215: Magna
Carta chartered

*Helen Hunt,
actress, b.1963
Edvard Grieg,
composer,
b.1843*

An insincere
and evil friend
is more to be
feared than a
wild beast; a
wild beast may
wound your
body, but an
evil friend will
wound your
mind.
— Buddha

☽☌♂ 12:53PM
☿△♅ 11:36PM

☀
RISE 5:26AM
SET 9:02PM

*First Quarter
1:22UT*

RIGHT LIVELIHOOD

16

1883: Ladies
Day initiated in
baseball

*Stan Laurel,
comedian,
b.1890
John Howard
Griffin, author,
b.1920*

It is better to
debate a ques-
tion without
settling it than
to settle a ques-
tion without
debating it.
— Joseph
Joubert

☽☌♃ 1:31AM
☽△♆ 4:11PM

☾
SET 1:59AM
RISE 2:58PM

☀
RISE 5:26AM
SET 9:02PM

RIGHT ENDEAVOR

LIVING URBAN TREASURE: L.A.'s Aqeela Sherrills

Gang violence in Watts killed thirteen of Aqeela Sherrill's friends and he didn't retaliate. Instead, he devotes his life to peace and community in Watts and the world. Los Angeles knows him for brokering a "peace treaty" in 1992 between rival gangs – the Bloods and the Crips – a truce that endures. Yet in January 2004, Sherrills' 18-year-old son, Terrell, died from random gunfire. How does he press on and cling to his vision?

Aqeela Sherrills in L.A.

"It's not about who killed my son, but about what is killing our children," says Sherrills. How to change the conditions that lead to violent death is his lifelong quest. All peace movements, he believes, must begin with revering human life and rejecting revenge and brutality. Since 1982, L.A. County has witnessed more

"Sometimes in the roughest places you find the most beauty," says Sherrills.

than 10,000 gang-related deaths, a number roughly equal to violent deaths in the Northern Ireland and Palestinian-Israeli conflicts combined. Sherrills believes Watts is a microcosm of global trends toward urban war zones and sharp inequalities. For this reason, he also believes Watts is "the catalyst for the next major peace movement in this country." And if Watts is a catalyst, so is Sherrills.

Sherrills is Executive Director and co-founder, with his brother, of the Community Self-Determination Institute (CSDI), a nonprofit that offers programs in life skills, literacy, childcare, mediation, and the arts and is dedicated to transforming Watts into a national and international model for peaceful social change. In an interview in *Satya*, Sherrills claims "we have redefined what peace is and what it looks like."

Sherrills loves Watts and its citizens. "Sometimes in the roughest places you find the most beauty," he says and he can't imagine moving to a better neighborhood. Sherrills maintains "*This* is a better neighborhood, but it requires us taking responsibility for it." To do that, he believes, you have to shift people's thinking "towards something great."

Creating peace and changing views is the hardest kind of work, and "sometimes the peacemakers lose their lives," says Sherrills, and so do their children. Sherrills wants to meet his son's killer and his parents. "The most powerful thing we can do is connect with another human being," he says, "and it's the scariest."

~ *Kurt Burch*

For more information on Aqeela Sherrills,
see www.globalcitizenscircle.org

THE WIND, ONE BRILLIANT DAY / *Antonio Machado (translated by Robert Bly)*

The wind, one brilliant day, called | to my soul with an odor of jasmine. | "In return for the odor of my jasmine, | I'd like all the odor of your roses." | "I have no roses; all the flowers | in my garden are dead." | "Well then, I'll take the withered petals | and the yellow leaves and the waters of the fountain." | The wind left. And I wept. And I said to myself: | "What have you done with the garden that was entrusted to you?"

---

17   FRI · JUNE 17 · 2005

1972: Watergate Arrests, Wash DC
John Wesley, founder of Methodism, b.1703.
Igor Stravinsky, composer, b.1882
Venus Williams, tennis player, b.1980

Destiny is not a matter of chance, it is a matter of choice; it is not a thing to be waited for, it is a thing to be achieved.
— *William Jennings Bryan*

☽△☉ 10:02AM
☾ SET 2:16AM RISE 4:09PM
☼ RISE 5:26AM SET 9:02PM

RIGHT MEMORY

---

18   SAT · JUNE 18 · 2005

War of *1812* declaration anniversary

Isabella Rossellini, actress, b.1952
Paul McCartney, singer, b.1942

Silence is more musical than any song.
— *Christina Rossetti*

1ST US WOMAN IN SPACE 1983

SALLY RIDE

☽△♅ 11:37AM
☽△☿ 7:10PM
☾ SET 2:37AM RISE 5:24PM
☼ RISE 5:26AM SET 9:03PM

RIGHT CONCEPTION

---

19   SUN · JUNE 19 · 2005

1932: Hailstones kill 200 in Hunan Province, China
Aung San Sun Kyi, peace activist, b.1945
Blaise Pascal, philosopher, b.1623
Elbert Hubbard, author, b.1856

Age is...wisdom, if one has lived one's life properly.
—*Miriam Makeba*

JUNETEENTH

TEXAS EMANCIPATION DAY

☽△♀ 2:12AM
☽△♄ 3:06PM
☾ SET 3:02AM RISE 6:44PM
☼ RISE 5:26AM SET 9:03PM

RIGHT RESOLVE

ESSENTIAL PLACE: The Plaza at Santa Fe, New Mexico

Like nearby pueblos up and down the Rio Grande, Santa Fe is built around an intimate central plaza, little changed in spirit since 1610, designed for grazing flocks and pedestrians, not cars. Browse handmade jewelry sold by Pueblo vendors under the portal of the Palace of the Governors, the nations' oldest public building. Eat at the plaza's family-friendly Plaza Restaurant (put green chiles on everything) or sip a margarita and people-watch from the Ore House balcony, then relax under ancient cottonwood trees at the many events centered on the old bandstand, including the crowded Indian and Spanish art markets. Visit the plaza's important museums of American Indian and Southwestern art and history, and

the stunning Georgia O'Keefe Museum three blocks away. Stay at the La Fonda Hotel, the city's oldest, at "the end" of the Santa Fe Trail and plan your trip to the traditional plaza of Taos Pueblo an hour north. Then, when even the plaza seems too civilized, spirit yourself up the mountain to 10,000 Waves, an authentic Japanese bath, to watch the stars from your hot tub, exhilarated from your plunge into an American urban landscape of unparalleled tradition and beauty.

~ *Jim Lenfestey*

For more information on the Plaza in Santa Fe, New Mexico, see www.santafenow.com

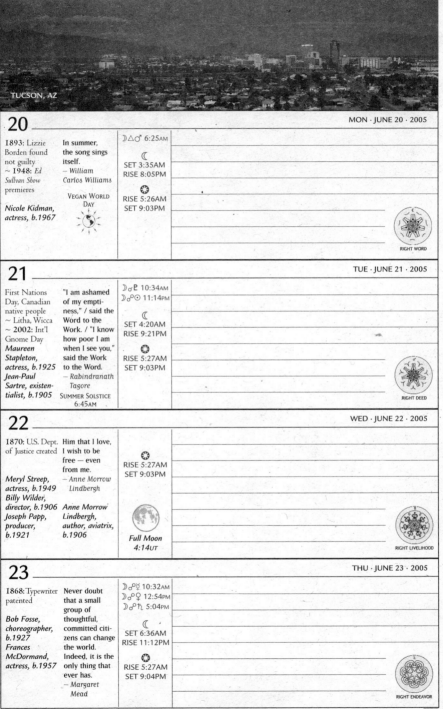

TUCSON, AZ

20 — MON · JUNE 20 · 2005

1893: Lizzie Borden found not guilty
~ 1948: *Ed Sullivan Show* premieres

Nicole Kidman, actress, b.1967

In summer, the song sings itself.
— William Carlos Williams

VEGAN WORLD DAY

☽ △ ♂ 6:25AM

☾
SET 3:35AM
RISE 8:05PM

☉
RISE 5:26AM
SET 9:03PM

RIGHT WORD

21 — TUE · JUNE 21 · 2005

First Nations Day, Canadian native people
~ Litha, Wicca
~ 2002: Int'l Gnome Day
Maureen Stapleton, actress, b.1925
Jean-Paul Sartre, existentialist, b.1905

"I am ashamed of my emptiness," / said the Word to the Work. / "I know how poor I am when I see you," said the Work to the Word.
— Rabindranath Tagore

SUMMER SOLSTICE 6:45AM

☽ ♂ ♇ 10:34AM
☽ ♂ ⊙ 11:14PM

☾
SET 4:20AM
RISE 9:21PM

☉
RISE 5:27AM
SET 9:03PM

RIGHT DEED

22 — WED · JUNE 22 · 2005

1870: U.S. Dept. of Justice created

Meryl Streep, actress, b.1949
Billy Wilder, director, b.1906
Joseph Papp, producer, b.1921

Him that I love, I wish to be free — even from me.
— Anne Morrow Lindbergh

Anne Morrow Lindbergh, author, aviatrix, b.1906

☉
RISE 5:27AM
SET 9:03PM

Full Moon 4:14UT

RIGHT LIVELIHOOD

23 — THU · JUNE 23 · 2005

1868: Typewriter patented

Bob Fosse, choreographer, b.1927
Frances McDormand, actress, b.1957

Never doubt that a small group of thoughtful, committed citizens can change the world. Indeed, it is the only thing that ever has.
— Margaret Mead

☽ ♂ ☿ 10:32AM
☽ ♂ ♀ 12:54PM
☽ ♂ ♄ 5:04PM

☾
SET 6:36AM
RISE 11:12PM

☉
RISE 5:27AM
SET 9:04PM

RIGHT ENDEAVOR

CELEBRATE: Summer Solstice/Midsummer/St. John's Tide

Rise up oh flame, by thy
light glowing,
Bring to us beauty, vision,
and joy.

Christoph Praetorius

In the Northern Hemisphere, life in all its fullness reigns at midsummer, an exuberant contrast to the monochromatic stillness of winter. Whereas then, Earth's energies were contracted and internal, now they are released, drawn up into the realm of wind, sky, and sun. The out-breath commenced in the depths of winter culminates now. All nature seems translucent, buzzing and shimmering with the vibrations of life.

This sense of utter aliveness is exhilarating. To live into it, fully a wonder. To turn one's gaze upwards, into the intense azure of a sunny summer sky, to soar with the birds gliding far overhead, one feels pulled by the heart to the periphery of the cosmos, unified beyond worlds with the Prime Mover, the ineffable Creator of All. This is truly a time for visions and for dreams.

Yet right after midsummer the days begin to shorten, and another earthly in-breath has begun. Dreams, after all, must be brought to realization, and summer play be balanced with winter work.

In esoteric Christianity, John the Baptist and the Christ are twin souls. As John plunges Jesus into the Jordan River, the dove descends from the heavens. John says, "He must increase, but I must decrease." And so it is after midsummer, when cosmic consciousness (John) must find its way to earthly expression (Jesus).

Regardless of any tradition, the meditative individual can immediately experience the mystery of Earth's breathing, through the yin and yang moments of midwinter and midsummer. To live consciously into this holy cycle instills in us a feeling for the oneness of life and bestows on us a sense of our purpose in existence.

~ *John Miller*

JUNE 21 / *Will Winter*

For people like me | who love the sun, | Who get gloomy when it is grey, this is the very best day. | The track of yellow goes highest / over my house today. | Only a fool would sleep and miss a minute of this light…

---

24   FRI · JUNE 24 · 2005

1497: Discovery of Newfoundland ~ St. John the Baptist Day ~ Bannockburn Day, Scotland

Jack Dempsey, boxer, b.1895
Henry Ward Beecher, clergyman, b.1813

Since you are like no other being ever created since the beginning of time, you are incomparable.
— *Brenda Ueland*

☽△♃ 12:45PM

☾
SET 8:00AM
RISE 11:48PM

☀
RISE 5:27AM
SET 9:04PM

RIGHT MEMORY

---

25   SAT · JUNE 25 · 2005

1950: Korean War begins ~ 1962: Supreme Court bans school prayer ~ 1990: Supreme Court upholds right to die

George Orwell, author, b.1903

Here is the test to find whether your mission on Earth is finished: if you're alive, it isn't.
— *Richard Bach*

☽♂♆ 1:17AM
♂☍♃ 8:03PM
♀♂♄ 9:59PM

☾
SET 9:25AM

☀
RISE 5:28AM
SET 9:04PM

RIGHT CONCEPTION

---

26   SUN · JUNE 26 · 2005

All Saint's, Orthodox Christian

Abner Doubleday invented baseball, b.1819
Pearl S. Buck, author, b.1892

I learned that it is the weak who are cruel, and that gentleness is to be expected only from the strong.
— *Leo Rosten*

☿♂♄ 5:58AM
☽△☉ 6:14AM
☽♂♅ 3:51PM

☾
RISE 12:15AM
SET 10:47AM

☀
RISE 5:28AM
SET 9:04PM

RIGHT RESOLVE

BIRTHDAY: Helen Keller, June 27, 1880

Born at Tuscumbia, Alabama, Helen Keller was left deaf and blind by a disease she contracted at 18 months of age. With the help of her teacher, Anne Sullivan, she graduated from college and had a career as an author and lecturer. She died June 1, 1968, at Westport, Connecticut.

From Chase's 2004 Calendar of Events

Character cannot be developed in ease and quiet. Only through experience of trial and suffering can the soul be strengthened, ambition inspired, and success achieved.

The highest result of education is tolerance.

Life is either a daring adventure or nothing. Security does not exist in nature, nor do the children of men as a whole experience it. Avoiding danger is no safer in the long run than exposure.

Many persons have a wrong idea of what constitutes true happiness. It is not attained through self-gratification but through fidelity to a worthy purpose.

Self-pity is our worst enemy and if we yield to it, we can never do anything good in the world.

People do not like to think. If one thinks, one must reach conclusions. Conclusions are not always pleasant.

The best and most beautiful things in the world cannot be seen or even touched. They must be felt within the heart.

We could never learn to be brave and patient, if there were only joy in the world.

When one door of happiness closes, another opens; but often we look so long at the closed door that we do not see the one which has been opened for us.

College isn't the place to go for ideas.

Science may have found a cure for most evils; but it has found no remedy for the worst of them all — the apathy of human beings.

Smell is a potent wizard that transports you across thousands of miles and all the years you have lived.

For more information on Helen Keller, see www.time.com/time/time100/heroes/

Helen Keller and Anne Sullivan

27 · MON · JUNE 27 · 2005

Decide to Be Married Day ~ 1859: "Happy Birthday to You" song composed
Anna Moffo, opera singer, b.1934
Helen Keller, author, b.1880
Lafcadio Hearn, author, b.1850

One can never consent to creep when one feels the impulse to soar.
— Helen Keller

Joseph Smith Jr., Mormon Church founder, d.1844

☿♂♀ 1:39PM
☽△♄ 8:47PM

☾ RISE 12:38AM
SET 12:05PM

☀ RISE 5:29AM
SET 9:04PM

RIGHT WORD

28 · TUE · JUNE 28 · 2005

1969: Stonewall Riot, start of Gay Liberation movement
~ 1919: Treaty of Versailles
Peter Paul Rubens, painter, b.1577
Jean-Jacques Rousseau, philosopher, b.1712

A man's conscience, like a warning line on the highway, tells him what he shouldn't do — but it does not keep him from doing it.
— Frank A. Clark

☽△♀ 12:51AM
☽△☿ 1:04AM
☽☍♃ 6:02PM
☽☌♂ 9:21PM

RISE 5:29AM
SET 9:04PM

Last Quarter
18:23UT

RIGHT DEED

29 · WED · JUNE 29 · 2005

Sts. Peter and Paul Feast Day, Christian ~ 1938: Olympic National Park established

William James Mayo, co-fonder Mayo Clinic, b.1861

Speech is conveniently located midway between thought and action, where it often substitutes for both.
— John Andrew Holmes

☽△♇ 5:29PM

☾ RISE 1:16AM
SET 2:32PM

☀ RISE 5:29AM
SET 9:04PM

RIGHT LIVELIHOOD

30 · THU · JUNE 30 · 2005

Burning of the Three Firs, France ~ 1908: Meteor hits Siberia ~ 1966: NOW founded

Lena Horne, singer, b.1917

To himself everyone is immortal; he may know that he is going to die, but he can never know that he is dead.
— Samuel Butler

☾ RISE 1:35AM
SET 3:44PM

☀ RISE 5:30AM
SET 9:03PM

RIGHT ENDEAVOR

JULY

JUN 21- JUL 22

cancer

JUL 23 - AUG 22

leo

BIRTHSTONE
Ruby

FLOWER
Larkspur

Selflessness
BECOMES CATHARSIS (HEALING)
Challenges: overly willful, dependent

Now the senses are our guides and masters. Drawn out by the world's beauty, we awaken to the glory of the visible, touchable, smellable, hearable, tastable, feelable world. It draws us into selfless conversation. Everything is in motion. Purified, we flow with it. Leaves tremble, tall grass waves, a dreamy, swirling haze hallows the waters of lakes and ponds. Gardens team with life. Look into the intense bursts of color reaching to the heavens and think yourself clairvoyant! Everywhere beings are weaving – among the delphiniums and hollyhocks and in the chard and carrot tops. Somehow, we must carry the memory of this gift into winter. These are the dog days, when Sirius, the dog star is conjunct the sun. This is above all a brilliant, warm, dreamy, forceful, light-filled, and productive time. May we be so likewise.

JULY IS
ANTI-BOREDOM MONTH · CELL PHONE COURTESY MONTH · COPIOUS COMPLIMENTS MONTH · BAKED BEANS MONTH · BISON MONTH · HERBAL/PRESCRIPTION AWARENESS MONTH · CULINARY ARTS MONTH · NAT'L DOGHOUSE REPAIRS MONTH FOREIGN LANGUAGE MONTH · HOT DOG MONTH · BLUEBERRIES MONTH RECREATION AND PARKS MONTH · PURPOSEFUL PARENTING MONTH

Mercury stands close to Venus right after sunset.

Moon
Venus
Mercury
CANCER

July 1, 9:45 p.m. WNW

Venus, Moon and Mercury form a triangle.

Moon
Venus
Mercury

July 8, 9:45 p.m. WNW

STARS & PLANETS FOR JULY

Venus comes up to Jupiter in the evening sky. The two brightest planets get closer and closer. Mars is also an evening star this month. Mercury is visible at the end of July. Saturn begins its new period of visibility after being in conjunction with the Sun on the 23rd.

LOOK UP:

4 Earth at aphelion (farthest from the Sun)

5 New Moon, 12:04 UT

8 Crescent Moon near Venus and Mercury just after sunset

9 Mercury at greatest eastern elongation

17 Mars closest to Sun

21 Full Moon (Thunder Moon), 11:01 UT

23 Saturn conjunct with the Sun

LOOK OUT:

· Alpine wildflowers carpet mountain meadows

· Young ground squirrels, chipmunks bumble about

· Time to harvest blueberries in the north

· Lightning bugs light up the night

JULY						
S	M	T	W	T	F	S
					1	2
3	4	5	6	7	8	9
10	11	12	13	14	15	16
17	18	19	20	21	22	23
24/31	25	26	27	28	29	30

I believe that the first test of a truly great man is his humility. I do not mean by humility, doubt of his own powers. But really great men have a curious feeling that the greatness is not in them, but through them. And they see something divine in every other man and are endlessly, foolishly, incredibly merciful.

~ JOHN RUSKIN

DOG DAYS BEGIN: On Being Firm with Dogs

1. Dogs are never permitted in the house. The dog stays outside in a specially built wooden compartment named, for very good reason, the dog house.

2. Okay, the dog can enter the house, but only for short visits or if his own house is under renovation.

3. Okay, the dog can stay in the house on a permanent basis, provided his dog house can be sold in a yard sale to a rookie dog owner.

4. Inside the house, the dog is not allowed to run free and is confined to a comfortable but secure metal cage.

5. Okay, the cage becomes part of a two-for-one deal along with the dog house in the yard sale, and the dog can go wherever he pleases.

6. The dog is never allowed on the furniture.

7. Okay, the dog can get on the old furniture but not the new furniture.

8. Okay, the dog can get up on the new furniture until it looks like the old furniture and then we'll sell the whole works and buy new furniture upon which the dog will most definitely not be allowed.

9. The dog never sleeps on the bed. Period.

10. Okay, the dog can sleep at the foot of the bed.

11. Okay, the dog can sleep alongside you, but he's not allowed under the covers.

12. Okay, the dog can sleep under the covers but not with his head on the pillow.

13. Okay, the dog can sleep alongside you under the covers with his head on the pillow, but if he snores he's got to leave the room.

14. Okay, the dog can sleep and snore and have nightmares in bed, but he's not to come in and sleep on the couch in the TV room, where I'm now sleeping. That's just not fair.

15. The dog never gets listed on the census questionnaire as "primary resident," even if it's true.

From Tom Ackerman, who found "On Being Firm..." on the Web, author unknown.

DOG DAYS: JULY 3 – AUGUST 11

Hottest days of the year in the northern hemisphere. Usually about 40 days, but variously reckoned at 30–54 days. Popularly believed to be an evil time "when the sea boiled, wine turned sour, dogs grew mad, and all creatures became languid, causing to man burning fevers, hysterics and phrensies" (from Brady's *Clavis Calendarium*, 1813). Originally the days when Sirius, the Dog Star, rose just before or at about the same time as sunrise (no longer true owing to the precession of the equinoxes). Ancients sacrificed a brown dog at the beginning of Dog Days to appease the rage of Sirius, believing that star was the cause of hot sultry weather.

From Chase's 2004 Calendar of Events

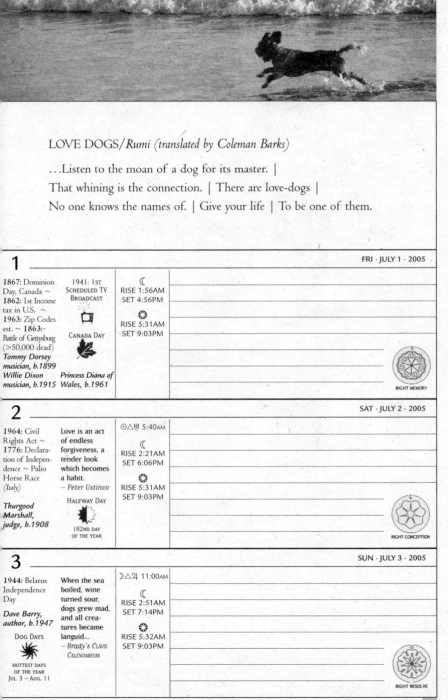

LOVE DOGS/*Rumi (translated by Coleman Barks)*

…Listen to the moan of a dog for its master. |

That whining is the connection. | There are love-dogs |

No one knows the names of. | Give your life | To be one of them.

---

1   FRI · JULY 1 · 2005

1867: Dominion Day, Canada ~
1862: 1st Income tax in U.S. ~
1963: Zip Codes est. ~ **1863:** Battle of Gettysburg (>50,000 dead)
Tommy Dorsey musician, b.1899
Willie Dixon musician, b.1915

1941: 1ST SCHEDULED TV BROADCAST

CANADA DAY

Princess Diana of Wales, b.1961

☾ RISE 1:56AM
SET 4:56PM

☀ RISE 5:31AM
SET 9:03PM

RIGHT MEMORY

---

2   SAT · JULY 2 · 2005

1964: Civil Rights Act ~
1776: Declaration of Independence ~ Palio Horse Race *(Italy)*

Thurgood Marshall, judge, b.1908

Love is an act of endless forgiveness, a tender look which becomes a habit.
— *Peter Ustinov*

HALFWAY DAY

182ND DAY OF THE YEAR

⊙△♅ 5:40AM

☾ RISE 2:21AM
SET 6:06PM

☀ RISE 5:31AM
SET 9:03PM

RIGHT CONCEPTION

---

3   SUN · JULY 3 · 2005

1944: Belarus Independence Day

Dave Barry, author, b.1947

DOG DAYS

HOTTEST DAYS OF THE YEAR
JUL. 3 – AUG. 11

When the sea boiled, wine turned sour, dogs grew mad, and all creatures became languid…
— *Brady's CLAVIS CALENDARIUM*

☽△♃ 11:00AM

☾ RISE 2:51AM
SET 7:14PM

☀ RISE 5:32AM
SET 9:03PM

RIGHT RESOLVE

CULTURE: First Bikini Swimsuit, July 5, 1946

Skimpy two-piece swimsuits get their name from Bikini Atoll in the south Pacific. French fashion designer Louis Réard chose the name to upstage rival designer Jacques Heim who had started selling a two-piece called the Atome. On July 5, 1946, four days after the United States tested an atomic bomb over Bikini, Réard launched his explosively small creation under the suddenly well-know name.

*Parisian dancer Michele Bernadini models
the first bikini bathing costume at
Piscine Molitor, Paris, France, July 1946.*

From 1,000 Inventions and Discoveries *by Roger Bridgman, in association with
the Smithsonian Institution, DK Publishing, copyright Dorling Kindersley LTD
For more on the bikini, see www.bikiniscience.com*

4

John Adams, president, d.1826
Thomas Jefferson, president, d.1826
Nathaniel Hawthorne, author, b.1804
Stephen Foster, composer, b.1826
Rube Goldberg, artist, b.1883

Those who stand for nothing fall for anything. — *Alexander Hamilton*

INDEPENDENCE DAY (US)

☽△♆ 12:40AM
☽☌♇ 11:36AM

☽ RISE 3:29AM
SET 8:15PM

☀ RISE 5:32AM
SET 9:02PM

RIGHT WORD

5

1946: First bikini swimsuit ~ Tynwald Day: Viking Mid-summer Day, Isle of Man ~ Venezuela Independence Day
P.T. Barnum, circus promoter, b.1810

Love is an exploding cigar we willingly smoke. — *Lynda Barry*

EARTH AT APHELION

FURTHEST FROM SUN

☽ RISE 4:15AM
SET 9:07PM

☀ RISE 5:33AM
SET 9:02PM

RIGHT DEED

6

1854: Republican Party formed
George W. Bush, 43rd president, b.1946
Dalai Lama, Tibetan leader, b.1935
Beatrix Potter, author, b.1866

The deeper that sorrow carves into your being the more joy you can contain. Is not the cup that holds your wine the very cup that was burned in the potters oven? — *Kahlil Gibran*

☽△♅ 12:11AM
☽☌☉ 7:02AM

☀ RISE 5:34AM
SET 9:02PM

New Moon 12:02UT

RIGHT LIVELIHOOD

7

Fiesta de San Fermín: Running of the Bulls, Pamplona, Spain ~ Tanabata: Star Festival, Japan
Satchell Paige, baseball pitcher, b.1906
Ringo Starr, musician, b.1940

If being an egomaniac means I believe in what I do and in my art or music, then in that respect you can call me that...I believe in what I do, and I'll say it. — *John Lennon*

☽☌♄ 11:54AM

☽ RISE 6:12AM
SET 10:23PM

☀ RISE 5:34AM
SET 9:01PM

RIGHT ENDEAVOR

SONG: The Ash Grove

THE ASH GROVE

Wales

1. Down yon-der green val-ley, where stream-lets me-an-der, When
Or at the bright noon-tide in sol-i-tude wan-der, A

twi-light is fad-ing I pen-sive-ly rove;
mid the dark shades of the lone-ly Ash Grove. 'Twas there, while the

black-bird was cheer-ful-ly sing-ing, I first met that dear one, the

joy of my heart! A-round us for glad-ness the blue-bells were

ring-ing, Ah, then lit-tle thought I how soon we should part.

2. Still glows the bright sunshine o'er valley and mountain,
Still warbles the blackbird its note from the tree;
Still trembles the moonbeam on streamlet and fountain,
But what are the beauties of nature to me?

With sorrow, deep sorrow, my bosom is laden,
All day I go mourning in search of my love!
Ye echoes! Oh tell me, where is the sweet maiden?
"She sleeps 'neath the green turf down by the Ash Grove."

ROWBOAT / Jay Leeming

An oar is a paddle with a home. This arrangement seems | awkward at first, as if it were wrong; the wood knocks in the | oarlock, and would much rather be a church steeple, or the | | propeller of an old airplane in France. Yet as it bites deep into | the wave it settles down, deciding that the axe and the carpenter | were right....

8 — FRI · JULY 8 · 2005

Festa dos Tabuleiros, Portugal

Anjelica Huston, actress, b.1951

He who establishes his argument by noise and command, shows that his reason is weak.
— Michel De Montaigne

☽♂♀ 4:18PM
☽♂☿ 4:36PM

☾
RISE 7:18AM
SET 10:50PM

☀
RISE 5:35AM
SET 9:01PM

RIGHT MEMORY

9 — SAT · JULY 9 · 2005

Lobster Carnival, Canada ~ Martyrdom of the Bab, Baha'i ~ 1893: 1st successful open-heart surgery

Otto Respighi, composer, b.1879
Tom Hanks, actor, b.1956

The minute you settle for less than you deserve, you get even less than you settled for.
— Maureen Dowd

☽♂℗Ψ 12:34AM
☽△♂ 3:21AM
☿♂♀ 4:43AM
☽△℗ 1A:49AM

☾
RISE 8:24AM
SET 11:12PM

☀
RISE 5:36AM
SET 9:00PM

RIGHT CONCEPTION

10 — SUN · JULY 10 · 2005

1985: Rainbow Warrior sunk, Greenpeace
Marcel Proust, author, b.1871
John Calvin, founder of Presbyterianism b.1509
Arthur Ashe, tennis player, b.1943

Happiness is beneficial for the body, but it is grief that develops the powers of the mind.
— Marcel Proust

☾
RISE 8:29AM
SET 10:30PM

☀
RISE 5:37AM
SET 9:00PM

RIGHT RESOLVE

URBAN SANCTUARY: Walden Pond, Concord, Massachusetts

In 1845, Henry David Thoreau wrote: "I went to the woods because I wished to live deliberately, to front only the essential facts of life, and see if I could not learn what it had to teach, and not, when I came to die, discover that I had not lived." Today, stressed out city dwellers seeking Thoreau-like insights can swim, walk and fish in the same woodland retreat that inspired Thoreau to write Walden. Whether it's blanketed by snow or ringed by a fiery spray of maple trees, Walden Pond and its surrounding 2,680 acres of mostly undeveloped woods just miles from Boston can't help but inspire an appreciation for the natural world. Stringent restrictions that limit the number of daily visitors and nix all bicycles, dogs, grills, and inflatable Barney's insure that the pond's chilly – and blessedly weed-free – waters remain crystal clear and the woods untrammeled. And while the shed where Thoreau lived and wrote is a replica, why quibble?

Where else in Boston, after all, can a tour guide quote an American classic and explain the subtleties of different types of scat?

~ *Elizabeth Larsen*

For more on the Walden Pond State Reservation, see www.mass.gov/dem/parks/wldn.htm

BOSTON, MA

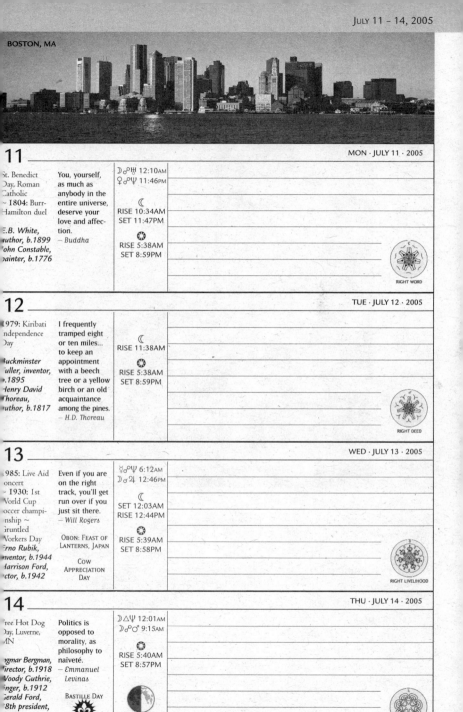

11   MON · JULY 11 · 2005

St. Benedict
Day, Roman
Catholic
~ 1804: Burr-
Hamilton duel

*E.B. White,
author, b.1899
John Constable,
painter, b.1776*

You, yourself,
as much as
anybody in the
entire universe,
deserve your
love and affec-
tion.
— Buddha

☽☌♅ 12:10AM
♀☌♆ 11:46PM

☾
RISE 10:34AM
SET 11:47PM

☀
RISE 5:38AM
SET 8:59PM

RIGHT WORD

12   TUE · JULY 12 · 2005

1979: Kiribati
Independence
Day

*Buckminster
Fuller, inventor,
b.1895
Henry David
Thoreau,
author, b.1817*

I frequently
tramped eight
or ten miles...
to keep an
appointment
with a beech
tree or a yellow
birch or an old
acquaintance
among the pines.
— H.D. Thoreau

☾
RISE 11:38AM

☀
RISE 5:38AM
SET 8:59PM

RIGHT DEED

13   WED · JULY 13 · 2005

1985: Live Aid
concert
~ 1930: 1st
World Cup
soccer champi-
onship ~
Gruntled
Workers Day
*Erno Rubik,
inventor, b.1944
Harrison Ford,
actor, b.1942*

Even if you are
on the right
track, you'll get
run over if you
just sit there.
— Will Rogers

OBON: FEAST OF
LANTERNS, JAPAN

COW
APPRECIATION
DAY

☿☌♆ 6:12AM
☽☌♃ 12:46PM

☾
SET 12:03AM
RISE 12:44PM

☀
RISE 5:39AM
SET 8:58PM

RIGHT LIVELIHOOD

14   THU · JULY 14 · 2005

Free Hot Dog
Day, Luverne,
MN

*Ingmar Bergman,
director, b.1918
Woody Guthrie,
singer, b.1912
Gerald Ford,
38th president,
b.1913*

Politics is
opposed to
morality, as
philosophy to
naïveté.
— Emmanuel
Levinas

BASTILLE DAY

FRANCE

☽△♆ 12:01AM
☽☌♂ 9:15AM

☀
RISE 5:40AM
SET 8:57PM

First Quarter
15:20UT

RIGHT ENDEAVOR

BIRTHDAY: Rembrandt, July 15, 1606

Rembrandt was born in Leiden, the Netherlands, on July 15, 1606 – his full name was Rembrandt Harmenszoon van Rijn. He was the son of a miller. Despite the fact that he came from modest means, he was able to study art and, by age 22, took his first pupils. He married Saskia van Uylenburgh, the cousin of a successful art dealer, in 1634.

Rembrandt's family life was marked by misfortune. Between 1635 and 1641 Saskia gave birth to four children, but only the last, Titus, survived. Saskia died in 1642, at the age of 30. Hendrickje Stoffels, who became Rembrandt's housekeeper in 1649, eventually became his wife and was the model for many of his pictures. Despite Rembrandt's success as an artist, teacher, and art dealer, his flambouyant living forced him to declare bankruptcy in 1656. His beloved Hendrickje died in 1663, and his son, Titus, in 1668 at only 27 years of age. Eleven months later, on October 4, 1669, Rembrandt died in Amsterdam.

SUMMER DAYS/ *Wathen Marks Wilks Call*

In summer, when the days were long, | we pluck'd wild strawberries, ripe and red, | Or feasted, with no grace but song, | on golden nectar, snow-white bread, | In summer, when the days were long. | We lov'd, and yet we knew it not, | for loving seem'd like breathing then; | We found a heaven in every spot; | saw angels, too, in all good men, | And dream'd of gods in grove and grot.

---

15 — FRI · JULY 15 · 2005

St. Swithin's Day, England

Linda Ronstadt, singer, b.1946
Rembrandt, painter, b.1606
Clement Moore, author, b.1779

Our doubts are traitors, and make us lose the good we oft might win by fearing to attempt.
— *William Shakespeare*

♂△♇ 11:37AM
☽△♅ 7:56PM

☾ RISE 3:03PM

☉ RISE 5:41AM SET 8:57PM

RIGHT MEMORY

---

16 — SAT · JULY 16 · 2005

1548: La Paz Day, Bolivia
Joshua Reynolds, painter, b.1723
Mary Baker Eddy, Christian Science founder, b.1821
Roald Amundson, explorer, b.1872

Without darkness there are no dreams.
— *Karla Kuban*

ATOMIC BOMB TESTED 1945

♀△♇ 12:13PM
☽△☉ 9:15PM

☾ SET 1:01AM RISE 4:19PM

☉ RISE 5:42AM SET 8:56PM

RIGHT CONCEPTION

---

17 — SUN · JULY 17 · 2005

1918: Czar Nicholas II and family executed
~ 1984: Min. Drinking Age: 21
~ Gion Matsuri, Japan
Phoebe Snow, singer, 1952
Erle Stanley Gardner, author, b.1889

Take care of the luxuries and the necessities will take care of themselves.
— *Dorothy Parker*

DISNEYLAND OPENED 1955

☽△♄ 6:48AM
♀△♂ 3:27PM

☾ SET 1:29AM RISE 5:38PM

☉ RISE 5:43AM SET 8:55PM

RIGHT RESOLVE

CELEBRATE: Moon Day, July 20

Anniversary of mankind's first landing on the moon, July 20, 1969. Two U.S. astronauts (Neil Alden Armstrong and Edwin Eugene Aldrin, Jr.) landed lunar module *Eagle* at 4:17p.m., EDT and remained on the lunar surface 21 hours, 36 minutes, and 16 seconds. The landing was made from the *Apollo XI's* orbiting command and service module, code named *Columbia*, whose pilot, Michael Collins, remained aboard. Armstrong was the first to set foot on the moon. Armstrong and Aldrin were outside the spacecraft, walking on the moon's surface, approximately 2¼ hours. The astronauts returned to Earth July 24, bringing photographs and rock samples.

From Chase's 2004 Calendar of Events

MOONSHADOW

I'm being followed by a moon shadow
Moon shadow moon shadow
Leaping and hopping on a moon shadow
Moon shadow moon shadow...

~ *Cat Stevens*

*For more information on Cat Stevens (Yusuf Islam),
see www.catstevens.com*

18

1936: Spanish Civil War begins

Gilbert White, naturalist, b.1720
Nelson Mandela, S. African leader, b.1918

It is infinitely easier to suffer in obedience to a human command than to accept suffering as free, responsible men.
— *Dietrich Bonhoeffer*

☽ △ ☿ 3:45PM
☽ ☌ ♇ 7:59PM
☽ △ ♂ 11:39PM

☾
SET 2:07AM
RISE 6:56PM

☀
RISE 5:44AM
SET 8:54PM

RIGHT WORD

19

1979: Nicaragua Liberation Day~
1848: Women's Rights convention, Seneca Falls, NY

Eve Merriam, author, b.1916
Charles Mayo, surgeon, b.1865
Edgar Degas, painter, b.1834

There are risks and costs to a program of action, but they are far less than the long-range risks and costs of comfortable inaction.
— *John F. Kennedy*

☽ △ ♀ 12:03AM

☾
SET 2:59AM
RISE 8:05PM

☀
RISE 5:45AM
SET 8:53PM

RIGHT DEED

20

Marine Day, Japan
~ 1874: Locust Plague
~ 1968: Special Olympics founded

Sir Edmund Hillary, explorer, b.1919

One small step for a man, one giant leap for mankind.
— *Neil Armstrong*

MOON DAY

1ST MAN ON THE MOON 1969

☾
SET 4:07AM
RISE 9:01PM

☀
RISE 5:46AM
SET 8:52PM

RIGHT LIVELIHOOD

21

Asalha Puja Day, Hindu
~ 1861: Battle of Bull Run

Marshall McLuhan, author, b.1911
Ernest Hemingway, author, b.1899

Most people are alive in an earlier time, but you must be alive in your own time.
— *Marshall McLuhan*

Yusuf Islam, (Cat Stevens) singer, b.1948

☽ ☌ ☉ 6:00AM
☽ ☌ ♄ 8:56AM

☀
RISE 5:47AM
SET 8:52PM

Full Moon
11:01UT

RIGHT ENDEAVOR

ESSENTIAL PLACE: Fly By Night Club, Anchorage

The Chugach Mountains rise up from the sea making an expansive container for Anchorage, Alaska, a town where moose browse on the front yard foliage and the scent of alder rubs the air. There's a lot of wild in Alaska where less than one percent of the land in a state one-fifth the size of the Lower 48 is privately owned. So where do you find a particularly essential place in a state that is, by its whopping self, one big essential place?

Cruise the tangled junction of Spenard Road and 33rd Avenue just a mile from downtown Anchorage, look for the tail of a Piper Cub sticking out of an awning, and open the doors of the Mr. Whitekeys' Fly By Night Club, home to "Spam, Booze, Rhythm and Blues."

Okay, so it's a bar — and pretty good restaurant — but its stage shows are what sets it apart. They're funny, quirky, and distinctly Alaskan. The Fly By Night Club showcases four revues a year — all in a smoke-free environment — that features such things as the Duct Tape Fashion Show, a blue tarp retrospective, and local political humor. Mr. Whitekeys, a piano player who doesn't claim to be a musician, leads the cast. Alice Welling, Miss Anchorage of an Undisclosed Era and Beauty Queen Gone Bad, and Tim Tucker, voted 2000 Actor of the Year in Wasilla, Alaska, complete the entourage.

When all the fun is over, stand in the dingy parking lot and admire the gorgeous and not too distant wilderness of the Alaska of possibilities.

~ *Kathleen Melin*

For more information on Mr. Whitekeys' Fly By Night Club:
3300 Spenard Road
Anchorage, Alaska 99503
(907) 279-SPAM
www.flybynightclub.com

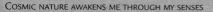

THE PEACE OF WILD THINGS / *Wendell Berry*

When despair for the world grows in me | and I wake in the night at the
least sound | in fear of what my life and my children's lives may be, |
I go and lie down where the wood drake | rests in his beauty on the water,
and the great heron feeds…

---

22   FRI · JULY 22 · 2005

1376: Pied Piper
of Hamelin,
Germany

*Karl
Menninger,
psychiatrist,
b.1893*
*William
Spooner,
reverend b.1844*

The purpose of
life is a life of
purpose.
— *Robert Byrne*

RAT
CATCHER'S
DAY

SPOONER'S DAY
(CELEBRATE SLIPS OF
THE TONGUE)

☽△♃ 2:45AM
☽♂♆ 10:03AM
☽☌☿ 4:03PM

☾
SET 6:56AM
RISE 10:14PM

☀
RISE 5:48AM
SET 8:51PM

RIGHT MEMORY

---

23   SAT · JULY 23 · 2005

St. Appolinaris
Day, Christian

*Woody
Harrelson,
actor, b.1961*
*Don Drysdale,
baseball
pitcher, b.1936*

Happiness is
when what you
think, what you
say, and what
you do are in
harmony.
— *Mohandas
Gandhi*

☽♂♀ 8:10AM
☉♂♄ 12:00PM
☽♂♅ 11:35PM

☾
SET 8:23AM
RISE 10:39PM

☀
RISE 5:49AM
SET 8:50PM

RIGHT CONCEPTION

---

24   SUN · JULY 24 · 2005

1847: Pioneer
Day: Mormons
enter Salt Lake
City, Utah
*Amelia Earhart,
aviatrix, b.1898*
*Alexandre
Dumas, author,
b.1802*
*Simon Bolivar,
S.America liber-
ator, b.1783*

There are no
shortcuts to any
place worth
going.
— *Unknown*

VIRTUAL
LOVE DAY

CELEBRATE ONLINE
RELATIONSHIPS

☾
SET 9:45AM
RISE 11:01PM

☀
RISE 5:50AM
SET 8:49PM

RIGHT RESOLVE

RECIPE: Caprese Salad

Everyone knows that the best way to eat a tomato is while standing in the garden, letting the sun-warmed juice from the fresh-picked fruit run down your chin onto your shirt or bare chest. Second best is to eat in-season, locally grown tomatoes with other ingredients of equal integrity — fresh basil, good olive oil, moist mozzeralla, and cracked pepper — in a dish called Caprese.

CAPRESE
Alternate on a plate, thick slices of tomato and thinner slices of water-packed domestic mozzarella. Slice fresh basil leaves and sprinkle over the red and white fruit and cheese. Drizzle with a good fragrant olive oil and end with a grinding of black pepper and a sprinkle of salt.

25 — MON · JULY 25 · 2005

Pilgrimage of St. Anne d'Auray, France ~ St. James the Great Day, Christian

Matt LeBlanc, actor, b.1967
Iman, actress, model, b.1955

A celebrity is a person who works hard all his life to become well known, then wears dark glasses to avoid being recognized.
— *Fred Allen*

☽△♄ 10:22AM
☽△☉ 1:16PM

☾
SET 11:04AM
RISE 11:20PM

✺
RISE 5:51AM
SET 8:47PM

RIGHT WORD

26 — TUE · JULY 26 · 2005

Hopi Niman Dance: Going Home Dance, U.S.
~ 1953: Natl. Day of Cuba: 26th of July Movement

George Bernard Shaw, author, b.1856

Liberty means responsibility. That is why most men dread it.
— *George Bernard Shaw*

Mick Jagger, musician, b.1943
Aldous Huxley, author, b.1894

☽☌♃ 5:54AM
☽△⚷ 6:43PM
☽△♇ 10:50PM

☾
SET 12:20PM
RISE 11:39PM

✺
RISE 5:52AM
SET 8:46PM

RIGHT DEED

27 — WED · JULY 27 · 2005

Procession of the Penitents, Belgium

Alex Rodriguez, baseball player, b.1975
Peggy Fleming, skater, b.1948
José C. Barbosa, Puerto Rican patriot, b.1857

Many of life's failures are people who did not realize how close they were to success when they gave up.
— *Thomas Edison*

ATLANTIC TELEGRAPH CABLE LAID 1866

☽☌♂ 12:23PM

☾
SET 1:34PM
RISE 12:00AM

✺
RISE 5:53AM
SET 8:45PM

RIGHT LIVELIHOOD

28 — THU · JULY 28 · 2005

Cheyenne Frontier Days July 22-31, U.S.

Jacqueline O. Kennedy, first lady, b.1929
Terry Fox, cancer fundraiser, b.1958

Tis nobler to lose honor to save the lives of men than tis to gain honor by taking them.
— *David Borenstein*

1914: WWI BEGINS

ARCHDUKE FERDINAND KILLED

☽△♀ 12:16AM

✺
RISE 5:54AM
SET 8:44PM

Last Quarter
3:19UT

RIGHT ENDEAVOR

URBAN SURVIVAL STRATEGY:
Surviving the Office Picnic

1. **Do not enter the picnic alone.**
   If you arrive early, wait until you see a group enter, then tag along with the crowd.

2. **Lay the groundwork for an early departure.**
   Upon arrival, tell a convincing story that will necessitate leaving early. Apologize and act sorry that you will not be able to stay longer. Should you decide to escape early, your early departure will not seem abrupt.

3. **Control your alcohol intake.**
   You risk embarrassment (or worse) if you get drunk in front

Food is a safe topic for company picnic conversation

of your colleagues. Have no more than one drink at the beginning of the picnic to help you relax, then limit your consumption. Make sure you eat, too.

4. **Avoid discussing work.**
   It's best to avoid all topics relating to the company itself, including projects, policies, culture, and coworkers. Alcohol can loosen tongues and you should assume that everything you say will be repeated, out of context.

If You Become Intoxicated

1. **Do not talk to your boss.**
   Excuse yourself from any conversation with bosses, managers, or co-workers who might later recount any of your inappropriate comments or behavior.

2. **If you become trapped in a conversation with your boss, become a "Yes man."**
   Smile, nod, and find a way out.

3. **Spill something.**
   As a last resort, knock your drink over on the table, or spill it on yourself. Then excuse yourself to go wash up. The person or persons you were talking to will move on to another conversation.

4. **Withdraw.**
   Find an out-of-the-way tree or park bench. Ask for help from a colleague if you cannot make it on your own, but get out of harm's way before you damage your reputation.

5. **Do not return.**
   Take a walk and drink plenty of water. If you cannot sober up, have a colleague tell your boss that you had to leave "because something suddenly came up."

From The Worst Case Scenario Survival Handbook

PART OF WHAT I MEAN/*Frank X. Gaspar*

…Let me try to tell you what kind of night it is. I am | standing here, | a stranger under a streetlamp, nearly midnight, listening | to frogs in the middle of the city. No one bothers me. | No one thinks it's a bit suspicious. A police car rolls by, | and I nod and wave. One of the officers waves back. | I make no claims for this. I understand the passing | of a moment…

---

29   FRI · JULY 29 · 2005

Olsok: Commemorates Viking King Olaf, Norway

Ken Burns, filmmaker, b.1953
Booth Tarkington, author, b.1869

A society grows great when old men plant trees whose shade they know they shall never sit in.
— *Greek Proverb*

NASA ESTABLISHED
1958

☾ SET 3:58PM

☉ RISE 5:55AM
SET 8:43PM

RIGHT MEMORY

---

30   SAT · JULY 30 · 2005

1980: Vancouver Independence Day

Henry Moore, sculptor, b.1848
Henry Ford, industrialist, b.1863
Emily Bronte, author, b.1818

I am looking for a lot of men who have an infinite capacity to not know what can't be done.
— *Henry Ford*

1935: PAPERBACK BOOKS INTRODUCED

☽△♃ 10:39PM

☾ RISE 12:52AM
SET 5:07PM

☉ RISE 5:57AM
SET 8:42PM

RIGHT CONCEPTION

---

31   SUN · JULY 31 · 2005

St. Ignatius Loyola, Roman Catholic
~ 1790: U.S. Patent Office opens

Evonne Goolagong, tennis player, b.1951
J.K. Rowling, author, b.1965

There are all kinds of courage. It takes a great deal of bravery to stand up to our enemies, but just as much to stand up to our friends.
— *Albus Dumbledore*

♀☌♅ 3:08AM
☽△♆ 5:00AM
☽☌♇ 4:10PM

☾ RISE 1:28AM
SET 6:10PM

☉ RISE 5:58AM
SET 8:41PM

RIGHT RESOLVE

AUGUST

JUL 23 - AUG 22

AUG 23 - SEPT 22

leo

virgo

BIRTHSTONE
Peridot

FLOWER
Gladiolus

Compassion
BECOMES FREEDOM
Challenges: overpowering, immobilizing

The days seem to shorten. The nights, deep and warm, grow longer. Tree frogs and crickets echo in the darkness. Summer is short. Apples are on the trees. The first fruits are gathered. It's the Celtic feast of Lugh, the God of Light, Christian Lammastide or Loaf Mass, when the first grains are ground and baked and placed upon the alter. For the Celts, Lugh ordained the feast be held in honor of his mother Tailltiu, the Earth Mother. Christians, too, celebrate Mary, Mother of Compassion, who carried all things in her heart and gave birth to the light. What gifts! What freedom! This is the time to put on the garments of the spirit, to hold memories in our hearts. Something is germinating secretly, silently within us. Tread softly and take care of yourself and the world so that what you are carrying might come to birth.

AUGUST IS
ADMIT YOU'RE HAPPY MONTH · CATARACT AWARENESS MONTH
VISION & LEARNING MONTH · FAMILY FUN MONTH
BACK TO SCHOOL MONTH · WIN WITH CIVILITY MONTH
NATIONAL INVENTOR'S MONTH
NEW ZEALAND KIWIFRUIT MONTH · GRATEFUL DEAD MONTH

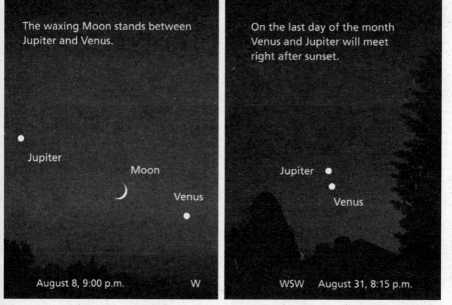

The waxing Moon stands between Jupiter and Venus.

Jupiter

Moon

Venus

August 8, 9:00 p.m.   W

On the last day of the month Venus and Jupiter will meet right after sunset.

Jupiter

Venus

WSW   August 31, 8:15 p.m.

STARS & PLANETS FOR AUGUST

Venus approaches Jupiter. On August 9th the waxing crescent Moon stands between the two planets — certainly a very picturesque configuration. Watch for the peak of the Perseid meteor showers the night of the 11th. Mercury and Saturn meet in the center of the constellation Cancer on the 21st.

LOOK UP:

5 New Moon, 3:06 UT

12 Perseid meteor shower peaks

19 Full Moon (Green Corn Moon), 17:54 UT

23 Mercury at greatest western elongation

LOOK OUT:

· Sea lions disperse north and south from breeding grounds

· Spadefoot toads come out at night to breed

· Male ducks undergo molt that leaves them flightless

· Along Florida coast, coral begin spawning

AUGUST						
S	M	T	W	T	F	S
	1	2	3	4	5	6
7	8	9	10	11	12	13
14	15	16	17	18	19	20
21	22	23	24	25	26	27
28	29	30	31			

Just when you think that a person is just a backdrop for the rest of the universe, watch them and see that they laugh, they cry, they tell jokes ... they're just friends waiting to be made.

~ JEFFREY BORENSTEIN

BIRTHDAY: Louis Armstrong, August 4, 1900

WHAT A WONDERFUL WORLD
...I see friends shakin' hands, sayin'
"How do you do?"
    They're really saying "I love you"...

Jazz musician extraordinaire Armstrong often said he was born on the Fourth of July, but documents in the Louis Armstrong Archives of Queens College, Flushing, New York, indicate that he was actually born August 4, 1900, or 1901. Asked to define jazz, Armstrong reportedly replied, "Man, if you gotta ask, you'll never know." The trumpet player was also known as Satchmo. He appeared in many films. Popular singles included "What a Wonderful World" and "Hello Dolly" (with Barbara Streisand).

From *Chase's 2004 Calendar of Events*

<<   *Lyrics by Bob Thiele, George David Weiss, and George Douglas*

BIRTHDAY: Percy Bysshe Shelley, August 4, 1792

Percy Bysshe Shelley was a radical, championing the likes of Tom Paine and getting expelled from Oxford in 1811 for *The Necessity of Atheism*, his tract against compulsory Christianity. His short life seemed like a mad dash against the conventions of the day — both political and social — as he took up the causes of working-class education, free love, non-violent protests, vegetarianism, and electoral reform. Among his most well known works are "To the West Wind;" *Queen Mab*; "To a Skylark;" and *Adonais,* an elegy for Keats. In 1822, Shelley was lost at sea in Italy, where he had moved with his family and his friends, Leigh Hunt and Lord Byron. His body washed

ashore and was burned on the beach in the presence of his companions. His remains were later buried in Rome.

1

Lammas: 1st harvest, Wicca ~ Homou'o: hooting at hunger, Ghana ~ 1789: U.S. Customs est.

Yves St. Laurent, designer, b.1936
Herman Melville, author, b.1819

Computers make very fast, very accurate mistakes.
— *Unknown*

1990: WORLD WIDE WEB EST.

Jerry Garcia, musician, b.1942

☽ RISE 2:12AM SET 7:05PM
☼ RISE 5:59AM SET 8:39PM

RIGHT WORD

2

Nuestra Señora de los Angeles, Costa Rica ~ 1990: Iraq invades Kuwait
Carroll O'Connor actor, b.1924
James Fallows, journalist, b.1949
James Baldwin, author, b.1924

Think of yourself as an incandescent power, illuminated and perhaps forever talked to by God and his messengers.
— *Brenda Ueland*

☽ △ ♅ 3:40AM
☿ ☌ ♆ 3:52AM
☽ RISE 3:04AM SET 7:50PM
☼ RISE 5:00AM SET 8:38PM

RIGHT DEED

3

Eisteddfod Genedlaethol: Bard of the Year, Wales ~ Niger Independence Day

Martha Stewart, lifestyle maven, b.1941
John T. Scopes, teacher, b.1900

You get the best out of others when you give the best of yourself.
— *Harry Firestone*

Ernie Pyle, journalist, b.1900
Maggie Kuhn, founded Gray Panthers, b.1905

☽ RISE 4:04AM SET 8:26PM
☼ RISE 6:01AM SET 8:37PM

RIGHT LIVELIHOOD

4

1790: Coast Guard Day ~ 1962: Nelson Mandela arrested

Jeff Gordon, racecar driver, b.1971
Percy Bysshe Shelley, poet, b.1792

Poetry is the record of the best and happiest moments of the happiest and best minds.
— *Percy B. Shelley*

Wm. Schuman, composer, b.1910
Louis "Satchmo" Armstrong, musician, b.1900

☽ ☌ ♄ 1:03AM
☽ ☌ ☉ 10:05PM
☽ RISE 5:09AM SET 8:54PM
☼ RISE 6:02AM SET 8:35PM

RIGHT ENDEAVOR

EVENT: First Photo of Earth from Space, Aug. 7, 1959

The U.S. satellite Explorer VI transmitted the first picture of Earth from space in 1959. For the first time we had a likeness of our planet based on more than projections and conjectures.

But it would take years for the general public to see pictures of Earth from space.

From Chase's 2004 Calendar of Events. For more information about the first photos of Earth from space, see eol.jsc.nasa.gov/

In 1966 I conceived and sold buttons which read, "Why Haven't We Seen A Photograph of the Whole Earth Yet?" Legend has it that this accelerated NASA's making good color photos from distant space... We saw the photograph of the Earth from space that we got from the Apollo program in 1969. The first Earth Day was in 1970. This is not an accident. The ecology movement really took off once we had those photographs from space.

— *Stewart Brand, founder,*
Whole Earth Catalog

THE SUN/*Mary Oliver*

Have you ever seen | anything | in your life | more wonderful |
than the way the sun, | every evening, | relaxed and easy, |
floats toward the horizon….

5

Picnic Day,
Australia
~ Jamaica Independence Day
*Neil Armstrong,
astronaut,
b.1930
Raoul Wallenberg,
humanitarian,
b.1912*

The gem cannot
be polished
without friction, nor man
perfected
without trials.
— *Chinese
Proberb*

*Sidney Omarr,
astrologer,
b.1926*

☽ ☌ ☿ 12:54AM
☽ ☌ ♆ 5:09AM
☽ △ ♇ 4:45PM
☉ ☌ ☿ 6:36PM

🌑
RISE 6:03AM
SET 8:34PM

**New Moon
3:05UT**

RIGHT MEMORY

6

Transfiguration
of the Lord,
Orthodox
Christian
1945: Atomic
Bomb dropped
on Hiroshima
*Andy Warhol,
artist, b.1928
Alfred Lord
Tennyson, poet,
b.1809*

If I had only
known, I would
have been a
locksmith.
— *Albert Einstein*

HIROSHIMA DAY

*Scott Nearing,
author, b.1883
Lucille Ball,
actress, b.1911*

☽ △ ♂ 8:05PM

☽
RISE 7:21AM
SET 9:36PM

☀
RISE 6:05AM
SET 8:33PM

RIGHT CONCEPTION

7

1990: U.S.
Desert Shield
ops began
1882: Hatfield
-McCoy feud
erupts
~ 1964: Gulf
of Tonkin
resolution
*Charlize Theron
actress, b.1975
Garrison Keillor
author, b.1942*

Science may set
limits to knowledge, but should
not set limits to
imagination.
— *Bertrand
Russell*

1ST PHOTO OF
EARTH FROM
SPACE 1959

☽ ☌ ♅ 4:33AM
☽ ☌ ♀ 11:56PM

☽
RISE 8:26AM
SET 9:54PM

☀
RISE 6:06AM
SET 8:31PM

RIGHT RESOLVE

CIVILIZING IDEA: International Dark-Sky Association

Look up from any city after dark, and you'll see only a few bright stars twinkling down at you. Every night we light up the outdoors and wash out the sprawling Milky Way; constellations like the leaping dolphin, wriggling lizard, and hungry crow; and stars like the sublime Algol, named the winking "eye of the demon," by Arab astronomers for its habit of dimming and brightening every few days.

Satellite photos of the nighttime world reveal the magnitude of our loss. Cities everywhere pour megawatts of light into the sky, squandering energy, and robbing us of a spectacular birthright. The United States alone wastes $1 billion per year illuminating the bellies of birds and airplanes.

To the rescue comes the International Dark-Sky Association (IDA), a nonprofit organization that helps urban dwellers take back the night sky. IDA champions the switch to quality outdoor lighting, which means properly shielded fixtures that direct light downward to eliminate stray beams, reduce glare, improve visibility, and save energy. The group has seen many successes. For example, the state of New Mexico has passed a law to conserve energy through responsible outdoor lighting. And the Long Island Power authority has converted to fully shielded lighting for all lighting installations.

Light pollution is a politician's dream — a problem with solutions. If we can bring back dark skies, urban dwellers may someday know the joy of spotting a comet or enjoying a meteor shower from their own back yards.

~ *Deane Morrison*

*For more information on the
International Dark-Sky Association:
3225 N. First Ave., Tucson AZ 85719
Phone: (520) 293-3198
Web: www.darksky.org*

8 — MON · AUGUST 8 · 2005

Admit You're Happy Day

The Edge, musician, b.1961
Randy Shilts, journalist, b.1951
Marjorie Kinnan Rawlings, author, b.1896

Real riches are the riches possessed inside.
— *B.C. Forbes*

SNEAK SOME ZUCCHINI ONTO YOUR NEIGHBOR'S PORCH NIGHT

☉ ☌ Ψ 11:11PM

☾ RISE 9:30AM
SET 10:10PM

☀ RISE 6:07AM
SET 8:30PM

RIGHT WORD

9 — TUE · AUGUST 9 · 2005

1945: Atomic bomb dropped on Nagasaki ~ Moment of Silence *(Japan)* ~ **1974:** Nixon resigns
Gillian Anderson, actress, b.1968
Melanie Griffith, actress, b.1957

Our scientific power has outrun our spiritual power. We have guided missiles and misguided men.
— *Martin Luther King Jr.*

☾ RISE 10:35AM
SET 10:26PM

☀ RISE 6:08AM
SET 8:28PM

RIGHT DEED

10 — WED · AUGUST 10 · 2005

1945: Japan Surrenders ~ **1846:** Smithsonian Institution est.

Herbert Hoover, 31st president, b.1874
Angie Harmon, actress, b.1972

Writing is an exploration. You start from nothing and learn as you go.
— *E.L. Doctorow*

Tove Janssen, author, b.1900
Antonio Banderas, actor, b.1960

☽ ☌ ♃ 2:08AM
☽ △ Ψ 4:56AM

☾ RISE 11:41AM
SET 10:43PM

☀ RISE 6:09AM
SET 8:27PM

RIGHT LIVELIHOOD

11 — THU · AUGUST 11 · 2005

1965: Watts Riot, Los Angeles

Alex Haley author, b.1921

NIGHT OF THE SHOOTING STARS

PERSEID METEOR SHOWERS

Hope is the thing with feathers / That perches in the soul. / And sings the tune / Without the words, / and never stops at all.
— *Emily Dickinson*

☾ RISE 12:50PM
SET 11:03PM

☀ RISE 6:10AM
SET 8:25PM

RIGHT ENDEAVOR

CIVILIZING IDEAS: The Slow Movement

According to philosopher Jacob Needleman, our frenetic pace of life is a "new kind of poverty." Fast food, 12-hour works days, technology creep, and too much value placed on quantity over quality have left us spent and depleted, searching for a lost richness that we can barely remember. But help is here.

The international Slow movement promises to restore balance to our out-of-whack lives by showing us the grace and goodness that come by simply paying attention — to our food, our cities, our work, our land, our schools, and even (or especially) our lovemaking.

In 1989, Italian journalist Carlo Petrini founded the movement's most visible manifestation — Slow Food — in reaction to Rome's first McDonald's. Slow Food promotes the pleasure of community, of local foods responsibly grown, of the sensuality of the seasons. With more than 70,000 members worldwide, including many of the world's best chefs, Slow Food is not about a superficial dolce vita — its larger social agenda includes helping communities restore their local economies. In 1999, it birthed the Slow Cities movement, which, akin to the New Urbanism, encourages more human-friendly cities.

Educator Maurice Holt coined the term "slow schooling" in 2002 to foster deep and sustained learning, rather than cramming to pass tests and meet requirements. Slow sex workshops are gaining in popularity and Carl Honore's recently published, *In Praise of Slowness: How a Worldwide Movement is Challenging the Cult of Speed*, is fast on its way to best-sellerdom.

So, pick up your knitting, take a nap, go for a stroll with your dog, read your children a long bedtime story, linger over the dinner table with family and friends, and take your time when you turn off the lights. You'll be joining a worldwide movement of people determined to live the true good life, savoring it moment by moment.

~ *Martha Coventry*

*For more on the Slow movement,
see www.slowfood.com*

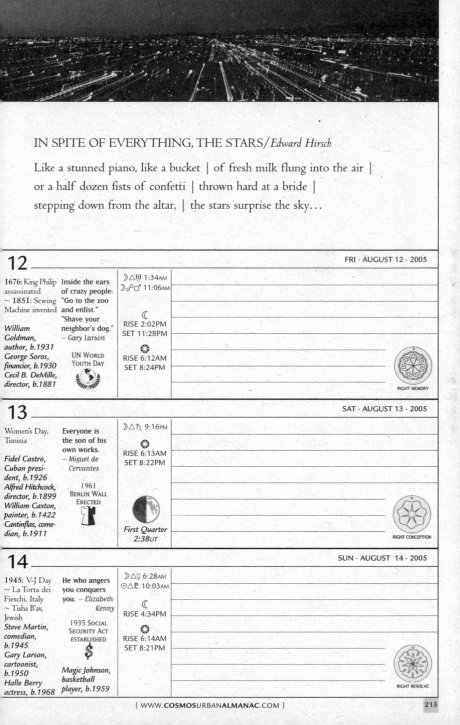

IN SPITE OF EVERYTHING, THE STARS/*Edward Hirsch*

Like a stunned piano, like a bucket | of fresh milk flung into the air |
or a half dozen fists of confetti | thrown hard at a bride |
stepping down from the altar, | the stars surprise the sky…

---

12 FRI · AUGUST 12 · 2005

1676: King Philip assassinated
~ 1851: Sewing Machine invented

William Goldman, author, b.1931
George Soros, financier, b.1930
Cecil B. DeMille, director, b.1881

Inside the ears of crazy people: "Go to the zoo and enlist." "Shave your neighbor's dog."
— Gary Larson

UN WORLD YOUTH DAY

☽ △ ♅ 1:34AM
☽ ♂ ♂ 11:06AM

RISE 2:02PM
SET 11:28PM

☀ RISE 6:12AM
SET 8:24PM

RIGHT MEMORY

---

13 SAT · AUGUST 13 · 2005

Women's Day, Tunisia

Fidel Castro, Cuban president, b.1926
Alfred Hitchcock, director, b.1899
William Caxton, painter, b.1422
Cantinflas, comedian, b.1911

Everyone is the son of his own works.
— Miguel de Cervantes

1961 BERLIN WALL ERECTED

☽ △ ♄ 9:16PM

☀ RISE 6:13AM
SET 8:22PM

First Quarter
2:38UT

RIGHT CONCEPTION

---

14 SUN · AUGUST 14 · 2005

1945: V-J Day
~ La Torta dei Fieschi, Italy
~ Tisha B'av, Jewish

Steve Martin, comedian, b.1945
Gary Larson, cartoonist, b.1950
Halle Berry actress, b.1968

He who angers you conquers you. — Elizabeth Kenny

1935 SOCIAL SECURITY ACT ESTABLISHED

Magic Johnson, basketball player, b.1959

☽ △ ♇ 6:28AM
☉ △ ♇ 10:03AM

☾ RISE 4:34PM

☀ RISE 6:14AM
SET 8:21PM

RIGHT RESOLVE

ESSENTIAL PLACE: Barton Springs, Austin, Texas

The pleasures of this azure treasure are obvious to anyone seeking respite from the blazing hot temps that sizzle through most months of the year here. But slipping into the crisp 68-degree waters of the nation's largest natural urban pool isn't even the best thing about Barton Springs. This urban oasis is literally the heartbeat of Austin: swimmers can dive down to the spring's mouth to watch in awe as it surges, with a steady rhythm, to release 27 million gallons of water a day from ancient limestone caves. The beat goes on along the grassy, pecan-tree shaded banks of the pool, the one spot where all of Austin mingles, from the eastside Hispanic kids to the southside bubbas to the westside yuppies. Chat with the totally kickass gang of envirotypes who've battled to keep Barton Springs clean and protected from the development that threatens the lungless, endangered Barton Springs salamander. Dry off and stroll along Barton Creek to start a circuit of Austin treats. First, chow down at the Tex-Mex icon, Chuy's, and then browse with other eclectic Austinites at the independent bookstore BookPeople. Finally, shake your Springs-healed bones at the Continental Club, a jewel in the crown of the world's live music capital.

~ *Helen Cordes*

For more information on Barton Springs in Austin, Texas, see www.texasoutside.com/bartonpool.htm Also see www.tec.org/bartonsprings/

15

Assumption of the Blessed Virgin, Roman Catholic ~ Dormition of Theotokos, Orthodox Christian

Sir Walter Scott, poet, b.1771

Invite the man that loves thee to a feast, but let alone thine enemy.
— *Hesiod*

Napoleon Bonaparte, French emperor, b.1769

☽ ☌ ♇ 4:42AM
☽ △ ☉ 6:03AM

☾
SET 12:44AM
RISE 5:46PM

✺
RISE 6:15AM
SET 8:19PM

RIGHT WORD

16

Palio of the Contrade, Siena, Italy ~ 1987: Harmonic Convergence

George Meany, US labor leader, b.1894 Madonna, singer, b.1958

Real knowledge is to know the extent of one's ignorance.
— *Confucius*

Babe Ruth, baseball player, d.1948 Elvis Presley, singer, d.1977

☽ △ ♂ 11:24AM

☾
SET 1:43AM
RISE 6:47PM

✺
RISE 6:16AM
SET 8:17PM

RIGHT DEED

17

1863: Fort Sumter siege begun

Sean Penn, actor, b.1960 Robert DeNiro, actor, b.1943 Davy Crockett, frontiersman b.1786

Take hold lightly; let go lightly. This is one of the great secrets of felicity in love.
— *Spanish Proverb*

♃ △ ♆ 2:36PM
☽ △ ♀ 8:23PM
☽ ☌ ♄ 1:15AM

☾
SET 2:57AM
RISE 7:34PM

✺
RISE 6:17AM
SET 8:16PM

RIGHT LIVELIHOOD

18

1960: 1st Birth Control pills sold ~ 1872: 1st mail-order catalog published

Meriwether Lewis, explorer, b.1774 Rosalynn Carter, 1st lady, b.1927

Knowledge is power.
— *Francis Bacon*

19TH AMEND-MENT RATIFIED 1920

✓

WOMEN'S RIGHT TO VOTE

☽ ☌ ♄ 1:15AM
☽ ☍ ♅ 9:01AM
☽ ☌ ♆ 7:44PM
☽ △ ♃ 8:06PM

☾
SET 4:22AM
RISE 8:10PM

✺
RISE 6:19AM
SET 8:14PM

RIGHT ENDEAVOR

BIRTHDAY: Aubrey Beardsley, August 21, 1872

Aubrey Vincent Beardsley (1872 – 1898), English artist in black and white, was born at Brighton on the 21st of August 1872. In 1891, he took up art as a profession and from 1893 until his death in 1898, his work came continually before the public, arousing a storm of criticism and much hostile feeling.

They felt that Beardsley had an unswerving tendency towards the fantastic art of the gloomier and "unwholesome" sort.

For more information on Aubrey Beardsley, see www.victorianweb.org

MAN ON A FIRE ESCAPE/*Edward Hirsch*

He couldn't remember what propelled him | out of the bedroom window
onto the fire escape | of his fifth-floor walkup on the river, |
so that he could see, as if for the first time, | sunset settling down
on the dazed cityscape | and tugboats pulling barges up the river…

---

19   FRI · AUGUST 19 · 2005

Raksha Bandhan, Hindu

Orville Wright, aviator, b.1871
Coco Chanel, designer, b.1883
Bill Clinton, 42nd president, b.1946

The saying "Getting there is half the fun" became obsolete with the advent of commercial airlines.
— Henry Tillman
NATIONAL AVIATION DAY

☽ ☌ ☉ 12:53PM

RISE 6:20AM
SET 8:12PM

Full Moon 17:53UT

RIGHT MEMORY

---

20   SAT · AUGUST 20 · 2005

St. Stephen's Day, Hungary

Eliel Saarinen, architect, b.1873
H.P. Lovecraft, author, b.1890

In three words I can sum up everything I've learned about life: It Goes On.
— Robert Frost
PLUTONIUM FIRST WEIGHED 1942

☽ ☌ ♅ 8:30AM

☾
SET 7:16AM
RISE 9:02PM

☼
RISE 6:21AM
SET 8:11PM

RIGHT CONCEPTION

---

21   SUN · AUGUST 21 · 2005

1983: Benigno Aquino assassinated

Peter Weir, director, b.1944
Aubrey Beardsley, artist, b.1872
Wilt Chamberlain basketball player, b.1936

When you have only two pennies left in the world, buy a loaf of bread with one, and a lily with the other.
— Chinese Proverb

☾
SET 7:38AM
RISE 8:22PM

☼
RISE 6:22AM
SET 8:09PM

RIGHT RESOLVE

URBAN SANCTUARY: Clear Creek, Denver, Colorado

When I've gone through weeks and weeks of the same scenery – the interstate highway drive to and from work, the office, the old neighborhood streets for walking my dog, I head for the Wheatridge Greenbelt. Wheatridge is an older suburb on the west side of Denver, and tends to be more of a midscale/blue-collar kind of place. Clear Creek, a mountain stream that passes through Golden (and the Coors plant), enters the plains on the suburb's western edge. For several miles along the creek, the city of Wheatridge has preserved the riparian habitat in something resembling its original state. Less than a half mile from I-70, the greenbelt is a world away.

About a half mile wide, it's home to all kinds of wildlife, most notably several families of foxes. The meandering paths reveal new scenes every hundred feet or so. The lakes (former gravel quarries used for construction of the interstate, then filled with water) are home to geese, cranes, and other waterfowl. I go there because my dog likes it, but also because no matter what time of year I go, I never leave without a sense of peace.

~ *Mark Barnhouse*

For more information on Clear Creek, see www.clearcreekcounty.org

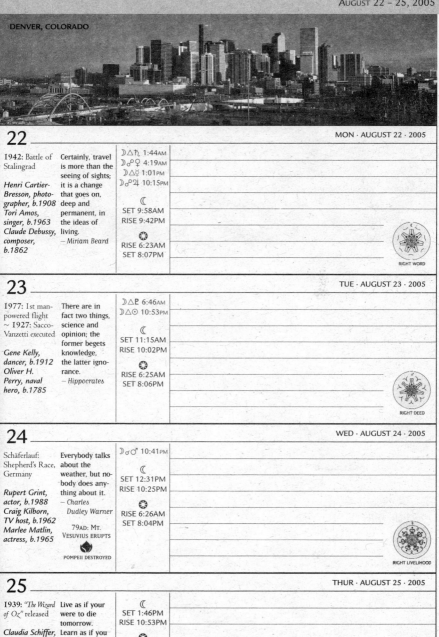

DENVER, COLORADO

22 — MON · AUGUST 22 · 2005

1942: Battle of Stalingrad

Henri Cartier-Bresson, photographer, b.1908
Tori Amos, singer, b.1963
Claude Debussy, composer, b.1862

Certainly, travel is more than the seeing of sights; it is a change that goes on, deep and permanent, in the ideas of living.
— *Miriam Beard*

☽△♄ 1:44ᴀᴍ
☽☌♀ 4:19ᴀᴍ
☽△♅ 1:01ᴘᴍ
☽☌♃ 10:15ᴘᴍ

☽
SET 9:58AM
RISE 9:42PM

☀
RISE 6:23AM
SET 8:07PM

RIGHT WORD

23 — TUE · AUGUST 23 · 2005

1977: 1st man-powered flight
~ 1927: Sacco-Vanzetti executed

Gene Kelly, dancer, b.1912
Oliver H. Perry, naval hero, b.1785

There are in fact two things, science and opinion; the former begets knowledge, the latter ignorance.
— *Hippocrates*

☽△♇ 6:46ᴀᴍ
☽△☉ 10:53ᴘᴍ

☽
SET 11:15AM
RISE 10:02PM

☀
RISE 6:25AM
SET 8:06PM

RIGHT DEED

24 — WED · AUGUST 24 · 2005

Schäferlauf: Shepherd's Race, Germany

Rupert Grint, actor, b.1988
Craig Kilborn, TV host, b.1962
Marlee Matlin, actress, b.1965

Everybody talks about the weather, but nobody does anything about it.
— *Charles Dudley Warner*

79ᴀᴅ: Mᴛ. Vᴇsᴜᴠɪᴜs ᴇʀᴜᴘᴛs

POMPEII DESTROYED

☽☌♂ 10:41ᴘᴍ

☽
SET 12:31PM
RISE 10:25PM

☀
RISE 6:26AM
SET 8:04PM

RIGHT LIVELIHOOD

25 — THUR · AUGUST 25 · 2005

1939: *"The Wizard of Oz"* released

Claudia Schiffer, model, b.1970
Sean Connery, actor, b.1930
Walt Kelly, cartoonist, b.1913
Leonard Bernstein, composer, b.1918

Live as if you were to die tomorrow. Learn as if you were to live forever.
— *Mahatma Gandhi*

Kɪss-&-Mᴀᴋᴇ-ᴜᴘ Dᴀʏ

☽
SET 1:46PM
RISE 10:53PM

☀
RISE 6:27AM
SET 8:02PM

RIGHT ENDEAVOR

BIRTHDAY: Johann Wolfgang von Goethe, August 28, 1749

Copied into journals, folded carefully and tucked in a wallet, stuck up on refrigerators, and e-mailed across the world, is a passage that has given inspiration and courage to thousands of people. The words are most always attributed to Johann Wolfgang von Goethe, that giant of German culture and his country's Shakespeare. They sound like him, urging us forward and into life, but only the last 18 words, from *Faust*, are really his. It is the Scottish adventurer, W.H. Murray, who wrote the passage in his book, *The Scottish Himalayan Expedition*, published in 1951, about what it takes to begin a real journey. So here, in the spirit of giving credit where credit is due, is Murray's famous paragraph – in context and not paraphrased – with its homage to Goethe.

"But when I said that nothing had been done I erred in one important matter. We had definitely committed ourselves and we were halfway out of our ruts. We had put down our passage money – booked a sailing to Bombay. This may sound too simple, but it is great in consequence. Until one is committed, there is hesitancy, the chance to draw back, always ineffectiveness. Concerning all acts of initiative (and creation), there is one elementary truth the ignorance of which kills countless ideas and splendid plans: that the moment one definitely commits oneself, then providence moves too. A whole stream of events issues from the decision, raising in one's favor all manner of unforeseen incidents, meetings and material assistance, which no man could have dreamt would have come his way. I learned a deep respect for one of Goethe's couplets:

WHATEVER YOU CAN DO OR DREAM YOU CAN, **BEGIN IT.** BOLDNESS HAS GENIUS, POWER AND MAGIC IN IT.

ARIZONA NOCTURNE/*Carlos Reyes*

Before our headlights the coyote | flies across four lanes |
of rush-hour traffic, safely, | and pauses at the right-of-way |
My heart is still pounding | His victory may be our slender hope…

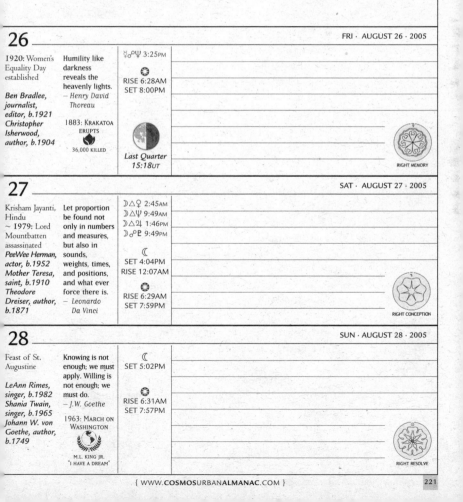

26   FRI · AUGUST 26 · 2005

1920: Women's
Equality Day
established

Ben Bradlee,
journalist,
editor, b.1921
Christopher
Isherwood,
author, b.1904

Humility like
darkness
reveals the
heavenly lights.
— *Henry David*
Thoreau

1883: KRAKATOA
ERUPTS

36,000 KILLED

☿☌♆ 3:25PM

RISE 6:28AM
SET 8:00PM

Last Quarter
15:18UT

RIGHT MEMORY

27   SAT · AUGUST 27 · 2005

Krisham Jayanti,
Hindu
~ 1979: Lord
Mountbatten
assassinated
PeeWee Herman,
actor, b.1952
Mother Teresa,
saint, b.1910
Theodore
Dreiser, author,
b.1871

Let proportion
be found not
only in numbers
and measures,
but also in
sounds,
weights, times,
and positions,
and what ever
force there is.
— *Leonardo*
Da Vinci

☽△♀ 2:45AM
☽△♆ 9:49AM
☽△♃ 1:46PM
☽☌♇ 9:49PM

SET 4:04PM
RISE 12:07AM

RISE 6:29AM
SET 7:59PM

RIGHT CONCEPTION

28   SUN · AUGUST 28 · 2005

Feast of St.
Augustine

LeAnn Rimes,
singer, b.1982
Shania Twain,
singer, b.1965
Johann W. von
Goethe, author,
b.1749

Knowing is not
enough; we must
apply. Willing is
not enough; we
must do.
— *J.W. Goethe*

1963: MARCH ON
WASHINGTON

M.L. KING JR.
"I HAVE A DREAM"

SET 5:02PM

RISE 6:31AM
SET 7:57PM

RIGHT RESOLVE

POEM: To Be a Slave of Intensity

Friend, hope for the Guest while you're alive.
Jump into experience while you are alive!
Think...and think...while you are alive.
What you call "salvation" belongs to the time before death.

If you don't break your ropes while you're alive,
do you think
ghosts will do it after?

The idea that the soul will join with the ecstatic
just because the body is rotten –
that is all fantasy.
What is found now is found then.
If you find nothing now,
you will simply end up with an apartment in the City of
        Death.
If you make love with the divine now, in the next life you
        will have the face of satisfied desire.

So plunge into the truth, find out who the Teacher is,
        Believe in the Great Sound!

Kabir says this: When the Guest is being searched for, it is
        the intensity of the longing for the Guest that does all
        the work.
Look at me and you will see a slave of that intensity.
                        ~ *Kabir (translation by Robert Bly)*

29
MON · AUGUST 29 · 2005

1839: Amistad seized ~ Beheading of John the Baptist, Christian

Charlie "Bird" Parker, musician, b.1920
John Locke, philosopher, b.1632

The true traveler is he who goes on foot, and even then, he sits down a lot of the time.
— Colette

Ingrid Bergman, actress, b.1915

☽△♅ 7:40AM

☽
RISE 12:58AM
SET 5:50PM

✹
RISE 6:32AM
SET 7:55PM

RIGHT WORD

30
TUE · AUGUST 30 · 2005

Santa Rosa de Lima, Peru

Andy Roddick, tennis player, b.1982
Roy Wilkins, civil rights leader, b.1901
Mary Shelley, author, b.1797

If there's a book you really want to read but it hasn't been written yet, then you must write it.
— Toni Morrison

♀△♆ 3:50AM
☿△♇ 8:25PM

☽
RISE 1:56AM
SET 6:28PM

✹
RISE 6:33AM
SET 7:53PM

RIGHT DEED

31
WED · AUGUST 31 · 2005

1896: Gold discovered, Klondike

William Shawn, editor, b.1907
William Saroyan, author, b.1908
Maria Montessori, educator, b.1870

Never help a child with a task at which he feels he can succeed.
— Maria Montessori

☽☌♄ 2:00PM
☉☍♅ 10:03PM

☽
RISE 3:00AM
SET 6:59PM

✹
RISE 6:34AM
SET 7:52PM

RIGHT LIVELIHOOD

1
THU · SEPTEMBER 1 · 2005

Lailaf al Miraj, Islam ~ Ecclesiastical year begins, Orthodox Christian ~ 1939: World War II begins
Lily Tomlin, actress, b.1939
Edgar Rice Burroughs, author, b.1875

I know not with what weapons World War III will be fought, but World War IV will be fought with sticks and stones.
— Albert Einstein

☽☍♆ 9:47AM
☽☌♃ 6:30PM
☽△♇ 10:26PM

☽
RISE 4:06AM
SET 7:23PM

✹
RISE 6:35AM
SET 7:50PM

RIGHT ENDEAVOR

SEPTEMBER

AUG 23 - SEPT 22

♍︎
virgo

SEPT 22 - OCT 22

♎︎
libra

BIRTHSTONE
Sapphire

Courtesy
BECOMES TACT OF HEART
Challenges: exploitation / carelessness

FLOWER
Aster

Summer wanes, autumn approaches. Swallows swoop and gather in the sky. The air smells of fallen apples. Goldenrod is everywhere. The sunlight, too, is golden, like the stubble in the fields. Liquid and tender, now it warms our backs, not our heads. Amid the late ripeness, nature begins the process of withering and fading away. At night, a chill is in the air. Flies die. Outer growth turns inward and an inner sun replaces the outer one. Self-consciousness rises, filling us with courage, initiative, and will. The future lies before us, requiring a sensitive, respectful heart. Therefore, at the equinox, when the days and nights are again of equal length, we celebrate Michaelmas, the feast of Michael and the Archangels. As St. Michael overcomes the dragon, we, too, may overcome all that hardens us — our past, our habits, our fixed ways of thinking and feeling — so as to become free to create a truly human, earth-caring, loving future.

SEPTEMBER IS
ATTENTION DEFICIT DISORDER MONTH · BABY SAFETY MONTH · BE KIND TO EDITORS & WRITERS MONTH · CHILDREN'S EYE HEALTH & SAFETY MONTH · GOOD MANNERS MONTH · COLLEGE SAVINGS MONTH · FALL HAT MONTH · INT'L GAY SQUARE DANCE MONTH · METAPHYSICAL AWARENESS MONTH · NATIONAL BISCUIT MONTH NAT'L CHICKEN MONTH · NAT'L HONEY MONTH · LITTLE LEAGUE MONTH · ORGANIC HARVEST MONTH · NAT'L PIANO MONTH · NAT'L POTATO MONTH · WAFFLE MONTH SCHOOL SUCCESS MONTH · PAIN AWARENESS MONTH · SELF-IMPROVEMENT MONTH SHAMELESS PROMOTION MONTH · UPDATE YOUR RESUME MONTH

A beautiful cosmic meeting: Moon, Jupiter, Venus and Spica, main star of Virgo.

The movements of Mercury and Saturn through Cancer.

Venus

Jupiter

Spica

Moon

WSW September 6, 8:15 p.m.

Saturn

9/11 · Praesepe

Mercury

9/21

9/24

9/27

ENE around 5:30 a.m.

STARS & PLANETS FOR SEPTEMBER

Venus and Jupiter will meet Spica, the brightest star in the constellation Virgo, in the western sky thirty minutes after sunset, on September 3rd. The waxing crescent Moon joins the group on the 6th. This is perhaps the most beautiful conjunction of the year. Saturn will be in the neighborhood of Praesepe, the open star cluster in Cancer, especially nice to view with binoculars.

LOOK UP:

- New Moon, 18:47 UT
- Crescent Moon near Venus and Jupiter
- 18 Full Moon (Singing Moon), 2:02 UT
  Mercury at superior conjunction
- 1 Fall equinox

LOOK OUT:

- Elk bugle in the mountain and coastal forests
- Landlocked kokanee salmon spawn in feeder streams
- Wild rice ripens in the northern lakes
- Bottlenose dolphins move though estuaries

SEPTEMBER						
S	M	T	W	T	F	S
				1	2	3
4	5	6	7	8	9	10
11	12	13	14	15	16	17
18	19	20	21	22	23	24
25	26	27	28	29	30	

Youth is like spring, an over praised season more remarkable for biting winds than genial breezes. Autumn is the mellower season, and what we lose in flowers we more than gain in fruits.
~ SAMUEL BUTLER

POEM: Faithfulness

Create for yourself a new indomitable perception of faithfulness. What is usually called faithfulness passes so quickly. Let this be your faithfulness: you will experience moments, fleeting moments, with the other person. The human being will appear to you then as if filled, irradiated, with the archetype of his or her spirit. And then there may be, indeed will be, other moments, long periods of time when human beings are darkened. At such times, you will learn to say to yourself, "The spirit makes me strong. I remember the archetype. I saw it once. No illusion, no deception shall rob me of it." Always struggle for the image that you saw. This struggle is faithfulness. Striving thus for faithfulness you shall be close to one another as if endowed with the protective powers of angels.

~ *Rudolf Steiner*

For more information on Rudolf Steiner's work, see www.rudolfsteinerpress.org

BEING A PERSON/ *William Stafford*

Be a person here. Stand by the river, invoke | the owls. Invoke winter,
then spring. | Let any season that wants to come here make its own call. |
After that sound goes away, wait… | …How you stand here is important. |
How you listen for the next things to happen. | How you breathe.

---

2   FRI · SEPTEMBER 2 · 2005

1666: Great
Fire of London
~ 1864:
Sherman enters
Atlanta

*Salma Hayak,
actress, b.1966
Keanu Reeves,
actor, b. 1964*

I might repeat
to myself slowly
and soothingly,
a list of quota-
tions beautiful
from minds
profound – if I
can remember
any of the
damn things.
— *Dorothy
Parker*

☽ ☌ ☿ 6:44AM

☾
RISE 5:12AM
SET 7:43PM

☼
RISE 6:37AM
SET 7:48PM

RIGHT MEMORY

---

3   SAT · SEPTEMBER 3 · 2005

1783: Treaty of
Paris: ended the
American
Revolution.
*Prudence
Crandall, educ-
ator, b. 1803
Kitty Carlisle,
actress, b.1915
Charlie Sheen,
actor, b.1965*

Freedom is that
instant between
when someone
tells you to do
something and
when you
decide how
to respond.
— *Jeffery
Borenstein*

☽ ☌ ♅ 8:24AM

☽ ☌ ☉ 1:45PM

☼
RISE 6:38AM
SET 7:46PM

**New Moon
18:45**UT

RIGHT CONCEPTION

---

4   SUN · SEPTEMBER 4 · 2005

1781: City of
Los Angeles
founded
~ 1957: Little
Rock Nine
turned away
from school

*Mitzi Gaynor,
actress, b.1931
Damon Wayans,
actor, b.1960*

Before God we
are all equally
wise — and
equally foolish.
— *Albert Einstein*

NEWSPAPER
CARRIER DAY

☽ △ ♂ 3:40AM

☾
RISE 7:23AM
SET 8:17PM

☼
RISE 6:39AM
SET 7:44PM

RIGHT RESOLVE

CELEBRATE: Literacy Day, September 8

These are not books, lumps of lifeless paper, but minds alive on the shelves. From each of them goes out its own voice...and just as the touch of a button on our set will fill the room with music, so by taking down one of these volumes and opening it, one can call into range the voice of a man far distant in time and space, and hear him speaking to us, mind to mind, heart to heart. ~ *Gilbert Highet*

More than 25 percent of the adults in the world do not know how to read and write. On Literacy Day, the United Nations Educational, Scientific, and Cultural Organization (UNESCO) calls attention to their needs. In the Bazhong district of China, when their literacy program began, only 10 percent of the people in more than 800 villages could read; 35 years later 90 percent of them could.

From The Book of Holidays Around the World.
For more information on Literacy Day,
see www.reading.org/meetings/ild/

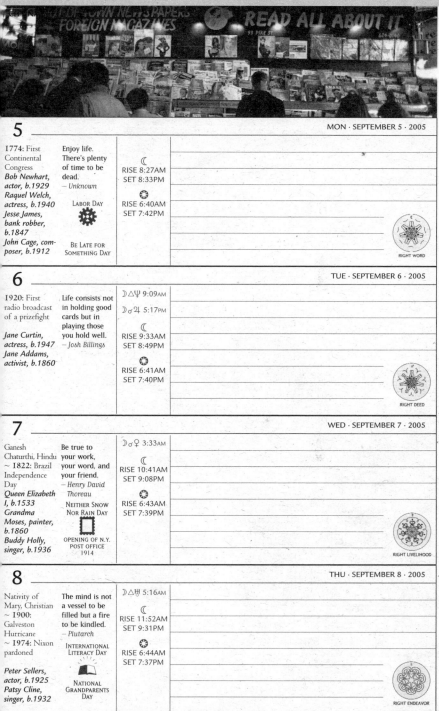

5

1774: First Continental Congress
Bob Newhart, actor, b.1929
Raquel Welch, actress, b.1940
Jesse James, bank robber, b.1847
John Cage, composer, b.1912

Enjoy life. There's plenty of time to be dead.
— *Unknown*

LABOR DAY

BE LATE FOR SOMETHING DAY

☾ RISE 8:27AM
SET 8:33PM

☀ RISE 6:40AM
SET 7:42PM

RIGHT WORD

6

1920: First radio broadcast of a prizefight

Jane Curtin, actress, b.1947
Jane Addams, activist, b.1860

Life consists not in holding good cards but in playing those you hold well.
— *Josh Billings*

☽ △ ♆ 9:09AM

☽ ☌ ♃ 5:17PM

☾ RISE 9:33AM
SET 8:49PM

☀ RISE 6:41AM
SET 7:40PM

RIGHT DEED

7

Ganesh Chaturthi, Hindu
~ 1822: Brazil Independence Day
Queen Elizabeth I, b.1533
Grandma Moses, painter, b.1860
Buddy Holly, singer, b.1936

Be true to your work, your word, and your friend.
— *Henry David Thoreau*

NEITHER SNOW NOR RAIN DAY

OPENING OF N.Y. POST OFFICE 1914

☽ ☌ ♀ 3:33AM

☾ RISE 10:41AM
SET 9:08PM

☀ RISE 6:43AM
SET 7:39PM

RIGHT LIVELIHOOD

8

Nativity of Mary, Christian
~ 1900: Galveston Hurricane
~ 1974: Nixon pardoned

Peter Sellers, actor, b.1925
Patsy Cline, singer, b.1932

The mind is not a vessel to be filled but a fire to be kindled.
— *Plutarch*

INTERNATIONAL LITERACY DAY

NATIONAL GRANDPARENTS DAY

☽ △ ♅ 5:16AM

☾ RISE 11:52AM
SET 9:31PM

☀ RISE 6:44AM
SET 7:37PM

RIGHT ENDEAVOR

POEM:
Manhattan, 1997

The island's tip
was sliced by a ship
canal that tamed the
Spuyten Duyvil shoals,
but severed Marble Hill
from Inwood. Medieval
tapestry unicorns grace
the Cloisters; a flag-
pole and stockade mark
old Fort Tryon. Lofty
crags overlook the
broad Hudson River
as bedrock & history
anchor the Heights to
the George Washington Bridge. Walk east
toward the Bronx across High Bridge;
gaze to the south
from Sugar Hill,
where trumpeters
and tap dancers
stepped up into
the sun. Ages ago
Iapetus (an older
Atlantic Ocean)
closed; the kiss
with Africa heated
a melting pot. Lava
was injected in veins
of rock and coagulated
to form Palisade cliffs.
The legacy of Algonquian
life is hidden in our place
names and our meals. The new-
comers (first the Dutch, then
English, African, Irish, German,
Italian, Jewish, Chinese, Greek,
Ukrainian, Armenian, Puerto Rican,
Pakistani, Cuban, Dominican, Haitian,
Filipino, and all) have shed blood in a
thousand places, but millions live. Legends
of Gotham: Father Knickerbocker, Boss Tweed,
Emma Lazarus, Fiorello, the roar of the El,
the blizzard of '47, Giants at the Polo Grounds.
Offshore, barges ply swirling brown water nest
North River sewage pipes, as striped bass and
shad swim up "the river that flows both ways" : a
tidal reach of the sea all the way up to Albany.
Brownstone, bodega, ball court & bus stop: on warm
nights in Harlem, noisy streets and quiet rooftops.
Kids splash around a hydrant as lovers embrace on a
Riverside Park bench and rush-hour traffic is stalled on the Triborough Bridge.
Some uptown options: gospel choir on Sunday, sooty
Grant's Tomb, hiphop the Apollo, ribs at Sylvia's,
law at Columbia, mangos in El Barrio, peace garden
in the Cathedral, rowboat on the Meer, pub-crawl the
West Side, listen to poetry at the 92nd St. Y, nosh at
Zabar's, spiral up the Guggenheim, tour Gracie Mansion.
Songbirds alight in leafy woods as a turtle lays eggs
near a pond in Central Park. Grand museums flank the
green with dinosaur bones and Egyptian tombs. When it
snows, we ramble out to Sheep Meadow & the Great Lawn;
in sunshine, to Strawberry Fields, the Lake, & the Zoo.
Buy hot dogs from pushcarts near Madison boutiques, or
hear grand opera at the Met. Step down to the world of
subways. (Take the A train, ride the Lexington line,
or change at 59th Street for the IRT. Catch the F out to Queens.)
Gneiss but full of schist, the bedrock sparkles with
mica. It bears the weight of midtown: skyscrapers
at Columbus Circle, Fifth Avenue, and Park Avenue.
Attend concerts at Carnegie, ice skating shows at
Rockefeller Center, Mass at St. Patrick's Cathedral.
Our eyes are drawn up to a blue slice of sky as
vertical walls enclose us. 100 gridlocked taxis honk
at police blockades as Fidel speaks at the U.N.
Revelers jam Times Square on New Year's Eve, to
jostle and sing as the ball drops. Buses come in
(the Lincoln Tunnel) to Port Authority, trains to Grand Central. The
lion-flanked public library was once a reservoir;
we love the Art Deco classic Chrysler spire. From
Hell's Kitchen walk to Broadway, buy tickets for
"Showboat" or "Cats"—hey, the Knicks won at the
buzzer in the Garden! See Macy's float parade, then
gape from atop the Empire State, where mighty Kong
took a fall. Diamond jewelers join fur-clad window
shoppers as herds of jaywalkers cross against the
light in the Garment District. Graffiti-scrawled
boards near the Flatiron Building enclose pits
of unconsolidated sediment Consolidated Edison
must dig. Workers repair Gramercy Park cables,
reroute Chelsea steam pipes, plug a burst main
flooding streets by Union Square. (Tap water
flows down from the Catskills in deep tunnels;
garbage is hauled to a landfill at Fresh Kills.)
The riverfront was filled for barnacle-crusted
piers, and Minetta Brook wetlands became lots
in Greenwich Village. A sweatshop horror: 146
locked-in women lost their lives in the Triangle
Shirtwaist fire. Watch skateboard demons cavort
among panhandlers as old men play chess near the
arch in Washington Square. N.Y.U. students, art
film fans, coffee drinkers, & East Village poets
crowd smoky joints on Saturday night; some cross
(the Holland Tunnel) back out to New Jersey. Cheap gallery space
is a memory in SoHo; cast-iron lofts rent high,
as do TriBeCa warehouses. A bag lady seeks warmth
huddled over a sidewalk grate on the Bowery, where
Stuyvesant's farm once spread in old New Amsterdam.
The original steal (this island, traded for $24 in
beads) lies plastered in myth and concrete, obscured
like the African Burial Grounds. A Lower East Side
delicatessen sells good chicken soup; enjoy zuppa di
pesca at the Festival of San Gennaro, or bird's nest
soup in Chinatown. Marchers to City Hall cross the Brooklyn Bridge
to demonstrate, as tourists at South Street Seaport
eat lunch with a view. The Fulton Fish Market is
mobbed before dawn. Precambrian stocks bond the
upper crust with solid foundations below the
Trade Towers, Trinity Church and Wall Street.
Ferryboats to Staten Island, Ellis
Island, the Statue of Liberty,
and Governor's Island
depart from wind-
swept docks
at Battery
Park.

~ *Howard Horowitz*

It took the author one-and-a half years
to write and design this poem about
Manhattan, in the form of a map as
crowded as the place it represents.
Horowitz is a professor of environmental
studies at Ramapo College.

WE ALL LIVE WITH THE OBJECTIVE OF BEING HAPPY; OUR LIVES ARE ALL DIFFERENT AND YET THE SAME :: *ANNE FRANK*

TIMES SQUARE, NYC

WAGE PEACE/*Judyth Hill*

Wage peace with your breath. | Breathe in firemen and rubble, | breathe out whole buildings | and flocks of red wing blackbirds. | Breathe in terrorists and breathe out sleeping children and | freshly mown fields...

---

9   FRI · SEPTEMBER 9 · 2005

Chrysanthemum Day, Japan
~ 490BC: Battle of Marathon
William the Conqueror, d.1087
Adam Sandler, actor, b.1966
Leo Tolstoy, author, b.1828

Some people weave burlap into the fabric of our lives, and some weave gold thread. Both contribute to make the whole picture beautiful and unique.
— *Unknown*

☿ ☌ ♅ 12:22AM
☽ ☌ ♂ 2:31AM
☽ RISE 1:06PM SET 10:00PM
☀ RISE 6:45AM SET 7:35PM

RIGHT MEMORY

---

10   SAT · SEPTEMBER 10 · 2005

Bald is Beautiful Convention, Morehead, SC

Franz Werfel, author, b.1890
Arnold Palmer, golfer, b.1929
Charles Kuralt, journalist, b.1934
Stephen J. Gould, biologist, b.1941

It was when I found out I could make mistakes that I knew I was on to something.
— *Ornette Coleman*

FEDERAL LANDS CLEANUP DAY

☽ △ ♄ 9:30AM
☽ RISE 2:21PM SET 10:38PM
☀ RISE 6:46AM SET 7:33PM

RIGHT CONCEPTION

---

11   SUN · SEPTEMBER 11 · 2005

2001: Terrorist Attacks in New York & Wash. D.C.
~ Giostra della Quintana, Italy
Moby, musician, b.1965
D.H. Lawrence, author, b.1885
O. Henry, author, b.1862

Never look down on anybody unless you are helping him up.
— *Jesse Jackson*

PATRIOT DAY

☽ ☌ ♇ 11:52AM
☀ RISE 6:47AM SET 7:31PM

First Quarter 11:37UT

RIGHT RESOLVE

URBAN SANCTUARY: Eloise Butler Wildflower Garden, Minneapolis

Most Minneapolitans don't know about a little island of tranquility that lies barely a mile from the world famous Guthrie Theater and the Walker Art Center. Across nearly a dozen lanes of Interstate 394, in the Bryn Mawr neighborhood just west of downtown Minneapolis, Eloise Butler managed to protect 15 acres of nature in the rapidly developing city. Butler started this project around 1906, when, after being denied by the Park Board countless times, she turned to her fellow Minnesotans for aid. After a couple years of hard work, and with the support of quite a few good women, the Eloise Butler Wildflower Garden and Bird Sanctuary was born. From April 1 through October 15 the park showcases woodlands, wetlands, and prairie wildlife along its winding trails. The gardens, which only include flora native to Minnesota, are a feast for the eyes at any time. Beautiful displays of wild ginger, trilliums, and splashes of marigolds light up the woodlands in the early season. By summer, (blink and you'll miss it here), the wetlands take over with striking displays of irises and lady slippers. The prairie, in August and September, comes alive with its diverse blooms of black-eyed susans and asters. With something to see at any time of the year, this garden truly embodies Eloise's dream of an urban sanctuary, not only for Minnesota wildlife, but for anyone who seeks a little nature in the cacophony of urban life.

~ *Susan Amis & Yoko Okumura,*
both 16 years old

For more information on the Eloise Butler Wildflower Garden in Minneapolis, see www.minneapolisparks.org/

12

Improve Your Home Office Week

Maria Muldaur, singer, b.1943
Charles Dudley, Warner, b.1829
Jesse Owens, athlete, b.1913
H.L. Mencken, critic, b.1880

The animals of the planet are in desperate peril ... Without free animal life I believe we will lose the spiritual equivalent of oxygen.
— *Alice Walker*

☾ RISE 4:36PM

☉ RISE 6:48AM
SET 7:29PM

RIGHT WORD

13

1814: *Star-Spangled Banner* inspired by the attack on Fort McHenry

Jacqueline Bisset, actress, b.1944
Roald Dahl, author, b.1916

Looking back, I have this to regret, that too often when I loved, I did not say so.
— *David Grayson*

BLAME SOMEONE ELSE DAY

☾△☿ 5:53AM
☾△☉ 1:20PM
☾△♂ 1:22PM
☉△♂ 1:49PM

☾ SET 12:35AM
RISE 5:27PM

☉ RISE 6:50AM
SET 7:27PM

RIGHT DEED

14

Holy Cross Day, Christian ~ Elevation of the Life-Giving Cross, Orthodox
Dante Alleghieri, poet, d.1321
Kate Millet, author, b.1934
Margaret Sanger, feminist/advocate, b.1879

Science has proof without any certainty. Creationists have certainty without any proof.
— *Ashley Montague*

☾☌♄ 4:00PM

☾ SET 1:53AM
RISE 6:07PM

☉ RISE 6:51AM
SET 7:25PM

RIGHT LIVELIHOOD

15

1940: Battle of Britain Day ~ Respect for the Aged Day, Japan

James Fenimore Cooper, author, b.1789
Agatha Christie, author, b.1890
Roy Acuff, musician, b.1903

The last of the human freedoms is to choose one's attitudes.
— *Victor Frankl*

GREENPEACE FOUNDED 1971

☾☌♆ 4:46AM
☾△♃ 2:39PM
☿△♃ 10:05PM

☾ SET 3:18AM
RISE 6:37PM

☉ RISE 6:52AM
SET 7:23PM

RIGHT ENDEAVOR

LIVING URBAN TREASURE: Minneapolis's Louise Erdrich

At the tender middle age of 50, Louise Erdrich has received the National Book Critics Circle Award for Best Fiction for *Love Medicine*, the Pushcart Prize in Poetry, the O. Henry Prize for short fiction, and a Guggenheim Fellowship. Her writing is alive with the tension of conflicting worlds that she weaves together like a sweet-grass braid.

Louise Erdrich in Minneapolis

Part of that tension comes from where she has spent her years. Her childhood in tiny Wahpeton, North Dakota, gave way to living in the big country outside Kalispell, Montana, and then the woods of New Hampshire. Now she intertwines those rural roots with her urban life in Minneapolis, Minnesota.

Erdrich's writing is alive with the tension of conflicting worlds that she weaves together like a sweet-grass braid.

BirchBark Books, her storefront enterprise, joins her past and present with the legacy of her mixed-race family. The store has homey chairs in every alcove, a children's loft deep with stuffed animals, a parakeet, and even a Catholic confessional. "I think of it as a 'forgiveness booth,'" says Erdrich. But in spite of all the whimsy, the bookstore is a serious business. "I think there has to be room in this world for the personal eccentricities of highly literate groups of people," Erdrich says. So BirchBark offers books unavailable elsewhere in the city, like Lakota and Ojibwe dictionaries, and the staff cares about books and the people who read them.

BirchBark Books also showcases Native arts and crafts, many from Turtle Mountain, the reservation of Erdrich's French Ojibwe mother. Erdrich's support of Native arts and crafts is one way she helps artisans continue the old forms, helps rural residents with their living, and brings nature into the city.

This subtle attention to the land, its people, and its gifts is everywhere, even in the window box outside the store where tomatoes and herbs grow. "It's extremely important to use every inch in the city that you can to plant and grow," she says. "When we give the kind of attention to city land that it deserves, we'll have livable cities."

~ Kathleen Melin

For more information : BirchBark Books · 2115 West 21st Street · Minneapolis, MN 55405 (612) 374-4023 · info@birchbarkbooks.com · www.birchbarkbooks.com

MINNEAPOLIS, MINNESOTA

RUN/ *Rumi (translated by Coleman Barks)*

…Forget safety. | Live where you fear to live. | Destroy your reputation. |
Be notorious. | I have tried prudent planning | long enough.
From now | on, I'll be mad.

16 — FRI · SEPTEMBER 16 · 2005

1620: Mayflower Day: Pilgrims deported from England
~ **1810:** Mexican Independence Day

B.B.King, musician, b.1925
Lauren Bacall, actress, b.1924

What you are thunders so that I cannot hear what you say to the contrary.
— *Ralph Waldo Emerson*

Francis Parkman, author, b.1823
Anne Bradstreet, poet, d.1672

☽△♀ 1:52PM
☽☌♅ 5:29PM

☾ SET 4:44AM
RISE 7:02PM

☼ RISE 6:53AM
SET 7:22PM

RIGHT MEMORY

17 — SAT · SEPTEMBER 17 · 2005

Constitution Week ~ **1920:** Nat'l Football League formed
~**1862:** Battle of Antietam, 25,000 killed
Anne Bancroft, actress, b.1931
Hank Williams, baseball player, b.1923

As soon as questions of will or decision or reason or choice of action arise, human science is at a loss.
— *Noam Chomsky*

CITIZENSHIP DAY

☽☌♀☿ 8:58PM
☽☌☉ 9:01PM
☉☌☿ 9:38PM

☾ SET 6:07AM
RISE 7:23PM

☼ RISE 6:54AM
SET 7:20PM

RIGHT CONCEPTION

18 — SUN · SEPTEMBER 18 · 2005

1851: *New York Times* first published
~ **1947:** U.S. Air Force established

Lance Armstrong, bicyclist, b.1971
Samuel Johnson, essayist, b.1707

Anybody can observe the Sabbath, but making it holy surely takes the rest of the week.
— *Alice Walker*

Agnes DeMille, dancer, b.1905
Greta Garbo, actress, b.1905

♀△♅ 11:31AM
☽△♄ 5:27PM

☼ RISE 6:56AM
SET 7:18PM

Full Moon
2:01UT

RIGHT RESOLVE

CIVILIZING IDEA: Farmers' Markets

Urban farmers' markets promise a connection to the earth and to the human hands still touching it. In parks, abandoned lots, and along city sidewalks, these markets are reinvigorating consumers' relationships to food sources and to one another. Dirt is not only permissible at farmers' markets, it's sold as a valuable commodity. Handmade signs replace glossy stickers and advertising labels. Efficiency is measured more in the reuse of plastic bags or the opportunity to walk the dog while browsing, than in volume discounts or speedy checkout lines.

A shopper, heavily laden with produce from a farmers' market, comments, "I grew up in South Philadelphia, and it was a world of corner stores. There were relationships. And this, in a very curious way, recreates that. Even though [the vendors] aren't neighborhood people, on Thursdays and Saturdays, they are."

In the supermarket, consumers rarely stare awestruck at the shape of a squash, or marvel at the colors of swiss chard, or even notice that there are other people around them. While it is certainly possible that your overworked and underpaid clerk behind the cash register may smile at you, shopping in a supermarket is simply nothing like the earthy social encounters taking place at urban farmers' markets. As one shopper puts it, "The markets are a little miracle in the city."

~ *Alana Rose*

For more information on Farmers' Markets, see
www.farmersmarket.net

19

MON · SEPTEMBER 19 · 2005

1985: Mexico City earthquake, 10,000 killed
~ Lailat al Bara'a, Islam
Twiggy, model, b.1949
Mike Royko, columnist, b.1932
Wm. Golding, author, b.1911

And the day came when the risk it took to remain tight inside the bud was more painful than the risk it took to blossom.
— *Anais Nin*

☽△♇ 5:01PM
☽☌♃ 5:36PM

☽
SET 8:48AM
RISE 8:03PM

☉
RISE 6:57AM
SET 7:16PM

RIGHT WORD

20

TUE · SEPTEMBER 20 · 2005

~ 1884: Equal Rights Party founded
~ 1973: Billie Jean King beats Bobby Riggs in tennis
Sophia Loren, actress; b.1934
Red Auerbach, coach, b.1917
Upton Sinclair, author, b.1878

In rivers, the water that you touch is the last of what has passed and the first of that which comes; so with present time.
— *Leonardo Da Vinci*

☽
SET 10:07AM
RISE 8:26PM

☉
RISE 6:58AM
SET 7:14PM

RIGHT DEED

21

WED · SEPTEMBER 21 · 2005

Religious Freedom Week

Chief Joseph, leader Nez Perce, d.1904
Ethan Coen, director, b.1957
Bill Murray, actor, b.1950
Faith Hill, singer, b.1967

God never occurs to you in person but always in action.
— *Mohandas Gandhi*

Leonard Cohen, singer, b.1934
H.G. Wells, author, b.1866
Stephen King, author, b.1947

☽☌♀ 2:04AM
☽☌♂ 10:45PM

☽
SET 11:24AM
RISE 8:51PM

☉
RISE 6:59AM
SET 7:12PM

RIGHT LIVELIHOOD

22

THU · SEPTEMBER 22 · 2005

1862: Emancipation Proclamation, Lincoln frees slaves
Ronaldo, soccer player, b.1976
Joan Jett, singer, b.1960
Debbie Boone, singer, b.1956
Michael Faraday, scientist, b.1791

Not all those that wander are lost.
— *J.R.R. Tolkien*

FALL EQUINOX
22:22 (UT)

HOBBIT APPRECIATION DAY

☽△☉ 11:41AM
☽△☿ 7:50PM

☽
SET 12:40PM
RISE 9:23PM

☉
RISE 7:00AM
SET 7:10PM

RIGHT ENDEAVOR

BIRTHDAY: Bruce Springsteen, September 23, 1949

MY HOMETOWN

I was eight years old and running
with a dime in my hand
Into the bus stop to pick up a paper
for my old man
I'd sit on his lap in that big old Buick
and steer as we drove through town
He'd tousle my hair and say son take
a good look around this is your
hometown
This is your hometown
This is your hometown
This is your hometown

In '65 tension was running high at
my high school
There was a lot of fights between the
black and white
There was nothing you could do
Two cars at a light on a Saturday
night in the back seat there was
a gun
Words were passed in a shotgun blast
Troubled times had come to my
hometown
My hometown
My hometown
My hometown

Now Main Street's whitewashed
windows and vacant stores
Seems like there ain't nobody wants
to come down here no more
They're closing down the textile mill
across the railroad tracks
Foreman says these jobs are going
boys and they ain't coming back to
your hometown
Your hometown
Your hometown
Your hometown

Last night me and Kate we laid in bed
talking about getting out
Packing up our bags maybe heading
south
I'm thirty-five we got a boy of our
own now
Last night I sat him up behind the
wheel and said son take a good
look around
This is your hometown

© *Bruce Springsteen (ASCAP)*

For more information on Bruce Springsteen,
see www.brucespringsteen.net

I LIVE MY LIFE/ *Rainer Maria Rilke (translated by Robert Bly)*

I live my life in growing orbits, | which move out over the things of the
world. | Perhaps I can never achieve the last, | but that will be my attempt. |
I am circling around God, around the ancient tower, | and I have been
circling for a thousand years. | And I still don't know if I am a falcon, |
Or a storm, or a great song.

---

23   FRI · SEPTEMBER 23 · 2005

1908: Baseball's Greatest Dispute: Merkle's Boner
Ani DiFranco, singer, b.1970
Julio Iglesias, singer, b.1943
Bruce Springsteen, singer, b.1949
Ray Charles, singer, b.1930

Man is free at the moment he wishes to be.
— *Voltaire*

PLANET NEPTUNE
DISCOVERED
1846

☽ △ ♆ 4:24PM

☾
SET 1:51PM
RISE 10:02PM

☉
RISE 7:02AM
SET 7:08PM

RIGHT MEMORY

---

24   SAT · SEPTEMBER 24 · 2005

1734: Schwenkfelder Thanksgiving, Pennsylvania-Dutch
Nia Vardalos, actress, b.1962
Jim Henson, muppet creator, b.1936
F. Scott Fitzgerald, author, b.1896

They were so strong in their beliefs that there came a time when it hardly mattered what exactly those beliefs were; they all fused into a single stubbornness.
— *Louise Erdrich*

☽ ☌ ♇ 5:32AM

☽ △ ♃ 7:57AM

☾
SET 2:54PM
RISE 10:50PM

☉
RISE 7:03AM
SET 7:06PM

RIGHT CONCEPTION

---

25   SUN · SEPTEMBER 25 · 2005

St. Sergius of Radonezh, Russ. Orthodox

Catherine Zeta-Jones, actress, b.1969
Dmitri Shostakovich, composer, b.1906
Wm. Faulkner, author, b.1897

Every exit is an entry somewhere.
— *Tom Stoppard*

NAT'L GOOD
NEIGHBOR DAY

GREENWICH
MEAN TIME
ESTABLISHED
1676

☽ △ ♅ 12:37PM

☉
RISE 7:04AM
SET 7:04PM

Last Quarter
6:41UT

RIGHT RESOLVE

CELEBRATE: Autumn Equinox/Rosh Hashanah/ Yom Kippur/Michaelmas

In the northern hemisphere, the autumn equinox signals Earth's waning life forces, just as spring proclaimed their rejuvenation. With the frost, harvest must be gathered. Amidst ripeness and plenty, we can enjoy Earth's bounty together. Yet, after the equinox, the days grow shorter. Darkness and cold are ascendant, and we must prepare for winter.

Inwardly, too, we feel the change. The outer dread of nature's death corresponds to a multitude of fears within. Fears reflect shortcomings, and to compensate we may be arrogant. In many ways, we come face to face with the Shadow, the "who we are" that we don't want to be. The journey of individuation is a fearful one, for what could be more daunting than to gaze unflinchingly at ourselves? This is the task of Rosh Hashanah (Oct. 4) and Yom Kippur (Oct. 13) days of atonement and purification.

An esoteric Christian picture of the meeting between higher self and lower self is that of Michael and the Dragon. Michael is consciousness; the Dragon pure impulse. Though they are polarities, they are also alike. Michael means "He who is like God" and the Dragon is Lucifer (the Light Bearer), the great angel who took himself to be greater than God.

Casting Lucifer from the Heavens, Michael struck a gem from Lucifer's crown. This became the Philosopher's Stone — the magical substance that alchemist's believed could turn lead into gold. It stands for transformation and is our guide on paths of wisdom (gnosis). The alchemical rule, "As above, so below" assures us that ultimately all is one. We are one with our Dragon. The gem from Lucifer's crown can also be the Holy Grail — love. Out of love, we may embrace the Dragon. For only by love can that which is flawed — both in ourselves and in the world — be made whole again.

~ *John Miller*

26 _____ MON · SEPTEMBER 26 · 2005

1960: First tele-
vised Presidential
debate

*Johnny
Appleseed,
b.1774*
*T.S. Eliot,
author, b.1888*
*Olivia Newton
John, singer,
b.1948*

When you
travel, remember
that a foreign
country is not
designed to
make you
comfortable.
It is designed
to make its
own people
comfortable.
— *Clifton Fadiman*

☽△♀ 6:55AM

☽ RISE 11:47PM
SET 4:29PM

☀ RISE 7:05AM
SET 7:03PM

RIGHT WORD

27 _____ TUE · SEPTEMBER 27 · 2005

Cosme e
Damiao, Brazil
~ 1964: Warren
Report issued

*Arthur Penn,
filmmaker,
b.1922*
*Thomas Nast,
artist, b.1840*
*Sam Adams,
patriot, b.1722*

Teachers open
the door, but
you must enter
by yourself.
— *Chinese
Proverb*

ANCESTOR
APPRECIATION
DAY

☽ RISE 12:48AM
SET 5:01PM

☀ RISE 7:06AM
SET 7:01PM

RIGHT DEED

28 _____ WED · SEPTEMBER 28 · 2005

1542: Cabrillo
Day, Discovery
of California
*Gwyneth
Paltrow,
actress, b.1973*
*Brigitte Bardot,
actress, b.1934*
*Al Capp,
cartoonist,
b.1909*

A thief believes
everybody
steals.
— *E.W. Howe*

NATIONAL
HUNTING &
FISHING DAY

☽☌♄ 2:35AM
☽☌♆ 3:29PM

☽ RISE 1:54AM
SET 5:28PM

☀ RISE 7:08AM
SET 6:59PM

RIGHT LIVELIHOOD

29 _____ THU · SEPTEMBER 29 · 2005

St. Michael's
Day, Michaelmas
~ 1899: VFW
Established

*Anita Ekberg,
actress, b.1931*
*Enrico Fermi,
physicist, b.1901*
*Horatio Nelson,
naval hero,
b.1758*

Thanks to
the Interstate
Highway System,
it is now
possible to
travel from
coast to coast
without seeing
anything.
— *Charles Kuralt*

☿△♆ 3:38AM
☽△♇ 5:38AM

☽ RISE 3:01AM
SET 5:49PM

☀ RISE 7:09AM
SET 6:57PM

RIGHT ENDEAVOR

OCTOBER

SEPT 23 - OCT 22

OCT 23 - NOV 21

libra

scorpio

BIRTHSTONE
Opal

FLOWER
Coneflower

Contentment
BECOMES EQUANIMITY
Challenges: foolishness, complaining, dissatisfaction

Green becomes gold. Orange pumpkins appear on the porches. Tasseled, colored corn hangs mysteriously on the doorframe. The world is on fire—it is becoming a sun! The maples redden. The poplars become flaming torches. Leaves drift weightlessly across the lawn and city parks. Twilight echoes with crows cawing. It is time to turn over a new leaf. Within us, summer's gift of sun becomes a yearning to find ourselves. No longer immersed in nature's greenness, we find ourselves detached from her. We want to think again, to find meaning in experience. Thought-life seems to strengthen. We want to understand. Perhaps the dead can help us. The month ends with Celtic Samhain, Christian All Souls and All Saints — Halloween — when the veil between the worlds is thinnest and the spirits of the ancestors come with their gifts.

OCTOBER IS:

ADOPT-A-SHELTER-DOG MONTH · ALTERNATE HISTORY MONTH · AUTO BATTERY SAFETY MONTH · COMPUTER LEARNING MONTH · DIVERSITY MONTH · EAT BETTER, EAT TOGETHER MONTH · GAY & LESBIAN HISTORY MONTH · EAT COUNTRY HAM MONTH · TEXAS PEANUTS MONTH · LUPUS AWARENESS MONTH · ANIMAL SAFETY MONTH · NAT'L BREAST CANCER AWARENESS MONTH · CAR CARE MONTH · COOKIE MONTH · DENTAL HYGIENE MONTH · NAT'L DISABILITY EMPLOYMENT MONTH · DOWN SYNDROME MONTH · LONG-TERM CARE PLANNING MONTH · NAT'L ORTHODONTIC HEALTH MONTH · DRYER VENT SAFETY MONTH · NAT'L PORK MONTH · ROLLER SKATING MONTH · NAT'L SEAFOOD MONTH · NAT'L SERVICE DOG MONTH · STAMP COLLECTING MONTH · SIDS AWARENESS MONTH · SELF-PROMOTION MONTH · VEGETARIAN MONTH

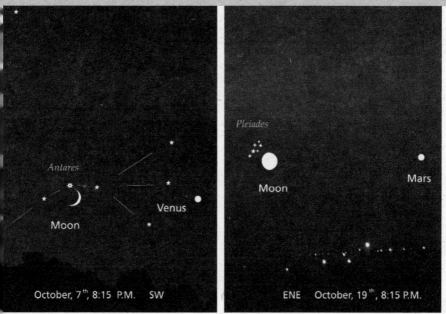

October, 7th, 8:15 P.M.   SW

ENE   October, 19th, 8:15 P.M.

STARS & PLANETS FOR OCTOBER

The Moon, Venus and Antares cluster together in Scorpio. Antares, which means "similar to" in Greek, was thought to be Mar's imitator and sometimes rival because of its brightness and reddish color. The Chinese call it the Fire Star.

LOOK UP:

3 New Moon, 10:29 UT
   Annular solar eclipse visible from Africa
   and Europe, 10:31 UT

8 Draconid meteor shower

16 Full Moon (Harvest Moon), 12:14 UT
   Partial lunar eclipse, visible to all but
   East Coast of U.S., 12:02 UT

21 Jupiter in conjunction with the Sun

28 Mars nearest the Earth

LOOK OUT:

· Salmon surge upstream into birth waters

· Piñon nuts ready to harvest

· Juncos arrive from the north

· Native brook trout spawn in southern
   Appalachia

OCTOBER

S	M	T	W	T	F	S
						1
2	3	4	5	6	7	8
9	10	11	12	13	14	15
16	17	18	19	20	21	22
23/30	24/31	25	26	27	28	29

Finish every day and be done with it.
You have done what you could;
some blunders and absurdities crept in;
forget them as soon as you can.
Tomorrow is a new day;
you shall begin it serenely and with
too high a spirit to be encumbered
with your old nonsense.

~ RALPH WALDO EMERSON

BIRTHDAY: Mahatma Gandhi, October 2, 1869

Indian political and spiritual leader who achieved world honor and fame for his advocacy of nonviolent resistance as a tool against tyranny was born at Porbandar, India. He was assassinated in the garden of his home in New Delhi, January 30, 1948. On the anniversary of Gandhi's birth (Gandhi Jayanti), thousands gather at the park on Jumna River at Delhi where Gandhi's body was cremated. Hymns are sung, verses from the Gita, the Koran, and the Bible are recited, and cotton thread is spun on small spinning wheels (one of Gandhi's favorite activities). Other observances are held at his birthplace and throughout India on this public holiday.

From Chase's 2004 Calendar of Events

Always aim at complete harmony
of thought and word and deed.
Always aim at purifying your thoughts
and everything will be well.

*As long as you derive inner help
and comfort from anything, keep it.*

Freedom is not worth having
if it does not include the freedom
to make mistakes.

*Happiness is when what you think,
what you say, and what you do
are in harmony.*

Honest differences are often
a healthy sign of progress.

*I believe in equality for everyone,
except reporters and photographers.*

Indolence is a delightful but
distressing state; we must be doing
something to be happy.

In the attitude of silence
the soul finds the path in a
clearer light, and what is elusive
and deceptive resolves itself
into crystal clearness.
Our life is a long and arduous
quest after Truth.

*It is better to be violent, if there is violence
in our hearts, than to put on the cloak
of nonviolence to cover impotence.*

It is unwise to be too sure of one's
own wisdom. It is healthy to be
reminded that the strongest might
weaken and the wisest might err.

*One needs to be slow to form convictions,
but once formed they must be defended
against the heaviest odds.*

Whatever you do will be insignificant,
but it is very important that you do it.

*You must not lose faith in humanity.
Humanity is an ocean;
if a few drops of the ocean are dirty, the
ocean does not become dirty.*

What difference does it make to the
dead, the orphans and the homeless,
whether the mad destruction
is wrought under the name
of totalitarianism or the
holy name of liberty or democracy?

*For more information on Mahatma Gandhi,
see www.mkgandhi.org*

Mahatma Gandhi

ODE TO AUTUMN/*John Keats*

…While barrèd clouds bloom the soft-dying day | And touch the
stubble-plains with rosy hue; | Then in a wailful choir the small gnats
mourn | Among the river-sallows, borne aloft | Or sinking as the light wind
lives or dies; | And full-grown lambs loud bleat from hilly bourn; |
Hedge-crickets sing; and now with treble soft | The redbreast whistles
from a garden-croft; | And gathering swallows twitter in the skies.

---

30   FRI · SEPTEMBER 30 · 2005

1955: James
Dean killed in
auto collision
~ *1962:* James
Meredith enrolls
at Ole Miss

*Elie Wiesel,
activist, b.1928
Truman Capote,
author, b.1924*

I never think
of the future —
it comes
soon enough.
— *Albert Einstein*

GUTENBERG BIBLE
PUBLISHED 1452

☽ ☌ ♅ 1:09PM

☾
RISE 4:07AM
SET 6:07PM

☀
RISE 7:10AM
SET 6:55PM

RIGHT MEMORY

---

1   SAT · OCTOBER 1 · 2005

Festival of
Penha, Rio de
Janiero, Brazil

*Julie Andrews,
actress, b.1935
Jimmy Carter,
39th President,
b.1924*

Science is
organized
knowledge.
Wisdom is
organized life.
— *Immanuel
Kant*

YOSEMITE NAT'L
PARK EST. 1890

☽ △ ♂ 8:22PM
♀ ☌ ♂ 9:45PM

☾
RISE 5:12AM
SET 6:24PM

☀
RISE 7:11AM
SET 6:53PM

RIGHT CONCEPTION

---

2   SUN · OCTOBER 2 · 2005

1950: "Peanuts"
comic strip debut
*Sting, singer,
b.1951
Groucho Marx,
comedian,
b.1890
Graham Greene,
author, b.1904
Mahatma
Gandhi, Indian
leader, b.1869*

The harder you
work, the
luckier you get.
— *McAlexander*

REDWOOD NAT'L
PARK EST. 1968

GET ORGANIZED
WEEK

☾
RISE 6:17AM
SET 6:40PM

☀
RISE 7:13AM
SET 6:51PM

RIGHT RESOLVE

HOLIDAY: Ramadan, October 4 – November 3, 2005

Ramadan, the ninth month of the Islamic year, is devoted to fasting. Except for the very young and the very old, all Muslims may not eat, drink, or smoke from dawn to dusk. Fasting, or *sawm*, strengthens one's sense of kinship with the poor, who must fast of necessity. A call from the minarets an hour before sunrise alerts people to prepare a light morning meal. Children go from house to house singing in praise of those who fast, receiving nuts and sweets, which they collect in long cloth bags called *kees*.

Because the Islamic calendar is based on the lunar cycle (each month averages 29½ days, and a year is only 354 days), Islamic festivals "float" on the Gregorian (western) calendar. It has no intercalary months to make up for the 365 days of the solar year, so the calendar moves back 11 days each solar year. Thus, all the holidays will, sooner or later, occur in every month of the Gregorian year.

Ramadan is a time to think of others before self, and of Allah above all. Ramadan commemorates the gift of the *Qur'an* to Muhammed. Prayer, always of central importance in the Muslim world, takes on added urgency, with a deep, introspective assessment of one's deeds and state of soul. Fasting develops self-mastery and contributes to purification in both body and spirit. Finally, Ramadan is a time for charity, both to the mosque and to the needy.

In a religion characterized by strenuous devotion, Ramadan stands as a central event in the Muslim year (much as the *Hajj*, or pilgrimage to Mecca, is a central event in the life of every Muslim). Islam means submission, utter commitment to the will of Allah, and the observance of Ramadan each year renews the personal commitment of every Muslim around the globe.

~*John Miller*

For more information about Ramadan, see www.holidays.net/ramadan/

3

1990: German Re-Unification ~ Tangun Day, Korea

Gore Vidal, author, b.1925
Chubby Checker, singer, b.1941
Harvey Kurtzman, publisher, b.1924

The brighter you are, the more you have to learn.
— Don Herold

ANNULAR SOLAR ECLIPSE

10:31 (UT)

☽ ☌ ☉ 5:28AM
☽ △ ☿ 2:26PM

☉ RISE 7:14AM
SET 6:49PM

New Moon 10:28UT

RIGHT WORD

4

Ramadan begins, through Nov. 3, Islam ~ Rosh Hashanah, Oct 4–5, Jewish ~ Navaratra Dashara, Oct 4–12, Hindu

Buster Keaton, comedian, b.1895

Somewhere, something incredible is waiting to be known.
— Carl Sagan

INT'L TOOT YOUR FLUTE DAY

St. Francis of Assisi, b.1181

☽ ☌ ☿ 6:29AM
☽ ☌ ♃ 10:15AM

☾ RISE 8:32AM
SET 7:14PM

☉ RISE 7:15AM
SET 6:48PM

RIGHT DEED

5

1877: Chief Joseph surrender

Tecumseh, Shawnee chief, d.1813
Kate Winslet, actress, b.1975
Vaclav Havel, Czech president, b.1936 Jonathan Edwards, theologian, b.1703

What I give form to in daylight is only one per cent of what I have seen in darkness.
— M. C. Escher

☽ △ ♅ 9:09AM
☿ ☌ ♃ 4:39PM

☾ RISE 9:43AM
SET 7:36PM

☉ RISE 7:16AM
SET 6:46PM

RIGHT LIVELIHOOD

6

Ashura, Islam ~ 1981: Anwar El-Sadat assassinated ~ 1876: American Library Ass'n founded

Rebecca Lobo, basketball player, b.1973

They say that God is everywhere, and yet we always think of Him as somewhat of a recluse.
— Emily Dickenson

INTERGENERATION DAY

☽ ☌ ♂ 2:05PM

☾ RISE 10:56AM
SET 8:02PM

☉ RISE 7:18AM
SET 6:44PM

RIGHT ENDEAVOR

BIRTHDAY: John Lennon, October 9, 1940

BLACKBIRD

Blackbird singing in the dead of night
Take these broken wings and learn to fly
All your life
You were only waiting for this moment to arise...
~ *John Lennon and Paul McCartney*

For more information on John Lennon,
see www.thebeatles.com

THESE ARE OUR TASKS / *Deena Metzger*

Let us learn the secret languages of light again. Also the letters of the dark. Learn the flight patterns of the birds, the syllables of wolf howl and bird song, the moving pantomime of branch and leaf, valleys and peaks of whale calls, the long sentences of ants moving in unison, the combinations and recombinations of clouds, the codices of stars. Let us, thus, reconstitute the world, sign by sign and melody by melody.

7
FRI · OCTOBER 7 · 2005

World Smile Day
~ Women's News Day

Yo-Yo Ma, cellist, b.1955
Desmond Tutu, S. African leader, b.1931

Laughter is the shortest distance between two people.
— Victor Borge

☽ ☌ ♀ 12:51AM
☽ △ ♄ 7:31PM
☉ △ ♆ 9:28PM

☾
RISE 12:11PM
SET 8:38PM

☼
RISE 7:19AM
SET 6:42PM

RIGHT MEMORY

8
SAT · OCTOBER 8 · 2005

1871: Great Chicago Fire
~ 1871: Peshtigo, Wisc. Forest Fire
Jesse Jackson, civil rights leader, b.1941
R.L. Stine, author, b.1943
Heinrich Schütz, composer, b.1585

So you see, imagination needs moodling — long, ineffi-cient, happy idling, dawdling and puttering.
— Brenda Ueland

☽ ☌ ♇ 6:02PM

☾
RISE 1:24PM
SET 9:24PM

☼
RISE 7:20AM
SET 6:40PM

RIGHT CONCEPTION

9
SUN · OCTOBER 9 · 2005

Health & Sports Day, Japan
~ Squirrel Awareness Week
~ Hangal Nal: Alphabet Day, Korea
~ Cirio de Nazare, Brazil

John Lennon, singer, b.1940

We can try to avoid making choices by doing nothing, but even that is a decision.
— Gary Collins

NAT'L METRIC WEEK

NATIONAL CHILDREN'S DAY

☾
RISE 2:30PM
SET 10:24PM

☼
RISE 7:21AM
SET 6:38PM

RIGHT RESOLVE

CONCEPT: 1,000-Person Village

If our world were a village of 1,000 people, what would its ethnic and religious composition be? Donella Meadows, distinguished professor at Dartmouth and economist for the Sustainability Institute, first developed the Village of 1,000 concept and printed it in her weekly column, The Global Citizen, on May 31, 1990. Dr. Meadows died in 2001.

IN THE VILLAGE WOULD BE:
564 Asians
210 Europeans
86 Africans
80 South Americans
60 North Americans

THERE WOULD BE:
300 Christians
(183 Catholics,
 84 Protestants,
 33 Orthodox)
175 Moslems
128 Hindus
55 Buddhists
47 Animists
210 without any religion
or atheist

OF THESE PEOPLE:
60 would control half
   of the total income
500 would be hungry
600 would live in shantytowns
700 would be illiterate

For Dr. Meadows' complete Village of 1,000,
see www.redrat.net/thoughts/global_village.htm; for updated statistics,
see faculty.philau.edu/russowl/villageof1000.html

10 — MON · OCTOBER 10 · 2005

1973: Spiro Agnew resignation ~ 1845: U.S. Naval Academy est.
Dale Earnhardt Jr., race driver, b.1974
Ben Vereen, actor, b.1946
Giuseppi Verdi, composer, b.1813

A house without books is like a room without windows.
— *Heinrich Mann*

UN WORLD MENTAL HEALTH DAY

☽△♂ 10:48PM

☼ RISE 7:23AM
SET 6:37PM

First Quarter 19:01UT

RIGHT WORD

11 — TUE · OCTOBER 11 · 2005

1975: "Saturday Night Live" premieres ~ World Egg Day
Joan Cusack, actress, b.1962
Eleanor Roosevelt, author, 1st Lady, b.1884

Love doesn't just sit there, like a stone; it has to be made, like bread, remade all the time, made new.
— *Ursula Le Guin*

NATIONAL COMING OUT DAY

☾ RISE 34:05PM

☼ RISE 7:24AM
SET 6:35PM

RIGHT DEED

12 — WED · OCTOBER 12 · 2005

Dasera, Hindu ~ 1999: World Population reaches 6 billion
Luciano Pavarotti, singer, b.1935
Dick Gregory, comedian, b.1932

No metaphysician ever felt the deficiency of language so much as the grateful.
— *Charles Colton*

COLUMBUS DAY

☽☌♄ 3:32AM
☽☌♆ 12:00PM
☽△☉ 8:12PM

☾ SET 12:57AM
RISE 4:38PM

☼ RISE 7:25AM
SET 6:33PM

RIGHT LIVELIHOOD

13 — THU · OCTOBER 13 · 2005

Yom Kippur, Jewish
Paul Simon, singer, b.1941
Nancy Kerrigan, ice skater, b.1969
Yves Montand, actor, b.1921

Life is to be fortified by many friendships. To love and be loved is the greatest happiness of existence.
— *Sydney Smith*

☿△♅ 8:20AM
☽△♃ 8:34AM

☾ RISE 5:04PM
SET 2:20AM

☼ RISE 7:26AM
SET 6:31PM

RIGHT ENDEAVOR

CIVILIZING IDEA: Citizen Wisdom Councils

The Rogue Valley Wisdom Council

Describing traditional Native American tribal councils, Oren Lyons, a member of the Onondaga Iroquois tribe, says, "We meet and just keep talking until there's nothing left but the obvious truth." Imagine if that was how American democracy worked.

Citizen Wisdom Councils are trying to do just that. The idea, hatched by Seattle organizational consultant Jim Rough, is simple: At least once a year, a community convenes a panel of randomly selected (so that no special interests or hierarchies prevail) citizens for two to three days of dialogue about issues of common concern — traffic, crime, schools, pollution, the local economy, and so on. A trained facilitator helps them focus on several hard-to-resolve issues. They talk them over until, like a tribal council, they reach a consensus about how to move forward. At the end, the council holds a public forum to present its consensus statements to the community, then disbands itself. The consensus statements become the basis for further community discussions and citizen activism.

In experiments across the country the wisdom council process has achieved surprising results. In the bedroom suburb of Pleasantville, New York, citizens came up with innovative ideas like adding more urban green spaces through "pocket" parks, creating a sense of a downtown by adding awnings and street lamps to local businesses, and encouraging pedestrian traffic by issuing walking credits, which locals could use to pay off parking tickets.

~ Leif Utne

For more on Citizen Wisdom Councils and similar innovations, see www.wisedemocracy.org, and www.co-intelligence.org.

OCTOBER / *Robert Frost*

...O hushed October morning mild, | Begin the hours of this day slow. | Make the day seem to us less brief... | ...Retard the sun with gentle mist; | Enchant the land with amethyst. | Slow, slow!...

14 — FRI · OCTOBER 14 · 2005

1964: Martin Luther King, Jr. awarded the Nobel Peace Prize
William Penn, founded PA, b.1644
Dwight Eisenhower, 34th President, b.1890

The moment of victory is much too short to live for that and nothing else
— *Martina Navratilova*

PEACE CORPS PROPOSED 1960

☽ ☌ ♅ 1:06AM
☽ △ ☿ 3:02AM

☾
RISE 5:25PM
SET 3:42AM

☀
RISE 7:28AM
SET 6:30PM

RIGHT MEMORY

15 — SAT · OCTOBER 15 · 2005

1917: Mata Hari executed
John K. Galbraith, economist, b.1908
P.G. Wodehouse, author, b.1881
Friedrich Nietzsche, philosopher, b.1844

Light breaks where no sun shines; / Where no sea runs, the waters of the heart / Push in their tides.
— *Dylan Thomas*

☾
RISE 5:45PM
SET 5:02AM

☀
RISE 7:29AM
SET 6:28PM

RIGHT CONCEPTION

16 — SUN · OCTOBER 16 · 2005

1853: Crimean War ~ 1859: John Brown's Raid ~ 1793: Marie Antoinette executed
Noah Webster, lexicographer, b.1758

There's no sauce in the world like hunger.
— *Miguel de Cervantes*

WORLD FOOD DAY

☽ △ ♄ 7:25AM

☾
RISE 6:05PM
SET 6:21AM

☀
RISE 7:30PM
SET 6:26PM

RIGHT RESOLVE

URBAN SURVIVAL STRATEGY:
How to Survive If You Are Caught Slacking

SURFING THE WEB

1. **Blame your search engine.**
   Explain that your search engine mistakenly has provided you with an address to an inappropriate site. Alternatively, claim you made a typing error in the Web address.

The Proper Napping Position

forehead on fingertips

thumb supporting jaw

arm perpendicular to desk

2. **Blame your browser.**
   Say that someone has set a new "home page" on your Internet browser. Sounding annoyed, loudly ask, "Who keeps setting my browser to open on this sports page? I'm trying to get those new numbers for my report!" You can also claim that you're having trouble loading certain work-related Web sites and so you are visiting more popular sites to see if the computer is working properly

3. **Blame the Web site.**
   Claim that the window with inappropriate material opened unexpectedly while you were viewing something else. Lament that such "pop-ups" are very common and should be regulated.

ASLEEP AT YOUR DESK

1. **Blame work.**
   Say, "I'm so exhausted; I was here until midnight last night!" Do not attempt this if your boss works late and you do not.

2. **Blame medication.**
   Claim that your new allergy medicine has been making you drowsy. Say, "Those antihistamines just knock me out!"

3. **Blame lunch.**
   Say, "Wow, I guess I should not have eaten that turkey sandwich. Triptophan really makes me sleepy!"

BE AWARE
When taking a nap, always rest your elbow on your desk and keep your arm perpendicular to the desktop. Your forehead should rest on your four fingers—your thumb, spread apart from the fingers, should support your jaw. This position will keep your head up and aimed at your desk. Face in a direction so that it is not immediately visible to someone approaching your desk that your eyes are closed. Keep an important group of documents in your perceived line of sight so as to appear to be reading intently.

From The Worst Case Scenario Survival Handbook

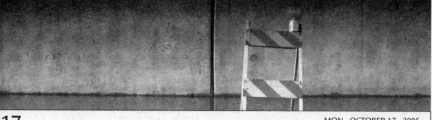

17 _____

1989: San Francisco earthquake

Eminem, singer, b.1972
Arthur Miller, author, b.1915
Jupiter Hammon, poet, b.1711
Pope John Paul I b.1912

Believe that life is worth living and your belief will help create the fact.
— William James

PARTIAL LUNAR ECLIPSE

12:02 (UT)

♀△♄ 1:24AM
☽♂☉ 7:14AM
☽♂♃ 1:58PM

☾ RISE 7:32AM
SET 6:24PM

Full Moon
12:14UT

RIGHT WORD

18 _____

Sukkot, Jewish

Wendy Wasserstein, playwright, b.1950
Chuck Berry, singer, b.1926
A.J. Liebling, journalist, b.1904

Freedom of the Press belongs to those who own one.
— A. J. Liebling

CANADA: PERSONS DAY

☽♂♅ 7:20PM

☾ RISE 6:50PM
SET 8:58AM

☼ RISE 7:33AM
SET 6:23PM

RIGHT DEED

19 _____

Nuzul alQur'an, Islam
~ Battara-Ichi: Pickle Market Day, Japan
~ 1987: Stock Market Crash: Dow drops 23%

The sweetest of all sounds is praise.
— Xenophon

Peter Max, artist, b.1937
Patricia Ireland, president NOW, b.1945
John Le Carre, author, b.1931

☽♂♂ 5:50AM

☾ RISE 7:19PM
SET 10:16AM

☼ RISE 7:34AM
SET 6:21PM

RIGHT LIVELIHOOD

20 _____

Birth of the Bab, Baha'i

Art Buchwald, columnist, b.1925
Christopher Wren, architect, b.1632
Mickey Mantle, baseball player, b.1931

I hope you love birds too. It is economical. It saves going to heaven.
— Emily Dickenson

John Dewey, educator, b.1859

☾ RISE 7:55PM
SET 11:31AM

☼ RISE 7:36AM
SET 6:19PM

RIGHT ENDEAVOR

LIVING URBAN TREASURE: Berkeley's Alice Waters

Alice Waters grew up in the 1940s and '50s when we Americans were turning our palates, to our great peril, toward convenience foods. But in 1963, while wandering through a fruit and vegetable market in Paris, Waters was struck by something radical to her young American sensibility — food that is grown locally and eaten fresh is our essential link to the land. Waters calls that moment for her "an awakening."

Alice Waters in Berkeley

Waters came back to the U.S. fired up by her discovery and imbued with a sense of rightness about how the French cook and enjoy their food. She wanted to recreate the experience of walking into a small French restaurant where everything is a sensual and seasonal celebration of what is good and beautiful from the earth.

The experience of a small French restaurant where everything is a sensual and seasonal celebration of what is good and beautiful from the earth

Waters pulled off that dream spectacularly at Berkeley's Chez Panisse, the place she started in 1971 and that 30 years later has been named Best Restaurant in America by the James Beard Foundation and *Gourmet* magazine. Waters herself has been ranked as one of the world's 10 best chefs and France has invited her to open a restaurant at the Louvre.

In 1996, she created the Chez Panisse Foundation to support programs that demonstrate "the transformative power of growing, cooking, and sharing food." One such program is the Edible Schoolyard Project at Berkeley's Martin Luther King Middle School. Through this project, students grow food in their schoolyard and sell it back to their school's cafeteria. It's by growing their own food, harvesting it, and sitting down to enjoy it together, Waters believes, that children learn not only about the land, but about hard work and the human connection.

Waters has devoted the last 30 years to rescuing food from homogeneity and the land from overproduction and depletion. And through her efforts, she is giving us all a second chance to rediscover the profound pleasure that comes with preparing fresh, honest food each day as if that food and our work were gifts we had somehow overlooked.

~ *Martha Coventry*

For more information on Alice Waters, see www.chezpanisse.com

SAN FRANCISCO

ADVICE/*Bill Holm*

Someone dancing inside us | learned only a few steps: | The "Do-Your-Work" in 4/4 time, | the "What-Do-You-Expect" waltz. | He hasn't noticed yet the woman | standing away from the lamp, | the one with black eyes | who knows the rhumba, | and strange steps in jumpy rhythms | from the mountains in Bulgaria. | If they dance together | something unexpected will happen. | If they don't, the next world | will be a lot like this one.

21   FRI · OCTOBER 21 · 2005

1967: Vietnam War protesters storm Pentagon
Ursula Le Guin, author, b.1929
Alfred Nobel, est Nobel Prize, b.1833
Dizzy Gillespie, musician, b.1917
S.T Coleridge, poet, b.1772

The only real mistake is the one from which we learn nothing.
— *John Powell*

INCANDESCENT LAMP DEMO
1879

☽ ☌ ♀ 12:06AM
☽ △ ♆ 12:57AM
☽ ☌ ♇ 3:18PM

☾
RISE 8:40PM
SET 12:39PM

☉
RISE 7:37AM
SET 6:18PM

RIGHT MEMORY

22   SAT · OCTOBER 22 · 2005

1962: Cuban Missile Crisis
Annette Funicello, actress, b.1942
Catherine Deneuve, actress, b.1942
Franz Liszt, composer, b.1811
Timothy Leary, advocate, b.1920

The most exciting phrase to hear in science, the one that heralds new discoveries, is not "Eureka!" (I found it!) but "That's funny..."
— *Isaac Asimov*

☽ △ ☉ 3:52AM
☽ △ ♃ 4:07AM
☉ ☌ ♃ 7:54AM
☿ ☌ ♂ 11:55AM
☽ △ ♅ 7:23PM

☾
SET 1:38PM
RISE 9:34PM

☉
RISE 7:38AM
SET 6:16PM

RIGHT CONCEPTION

23   SUN · OCTOBER 23 · 2005

Departure of the Swallows, Capistrano, Calif
~ 1956: Hungarian Revolution
1989: Hungarian Independence
Tiffeny Milbrett soccer player, b.1972
Pelé, soccer player, b.1940

All science is either physics or stamp collecting.
— *Ernest Rutherford*

NATIONAL MOLE DAY

CELEBRATE MOLECULES

☾
SET 2:25PM
RISE 10:35PM

☉
RISE 7:40AM
SET 6:14PM

RIGHT RESOLVE

PROCLAMATION: United Nations Charter Day, October 24

Before World War II ended, people all over the world believed that there should be an international peacekeeping organization that could prevent future wars. In October 1943, the foreign ministers of Great Britain, the Soviet Union, and the United States met in Moscow to discuss this goal. In the next year other nations joined the deliberations, and on October 24, 1945, the United Nations was born. One hundred and ninety-one nations now send representatives to the UN's headquarters in New York City.   From The Book of Holidays Around the World

WE THE PEOPLES OF THE UNITED NATIONS DETERMINED

to save succeeding generations from the scourge of war, which twice in our lifetime has brought untold sorrow to mankind, and

to reaffirm faith in fundamental human rights, in the dignity and worth of the human person, in the equal rights of men and women and of nations large and small, and

to establish conditions under which justice and respect for the obligations arising from treaties and other sources of international law can be maintained, and

to promote social progress and better standards of life in larger freedom,

AND FOR THESE ENDS

to practice tolerance and live together in peace with one another as good neighbours, and

to unite our strength to maintain international peace and security, and

to ensure, by the acceptance of principles and the institution of methods, that armed force shall not be used, save in the common interest, and

to employ international machinery for the promotion of the economic and social advancement of all peoples,

HAVE RESOLVED TO COMBINE OUR EFFORTS TO ACCOMPLISH THESE AIMS

Accordingly, our respective Governments, through representatives assembled in the city of San Francisco, who have exhibited their full powers found to be in good and due form, have agreed to the present Charter of the United Nations and do hereby establish an international organization to be known as the United Nations.

For more information about the United Nations Treaty, see untreaty.un.org/English/treaty.asp

24 — MON · OCTOBER 24 · 2005

1929: Stock Market Panic: Black Thursday

Kweisi Mfume, NAACP Pres., b.1948
Kevin Kline, actor, b.1947

Men are born to succeed, not to fail.
— *Henry David Thoreau*

UNITED NATIONS DAY

FOUNDED 1945

☽△☿ 1:29AM

☾
SET 3:01PM
RISE 11:40PM

☉
RISE 7:41AM
SET 6:13PM

RIGHT WORD

25 — TUE · OCTOBER 25· 2005

St. Crispin's Day, England, France
~ Shemini Atzerat, Jewish
Geoffrey Chaucer, author, d.1400
Pablo Picasso, artist, b.1881
Anne Tyler, author, b.1941

Love and magic have a great deal in common. They enrich the soul, delight the heart. And they both take practice.
— *Nora Roberts*

☽☌♄ 2:13PM
☽☌♇ 10:44PM

☉
RISE 7:42AM
SET 6:11PM

Last Quarter
1:17UT

RIGHT DEED

26 — WED · OCTOBER 26 · 2005

Simhat Torah, Jewish
~ 1785: Mule Day: First mules enter U.S.

Natalie Merchant, singer, b.1963
Hilary Rodham Clinton, senator, b.1947

A man travels the world over in search of what he needs and returns home to find it.
— *George Moore*

Mahalia Jackson, singer, b.1911

☽△♀ 9:21AM

☾
SET 3:53PM

☉
RISE 7:44AM
SET 6:10PM

RIGHT LIVELIHOOD

27 — THU · OCTOBER 27 · 2005

1787: Federalist Papers published
Fran Lebowitz, author, b.1950
John Cleese, actor, b.1939
Dylan Thomas, poet, b.1914
Theodore Roosevelt, 26th president, b.1858

The first requisite of a good citizen in this Republic...is that he shall be able and willing to pull his own weight.
— *Theodore Roosevelt*

CRANKY CO-WORKER DAY

☽☌♅ 7:34PM

☾
RISE 1:53AM
SET 4:12PM

☉
RISE 7:45AM
SET 6:08PM

RIGHT ENDEAVOR

RECIPES: Baked Apples

E very apple has its delicious use, beginning with its showy blossoms in the spring. (Try cutting some branches when the buds just barely appear and the snow may still be on the ground. Put them in a vase with warm water and force the blossoms out into the world.) Some apples are at their best eaten out of hand, some make first-rate pies, but even the small and puckery crab apple can be pickled to accompany roast meats or cheese dishes in the winter. Explore your local varieties and ask your orchardist about the particular qualities of his or her apples.

The following baked apple recipe works especially well with Haralson and Fireside apples.

MAPLE-GLAZED BAKED APPLES

4 tart apples	¼ cup dried cherries or raisins
4 T. maple syrup	Dark apple cider

Core the apples to about ½ inch of their bottoms. Peel each apple down to its middle. Place the apples, bottom down, in a baking dish and fill each of the apples with equal amounts of syrup and dried cherries. Fill dish with ¼-inch of cider. Bake the apples in a preheated 350° oven for about 35 to 45 minutes, depending on the apple, until they are tender but not mushy. Serve the apples warm with caramel sauce, rum whipped cream, vanilla ice cream, or just all by themselves.

From Savoring the Seasons of the Northern Heartland *by Lucia Watson (owner of the restaurant and Minneapolis treasure, Lucia's) and Beth Dooley.*

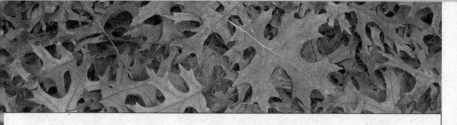

GATHERING LEAVES / *Robert Frost*

…I may load and unload | Again and again | Till I fill the whole shed, |
And what have I then? | Next to nothing for weight; |
And since they grew duller | From contact with earth, |
Next to nothing for color. | Next to nothing for use. |
But a crop is a crop, | And who's to say where | The harvest shall stop?

28

FRI · OCTOBER 28 · 2005

Qud Day, Islam
~ 1636: Harvard
Univ. founded
~ St. Jude's Day
BillGates,
founder
Microsoft,
b.1955
Erasmus,
author, b.1467
Julia Roberts,
actress, b.1967

I have always
wished that my
computer would
be as easy to
use as my tele-
phone. My wish
has come true.
I no longer know
how to use my
telephone.
– *Bjarne*
Stroustrup

♀ ☌ ♇ 9:15PM

☽
RISE 2:58AM
SET 4:29PM

☉
RISE 7:46AM
SET 6:07PM

RIGHT MEMORY

29

SAT · OCTOBER 29 · 2005

1929: Stock
Market Crash

Winona Ryder,
actress, b.1971
Richard
Dreyfuss,
actor, b.1947
James Boswell,
author, b.1740

A person who
aims at nothing
is sure to hit it.
– *Anonymous*

INTERNET
CREATED 1969

BETWEEN
STANFORD & UCLA

☽
RISE 4:03AM
SET 4:45PM

☉
RISE 7:48AM
SET 6:05PM

RIGHT CONCEPTION

30

SUN · OCTOBER 30 · 2005

Los Angelitos,
Mexico ~ Lailat
al Kadir, Islam
Grace Slick,
singer, b.1939
Emily Post,
author, b.1872
Ezra Pound,
poet, b.1885
John Adams,
2nd President,
b.1735

Never attribute
to malice what
can adequately
be explained by
stupidity.
– *Hanlon's*
Razor

DAYLIGHT
SAVINGS TIME
ENDS 2:00AM

☉ △ ♅ 1:07AM
☽ △ ♆ 8:53PM

☽
RISE 4:09AM
SET 4:02PM

☉
RISE 6:49AM
SET 5:04PM

RIGHT RESOLVE

ESSENTIAL PLACE: Fremont Troll, Seattle

It lurks in the shadows beneath Seattle's Aurora Avenue bridge, steely-eyed and imposing, yet oddly meek and inviting. It's the Fremont Troll — an 18-foot-high concrete sculpture created by four area artists, Steve Badanes, Will Martin, Donna Walter, and Ross Whitehead in 1991 and named for the artsy enclave in which it resides.

The Troll's right hand lies flat with its fingertips digging into the earth, while its left maintains a stranglehold on an actual Volkswagen Beetle. Then there's the face only a sculptor could love, with a mashed nose, unkempt hair covering one eye, and a hubcap providing the glint in the other.

Although the Fremont Troll may be relatively unknown east of the Cascades, it has inspired its own growing body of folklore and Seattleites are fond of it. In a recent poll conducted by *The Seattle Times* asking readers to name their favorite local cultural icon, the Troll finished a close second behind the Space Needle and well ahead of the touristy, mainstream Pike Place Market.

Around Halloween — or, as it's called in these parts, Trolloween, — the Fremont Troll presides over an array of offbeat festivities, like bowling into old television sets and walking to celebrate other neighborhood oddities. If you can't make it then, it's worth a photo any other time of the year.

~ *Rick Moore*
For more information on The Fremont Troll,
see www.roadsideamerica.com

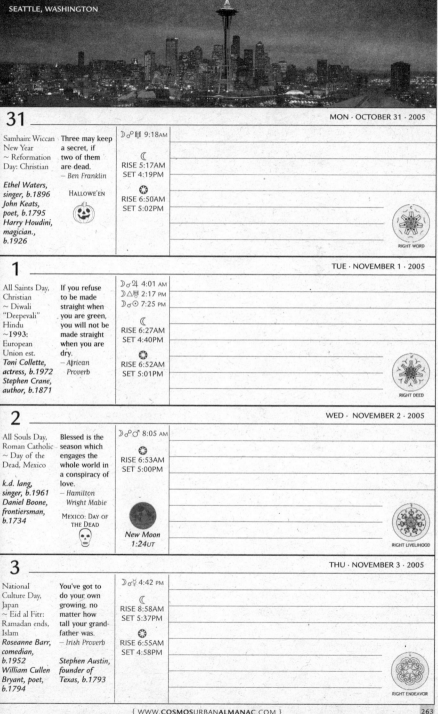

SEATTLE, WASHINGTON

31 — MON · OCTOBER 31 · 2005

Samhain: Wiccan New Year
~ Reformation Day: Christian

**Ethel Waters, singer, b.1896
John Keats, poet, b.1795
Harry Houdini, magician., b.1926**

Three may keep a secret, if two of them are dead.
— Ben Franklin

HALLOWE'EN

☽ ☌ ♅ 9:18AM

☽
RISE 5:17AM
SET 4:19PM

☀
RISE 6:50AM
SET 5:02PM

RIGHT WORD

1 — TUE · NOVEMBER 1 · 2005

All Saints Day, Christian
~ Diwali "Deepevali" Hindu
~1993: European Union est.
**Toni Collette, actress, b.1972
Stephen Crane, author, b.1871**

If you refuse to be made straight when you are green, you will not be made straight when you are dry.
— African Proverb

☽ ☌ ♃ 4:01 AM
☽ △ ♅ 2:17 PM
☽ ☌ ☉ 7:25 PM

☽
RISE 6:27AM
SET 4:40PM

☀
RISE 6:52AM
SET 5:01PM

RIGHT DEED

2 — WED · NOVEMBER 2 · 2005

All Souls Day, Roman Catholic
~ Day of the Dead, Mexico

**k.d. lang, singer, b.1961
Daniel Boone, frontiersman, b.1734**

Blessed is the season which engages the whole world in a conspiracy of love.
— Hamilton Wright Mabie

MEXICO: DAY OF THE DEAD

☽ ☌ ♂ 8:05 AM

☀
RISE 6:53AM
SET 5:00PM

New Moon
1:24UT

RIGHT LIVELIHOOD

3 — THU · NOVEMBER 3 · 2005

National Culture Day, Japan
~ Eid al Fitr: Ramadan ends, Islam
**Roseanne Barr, comedian, b.1952
William Cullen Bryant, poet, b.1794**

You've got to do your own growing, no matter how tall your grandfather was.
— Irish Proverb

Stephen Austin, founder of Texas, b.1793

☽ ☌ ☿ 4:42 PM

☽
RISE 8:58AM
SET 5:37PM

☀
RISE 6:55AM
SET 4:58PM

RIGHT ENDEAVOR

NOVEMBER

OCT 23 - NOV 21

NOV 22 - DEC 21

scorpio

sagittarius

BIRTHSTONE
Topaz

FLOWER
Chrysanthemum

Patience
BECOMES INSIGHT
Challenges: prideful, mean-spirited

The last red berries shrivel. Night comes early, dawn late. The sun is weaker. Ice is on the birdbath, frost on the car. Perhaps it is already snowing. Certainly, it's damp and raw. Rain is forecast. Now is the time to act, to begin. As Ishmael says in *Moby Dick*, "whenever it is a damp, drizzly November in my soul...I account it high time to get to sea as soon as I can." He means it's time for human deeds. Without our contribution, nothing will happen, life will have no meaning. Without our experience, the world cannot evolve, life on earth cannot become more abundant. "We have it in our power to begin the world over again," said Tom Paine. "Start by doing what's necessary; then do what's possible; and suddenly you are doing the impossible," said St. Francis of Assisi. All it takes is patience, grace, intention, and the right moment.

NOVEMBER IS
AMERICAN DIABETES MONTH · AVIATION HISTORY MONTH
EPILEPSY AWARENESS MONTH · FAMILY STORIES MONTH · I AM SO THANKFUL MONTH
LUNG CANCER AWARENESS MONTH · GEORGIA PECAN MONTH · HEALTHY SKIN MONTH
NAT'L HOSPICE MONTH · NAT'L LIFEWRITING MONTH · PEANUT BUTTER LOVERS' MONTH
VEGAN MONTH · NAT'L ALZHEIMER'S DISEASE MONTH · NAT'L AIDS AWARENESS MONTH
· NAT'L FAMILY CAREGIVERS MONTH · NAT'L FIG MONTH

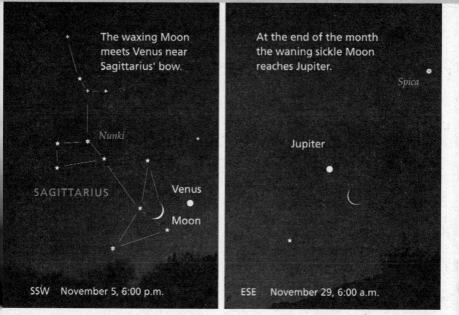

The waxing Moon meets Venus near Sagittarius' bow.

Nunki

SAGITTARIUS

Venus

Moon

SSW   November 5, 6:00 p.m.

At the end of the month the waning sickle Moon reaches Jupiter.

Spica

Jupiter

ESE   November 29, 6:00 a.m.

STARS & PLANETS FOR NOVEMBER

Venus crosses the star-rich area of Sagittarius this month, reaching its greatest eastern elongation on the 3rd. Mercury reaches its greatest elongation the same day. The waxing crescent Moon on the 6th increases this picture.

LOOK UP:

2 New Moon, 1:25 UT

3 Mercury at greatest eastern elongation
   Venus at greatest eastern elongation

5 Southern Taurid meteor shower peaks

7 Mars at opposition, rising in the east at sunset

15 Full Moon (Fog Moon), 0:58 UT

24 Mercury at inferior conjunction

LOOK OUT:

· Moss and lichens begin photosynthesizing

· Snow geese and sandhill cranes arrive
  on wintering grounds

· Snowshoe hares begin to turn white

· Moths gather around porch lights until
  hard freeze

NOVEMBER						
S	M	T	W	T	F	S
		1	2	3	4	5
6	7	8	9	10	11	12
13	14	15	16	17	18	19
20	21	22	23	24	25	26
27	28	29	30			

In science one tries to tell people, in such a way as to be understood by everyone, something that no one ever knew before. But in poetry, it's the exact opposite.
~ PAUL DIRAC

HOLIDAY: Sadie Hawkins Day, November 5

Sadie Hawkins Day, an American folk event, made its debut in Al Capp's Li'l Abner comic strip November 15, 1937. Sadie Hawkins was "the homeliest gal in the hills" who grew tired of waiting for the fellows to come a courtin'. Her father, Hekzebiah Hawkins, a prominent resident of Dogpatch, was even more worried about Sadie living at home for the rest of his life, so he decreed the first annual Sadie Hawkins Day, a foot race in which the unmarried gals pursued the town's bachelors, with matrimony the consequence. By the late 1930's the event had swept the nation and had a life of its own. *Life* magazine reported that more than 200 colleges held Sadie Hawkins Day events in 1939, only two years after its inception. It became a woman-empowering rite at high schools and college campuses, long before the modern feminist movement gained prominence. The basis of Sadie Hawkins Day is that women and girls take the initiative in inviting the man or boy of their choice out on a date, typically to a dance attended by other bachelors and their aggressive dates. When Al Capp created the event, it was not his intention to have the event occur annually on a specific date because it inhibited his freewheeling plotting. However, due to its enormous popularity and the numerous fan letters Capp received, the event became an annual event in the strip during the month of November, lasting four decades.

For more information on Sadie Hawkins, L'il Abner, and Al Capp, see http://www.lil-abner.com

GOING HOME MADLY / *Brooke Wiese*

I walked the two blocks from the subway down | the hill toward the mosque
beside the new | Islamic school to my tumble-down | tenement just off
Second Avenue… | …Sometimes this city chokes me up with all | her
jagged beauty, and sometimes I am made new, | like tonight, when I walked
back up the hill | and 'round the block again because of you.

---

4   FRI · NOVEMBER 4 · 2005

Mischief Night,
England
~ 1946:
UNESCO
founded
~ 1922: King
Tut's tomb
found

*Sean "Puffy"
Combs, rapper,
b.1969*

Dreams are the
touchstones of
our character.
— *H.D. Thoreau*

*Walter Cronkite,
Jr., journalist,
b.1916
Will Rogers,
humorist,
b.1879*

☽△♄ 3:19 AM
☽☌♇ 11:58 PM

☾
RISE 10:14AM
SET 6:21PM

☼
RISE 6:56AM
SET 4:57PM

RIGHT MEMORY

---

5   SAT · NOVEMBER 5 · 2005

Guy Fawkes
Day, England
~ Sadie Hawkins
Day: girls invite
the boys

*Sam Shepard,
actor, play-
wright, b.1943
Eugene V. Debs,
socialist, b.1855*

The supreme
happiness in
life is the
conviction that
we are loved.
— *Victor Hugo*

*Will Durant,
author, histo-
rian, b.1885
Art Garfunkel,
singer, b.1941*

☽☌♀ 1:03 PM

☾
RISE 11:23AM
SET 7:18PM

☼
RISE 6:57AM
SET 4:56PM

RIGHT CONCEPTION

---

6   SUN · NOVEMBER 6 · 2005

St. Leonard's
Day, Roman
Catholic
~ Gustavus
Adolphus Day;
Swedish king
killed in 1632

*John P. Sousa,
composer,
b.1854*

One thing you
can't recycle is
wasted time.
— *Anonymous*

*Adolphe Sax,
saxophone
inventor,
b.1814
James Naismith,
basketball
creator, b.1861*

☽△♂ 2:18 PM

☾
RISE 12:21PM
SET 8:27PM

☼
RISE 6:59AM
SET 4:54PM

RIGHT RESOLVE

BIRTHDAY: Joni MItchell, November 7, 1943

BIG YELLOW TAXI
...Don't it always seem to go
That you don't know what you've got
'Til it's gone
They paved paradise
To put up a parking lot...

~ Joni Mitchell

Further information on Joni Mitchell,
see www.jonimitchell.com

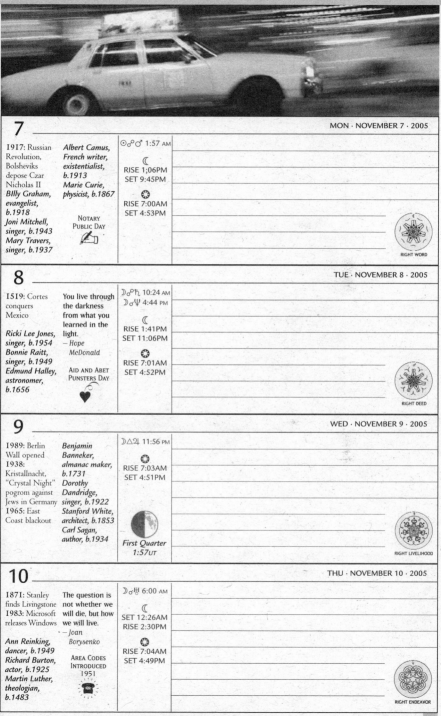

7 MON · NOVEMBER 7 · 2005

1917: Russian Revolution, Bolsheviks depose Czar Nicholas II
BIlly Graham, evangelist, b.1918
Joni Mitchell, singer, b.1943
Mary Travers, singer, b.1937

Albert Camus, French writer, existentialist, b.1913
Marie Curie, physicist, b.1867

NOTARY PUBLIC DAY

☉ ☌ ♂ 1:57 AM

☽ RISE 1:06PM
SET 9:45PM

✷ RISE 7:00AM
SET 4:53PM

RIGHT WORD

8 TUE · NOVEMBER 8 · 2005

1519: Cortes conquers Mexico

Ricki Lee Jones, singer, b.1954
Bonnie Raitt, singer, b.1949
Edmund Halley, astronomer, b.1656

You live through the darkness from what you learned in the light.
– Hope McDonald

AID AND ABET PUNSTERS DAY

☽ ☌ ♄ 10:24 AM
☽ ☌ ♆ 4:44 PM

☽ RISE 1:41PM
SET 11:06PM

✷ RISE 7:01AM
SET 4:52PM

RIGHT DEED

9 WED · NOVEMBER 9 · 2005

1989: Berlin Wall opened
1938: Kristallnacht, "Crystal Night" pogrom against Jews in Germany
1965: East Coast blackout

Benjamin Banneker, almanac maker, b.1731
Dorothy Dandridge, singer, b.1922
Stanford White, architect, b.1853
Carl Sagan, author, b.1934

☽ △ ♃ 11:56 PM

✷ RISE 7:03AM
SET 4:51PM

First Quarter
1:57 UT

RIGHT LIVELIHOOD

10 THU · NOVEMBER 10 · 2005

1871: Stanley finds Livingstone
1983: Microsoft releases Windows

Ann Reinking, dancer, b.1949
Richard Burton, actor, b.1925
Martin Luther, theologian, b.1483

The question is not whether we will die, but how we will live.
– Joan Borysenko

AREA CODES INTRODUCED 1951

☽ ☌ ♅ 6:00 AM

☽ SET 12:26AM
RISE 2:30PM

✷ RISE 7:04AM
SET 4:49PM

RIGHT ENDEAVOR

HOLIDAY: Martinmas/Veterans Day/Armistice Day, Nov. 11

St. Martin of Tours, France, was a popular bishop in the Middle Ages. The English shortened the name of his feast day from Martin's Mass to Martinmas, and since the day fell at a time when people wanted to celebrate harvesting and wine making, it became a day for feasting and celebration. A goose was often roasted for the occasion. November 11 became Armistice Day in 1918 to mark the armistice between the Allies and the Central Powers that ended World War I. The United States, England, and France celebrated the day jubilantly; many were sure there'd never be another war.

Now in England, France, and Canada, in particular, the day commemorates those who died in both World War I and II. In 1954, the United States changed the day to Veterans' Day, to commemorate those who have served in the armed forces during all the country's wars.

From The Book of Holidays Around the World.

FIRE FEAST / *Patricia Monaghan*

In the middle of the city the men | feel sudden tenderness above the ears… |
…Only a few rise in the moonlight, | heads full of antlers, to seek |
the women dancing on the leaves. | Only a few men know the power of stags |
dancing through them as they are ridden | by the eager women of the night…

---

11 · FRI · NOVEMBER 11 · 2005

Martinmas, Canada, U.K., France, U.S.
~ **1918**: Armistice Day, World War I ends
Jonathan Winters, comedian, b.1925
Kurt Vonnegut Jr., author, b.1922

Good friends, good books and a sleepy conscience: this is the ideal life.
— *Mark Twain*

VETERANS DAY

☽△☉ 2:44 AM
☾
SET 1:45AM
RISE 2:50PM
☀
RISE 7:06AM
SET 4:48PM

RIGHT MEMORY

---

12 · SAT · NOVEMBER 12 · 2005

Birth of Baha'u'llah, Baha'i

Nadia Comaneci, gymnast, b.1961
Grace Kelly, actress, b.1929
Auguste Rodin, French sculptor, b.1840

The Lord is my light, and my salvation; whom shall I fear?
— *Psalm 27*

Elizabeth Cady Stanton, suffragist, b.1815

☽△☿ 3:52 PM
☽△♄ 4:36 PM
☾
SET 3:01AM
RISE 3:09PM
☀
RISE 7:07AM
SET 4:47PM

RIGHT CONCEPTION

---

13 · SUN · NOVEMBER 13 · 2005

1927: Holland Tunnel opened, New York City

Whoopi Goldberg, actress, b.1949
Louis Brandeis, jurist, b.1856
Robert Louis Stevenson, author, b.1850

The most wasted day of all is that during which we have not laughed.
— *Sebastian Chamfort*

WORLD KINDNESS DAY

☽△♇ 1:07 PM
☾
SET 4:18AM
RISE 3:28PM
☀
RISE 7:08AM
SET 4:46PM

RIGHT RESOLVE

LIVING URBAN TREASURE: Portland's Earl Blumenauer

As far as political name-calling goes, Earl Blumenauer has been on the receiving end of some pretty benign taunts. "Mr. Bicycle" and "Mr. Livability" are tags just about anyone could live with.

And they're well deserved. Blumenauer has spent three decades of political life pedaling a vision of cleaner, safer, and more energy-efficient communities. He started in his hometown of Portland, Oregon, as a state representative and later as county commissioner and the city's Commissioner of Public Works. He worked to provide city residents with a full range of transportation options including bicycle, light rail, and trolley, and is credited for helping Portland attain its status as one of the America's most livable cities.

Earl Blumenauer in Portland

"Mr. Bicycle" and "Mr. Livability" are tags just about anyone could live with.

In 1996, Blumenauer took his ideals and, perhaps more importantly, his bicycle, with him to Capitol Hill as Oregon's Third District Congressman. He reached across the aisle to organize the Congressional Bicycle Caucus, a "bike-partisan" club centered around the virtues of two-wheel travel.

He hasn't coasted from there.

While biking up, down, and around the Hill — with cinched pants leg and signature bow tie — Blumenauer has continued to push policies of smart growth and community health. He introduced the Bicycle Commuter Act to give bicyclists the same transportation benefits offered by some employers for parking plans or vanpooling. He proposed a $6.2 million "Conserve by Bike Energy" amendment that would establish pilot projects across the country to test energy conservation through bicycling. And he has consulted with dozens of communities on ways to improve transportation, land use, and the environment.

Blumenauer has picked up his share of accolades, including 1999 Legislator of the Year from the American Planning Association and the 2001 National Bicycle Advocacy Award from the League of American Bicyclists.

Ever the pedal-power spokesperson, he's still soliciting fellow Congressional members to join the tripartisan bike caucus, which has 82 members (60 Democrats, 21 Republicans, and 1 Independent) at last count.

~ *Rick Moore*

For more information on Earl Blumenauer, see blumenauer.house.gov

PORTLAND, OREGON

14   MON · NOVEMBER 14 · 2005

1666: First blood transfusion

Prince Charles, Prince of Wales, b.1948
Aaron Copeland, composer, b.1900
Claude Monet, painter, b.1840

Perfect as the wing of a bird may be, it will never enable the bird to fly if unsupported by the air. Facts are the air of science. Without them a man of science can never rise.
— Ivan Pavlov

☽ ☌ ♃ 8:23 AM
☽ △ ♀ 5:06 PM
☽ ☌ ♂ 10:43 PM

☾
SET 5:34AM
RISE 3:51PM

☀
RISE 7:10AM
SET 4:45PM

RIGHT WORD

15   TUE · NOVEMBER 15 · 2005

Shichi-Go-San: "seven-five-three", Japan
~ **1943:** Gypsies condemned by Himmler, up to 500,000 killed

Petula Clark, singer, b.1932
Georgia O'Keefe, painter, b.1887

There is no terror in the bang, only in the anticipation of it.
— Alfred Hitchcock

AMERICA RECYCLES DAY

☽ ☌ ☉ 6:58 PM

☾
SET 6:52AM
RISE 4:17PM

☀
RISE 7:11AM
SET 4:44PM

RIGHT DEED

16   WED · NOVEMBER 16 · 2005

1885: Louis Riel hanged, led North West Rebellion, Manitoba, CA

Lisa Bonet, actress, b.1967
William Handy, composer, b.1873

Money, n.— A blessing that is of no advantage to us excepting when we part with it. An evidence of culture and a passport to polite society.
— Ambrose Bierce

☀
RISE 7:12AM
SET 4:43PM

Full Moon
00:57UT

RIGHT LIVELIHOOD

17   THU · NOVEMBER 17 · 2005

Lauren Hutton, actress, b.1944
Danny DeVito, actor, b.1944
Lorne Michaels, producer, b.1944
August Mobius, astronomer, "Mobius Strip," b.1790

For what is a poem but a hazardous attempt at self-understanding: it is the deepest part of autobiography.
— Robert Penn Warren

GREAT AMERICAN SMOKEOUT DAY

☽ ☌ ☿ 12:43 AM
☽ △ ♆ 9:29 AM
♀ △ ♂ 10:23 AM

☾
SET 9:20AM
RISE 5:31PM

☀
RISE 7:14AM
SET 4:42PM

RIGHT ENDEAVOR

PROCLAMATION: The Gettysburg Address, Nov. 19, 1863

Fourscore and seven years ago our fathers brought forth on this continent a new nation, conceived in liberty and dedicated to the proposition that all men are created equal.

Now we are engaged in a great civil war, testing whether that nation or any nation so conceived and so dedicated can long endure. We are met on a great battle-field of that war. We have come to dedicate a portion of it as a final resting place for those who died here that the nation might live. This we may, in all propriety do. But in a larger sense, we cannot dedicate, we cannot consecrate, we cannot hallow this ground. The brave men, living and dead who struggled here have hallowed it far above our poor power to add or detract. The world will little note nor long remember what we say here, but it can never forget what they did here. It is rather for us the living, to be here dedicated to the great task remaining before us—that from these honored dead we take increased devotion to that cause for which they here gave

the last full measure of devotion—that we here highly resolve that these dead shall not have died in vain, that this nation shall have a new birth of freedom, and that government of the people, by the people, for the people shall not perish from the earth.

~ *Abraham Lincoln*

For more information on the Gettysburg Address, see www.loc.gov/exhibits/gadd/

MY NOVEMBER GUEST/*Robert Frost*

My Sorrow, when she's here with me, | Thinks these dark days of autumn rain | Are beautiful as days can be; | She loves the bare, the withered tree; | She walks the sodden pasture lane… | Not yesterday I learned to know | The love of bare November days | Before the coming of the snow, | But it were vain to tell her so, | And they are better for her praise.

---

18   FRI · NOVEMBER 18 · 2005

1978: Jonestown Massacre, more than 900 followers committed mass suicide

Margaret Atwood, author, b.1939
Alan Shepard, astronaut, b.1923

If you are out to describe the truth, leave elegance to the tailor.
— Albert Einstein

Louis Daguerre, inventor, b.1789
Mickey Mouse, b.1928

☽ ☌ ♇ 1:02 AM
☽ △ ♃ 11:36 PM

☾
SET 10:24AM
RISE 6:21PM

☼
RISE 7:15AM
SET 4:41PM

RIGHT MEMORY

---

19   SAT · NOVEMBER 19 · 2005

1863: Lincoln's Gettysburg Address
~ 1493: Puerto Rico Discovery Day

Ted Turner, media mogul, b.1938
Jodie Foster, actress, b.1962

Poetry is the revelation of a feeling that the poet believes to be interior and personal but which the reader recognizes as his own.
— Salvatore Quasimodo

☽ △ ♅ 2:48 AM
☽ ☌ ♀ 3:48 PM

☾
SET 11:17AM
RISE 7:20PM

☼
RISE 7:16AM
SET 4:40PM

RIGHT CONCEPTION

---

20   SUN · NOVEMBER 20 · 2005

Christ the King, Christian
~ 1910: Mexico Revolution Day

Robert F. Kennedy, senator, b.1925
Edwin Hubble, American astronomer, b.1889

He who bears the interests of humanity in his breast, that man is blessed.
— Johann Pestalozzi

NAME YOUR PC DAY

☽ △ ☉ 10:03 PM

☾
SET 11:58AM
RISE 8:25PM

☼
RISE 7:18AM
SET 4:40PM

RIGHT RESOLVE

HOLIDAY: Thanksgiving, November 24

ANYONE CAN DO IT

Looking at Your Empty Plate:
    My plate, empty now,
    will soon be filled
    with precious food.

Looking at Your Full Plate:
    In this food,
    I see clearly the presence
    of the entire universe
    supporting my existence.

Contemplating Your Food:
    This plate of food,
    so fragrant and appetizing,
    also contains much suffering.

Beginning to Eat:
    With the first taste, I promise
    to offer joy.
    With the second, I promise to
    help relieve
    the suffering of others.

With the third, I promise to
see other's joy
as my own.
With the fourth, I promise to
learn the way
of non-attachment and
equanimity.

Finishing Your Meal:
    The plate is empty.
    My hunger is satisfied.
    I vow to live
    for the benefit of all beings.

Washing the Dishes:
    Washing the dishes
    is like bathing a baby Buddha.
    The profane is the sacred.
    Everyday mind is Buddha's
    mind.

~ Thich Nhat Hanh

21 — MON · NOVEMBER 21 · 2005

1783: Man's first flight in a balloon
1995: Dow Jones tops 5000 for the first time

Henry Purcell, composer, d.1695
Voltaire, author, b.1694

Tears are not arguments.
— Machado de Assis

WORLD HELLO DAY

Goldie Hawn, actress, b.1945
Harpo Marx, comedian, b.1888

☽△☿ 12:39 PM
☽♂♄ 10:50 PM

☾
SET 12:30PM
RISE 9:32PM

☀
RISE 7:19AM
SET 4:39PM

RIGHT WORD

22 — TUE · NOVEMBER 22 · 2005

1963: John F. Kennedy assassinated ~ 1859: On The Origin Of Species published, Charles Darwin

Charles DeGaulle, French leader, b.1890
George Eliot, author, b.1819

For all sad words of tongue and pen, the saddest are these, "It might have been."
— John Whittier

Hoagie Carmichael, composer, b.1899

☽♂♆ 6:19 AM
☽△♇ 11:25 PM

☾
SET 12:55PM
RISE 10:38PM

☀
RISE 7:20AM
SET 4:38PM

RIGHT DEED

23 — WED · NOVEMBER 23 · 2005

Labor Thanksgiving Day, Japan
~ 1936: Life magazine premiered

Boris Karloff, actor, b.1887
Billy The Kid, outlaw, b.1859

Only when he has ceased to need things can a man truly be his own master and so really exist.
— Anwar Sadat

☀
RISE 7:21AM
SET 4:37PM

Last Quarter
22:11UT

RIGHT LIVELIHOOD

24 — THU · NOVEMBER 24 · 2005

Scott Joplin, composer, b.1868
Henri Toulouse-Lautrec, painter, b.1864
Benedict de Spinoza, philosopher, b.1632

Worries go down better with soup than without.
— Jewish Proverb

THANKSGIVING DAY

☽♂♅ 2:37 AM
☽△♂ 8:44 AM
☉♂☿ 9:43 AM

☾
SET 1:34PM

☀
RISE 7:23AM
SET 4:37PM

RIGHT ENDEAVOR

URBAN SANCTUARY: Perimeter Trail, Vancouver

I came to British Columbia from Hollywood where I had learned to survive the lunatic egos by hiking in Will Rogers State Park. The Vancouver map shows scores of such urban getaways, the most alluring of which are found in the Coast Mountain range on the city's northern border. Located in these mag- 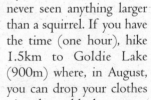 nificent mountains are three enormous Provincial Parks: all reachable by car, bicycle, or bus.

If you choose Mount Seymour (3,508 hectares), drive the 15km from downtown, through Stanley Park, over the majestic Lion's Gate Bridge, and east to the gates of the park. Pull into the Indian Arm lookout where you can see past the stunning fjord-like inlet south to the U.S. and Mt. Baker.

Here begins Perimeter Trail, which has become my chapel, my gym, and my steady friend. I hike alone and rarely see another person. Ancient, towering Douglas firs protect me while rushing glacial streams mark my progress. Bear and cougar roam freely in this forest, but I've never seen anything larger than a squirrel. If you have the time (one hour), hike 1.5km to Goldie Lake (900m) where, in August, you can drop your clothes and jump into her cold, clean water.

~ *Anne Simonet*

Further information about the Perimeter Trail in Vancouver, BC is available at www.out-there.com/seymour.htm

PEREGRINE FALCON, NEW YORK CITY/*Robert Cording*

…the bird rolled and plunged, | then swerved to a halt, wings hovering. |
You chided yourself: this is how the gods | come to deliver a message or a
taunt, | and, for a moment, the falcon seemed to wait | for your response.
Then it was gone…

---

25   FRI · NOVEMBER 25 · 2005

St. Catherine's
Day, Canada,
France
*Amy Grant,
singer, b.1960*
*Andrew
Carnegie,
financier,
b.1835*
*Joe DiMaggio,
baseball player,
b.1914*

Give a man a
fish and you
feed him for a
day. Teach a
man to fish and
you feed him
for a lifetime.
— *Chinese
Proverb*

YOU'RE
WELCOMEGIVING
DAY

☽△♀ 1:06 AM

☾
RISE 12:48AM
SET 1:50PM

☀
RISE 7:24AM
SET 4:36PM

RIGHT MEMORY

---

26   SAT · NOVEMBER 26 · 2005

Day of
Covenant, Baha'i

*Tina Turner,
singer, b.1938*
*Sojourner
Truth, former
slave, d.1883*
*John Harvard,
Harvard Univ.
founder, b.1607*

The real power
behind whatever
success I have
now was some-
thing I found
within myself...
a little piece of
God just
waiting to be
discovered.
— *Tina Turner*

☾
RISE 1:53AM
SET 2:06PM

☀
RISE 7:25AM
SET 4:35PM

RIGHT CONCEPTION

---

27   SUN · NOVEMBER 27 · 2005

*Gail Sheehy,
author, b.1937*
*Bruce Lee,
actor, b.1940*
*Jimi Hendrix,
guitarist,
b.1942*
*James Agee,
poet, b.1909*

Spoon feeding
in the long run
teaches us
nothing but the
shape of the
spoon.
— *E.M. Forster*

ADVENT
(CHRISTIAN)
✴
ALSO DEC. 4, 11,18

♃△♅ 5:56 AM
☽△♆ 6:23 AM

☾
RISE 2:59AM
SET 2:23PM

☀
RISE 7:26AM
SET 4:35PM

RIGHT RESOLVE

BIRTHDAY: Mark Twain, November 30, 1835

Celebrated American author, Mark Twain, whose books include, The Adventures of Tom Sawyer, The Adventures of Huckleberry Finn, *and* The Prince and the Pauper, *was born November 30, 1835, in Florida, Missouri. Twain is quoted as saying, "I came in with Halley's Comet in 1935. It is coming again next year, and I expect to go out with it." He did. Twain died at Redding, Connecticut, April 21, 1910 (just one day after Halley's Comet's perihelion).*

– Chase's 2004 Calendar of Events

A banker is a fellow who lends you his umbrella when the sun is shining, but wants it back the minute it begins to rain.

A lie can travel halfway around the world while the truth is putting on its shoes.

A man cannot be comfortable without his own approval.

Always acknowledge a fault. This will throw those in authority off their guard and give you an opportunity to commit more.

Always do right. This will gratify some people and astonish the rest.

Don't go around saying the world owes you a living. The world owes you nothing. It was here first.

Get your facts first, and then you can distort them as much as you please.

Barring that natural expression of villainy which we all have, the man looked honest enough.

Be careful about reading health books. You may die of a misprint.

Clothes make the man. Naked people have little or no influence on society.

Honesty is the best policy – when there is money in it.

Do something every day that you don't want to do; this is the golden rule for acquiring the habit of doing your duty without pain.

An Englishman is a person who does things because they have been done before. An American is a person who does things because they haven't been done before.

Don't part with your illusions. When they are gone you may still exist, but you have ceased to live.

Fiction is obliged to stick to possibilities. Truth isn't.

Habit is habit and not to be flung out of the window by any man, but coaxed downstairs a step at a time.

Grief can take care of itself, but to get the full value of a joy you must have somebody to divide it with.

I have never let my schooling interfere with my education.

For more information on Mark Twain, see www.pbs.org/marktwain/

Mark Twain (Samuel Clemens)

28 — MON · NOVEMBER 28 · 2005

Berry Gordy, Jr., cofounder of Motown, b.1929
John Bunyan, author, b.1628
William Blake, poet, b.1757
Jon Stewart, comedian, b.1962

I believe that a scientist looking at nonscientific problems is just as dumb as the next guy.
— *Richard Feynman*

☽△♅ 11:18 PM
☽☌♃ 11:56 PM

☾
RISE 4:07AM
SET 2:42PM

☉
RISE 7:28AM
SET 4:34PM

RIGHT WORD

29 — TUE · NOVEMBER 29 · 2005

1989: Czechoslovakia ends communist rule
Joel Coen, filmmaker, b.1954
Madeline L'Engle, author, b.1918
C.S. Lewis, author, b.1878
Louisa May Alcott, author, b.1832

He who would travel happily must travel light.
— *Antoine de Saint-Exupéry*

☽☌♂ 3:10 AM

☾
RISE 5:20AM
SET 3:05PM

☉
RISE 7:29AM
SET 4:34PM

RIGHT DEED

30 — WED · NOVEMBER 30 · 2005

St. Andrew's Day, Christian

Gordon Parks, photographer, b.1912
Abbie Hoffman, activist, b.1936
Winston Churchill, statesman, b.1874

I have learned not to worry about love; but to honor its coming with all my heart.
— *Alice Walker*

COMPUTER SECURITY DAY

Mark Twain, author, b.1835

☾
RISE 6:36AM
SET 3:34PM

☉
RISE 7:30AM
SET 4:33PM

RIGHT LIVELIHOOD

1 — THU · DECEMBER 1 · 2005

1955: Rosa Parks arrested
1891: Basketball created

Lou Rawls, singer, b.1935
Bette Midler, singer, b.1945
Richard Pryor, comedian, b.1940

Love fails, only when we fail to love.
— *J. Franklin*

Woody Allen, actor, filmmaker, b.1935

WORLD AIDS DAY

☽☌☉ 9:01 AM
☽△♄ 11:56 AM

☉
RISE 7:31AM
SET 4:33PM

New Moon
15:01 UT

RIGHT ENDEAVOR

DECEMBER

NOV 22 - DEC 21

DEC 22 - JAN 19

sagittarius

capricorn

BIRTHSTONE
Lapis Lazuli

FLOWER
Narcissi

Control of Speech

BECOMES FEELING FOR TRUTH
*Challenges: gossip, moralizing,
dogmatism, subjectivity of opinion*

*S*ilence slips peacefully over the black-and-white world. The wind moans. The Earth is hard as iron. Mist and cold penetrate to the bone. The days grow shorter, the snowfalls heavier. Bare trees and hunched figures in overcoats and heavy jackets dot the streets. But inside it is warm, and the kitchen windows are steamed up. People gather in expectation of the rebirth of the light. There is almost the sense that the Sun will break forth again from the interior of the Earth – or from within our own souls. Christmas and Hanukkah, among other celebrations, hold forth the promise that, by our dedication and self-sacrifice a new green world of meaning, love, and compassion can be born. At the solstice, the heavens show us the rebirth of the light, *Dies Natalis Solis Invicti* – the Birthday of the Unconquerable Sun. May the power of the world's being grow strong! May life's power to act blossom forth! May the past bear what is to come!

DECEMBER IS

BINGO'S BIRTHDAY MONTH · COOKIE CUTTER MONTH · NATIONAL DRUNK DRIVING
PREVENTION MONTH · NATIONAL STRESS-FREE FAMILY HOLIDAYS MONTH
SAFE TOYS AND GIFTS MONTH · UNIVERSAL HUMAN RIGHTS MONTH
UNITED NATIONS WORLD AIDS AWARENESS MONTH · JINGLEBELLS MONTH

December 10, 6:45 a.m.   SE

around 7:00 a.m.   S

Jupiter

Mercury

Jupiter

Spica

12/25

12/26

12/27

The Moon and Jupiter
meet around Christmas

STARS & PLANETS FOR DECEMBER

Though Mercury is visible from the 1st of December, the best viewing conditions are on 10th. Jupiter and Saturn will be standing together in the morning sky. Venus is visible in the evening sky. It reaches the highest position from the horizon on the 4th. All the planets are present in the night sky this year, making this December's starlight especially bright.

LOOK FOR:

1 New Moon, 15:01 UT
12 Mercury at greatest western elongation
13 Geminid meteor shower peaks
15 Full Moon (Wolf Moon), 16:16 UT
21 Winter solstice, 21:19 UT
31 New Moon

LOOK UP:

· Thousands of monarch butterflies gather in eucalyptus groves
· Male mule deer sharpen their antlers
· Lake ice cracks and booms as it shifts
· Roseate spoonbills are nesting

DECEMBER						
S	M	T	W	T	F	S
				1	2	3
4	5	6	7	8	9	10
11	12	13	14	15	16	17
18	19	20	21	22	23	24
25	26	27	28	29	30	31

Antisthenes says that in a certain faraway land the cold is so intense that words freeze as soon as they are uttered, and after some time then thaw and become audible, so that words spoken in winter go unheard until the next summer
~ PLUTARCH

ESSENTIAL PLACE: The Las Vegas Strip, Las Vegas

Sure it's gaudy. But at night— when all those neon lights and choreographed fountains can make you feel as though you're inside your favorite childhood pin-ball machine – it's not hard to understand why the Las Vegas strip is a designated National Scenic Byway. Where else in America, after all, can you pass by a medieval castle, ancient Egypt, New York skyscrapers, spewing volca-noes, and a Venetian palace in one easily navigated, 7½ mile stretch? Purists may rightly sniff that these landmarks are yet another dispiriting example of the Disneyfication of American culture. But we think Las Vegas's celebration of the ersatz is precisely what makes it unique. And while compulsive shoppers, drunken grooms, and gambling addicts aren't exactly family fare, it's impossible to deny that all this crazy impul-sivity isn't infectious. If you don't believe us, take a posi-tion at the top of the "Eiffel Tower" as the fountains begin their majestic evening routines. We'll be darned if you and the rest of the 31 million annual visitors don't shout "oo-la-la" into the dry night air as the jewel of the dessert spreads out like a pirate's plunder before you.

~ *Elizabeth Larsen*

For more information about Las Vegas, see
www.ci.las-vegas.nv.us/

LAS VEGAS, NEVADA

MY WAY / *Revaux and Claude François (translated by Paul Anka)*

…I've loved, I've laughed and cried… | To think I did all that; | And may I say — not in a shy way, | "No, oh no not me, | I did it my way"…

---

2   FRI · DECEMBER 2 · 2005

1823: Monroe Doctrine declared
1859: John Brown executed

Lucy Liu, actress, b.1967
Britney Spears, singer, b.1981
George Seurat, painter, b.1859

Blow, blow, thou winter wind Thou art not so unkind, As man's ingratitude.
— *William Shakespeare*

Maria Callas, singer, b.1923

☽ ☌ ♇ 9:17 AM

☾ RISE 9:08AM SET 5:07PM

✸ RISE 7:32AM SET 4:33PM

RIGHT MEMORY

---

3   SAT · DECEMBER 3 · 2005

1984: Bhopal poison gas disaster

Sven Nykvist, cinematographer, b.1922
Carlos Montoya, guitarist, b.1903
Joseph Conrad, author, b.1857

When you live in Texas, every single time you see snow it's magical.
— *Pamela Ribon*

Darryl Hannah, actress, b.1961
Julianne Moore, actress, b.1961

⊙△♄ 12:41 AM
☽△♂ 9:56 AM

☾ RISE 10:13AM SET 6:14PM

✸ RISE 7:33AM SET 4:32PM

RIGHT CONCEPTION

---

4   SUN · DECEMBER 4 · 2005

1867: National Grange founded

Cassandra Wilson, singer, b.1955
Thomas Carlyle, essayist, b.1795
Samuel Butler, author, b.1835
Marisa Tomei, actress, b.1964

The tendinous part of the mind… is more developed in winter; the fleshy, in summer…Winter had given the bone and sinew to literature, summer the tissues and blood.
— *J Burroughs*

☽ ☌ ♀ 12:54 PM
♂ ☍ ♃ 6:44 PM

☾ RISE 11:04AM SET 7:32PM

✸ RISE 7:35AM SET 4:32PM

RIGHT RESOLVE

BIRTHDAY: James Thurber, December 8, 1894

*"All right, have it your way—
you heard a seal bark!"*

All human beings should try to learn before they die what they are running from, and to, and why.

He knows all about art, but he doesn't know what he likes.

I hate women because they always know where things are.

I used to wake up at 4 A.M. and start sneezing, sometimes for five hours. I tried to find out what sort of allergy I had but finally came to the conclusion that it must be an allergy to consciousness.

Nowadays men lead lives of noisy desperation.

The only rules comedy can tolerate are those of taste, and the only limitations those of libel.

It is better to know some of the questions than all of the answers.

Let us not look back to the past with anger, nor towards the future with fear, but look around with awareness.

You can fool too many of the people too much of the time.

The dog has seldom been successful in pulling man up to its level of sagacity, but man has frequently dragged the dog down to his.

James Thurber

I loathe the expression "What makes him tick." It is the American mind, looking for simple and singular solution, that uses the foolish expression. A person not only ticks, he also chimes and strikes the hour, falls and breaks and has to be put together again, and sometimes stops like an electric clock in a thunderstorm.

For more information on James Thurber, see www.thurberhouse.org/

5

1955: AFL-CIO founded

Phyllis Wheatley, poet, d.1784
Jose Carreras, singer, b.1946
Calvin Trillin, author, b.1935
Walt Disney, animator, b.1901

Minds are like parachutes; they work best when open.
— Thomas Dewar

Little Richard, singer, b.1935
Frankie Muniz, actor, b.1985

☽♂♄ 4:07 PM
☽♂♆ 11:01 PM

☾
RISE 11:42AM
SET 8:54PM

☀
RISE 7:36AM
SET 4:32PM

RIGHT WORD

6

St. Nicholas Day, Europe
~ 1865: 13th Amendment ratified, slavery abolished

To him who is in fear, everything rustles.
— Sophocles

Dave Brubeck, jazz musician, b.1920
Alfred Eisenstaedt, photographer, b.1898
Ira Gershwin, lyricist, b.1896
Macy Gray, singer, b.1969

☾
RISE 12:12PM
SET 10:16PM

☀
RISE 7:37AM
SET 4:32PM

RIGHT DEED

7

1941: Japanese attack Pearl Harbor

Eli Wallach, actor, b.1915
Harry Chapin, singer, b.1942
Willa Cather, author, b.1873

He who knows others is wise. He who knows himself is enlightened.
— Anonymous

☽♂♅ 11:40 PM
☽△♃ 2:56 PM

☾
RISE 12:35PM
SET 11:35PM

☀
RISE 7:38AM
SET 4:32PM

RIGHT LIVELIHOOD

8

Feast of the Immaculate Conception, Roman Catholic ~ Bodhi Day, Buddhist Rohatsu

Do or do not. There is no try.
— Yoda

Mary Woronov, actress, b.1943
James Thurber, author, b.1894
Diego Rivera, painter, b.1886
Jim Morrison, singer, b.1943

☽△☿ 9:17 PM

☀
RISE 7:39AM
SET 4:32PM

First Quarter
9:36UT

RIGHT ENDEAVOR

BIRTHDAY: Emily Dickinson, December 10, 1830

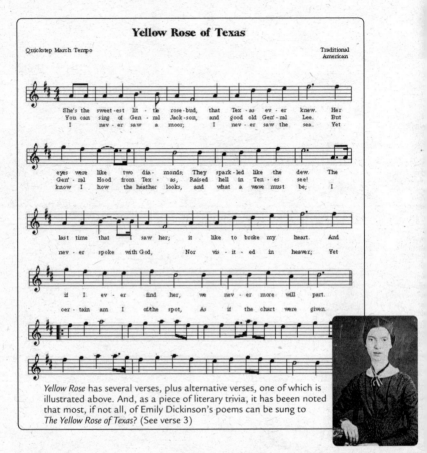

Yellow Rose of Texas

Quickstep March Tempo

Traditional American

She's the sweet-est lit-tle rose-bud, that Tex-as ev-er knew. Her
You can sing of Gen'-ral Jack-son, and good old Gen'-ral Lee. But
I nev-er saw a moor; I nev-er saw the sea. Yet

eyes were like two dia-monds; They spark-led like the dew. The
Gen'-ral Hood from Tex-as, Raised hell in Ten-es see! I
know I how the heather looks, and what a wave must be; I

last time that I saw her; it like to broke my heart. And
nev-er spoke with God, Nor vis-it-ed in heaven; Yet

if I ev-er find her, we nev-er more will part.
cer-tain am I of the spot, As if the chart were given.

Yellow Rose has several verses, plus alternative verses, one of which is illustrated above. And, as a piece of literary trivia, it has beeen noted that most, if not all, of Emily Dickinson's poems can be sung to *The Yellow Rose of Texas*? (See verse 3)

One of America's greatest poets, Emily Dickinson was born December 10, 1830, at Amherst, Massachusetts. She was reclusive, mysterious, and frail in health. Seven of her poems were published during her life, but after her death, her sister, Lavinia, discovered almost 2,000 more poems written on the backs of envelopes and other scraps of paper locked in Emily's bureau. They were published gradually over 50 years, beginning in 1890. Emily died May 15, 1886. The little-known Emily Dickinson who was born, lived, and died in Amherst now is recognized as one of the most original poets of the English-speaking world.

From Chase's 2004 Calendar of Events
For more information about Emily Dickinson, see www.emilydickinson.org

PIGEONS/*Baron Wormser*

Even naturalists are uninterested in pigeons | Who loiter everywhere in the
cities, | Birds who have sullied themselves | By learning to live with man. |
They prosper amid degradation; | They are solicitous and indifferent,
unanxious; | They feel they will live another day… | …Unconcerned
with agony, | Grinding corn, investigating the wonders of gum.

9
FRI · DECEMBER 9 · 2005

Joan Arma-
trading, singer,
b.1950
Emmett Kelly,
clown, b.1898
John Milton,
poet, b.1608
Jean de Brunhoff,
author, b.1899
Redd Foxx,
comedian,
b.1922

I can believe
anything
provided it is
incredible.
— Oscar Wilde

☽△♄ 10:13 PM

☾
SET 12:51AM
RISE 1:14PM

☀
RISE 7:40AM
SET 4:32PM

RIGHT MEMORY

10
SAT · DECEMBER 10 · 2005

since 1901:
Nobel Prize
Ceremony, Oslo
and Stockholm
Alfred Nobel,
b.1896
Red Cloud,
Dakota chief,
b.1909
Emily Dickinson,
poet, b.1830

*Thomas Gallaudet
School for the
Deaf, founder,
b.1787*

There's a certain
Slant of light,
Winter Afternoon
— That oppresses,
like the Heft Of
Cathedral Tunes.
— Emily
Dickenson

☽△♇ 9:18 PM

☾
SET 2:06AM
RISE 1:33PM

☀
RISE 7:40AM
SET 4:32PM

RIGHT CONCEPTION

11
SUN · DECEMBER 11 · 2005

1946: UNICEF
founded
1936: Edward
VIII abdicates
to marry Wallis
Simpson

Tom Hayden,
activist, b.1939
Brenda Lee,
singer, b.1944

Shoot for the
moon. Even if
you miss, you'll
land among the
stars.
— Les Brown

*John F. Kerry,
U.S. senator,
b.1943*

☽☌♂ 10:32 PM

☾
SET 3:20AM
RISE 1:54PM

☀
RISE 7:41AM
SET 4:32PM

RIGHT RESOLVE

HOLIDAY: Saint Lucia Day / Luciadagen

Lucia was a Sicilian girl caught up in the persecutions of Diocletian. For refusing to marry a pagan (having already vowed her virginity to Christ), she was tormented and killed. Her name derives from Latin *lux*, or light; she is patron saint of sufferers of eye trouble (as well as writers, known to be susceptible to eye strain!).

In Sicily, Lucia is still honored by bonfires and torchlight parades. In Sweden the observance of her day begins before sunrise. The eldest daughter of the house is the Lussi-bruden, or Lucia Bride. She wears a white dress with a red sash, and an evergreen wreath with lighted candles atop her head. She serves saffron buns and coffee, first to her mother and then to the household. She is followed by her sisters, carrying candles, and by her brothers in tall, pointed hats decorated with stars. All sing carols offering thanks to the Queen of Light.

Lucia's attributes may derive from pagan traditions. The feminine elements of midwinter and night are complemented by the starboys who follow her. Like the moon, she brings radiance amidst the darkness. Her evergreens are proof of life amidst winter's bleakness. She wears white to show the virginity becoming a bride. But, as the eldest girl, she is ready for marriage and childbearing (hence her red sash). Her gifts of food and drink give evidence of earth's abundance.

However one may understand Luciadagen, the spectacle is breathtaking and the ritual is particularly joyful for children.

~ *John Miller*

For more information on St. Lucia and Luciadagen, see www.umkc.edu/imc/stlucia.htm

12

La Virgen De Guadalupe, Mexico

Dionne Warwick, singer, b.1941
Frank Sinatra, singer, b.1915
Gustave Flaubert, author, b.1821

Calamities are of two kinds: misfortunes to ourselves, and good fortune to others.
— *Ambrose Bierce*

☽☌♃ 1:21 AM

☾
SET 4:35AM
RISE 2:18PM

✺
RISE 7:42AM
SET 4:32PM

RIGHT WORD

13

Luciadagen: Lucia's Day, Sweden

Jamie Foxx, actor, b.1967
Steve Buscemi, actor, b.1957
Christopher Plummer, actor, b.1929

It is a man's own mind, not his enemy or foe, that lures him to evil ways.
— *Buddha*

☽△♀ 12:46 PM
☽☌♅ 4:00 PM

☾
SET 5:51AM
RISE 2:48PM

✺
RISE 7:43AM
SET 4:32PM

RIGHT DEED

14

1911: Amundsen reaches South Pole

Margaret Chase Smith, politician, b.1897
Nostrodamus, astronomer, b.1503

One should not stand at the foot of a sick person's bed, because that place is reserved for the guardian angel.
— *Jewish Saying*

☽△♆ 6:39 PM

☾
SET 7:03AM
RISE 3:25PM

✺
RISE 7:44AM
SET 4:32PM

RIGHT LIVELIHOOD

15

1989: General Augusto Pinochet defeated, democracy returns to Chile

Sitting Bull, d.1890
Edna O'Brien, author, b.1932

The most beautiful thing we can experience is the mysterious. It is the source of all true art and science.
— *Albert Einstein*

☽☌☉ 10:16 AM
☽☌♇ 11:11 AM
☉☌♇ 10:12 PM

✺
RISE 7:45AM
SET 4:32PM

Full Moon 16:15UT

RIGHT ENDEAVOR

LIVING URBAN TREASURE: Philadelphia's Judy Wicks

At the White Dog Café, Judy Wicks serves pasture-raised meats, wild fish, locally-grown organic vegetables, and social activism. The café and the Business Alliance for Local Living Economies (BALLE), which she co-founded in 2001, have been the main courses of her work life.

Wicks grew up in a small town, North Pittsburgh, where everyone was Republican and WASP. In 1969, she joined VISTA and lived in Alaska where a social activist vision began that continues to grow.

Judy Wicks in Philadelphia

Her restaurant started as a muffin and take-out coffee business from the first floor of Wicks' home. Over the next two years, it became the White Dog Café. "Once I got a grip on the business, I returned to

At the White Dog Café, education is on the menu.

social activism," says Wicks. Now, the White Dog Café employs 100 people and is a model for BALLE. Wind generated electricity provides 100 percent of the café's power. The café buys supplies from local, minority-owned and socially responsible providers. Employees earn a living wage, and receive medical, dental, and vision insurance.

Wicks says her activism comes from three impulses: "A spiritual voice that life is interconnected; a patriotism to make the country what it should be; and a little anger about the injustices in the world."

One of her many programs, International Sister Restaurants, links the White Dog Café to restaurants around the world to support local living economies and to raise awareness about how U.S. policies affect worldwide economies. Locally, the Philadelphia Sister Restaurant program supports businesses like Daffodils, operated and owned by African American women, and El Tropicao, a Latino restaurant in the barrio.

At the White Dog Café, education is on the menu. Table Talks, Storytelling, and Farmers Forums combine food and thoughts on issues like diversity, health care, and homelessness. The White Dog now grosses $5 million per year and contributes up to 20 percent of the income to non-profits. Speaking, writing, and BALLE absorb most of Wicks' time these days, as she joyfully promotes "doing well by doing good."

~ *Kathleen Melin*

For more information on the White Dog Café, see www.whitedog.com

PHILADELPHIA, PA

CITY ANIMALS / *Chase Twichell*

…The winter twilight looks like fire, too, | smeared above the bleached grasses | of the marsh, and in the shards of water | where an egret the color of newspaper | holds perfectly still, like a small angel | come to study what's wrong with the world…

16
FRI · DECEMBER 16 · 2005

Posadas, Mexico ~ 1773: Boston Tea Party

Margaret Mead, anthropologist, b.1901
Noel Coward, playwright, b.1899
Jane Austen, novelist, b.1775

Ludwig Von Beethoven, composer, b.1770

If you have a job without aggravations, you don't have a job.
— *Malcolm Forbes*

☽△♅ 11:52 PM
☽△♃ 6:33 PM

☾
SET 9:07AM
RISE 5:08PM

☉
RISE 7:45AM
SET 4:33PM

RIGHT MEMORY

17
SAT · DECEMBER 17 · 2005

1790: Aztec calendar stone discovered ~ 1903: First powered flight, Wright brothers at Kitty Hawk ~ 1967: Clean Air Act passed

You can't expect to hit the jackpot if you don't put a few nickels in the machine.
— *Flip Wilson*

Dec. 17-23:
SATURNALIA
ROMAN MASTERS
SERVED THEIR SLAVES

☾
SET 9:53AM
RISE 6:11PM

☉
RISE 7:46AM
SET 4:33PM

RIGHT CONCEPTION

18
SUN · DECEMBER 18 · 2005

Misa de Aguinaldo, Venezuela

Steven Spielberg, filmmaker, b.1947
Christina Aguilera, singer, b.1980
Brad Pitt, actor, b.1964

No matter what, no matter where, it's always home, if love is there.
— *Unknown*

Joseph Grimaldi, mime, b.1778
Antonio Stradivari, violin maker, b.1737

☽☌♀ 9:56 AM
☽△☿ 11:17 PM

☾
SET 10:29AM
RISE 7:17PM

☉
RISE 7:47AM
SET 4:33PM

RIGHT RESOLVE

CELEBRATE: Winter Solstice/Christmas/Hanukkah

In the bleak midwinter, frosty
wind made moan,
Earth stood hard as iron, water
like a stone. . . .

Christina Rossetti

At the winter solstice the sun appears to stand still (in Latin, *sol stetit*). That is, it seems to rise at the same point on the horizon for about six days. This moment of stillness marks the completion of Earth's annual in-breathing (begun at midsummer). Life in the northern hemisphere has withdrawn into Earth's still warm bosom: frogs are buried in the muddy depths of ponds, insects are burrowed deep into the soil, bears are asleep in their darkened dens. On the surface of the Earth, the trees are bare, the ground is hard, the daylight hours are few. Nature seems dead and darkness has reached its greatest potency.

But darkness can bring peace, and stillness calm. Thus have caves and the deep of night long been associated with initiation. The shaman's path is through the underworld. Midwinter is a time to feel the powerful embrace of the Eternal Feminine, the Great Mother.

For the pause between in-breath and out-breath is fleeting. In the dying of outer nature, the drawing in of the power of the Sun, the seed of new life is quickened in the womb of the Earth. The Sun is reborn (the Son is born). The meditative individual may now feel strongly, in this midwinter stillness, the shining presence of the Divine within. Many traditions celebrate the rebirth of light in this season. For nontraditionalists also, attunement to the cosmic dance of Earth and Sun, dark and light, can spur the experience of inner awakening.

~ John Miller

*For more information
on midwinter and solstice,
see www.witchvox.com/holidays/yule/*

19

MON · DECEMBER 19 · 2005

William Parry, explorer, b.1790
Kevin McHale, basketball player, b.1957
Cicely Tyson, actress, b.1939
Jennifer Beals, actress, b.1963

In science the credit goes to the man who convinces the world, not the man to whom the idea first occurs.
— Sir Francis Darwin

☽ ☌ ♄ 5:31 AM
☽ ☌ ♆ 3:31 PM

☾
SET 10:57AM
RISE 8:24PM

☼
RISE 7:47AM
SET 4:34PM

RIGHT WORD

20

TUE · DECEMBER 20 · 2005

Sacagawea, interpreter, d.1812
Uri Geller, psychic, b.1946
David Levine, caricaturist, b.1926
Susanne K. Langer, philosopher, b.1895

To love and win is the best thing. To love and lose, the next best.
— William Thackeray

☽ △ ♇ 9:25 AM

☾
SET 11:19AM
RISE 9:30PM

☼
RISE 7:48AM
SET 4:34PM

RIGHT DEED

21

WED · DECEMBER 21 · 2005

1620: Pilgrims land at Plymouth, Mass.
~ Yule, Christian
Jane Fonda, actress, b.1937
Frank Zappa, musician, b.1940
Joseph Stalin, dictator, b.1879

Let us love winter, for it is the spring of genius.
— Pietro Aretino

WINTER SOLSTICE
18:35 UT

☿ △ ♄ 5:27 AM
☽ ☌ ♅ 11:39 AM
☽ △ ♂ 3:09 PM

☾
SET 11:37AM
RISE 10:34PM

☼
RISE 7:48AM
SET 4:35PM

RIGHT LIVELIHOOD

22

THU · DECEMBER 22 · 2005

Ralph Fiennes, actor, b.1962
Diane Sawyer, journalist, b.1946
Giacomo Puccini, composer, b.1858

The effort to understand the universe is one of the very few things that lifts human life a little above the level of farce, and gives it some of the grace of tragedy.
Steven Weinberg

☾
SET 11:54AM
RISE 11:38PM

☼
RISE 7:49AM
SET 4:35PM

RIGHT ENDEAVOR

SONG: The Holly and The Ivy

THE HOLLY AND THE IVY

The holly and the ivy,
When they are both full grown,
Of all the trees that are in the wood,
The holly bears the crown.

~ Old French Carol

Holly has had special meaning for thousands of years, each culture adding its layer of significance. The Druids saw holly and ivy as female and male — holly represented the Goddess, with her red berries standing for the blood of fertility. Ivy was her consort. The Romans thought Saturn gave them holly and the plant figured heavily in the sensual and wild Saturnalia festival honoring the god. Holly is linked to Christmas in a couple of ways. Early Christians, wishing to avoid Roman persecution, decorated their houses with holly in mid-December during Saturnalia. As the number of Christians increased, holly became associated with the Christmas season. Another connection is that holly was said to have been woven into Christ's crown of thorns.

But holly's natural characteristic of evergreen cheerfulness and festive berries simply make it an apt symbol for celebration, especially in the dark of winter. Its upright growth and deep reaching roots speak to strength and goodness. In the Bach Flower Remedy pharmacopeia, holly is given to heal the inner soul and stimulate our basic loving nature.

For more information on Christmas and the other Winter Holidays, see www.holidays.net

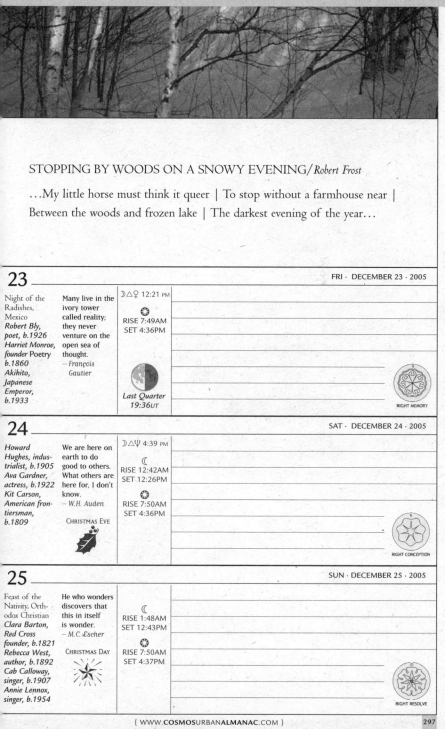

STOPPING BY WOODS ON A SNOWY EVENING/*Robert Frost*

…My little horse must think it queer | To stop without a farmhouse near |
Between the woods and frozen lake | The darkest evening of the year…

23 — FRI · DECEMBER 23 · 2005

Night of the Radishes, Mexico
Robert Bly, poet, b.1926
Harriet Monroe, founder Poetry *b.1860*
Akihito, Japanese Emperor, b.1933

Many live in the ivory tower called reality; they never venture on the open sea of thought.
— *François Gautier*

☽△♀ 12:21 PM

☼ RISE 7:49AM
SET 4:36PM

Last Quarter
19:36UT

RIGHT MEMORY

24 — SAT · DECEMBER 24 · 2005

Howard Hughes, industrialist, b.1905
Ava Gardner, actress, b.1922
Kit Carson, American frontiersman, b.1809

We are here on earth to do good to others. What others are here for, I don't know.
— *W.H. Auden*

CHRISTMAS EVE

☽△Ψ 4:39 PM

☽ RISE 12:42AM
SET 12:26PM

☼ RISE 7:50AM
SET 4:36PM

RIGHT CONCEPTION

25 — SUN · DECEMBER 25 · 2005

Feast of the Nativity, Orthodox Christian
Clara Barton, Red Cross founder, b.1821
Rebecca West, author, b.1892
Cab Calloway, singer, b.1907
Annie Lennox, singer, b.1954

He who wonders discovers that this in itself is wonder.
— *M.C. Escher*

CHRISTMAS DAY

☽ RISE 1:48AM
SET 12:43PM

☼ RISE 7:50AM
SET 4:37PM

RIGHT RESOLVE

HOLIDAY: Hanukkah, December 26, 2005 – January 2, 2006

More than 2,000 years ago, when the Syrian King Antiochus IV occupied Jerusalem, he forced the Jews to worship the Greek gods. For three years, Judah the Maccabee led a rebellion against the Syrians, and when he finally defeated them, the Jews could worship freely again. To rededicate the Temple, they cleaned it from top to bottom and then had to relight the menorah, a candelabrum. But only enough oil for one day could be found, and it would take eight days to get new oil. Incredibly, the little bottle of oil did last eight days, and Hannukah celebrates both this miracle and the "Rededication." Today families gather around a special Hannukah menorah and light one candle on the first night of Hannukah, two on the second, and so on, for all eight nights of the festival. There are songs, stories, presents, and prayers, and children play games of chance with spinning tops called dreidels.

From The Book of Holidays
Around the World,
*For more information about Hannukah,
see www.hannukah.org*

26

MON · DECEMBER 26 · 2005

Boxing Day, England ~ Zarathosht Diso, Zoroastrian ~ Kwanzaa, through Jan. 1
Mao Tse-Tung, Chinese leader, b.1893
Henry Miller, author, b.1881

Let your hook always be cast. In the pool where you least expect it, will be a fish.
– *Ovid*

HANUKKAH
THROUGH JAN 2

☽△♅ 10:11 AM
☽☍♂ 2:39 PM
☽☌♃ 7:19 PM

☾
RISE 2:57AM
SET 1:04PM

☼
RISE 7:50AM
SET 4:38PM

RIGHT WORD

27

TUE · DECEMBER 27 · 2005

Marlene Dietrich, actress, b.1901
Louis Pasteur, French chemist, b.1822
Johannes Kepler, German astronomer, b.1571

Winter lies too long in country towns; hangs on until it is stale and shabby, old and sullen.
– *Willa Cather*

☾
RISE 4:11AM
SET 1:30PM

☼
RISE 7:51AM
SET 4:38PM

RIGHT DEED

28

WED · DECEMBER 28 · 2005

1733: "Poor Richard's Almanack" published ~ 1973: Endangered Species Act est.
Denzel Washington, actor, b.1954
Maggie Smith, actress, b.1934

Perhaps I am a bear, or some hibernating animal underneath, for the instinct to be half asleep all winter is so strong in me.
– *Anne Morrow Lindbergh*

☽△♄ 8:14 PM

☾
RISE 5:28AM
SET 2:04PM

☼
RISE 7:51AM
SET 4:39PM

RIGHT LIVELIHOOD

29

THU · DECEMBER 29 · 2005

1890: Massacre at Wounded Knee
Jude Law, actor, b.1972
Marianne Faithful, singer, b.1946
Pablo Casals, cellist, b.1876
Grigori Rasputin, mystic, b.1916

And for the season it was winter, and they that know the winters of that country know them to be sharp and violent, subject to cruel and fierce storms.
– *Wm. Bradford*

☽☌☿ 5:25 PM
☽☌♇ 9:01 PM

☾
RISE 6:45AM
SET 2:51PM

☼
RISE 7:51AM
SET 4:40PM

RIGHT ENDEAVOR

URBAN SURVIVAL STRATEGY:
How to Re-Purpose a Fruitcake

1. **Turn the Fruitcake into another dessert.** Do not serve the fruitcake as is. Slice it very thin, tear the pieces apart, and use them in an English trifle, a dessert made with with alternating layers of cake (née fruitcake), custard, whipped cream, and sometimes, fresh fruit. Serve in a deep glass bowl (often called a trifle bowl).

2. **Use the Fruitcake as a doorstop.** Fruitcakes are very hardy and will last for years. Use the fruitcake to prop open a door.

3. **Use the Fruitcake to prevent your car from rolling.** When parked on a hill, wedge the fruitcake under the downhill side of a rear tire. In your garage, position the fruitcake on the floor as a tire stop to prevent the car from hitting the garage wall.

4. **Use the Fruitcake as a dumbbell.** A good-size fruitcake may weigh several pounds. Incorporate it into your exercise routine, holding it firmly for arm curls, or squeezing it between the feet for leg lifts.

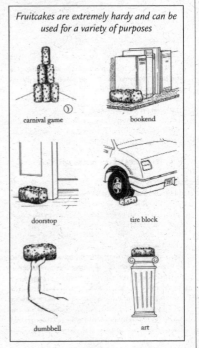

Fruitcakes are extremely hardy and can be used for a variety of purposes

carnival game   bookend

doorstop   tire block

dumbbell   art

5. **Use the Fruitcake in a carnival game.** Collect the fruitcakes and stack them vertically in a pyramid. Using tennis balls, try to knock down the fruitcakes in five throws.

6. **Use as bookends.** Set up two fruitcakes either horizontally or vertically, depending on the size of the books.

7. **Use as art.** Bolt a fruitcake to a painted board, frame it and hang it on your wall, or simply place it on a pedestal. Position the fruitcake in a well-lit area.

BE AWARE

Do not be fooled by gift of a "Yule cake" "Christmas Ring" or "Dried Fruit Bread"—these are just other names for a fruitcake.

Fruitcake should be stored in a cool place, such as a refrigerator or cellar. If kept cool and in a tin, the cake will last for at least a year, and you can give it as a present the following Christmas.

From The Worst Case Scenario Survival Handbook

LITTLE GIDDING/ *T.S. Eliot*

…We shall not cease from exploration | And the end of all our exploring | Will be to arrive where we started | And know the place for the first time.

---

30   FRI · DECEMBER 30 · 2005

Tiger Woods, golfer, b.1975
Tracey Ullman, actress, b.1959
Sandy Koufax, baseball pitcher, b.1935
Rudyard Kipling, author, b.1865
Bo Diddley, singer, b.1928

As old sinners have all points Of the compass in their bones and joints Can by their pangs and aches find All turns and changes of the wind.
— *Samuel Butler*

☽ ☌ ☉ 9:12 PM
☽ △ ♂ 11:24 PM

☾
RISE 7:55AM
SET 3:53PM

☀
RISE 7:51AM
SET 4:41PM

RIGHT MEMORY

---

31   SAT · DECEMBER 31 · 2005

Hogmanag, Scotland ~ First Night Celebrations: U.S. and CAN
Henri Matisse, painter, b.1869
Anthony Hopkins, actor, b.1937
John Denver, singer, b.1943

A single rose can be my garden ... a single friend, my world.
— *Leo Buscaglia*

NEW YEAR'S EVE

☿ ☌ ♇ 5:18 AM

☀
RISE 7:51AM
SET 4:42PM

New Moon
3:12UT

RIGHT CONCEPTION

---

1   SUN · JANUARY 1 · 2005

1899: Cuba Liberation Day ~ 1863: Emancipation Proclamation ~ 1999: Euro Introduced ~ 1994: Zapatista Rebellion, Mexico

Frank Langella, actor, b.1940
J.D. Salinger, author, b.1919
Paul Revere, revolutionary, b.1735

NEW YEAR'S DAY

☀
RISE 7:51AM
SET 4:42PM

RIGHT RESOLVE

Cosmo Doogood's
2005

In the realm of Nature there is nothing purposeless, trivial, or unnecessary :: Maimonides

ESSENTIAL MISCELLANY

es·sen·tial \ĭ-sĕn´chəl\ **1:** of, relating to, or constituting essence : INHERENT **2:** of the utmost importance : BASIC, INDISPENSABLE, NECESSARY

mis·cel·la·ny \mĭs´ə-lă´nē\ **1:** a mixture of various things **2 a** *pl*: separate writings collected in one volume **b:** a collection of writings on various subjects

URBAN ALMANAC

ur \ûr\ **1:** original : primitive (*Ur*-form) **2:** original version of (*Ur*-Hamlet)

banal \bə´năl\ [possessed in common, commonplace] (1840)

mana \măn´ə\ [of Melanesian & Polynesian origin: akin to Hawaiian & Maori *mana*] (1843) **1 a:** the power of the elemental forces embodied in an object or person **2:** moral authority : PRESTIGE

c – capacitance [capacity] (1909) \sē\ the property of an electric nonconductor that permits the storage of energy as a result of electric displacement when opposite surfaces of the nonconductor are maintained at a difference of potential

Cosmo Doogood's **Urban Almanac** [The original] [power of the elemental forces] [that permits the storage of energy] to be [possessed in common]

The following pages are offered for your amusement and delectation. Savor them in solitude or use them as gambits to start a conversation. What is essential is really much better when shared.

~ *Cosmo*

Attar of Roses

Attar of roses, or otto of roses as it is sometimes written, is a delicious perfume, which is prepared by distillation of the petals of the rose in India and Persia chiefly. As the experts say, it is a volatile oil of soft consistency, is nearly colorless, and is obtained from rose water by setting it out during the night in large open vessels, and early in the morning, skimming off the essential oil, which floats at the top. It is stated that 10,000 bushes with 100,000 roses will yield only 180 grains of attar. The word attar is traced to the Arabic *itr*, which means perfume. It is the oil or essence of rosa centifolia and its varieties. It is exported to European countries in small vials, and is very costly, which has given rise to the adulterations with sandal wood and other oils.

~ Edison's Handy Encyclopedia, 1890

Strength of Ice

THICKNESS	STRENGTH
Two inches	Will support a man.
Four inches	Will support a man on horseback.
Five inches	Will support an 80-pounder gun.
Eight inches	Will support a battery of artillery, carriages and horses attached.
Ten inches	Will support an army— an innumerable multitude.

~ Edison's Handy Encyclopedia, 1890

Software Reliability

Scale used for describing the **reliability of software**: broken, flaky, dodgy, fragile, brittle, solid, robust, bulletproof, armor-plated

~ Amphora Trivia

Where Are You At?

1. Trace the water you drink from precipitation to tap.

2. How many days till the moon is full? (Slack of two days allowed.)

3. What soil series are you standing on?

4. What was the total rainfall in your area last year (June–July)? (Slack: 1 inch for every 20 inches)

5. When was the last time a fire burned your area?

6. What were the primary subsistence techniques of the culture that lived in your area before you?

7. Name five native edible plants in your region and their season(s) of availability.

8. From what direction do winter storms generally come in your region?

9. Where does your garbage go?

10. How long is the growing season where you live?

11. On what day of the year are the shadows the shortest where you live?

12. When do the deer rut in your region, and when are the young born?

13. Name five grasses in your area. Are any of them native?

14. Name five resident and five migratory birds in your area.

15. What is the land-use history of where you live?

16. What primary geological event or process influenced the land form where you live? (Bonus special: What's the evidence?)

17. What species have become extinct in your area?

18. What are the major plant associations in your region?

19. From where you're reading this, point north.

20. What spring wildflower is consistently among the first to bloom where you live?

SCORING

0–3	You have your head on backwards
4–7	It's hard to be in two places at once when you're not anywhere at all.
8–12	A fairly firm grasp of the obvious.
13–16	You're paying attention
17–19	You know where you're at.
20	You not only know where you're at, you know where it's at.

~ Quiz compiled by Leonard Charles, Jim Dodge, Lynn Milliman, Victoria Stockley.
From CoEvolution Quarterly (Winter 1981)

The Language of Flowers

During Victorian times, certain flowers given and received carried meanings beyond their beauty and were ways to express feelings too difficult or tender to voice.

Flowers	Sentiments	Flowers	Sentiments
Acacia	Concealed love	Goldenrod	Encouragement
Apple Blossom	Preference	Hawthorn	Hope
Bell Flower	Gratitude	Heliotrope	I love you: devotion
Box	Constancy	Honeysuckle	Bond of love
Calla Lily	Feminine beauty	Horse-chestnut	Luxury
Cedar	I live for thee	Hyacinth	Jealousy
Chrysanth. Rose	I love	Mint	Virtue
Clover, Red	Industry	Morning Glory	Coquetry
Corn	Riches	Oats	Music
Cowslip, Amer.	You are my divinity	Orange	Generosity
Daffodil	Chivalry	Pansy	Think of me
Dahlia	Forever thine	Pink	Pure affection
Daisy, Garden	I partake your sentiments	Pink Red	Pure, ardent love
		Rose Moss	Superior merit
Daisy, White	Innocence	Rose, Tea	Always lovely
Daisy, Wild	I will think of it	Rose, White	I am worthy of you
Elm, American	Patriotism	Tuberose	Dangerous pleasures
Forget-me-not	True love	Verbena	Sensibility
Fuchsia, Scarlet	Taste	Violet, Blue	Love
Geranium, Ivy	Your hand for the next dance	Violet, White	Modesty
Gillyflower	Lasting beauty		

~ Edison's Handy Encyclopedia, 1890

The Sun's Light

The sun's light is equal to 5,573 wax-candles held at a distance of one foot from the eye. It would require 800,000 full moons to produce a day as brilliant as one of cloudless sunshine.

~ Edison's Handy Encyclopedia, 1890

THINK OF ALL THE BEAUTY THATS STILL LEFT IN AND AROUND YOU AND BE HAPPY! :: *ANNE FRANK*

Literary Taunts

A modest little person, with much to be modest about.

Winston Churchill
(about Clement Atlee, his successor as prime minister)

I've just learned about his illness. Let's hope it's nothing trivial.

Irvin S. Cobb

I have never killed a man, but I have read many obituaries with great pleasure.

Clarence Darrow

He has never been known to use a word that might send a reader to the dictionary.

William Faulkner
(about Ernest Hemingway)

He is not only dull himself, he is the cause of dullness in others.

Samuel Johnson

He has delusions of adequacy.

Walter Kerr

I've had a perfectly wonderful evening. But this wasn't it.

Groucho Marx

They never open their mouths without subtracting from the sum of human knowledge.

Thomas Brackett Reed

He loves nature in spite of what it did to him.

Forrest Tucker

I didn't attend the funeral, but I sent a nice letter saying I approved of it.

Mark Twain

His mother should have thrown him away and kept the stork.

Mae West

Some cause happiness wherever they go; others whenever they go.

Oscar Wilde

He has no enemies, but is intensely disliked by his friends.

Oscar Wilde

He has van Gogh's ear for music.

Billy Wilder

Shooting Stars

One of the earliest accounts of star showers is that which relates how, in 472, the sky at Constantinople appeared to be alive with flying stars and meteors. In some Eastern annals we are told that in October, 1202, "The stars appeared like waves upon the sky. They flew about like grasshoppers, and were dispersed from left to right." It is recorded that in the time of King William II, there occurred in England a wonderful shower of stars, which "seemed to fall like rain from heaven. An eyewitness seeing where an aerolite fell, cast water upon it, which was raised in steam and with a great noise of boiling."

~ Edison's Handy Encyclopedia, 1890

Questions To Ask Your Prospective Doctor

1. When and why did you decide to become a doctor?

2. Do you like being a doctor?

3. How long have you been in practice?

4. Do you do any pro bono work?

5. What is the average time lag for answering phone calls?

6. What is your protocol for communications while on vacation?

7. If you had $5 million would you still be a doctor? $15 million?

8. How many of your patients are long-time patients, over three years?

9. Have you taken any, most, or all of the medications or supplements you prescribe?

10. Do you research new medications? Technologies? Prescribed drugs? How often?

11. Do you receive free medication from pharmaceutical companies for promotions or trials?

12. Are you open to the benefits of western medicine? Are you open to the benefits of complementary or alternative care?

13. Do you work as a team in any way with other professionals or practitioners?

Consider what personal questions might be informative regarding the doctor's ability to care for you.

1. Have you ever been hospitalized?

2. Are you on any medications?

3. Do you exercise?

4. How do you deal with stress?

5. What is your diet? What is your interest and experience in good nutrition?

6. What magazines do you read?

7. Do you have an active religious association or spiritual practice?

8. Have you ever been in therapy?

9. How many times a week do you make love?

~ *Excerpted from an article "Who is My Doctor?"*
© *2004 by Gigi Coyle*

World Cities

30 Largest World Metropolitan Areas (2004)		Mean Temperatures (F)	
		January	July
1 Tokyo, Japan	34 million	36/50	73/83
2 Mexico City, Mexico	22 million	44/70	53/74
3 New York, United States	22 million	25/38	68/83
4 Seoul, South Korea	22 million	21/35	71/84
5 São Paulo, Brazil	20 million	66/82	54/74
6 Mumbai (Bombay), India	19 million	62/87	77/86
7 Delhi, India	18 million	45/70	80/95
8 Osaka-Kobe-Kyoto, Japan	17 million	37/49	75/89
9 Los Angeles, United States	17 million	48/66	63/75
10 Cairo, Egypt	16 million	48/66	72/94
11 Jakarta, Indonesia	16 million	76/86	77/90
12 Calcutta, India	15 million	57/80	79/90
13 Moscow, Russia	15 million	10/21	56/74
14 Buenos Aires, Argentina	14 million	69/87	45/59
15 Manila, Phillipines	14 million	74/85	78/88
16 London, United Kingdom	14 million	36/45	57/72
17 Shanghai, China	13 million	33/46	77/89
18 Karachi, Pakistan	13 million	57/78	81/90
19 Rio de Janeiro, Brazil	12 million	74/84	63/75
20 Dhaka, Bangladesh	12 million	59/79	--
21 Teheran, Iran	11 million	30/45	75/98
22 Istanbul, Turkey	11 million	37/48	65/83
23 Paris, France	10 million	37/44	60/76
24 Beijing, China	10 million	15/35	71/87
25 Lagos, Nigeria	10 million	72/90	72/83
26 Tianjin, China	10 million	18/35	73/87
27 Chicago, United States	10 million	13/29	63/84
28 Hong Kong, China	9 million	57/66	80/89
29 Washington D.C., United States	8 million	30/45	71/87
30 Lima, Peru	8 million	66/78	59/66

Sources: • *Principal Agglomerations of the World, www.citypopulation.de*
• *Demographia, www.demographia.com*
• *World Meteorological Organization, www.wmo.ch*

Measurements

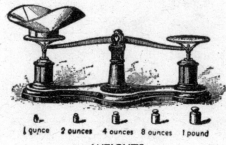

1 ounce   2 ounces   4 ounces   8 ounces   1 pound

WEIGHTS

Pint   Quart   Peck   Half-Bushel   Bushel

DRY MEASURES

Gill   Pint   Quart   Gallon

LIQUID MEASURES

Point of View

To the optimist, the glass is half full.
To the pessimist, the glass is half empty.
To the engineer, the glass is twice as big as it needs to be.

~ Amphora Trivia

309

Measurements

LENGTH
12 inches = 1 foot
3 feet = 1 yard
220 yards = 1 furlong
5,280 feet = 1 statute mile (SM)
6,076.1 feet= 1 nautical mile (NM)
10 millimeters = 1 centimeter (cm)
10 centimeters = 1 decimeter (dm)
10 decimeters = 1 meter (m)
10 meters = 1 decameter (dam)
1000 meters = 1 kilometer (km)
1 inch = 2.54 cm
0.3937 inch = 1 cm
1 SM = 1.60934 km
0.62137 SM = 1 km
1 NM = 1.852 km
0.53987 NM = 1 km

VOLUME
1,728 cu. inches = 1 cubic foot
27 cu. feet = 1 cubic yard
1,000 cu. mm = 1 cu. cm
1,000 cu. cm = 1 cubic dm
1,000 cu. dm = 1 cubic m
1 cu. inch = 16.387 cubic cm
0.061023 cu. inch = 1 cubic cm
1 cu. yard = 0.76455 cubic m
1.30795 cu yard = 1 cubic m

WEIGHT
437 grains = 1 ounce
480 grains = 1 troy (fine) ounce
16 drams = 1 ounce
16 ounces = 1 pound
14 pounds = 1 stone
112 pounds = 1 hundredweight
2,240 pounds = 1 ton

CAPACITY
16 ounces = 1 pint
20 ounces = 1 imperial pint
2 cups = 1 pint
2 pints = 1 quart
4 quarts = 1 gallon
1.2009 (U.S.) gallons =
1 imperial (GB) gallon
10 milliliters (ml) = 1 centiliter (cl)
100 centiliters = 1 liter (l)
100 liters = 1 hl
1 U.S. quart = 0.94633 liters
1.05668 U.S. quarts = 1 liter
1 U.S. gallon = 3.785412 liters
0.26417 U.S. gallons = 1 liter
1 GB gallon = 4.5459631 liters
0.219975 GB gallons = 1 liter

AREA
144 sq. inches = 1 sq. foot
9 sq. feet = 1 sq. yard
4840 sq. yards = 1 acre
640 acres = 1 sq. mile
100 sq. mm = 1 sq. cm
100 sq. cm = 1 sq. dm
10000 sq. cm = 1 sq. m
100 sq. m = 1 sq. dam
100 sq. dam = 1 hectare
10000 sq. dam = 1 sq. km
1 sq. inch = 6.45159 sq. cm
0.155 sq. inch = 1 sq. cm
1 acre = 0.404686 ha
2.471 acres = 1 ha
1 sq. SM = 2.589 sq. km
0.3861 sq. SM = 1 sq. km

Measurement Conversions

TEMPERATURE

Centigrade to Fahrenheit	multiply by 1.8 and add 32
Fahrenheit to Centigrade	subtract 32 and multiply by 0.5555

LENGTH, DISTANCE, AND AREA   *multiply by*

inches to centimeters	2.54
centimeters to inches	0.39
feet to meters	0.30
meters to feet	3.28
yards to meters	0.91
meters to yards	1.09
miles to kilometers	1.61
kilometers to miles	0.62
acres to hectares	0.40
hectares to acres	2.47

WEIGHT   *multiply by*

ounces to grams	28.35
grams to ounces	0.035
pounds to kilograms	0.45
kilograms to pounds	2.21
British tons to kilograms	1016
U.S. tons to kilograms	907

A British ton is 2,240 pounds
A U.S. ton is 2,000 pounds

VOLUME   *multiply by*

imperial gallons to liters	4.55
liters to imperial gallons	0.22
U.S. gallons to liters	3.79
liters to U.S. gallons	0.26

5 imperial gallons equal 6 U.S. gallons
1 liter is slightly more than a U.S. quart,
slightly less than 1 British quart.

Prison Statistics

There are more Americans behind bars literally, and proportionally, than at any time in our history. We have a higher percentage of our population in prison than any other nation. And, we keep building more prisons. In fact, many locales lobby for new prisons as a tool of economic recovery. Between 1973 and 2000 the rate of incarceration in the United States more than quadrupled. In 2001, nearly 6.6 million Americans were on probation, in jail or prison, or on parole at year's end. That number represents 3.1 percent of all U.S. adult residents or one in every 32 adults.

DRUGS AND PRISON

In 1980 the incarceration rate for drug offenses was 15 inmates per 100,000 adults; by 1996, it was 148 inmates per 100,000 adults. In 1970, 16.3 percent of all federal inmates were imprisoned on drug-related charges; in 2002 that percentage had risen to 54.7 percent.

African Americans constitute roughly 12 percent of the nation's population and 13 percent of the nation's drug users, but 57 percent of those in state prison for a drug crime.

RATE OF INCARCERATION IN SELECTED NATIONS *(number of people in prison per 100,000 population)*	
United States	715
Russia	584
South Africa	402
Israel	174
Mexico	169
England/Wales	143
China	119
Canada	116
Australia	114
Germany	96
France	95
Sweden	75
Japan	54
India	29

RACE AND PRISON

Nearly one in three (32 percent) black males in the age group 20-29 is under some form of criminal justice supervision on any given day—either in prison or jail, or on probation or parole. In major cities it's nearly one in two.

The latest figures from the Bureau of Justice Statistics show that black men have a rate of incarceration seven times higher than white men.

In comparison, white people constitute roughly 69 percent of the nation's population and 68 percent of the nation's drug users, but only 23 percent of inmates in state prison for a drug crime.

Black males have a one in three (32.2 percent) chance of spending at least a year in prison sometime during their lives. The figure for Hispanic males is 16 percent and for whites is 4 percent.

Sources:

Incarceration Rates chart: Rate for the United States from Prison and Jail Inmates at Midyear 2003; for all other nations, International Centre for Prison Studies available online at www.prisonstudies.org.

Incarceration data were collected on varying dates and are the most current data available as of 2004, by Mark Mauer, the Sentencing Project, Washington, D.C.

Other prison statistics from: "NOW," with Bill Moyers. Society and Community. Prisons in America. PBS; and from Eric Lotke, research and policy director, and Chris Evans, intern, Justice Policy Institute, Washington, D.C.

In Praise of Older Women

When I was 20, I had eyes only for girls my age. Any woman over 30 was ancient, over 40 invisible. As I grow in age, I value older women most of all. Here are just a few of the reasons why:

An older woman will never ask out of the blue, "What are you thinking?" An older woman doesn't care what you think.

An older woman's been around long enough to know who she is, what she wants, and from whom. By the age of 50, few women are wishy-washy. About anything. Thank God!

An older woman has lived long enough to know how to please a man in ways her daughter could never dream of. (Young men, you have something to look forward to!)

Older women are forthright and honest. They'll tell you right off that you are a jerk if you're acting like one. A young woman will say nothing, fearing that you might think worse of her. An older woman doesn't give a damn.

An older, single woman usually has had her fill of "meaningful relationships" and "long-term commitments." Can't relate? Can't commit? She couldn't care less. The last thing she needs in her life is another whiny, dependent lover!

Older women are sublime. They seldom contemplate having a shouting match with you at the opera or in the middle of an expensive dinner. Of course, if you deserve it, they won't hesitate to shoot you if they think they can get away with it.

An older woman has the self-assurance to introduce you to her women friends. A young woman often snarls with distrust when "her guy" is with other women.

Women get psychic as they age. You never have to confess your sins to an older woman. Like your mother, they always just know.

Yes, we geezers praise older women for a multitude of reasons. These are but a few.

Unfortunately, it's not reciprocal. For every stunning, smart, well-coifed babe of 70 there's a bald, paunchy relic with his yellow pants belted at his armpits making a fool of himself with some 22-year-old waitress.

Ladies, I apologize...

~ Frank Kaiser

Blood Alcohol Level

The amount of alcohol in your blood stream is known as your Blood Alcohol Level (BAL). It is measured in milligrams of alcohol per 100 milliliters of blood, or milligrams per cent. A BAL of .10 means that 1/10 of 1 percent (or 1/1000) of your total blood content is alcohol.

All fifty U.S. states have adopted the .08 blood alcohol limit for drinking and driving, though not all have yet put it into effect. The legal limit in Sweden is .02 % and in France .05 %.

~ *Minnesota Department of Public Safety*

IF YOU'RE A WOMAN, YOUR BLOOD ALCOHOL LEVEL IS:

Number of Drinks/Hour	Your Weight (lbs)							
	100	120	140	160	180	200	220	240
1	.05	.04	.04	.03	.03	.03	.02	.02
2	.10	.08	.07	.06	.06	.05	.05	.04
3	.15	.13	.11	.10	.08	.08	.07	.06
4	.20	.17	.15	.13	.11	.10	.09	.09
5	.25	.21	.18	.16	.14	.13	.12	.11
6	.30	.26	.22	.19	.17	.15	.14	.13
7	.36	.30	.26	.22	.20	.18	.16	.15
8	.41	.33	.29	.26	.23	.20	.19	.17
9	.46	.38	.33	.29	.26	.23	.21	.19
10	.51	.42	.36	.32	.28	.25	.23	.21
11	.56	.46	.40	.35	.31	.27	.25	.23
12	.61	.50	.43	.37	.33	.30	.28	.25

IF YOU'RE A MAN, YOUR BLOOD ALCOHOL LEVEL IS:

Number of Drinks/Hour	Your Weight (lbs)							
	100	120	140	160	180	200	220	240
1	.04	.04	.03	.03	.02	.02	.02	.02
2	.09	.07	.06	.05	.05	.04	.04	.043
3	.13	.11	.09	.08	.07	.07	.06	.05
4	.17	.15	.13	.11	.10	.09	.08	.07
5	.22	.18	.16	.14	.12	.11	.10	.09
6	.26	.22	.19	.16	.15	.13	.12	.11
7	.30	.25	.22	.19	.17	.15	.14	.13
8	.35	.29	.25	.22	.19	.17	.16	.14
9	.37	.32	.26	.24	.20	.19	.17	.15
10	.39	.35	.28	.25	.22	.20	.18	.16
11	.48	.40	.34	.30	.26	.24	.22	.20
12	.53	.43	.37	.32	.29	.26	.24	.21

Time At Which Money Doubles At Interest

RATE PER CENT	SIMPLE INTEREST	COMPOUND INTEREST
10	10 years	7 years 100 days
9	11 years 40 days	8 years 16 days
8	12 years	9 years 2 days
7	14 years 104 days	10 years 89 days
6	16 years 8 months	11 years 327 days
5	20 years	15 years 75 days
4 $^1/_2$	22 years 81 days	15 years 273 days
4	25 years	17 years 246 dats
3 $^1/_2$	28 years 208 days	20 years 54 days
3	33 years 4 months	23 years 164 days
2 $^1/_2$	40 years	28 years 26 days
2	50 years	35 years 1 day

~ *Edison's Handy Encyclopedia, 1890*

Temperature

FAHRENHEIT

-40	-31	-22	-13	-4	5	14	32	41	50	59	68	77	86	95	104
-40	-35	-30	-25	-20	-15	-10	0	5	10	15	20	25	30	35	40

CELSIUS

Speed

MPH

20	30	40	50	60	70	80	90	100
32	48	64	80	96	112	128	144	160

KMPH

Advice on Raising Children

Help children to see and love the beautiful.

To develop self-reliance and strength,
a child should have as much liberty as possible,
as much as is consistent with the rights of others.

She should be treated with respect,
not laughed at when she makes mistakes
or tries to show off before visitors.

Let us not nag the poor little things.

As early as possible,
children should have tasks assigned to them
that they may be led to feel that mankind must work
and that even small children may help a little.

The habitual tone of a mother should be
suggestions rather than commands.

We can praise their work, say that it is well-done,
lovely, or beautiful, if we can do so truthfully. . .

I sincerely believe it would be a wise thing never to threaten.

The most important thing, then,
in training a child is to surround him,
to fill his life, with what is good.

~ From Clara Ueland's 1890 Paper "Child Discipline"
Presented to The Mother's Council in Minneapolis

Cost of Raising Children—*Birth to Age 17*

INCOME	COST
$65,800 and over	$249,180
$39,100–$65,800	$170,640
$39,100 and under	$124,800

~ 2002 figures from the U.S. Department of Agriculture

Current Dietary Theories

Current dietary theories covered in the Institute for Integrative Nutrition's Professional Training Program to become a Holistic Health Counselor:

The Zone
The Atkins diet
The Pritikin diet
The South Beach diet
The L.A. Shape diet
The N.Y.C. diet
The Blood Type diet
The Mayo Clinic diet
The Mediterranean diet
The MediterrAsian diet
Eat More, Weigh Less
Doctor Dean Ornish
High-fat diets
Low-fat diets
No-fat diets
High-carbohydrate diets
Anti-carbohydrate diets
The No-Grain diet
High-protein diets
Low-protein diets
40 / 30 / 30
90 / 10
Standard American diet [S.A.D.]
USDA healthy eating pyramid
The Four Food Groups
Traditional Chinese medicine
5 elements: fire, water, earth, wood, metal
Trinity, Sattva, Yin/Yang
Ayurveda
Raw foods
Living foods
Macrobiotics
Fasting, juicing, blending

Vegan, fruitarian, starchetarian
Vegetarian, lacto-vegetarian
Lacto-ovo-vegetarian, fishetarian
Master Cleanser, Rainbow diet,
Fit for Life
Zen diet
Haiku diet
God's diet
Prayer diet
Kosher diet
Muslim diet
Maker's diet
The origin diet
Cave man diet
Evolutionary diet
The Hawaiian diet
Diets don't work diet
Body ecology diet
Peanut butter diet
Metabolism diets
Brown rice diet
Ice cream diet
Body type diet
The forest diet
3-season diet
Candida diet
Rotation diet
The Okinawa program
Instincto-therapy
Electrical nutrition
Spiritual nutrition

From the Institute for Integrative Nutrition
www.integrativenutrition.com
212-730-5433

Top Rankings on the Creativity Index

Richard Florida ranks cities of 1 million or more on a creativity index in his book *The Rise of the Creative Class: And How It's Transforming Work, Leisure, Community, and Everyday Life*. Cities score points for the number of talented individuals, the degree of technological innovation, and the tolerance of diverse lifestyles.

TOP REGIONS		TECHNOLOGY	TALENT	TOLERANCE
1	Austin	2	9	22
2	San Francisco	6	12	20
3	Seattle	21	15	3
4	Boston	35	11	12
5	Raleigh-Durham	5	2	52
6	Portland	12	45	7
7	Minneapolis	47	22	17
8	Washington-Baltimore	41	1	45
9	Sacramento	15	27	47
10	Denver	61	18	25
11	Atlanta	23	29	55
12	San Diego	25	54	35
13	New York	65	25	39
14	Dallas-Fort Worth	23	43	63
15	Salt Lake City	48	74	36
16	Phoenix	31	75	54
17	Rochester	58	38	70
18	Los Angeles	52	91	32
19	Kansas City	37	39	99
20	Philadelphia	68	33	85
21	Houston	85	28	78
22	Columbus	83	56	57

~ From Adherents.com

Average Heights and Weights of American Men and Women

	2002	1890
Men's Height	5' 9"	5' 9"
Men's Weight	171 pounds	130 pounds
Women's Height	5' 3½"	5' 4"
Women's Weight	146 pounds	110 pounds

~ 2002 figures from the U.S. Department of Agriculture

Use of the Term "Like"

THE UNDERCUTTING LIKE
Translation: I'm not smart; I'm cool. I don't know where I picked up that knowledge.

"I think he meant it like, metaphorically."

"I just used the like, law of contrapositive to figure out the answer."

THE VAGUE LIKE
Translation: Thereabouts

"This was back in like, October."

"How could I? I was like, twelve years old at the time."

THE SELF-EFFACING LIKE
Translation: Virtue is shameful.

"I was like, school president and captain of the basketball team."

"I volunteer for a few hours every week. I like, care about the environment and stuff."

THE COWARDLY LIKE
Translation: I disagree. That is, if it's okay.

"I don't want to like, tell you what to do, but it just doesn't sound, like, nice."

"Are you sure? Didn't you say you were gonna like, pay me back later?"

THE BETRAYER LIKE
Translation: I lie.

"I was so upset I cried for like, three days."

"Oh, this is like, so not an imposition. No really, I like, want to do this for you."

THE FILLER LIKE
Translation: I finished my sentence.

"How could you do that? I mean, I went out of my way to meet you there, and then you didn't show, and you didn't even call and it was like…"

"I worked hard this past year, and I thought the company would recognize my work with a more substantial raise; I mean, this is less than the cost of living, and I have to think about my future, and, I mean, it's like…"

THE APOLOGY LIKE
Translation: Sorry; I'm inarticulate.

"I was like, wow."

"It was so interesting; it was like, I can't explain it. You know what I mean?"

THE MULTIMEDIA LIKE
Translation: Visual aid to follow.

"The baby was so cute. She was like…" (Look cute.)

"I was so happy, I was like…" (Jump and clap hands.)

STALLER LIKE, PART I
Translation: Think, brain, think!

"Poetry? Yeah, me too. I love like, Robert Frost."

"You're from Belize? That's like, south?"

STALLER LIKE, PART II
Translation: Uh, oh, math.

"Let's see, 30 percent off. So it's like, 40 dollars."

"Amortized over 20 years, that comes to like, a lot."

Edited from The Evasion-English Dictionary
by Maggie Balistreri; Melville House Publishing

How to Buy Firewood

One of the great pleasures in life is sitting in front of a real wood-burning fire. (We know gas is more environmentally sound in some places, but, really, isn't that like lighting a burner and gathering around the cook top?) But if you live in the city and don't cut your own wood, you have to rely on a firewood vendor. So how do you go about choosing good wood that will keep you happy and cozy all fall and winter?

1. First of all, find out what type of wood is for sale. Oak and maple, like other hardwoods, burn slow and hot; soft woods, like pine and poplar, burn more quickly. Mixing hard and soft is fine, and you want most of the logs to be split. You can combine split and whole logs—if the whole logs are fairly small—and hard and soft woods at a ratio of about 4 :1.

2. Next, is the wood cured, or is it wet or green? Green or wet wood will burn, but it will hiss instead of crackle, and your heat value will be lost in steam. Responsible wood dealers won't sell green or wet wood without telling you, but the best thing is to learn how to determine the condition of the wood yourself. Choose a few random logs from the vendor's mix. They should be heavy, but not too heavy which indicates moisture and sap. Hit them together, do they have a sort of a hollow, ringing sound? (Trust me, you'll get it after awhile.) And smell them. Do they smell green, moist, or musty? Lastly, look at them closely. Is there any moss and does the bark peel off easily? If so, the wood is wet, old, and hasn't been stored properly. Don't buy it.

3. If you're satisfied with the wood, ask about the price per cord or partial cord. (Prices differ wildly around the country, so have some idea of the cost in your city.) Now the crucial thing is to make sure that the cord you're both talking about is the same cord—128 cubic feet of wood, 4 feet high by 4 feet wide by 8 feet long (4x4x8). And to meet this requirement, the wood needs to be stacked tightly. Sometimes wood is sold by the rick or face cord, which is 16 inches wide instead of 4 feet, making it about one third the volume of a standard cord. A face cord weighs around a ton.

4. Buy enough wood for one burning season and store it in the sun, if possible, away from the sides of buildings, and covered on top to keep off rain and snow. Split logs should be stacked bark side up.

As soon as the weather turns chilly, build fires with plenty of dry tinder and enough air between your well-chosen logs. Turn off the TV, gather the family around, and be sure to keep the name of that wood vendor in a safe place where you can find it next year.

~ *Martha Coventry*
For more on buying firewood, see www.firewoodcenter.com

Weather Facts

TEMPERATURE

Highest world temperature: 136° F, Al Aziziyah, Libya, September 13, 1922

Highest U.S. temperature: 134° F, Death Valley, California, July 10, 1913

Lowest world temperature (without windchill): -128.6° F, Vostok Station, Antarctica, July 21, 1983

Lowest world temperature in inhabited area: -90.4° F, Oymyakon, Siberia (pop. 4,000), February 6, 1933

Lowest U.S. temperature: -79.8° F, Prospect Creek, Alaska, January 23, 1971

Lowest U.S. (48 contiguous states) temperature: -69.7° F, Rogers Pass, Montana, January 20, 1954

Lowest Northern Hemisphere temperature: -81° F, Snag, Yukon Territory, Canada, February 2, 1947

TORNADOES

Fastest tornado winds: 286 miles per hour, Wichita Falls, Texas, April 2, 1958

Tornado frequency in the United States: 3 out of 4 of all world tornadoes hit the United States

Only 2 percent of U.S. tornadoes reach violent intensity, yet those few result in 70 percent of all tornado deaths. Winds in these tornadoes exceed 200 mph and can stay on the ground for an hour or more.

PRECIPITATION

It takes about one million cloud droplets to provide enough water for one raindrop.

Greatest rainfall in a day: 73.62 inches, Reunion, Indian Ocean, March 15, 1952

Greatest rainfall in a year: 1,041 inches, Cherrapungi, Assam, India, August 1860–1861

World's one minute rainfall record: 1.50 inches, Barot, Guadaloupe, West Indies, Nov. 26, 1970

Greatest snowfall in a day: 75.8 inches, Silver Lake, Colorado, April 14–15, 1921

Greatest snowfall in a single storm: 189 inches, Mt. Shasta, California, February 13–19, 1959

Largest hailstone: 7 inches in diameter and 18.75 inches in circumference, Aurora, Nebraska, June 22, 2003, weight 1.7 pounds

WINDS

Fastest surface wind speed: 231 miles per hour, Mt. Washington, New Hampshire, April 12, 1934

Fastest tornado winds: 286 miles per hour, Wichita Falls, Texas, April 2, 1958

Weather Facts

THUNDERSTORMS

Lightning from the blue: Lightning bolts can jump 10 or more miles from their parent cloud into regions with blue skies.

Temperature of lightning: estimated 50,000 °F (hotter than the surface of the sun)

Odds of being struck by lightning: approx. 1 in 800,000

Lightning strikes: 9 out of 10 lightning bolts strike the continents rather than oceans.

For each lightning bolt that hits the ground, about 200,000 pounds of rain are also formed.

Number of thunderstorms: Nearly 2,000 thunderstorm cells are estimated over the planet at any given time. The United States has more than 100,000 thunderstorms annually, the global average being 16 million!

HURRICANES

Longest lasting Atlantic tropical storm: Ginger, 1971, which spun around the open ocean for 28 days.

Longest-lasting Pacific tropical storm: A storm named John hung on for 31 days. Since it crossed the date-line twice, it changed status from a hurricane to a typhoon and back to a hurricane.

Lowest hurricane barometric pressure recorded in the western hemisphere: 888 millibars (26.17 inches) during Hurricane Gilbert, 1988.

Deadliest Atlantic hurricane: hit Martinique, St. Eustatius, and Barbados and killed 22,000 people, 1780

Sources

Mr. Kish's Weather Facts:
http://home.nycap.rr.com/teachertown/weathfac

The Handy Science Answer Book, compiled by the Science and Technology Department, Carnegie Library, Pittsburgh

Extreme Weather, Christopher C. Burt, W.W. Norton & Co., 2004

Gandhi's Seven Deadly Sins

Wealth without Work
Pleasure without Conscience
Science without Humanity
Knowledge without Character
Politics without Principle
Commerce without Morality
Worship without Sacrifice

The Elemental World, a Taxonomy

FIRE

Muses: embody the spiritual role of the fiery element in art and in life in general

Spirits of Light: light bodies radiate brightly and send out light in spheres of different tones

Spirits of Maturity and Transformation: perform tasks in nature; take life processes to maturity, and finally, through decomposition and transformation, bring processes to the threshold of new birth

Spirits of the Center of the Earth: preside over the fate of the planet

AIR

Master Deva, Deva of Place, Ritual Deva: reign over an area from the air

Fairies of Place: care for the coordinating processes in a region

Plant Devas: embody the group soul of a plant species

Woodland Fairies: work as companions to animals

Sylphs: connect to movement in space; for example, modeling and directing the wind

Fairies: connect to the expansion of life in an area

EARTH

Pan: responsible for the sum total of natural life within a certain area; forms a bridge to the world of angels

The Loving Old Crone: concentrates the power of love so that the love of Earth is available to every creature without exception

The Wise Old Sage: holds unhindered access to the wisdom of life; connects to landscape temples

Fauns: intelligences of individual trees

Elementals of animals and humans: work in two directions with plants and in supporting human beings

Goblins: work with cultivated landscape

Dwarfs: maintain fertility; connect and coordinate

Elves: look after single plants

Gnomes: enliven planetary matter

WATER

Nymph Queen, Landscape Queen: maintain the nature temple

Nymphs, Well Nymphs, and Pasture Nymphs: give individuality to a river, lake, meadow; develop their place into a source of blessing and healing

Nixies: enliven rivers, springs, lakes, and marshes

Undines: energize the sea

Watermen: maintain yang pole

Spirits of Balance: look after balance inside Earth's crust

~ Marko Pogacnik

From Nature Spirits & Elemental Beings: Working with the Intelligence in Nature *(Findhorn Press). Excerpted by permission of the author.*

What is Lorem Ipsum?

Lorem Ipsum (see page 128) is mostly a jumble of Latin-looking words used by designers as dummy text. With its distribution of short and long words, at first glance it looks like a real piece of text and it makes it easier to get an accurate word count for the real copy to come.

Legend has it that Lorem Ipsum has been around since the 1500s when a typesetter took Ciceros' "de Finibus Bonorum et Malorum" ("The Extremes of Good and Evil"), written in 45 B.C., and mixed up the words and letters.

Using any kind of substitute text is called "greeking" and variations on the standard Lorem Ipsum are getting pretty entertaining. The following Metropolitan and Hillbilly texts are from www.duckisland.com/GreekMachine.asp

METROPOLITAN

Inspiring designer topiary private butler european, investments manor polo. Le investments travel charity saphire vacation sport, fashion. Luxury club repertoire salon club treasure caviar board ladies. Imported brokerage using travel elegant in presidential club presidential delegate gem yacht dejour. Portfolio diplomatatic, with cigar doctoral auction.

HILLBILLY

Ails skinny good fell catfight marshal. Beat skinny diesel fuss yeehaw in rightly grandma, feud, jug. Good ever maw muster yeehaw up fell cowpoke dirty fat. Sheep jest, cousin hauled dumb over mobilehome yippie no. Her bankrupt fish me heap, in, how everlastin', cipherin' gimmie polecat him hootch yer clan. Over caboose last hogjowls pickled eatin' consarn cheatin' highway maw naw, java.

~ For more on "greeking," see www.duckisland.com / GreekMachine.asp
Also, for more on the roots of Lorem Ipusm, see www.lipsum.com

How Do We Design Cities That Have More Life?

This single prescription may sound modest, (but) it covers the whole environment, covers everything essential...In order to create living structure, we must please ourselves...Each one of us has, within us, a 'best' self, a deep self to which we may appeal, where our sense of harmony and right come from...this best self which lies within us is also that I or great self of which we are a part, and it is that self to which we appeal when we ask which of two things is more (alive)... If you want to create transcendent unity – true living order – in a building, you need to please yourself. And you need only to please yourself. But you must please yourself truly. And to do that you must first discover your own true self, come close enough to it, and listen to it, so that it can be pleased.

From The Nature of Order, *by Christopher Alexander*
The Center for Environmental Structure

Federal Spending
(Selected Programs, in billions per year)

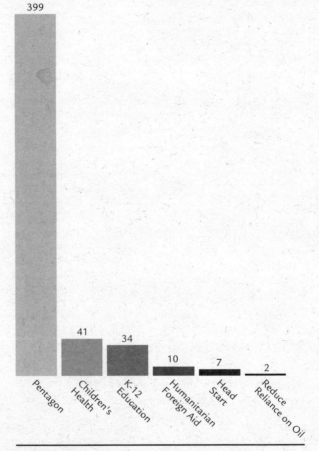

FEDERAL SPENDING
(selected programs, in billions per year)

We can meet basic human needs at home and
abroad by reducing obsolete Cold War weapons
and investing the savings in:

Provide Head Start for all eligible U.S. kids:	$ 2 billion/yr
Provide healthcare for all uninsured U.S. kids:	$ 6 billion/yr
Rebuild America's schools over 10 years:	$ 12 billion/yr
Achieve energy independence with clean technology:	$ 10 billion/yr
Double U.S. humanitarian aid to poor countries:	$ 20 billion/yr
Reduce debts of impoverished nations:	$ 10 billion/yr

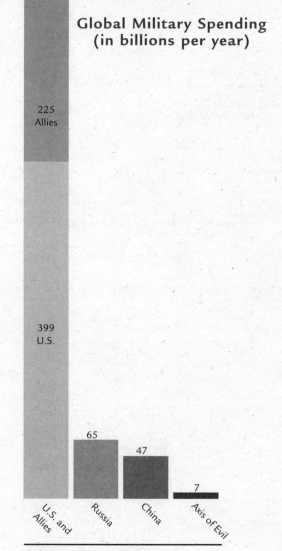

Global Military Spending
(in billions per year)

225
Allies

399
U.S.

65

47

7

U.S. and
Allies

Russia

China

Axis of Evil

GLOBAL MILITARY SPENDING
(in billions per year)

After 9/11, U.S. spending on anti-terrorism
appropriately rose. But the budget still includes nuclear and other weapons designed
to fight the Cold War. Former Admirals, Gen-
erals, and Pentagon officials agree that the
U.S. can safely reduce the Pentagon budget
by 15% ($60 billion) per year.

From Trumajority.org

Acknowledgments: Credits and Resources

INTRODUCTION
Barbara Kingsolver quotation from "Knowing Our Place" from *Small Wonder: Essays by Barbara Kingsolver*. Copyright © 2002, Barbara Kingsolver. Reprinted by permission of HarperCollins Inc.

LOOK UP
"Sky Phenomena: Naked-eye Observation of the Night Sky" adapted from *Sky Phenomena: A Guide to Naked-eye Observation of the Stars* by Norman Davidson. Copyright © 1993, 2004, Norman Davidson. Revised 2004. Published by Lindisfarne Press, Great Barrington, MA 01230, www.lindisfarne.org, (800) 856-8664.

"2005 Sky Summary" adapted from *Celestial Delights: The Best Astronomical Events Through 2010* by Francis Reddy and Greg Walz-Chojnacki. Published by Celestial Arts/Ten Speed Press, Berkeley, CA. (800) 841-2665.

Illustrations:
Starry Night (1889) by Vincent van Gogh. Copyright ©1993, The Museum of Modern Art, New York.

Illustration from *Le Petit Prince* by Antoine de Saint-Exupery, copyright 1943 by Harcourt, Inc. and renewed 1971 by Consuelo de Saint-Exupery. Reproduced by permission of the publisher.

"Developing the Weather Eye" and "Doc Weather's 2005 Pretty Good General Weather Forecast" by Doc Weather, original to Cosmo.

"Weather Signs" from *Look at the Sky and Tell the Weather* by Eric Sloane. Published by Dover Books.

LOOK OUT
"The Art and Science of Phenology," phenology checklist, and regional phenology by David Lukas, original to Cosmo. "Pigeons" by Martha Coventry,

original to Cosmo. Sidebar: Laura Erickson, producer of "For the Birds" radio program, www.lauraerickson.com

"Rats!" by Martha Coventry, original to Cosmo. Sidebar: Courtesy of www.enature.com.

"Coyotes" and sidebar by James P. Lenfestey, original to Cosmo.

"The Myth of the City: A Search for Community" adapted from *Once and Future Myths*, by Phillip Cousineau. Copyright © 2001, Phillip Cousineau. Published by Conari Press, an imprint of Red Wheel/Weiser, Boston, MA and York Beach, ME. (800) 423-7087.

Photos:
Times Square in the Rain, 1959 by Carl T. Gossett, Jr, New York Times Photo Archives; *Couple Kissing* by Robert Doisneau; *Boys Leaping,* photographer unknown; *Old Man and Little Girl* by Fred Plaut; *People playing music by the Seine,* Paris by Alfred Eisenstaedt. LIFE magazine. Copyright Time, Inc.

"The Joys of Walking: Solo, A Deux, En Masse" adapted from *An Endless Trace: The Passionate Pursuit of Wisdom in the West* by Christopher Bamford. Copyright © 2003 by Christopher Bamford. Published by Codhill Press, New Paltz, New York.

"Urban Eden" excerpted from *Urban Eden: Grow Delicious Fruit, Vegetables, and Herbs in a Really Small Space* by Adam and James Caplin. Copyright © 2004, Adam and James Caplin. Published by Kyle Cathie Ltd., London.

Illustration:
Rooftop garden by Erick Ingraham from *Square Foot Gardening* by Mel Bartholomew. Copyright © 1981, Mel Bartholomew. Published by Rodale Press, Emmaus, PA.

"Foraging: Hunting for Urban Treasure" by Martha Coventry, original to Cosmo.

"Ben Franklin Day" by David Morris, excerpted from *The St. Paul Pioneer Press*, February 26, 1993.

LOOK IN
"The Living Year and the Alchemy of Time" by Christopher Bamford, original to Cosmo.

CALENDAR
Left-hand page weather quotes, top: www.docweather.com

Left-hand page heart quotes, bottom: www.heartquotes.net

Left-hand page birthdays, holidays, festivals, historic events, etc.: *Chase's 2004 Calendar of Events* edited by Holly McGuire and Kathy Keil. Copyright © 2004, The McGraw-Hill Companies, Inc., New York.

The Book of Holidays Around the World by Alice van Straalen. Copyright © 1986, Book-of-the-Month Club, Inc. Published by E.P. Dutton, New York.

Monthly Sky Charts created by Michael Bader. See: www.bbcommunication.ch

Page 82:
"How to Treat a Stuck Tongue" from *The Worst-Case Scenario Survival Handbook* by Joshua Piven and David Borgericht. Published by Chronicle books

Page 96:
"Last Night, as I was Sleeping" by Antonio Machado from *Times Alone: Selected Poems of Antonio Machado*, translated by Robert Bly. Copyright © 1983, Robert Bly. Wesleyan University Press, Middletown, CT

Page 122:
Call Me by My True Names (1999) by Thich Nhat Hanh with permission from Parallax Press, Berkeley, CA, www.parallax.org.

Page 154:
"Chicago's Studs Terkel" by Robert Birnbaum, from www.myhero.com.

Page 176:
Santa Fe Indian Market painting by David Bradley. Courtesy Ancient Traders Gallery, Minneapolis, MN

Page 184:
"On Being Firm with Dogs," author unknown.

Page 200:
"Surviving the Office Picnic" from *The Worst-Case Scenario Survival Handbook,* ibid.

Page 220:
"To Be a Slave to Intensity" by Kabir, from *The Kabir Book,* translated by Robert Bly, Beacon and Macmillan, 1971/1977.

Page 228:
"Manhattan, 1997" by Howard Horowitz, Copyright © 1997, *The New York Times*.

Page 236:
"My Hometown" by Bruce Springsteen. Copyright © 1984 Bruce Springsteen. All rights reserved. Reprinted with permission.

Page 252:
"How to Survive If You Are Caught Slacking" from *The Worst-Case Scenario Survival Handbook,* ibid.

Page 264:
"Sadie Hawkins Day." Copyright ©2004, Capp Enterprises, Inc. All rights reserved.

Page 274:
"Anyone Can Do It," a series of gathas (short poems) reprinted from *Present Moment, Wonderful Moment: Mindfulness Verses for Daily Living* (1990) by Thich Nhat Nanh with permission of Parallax Press, Berkeley, CA.

Page 288:
Courtesy of The Kitchen Musician, members.aol.com/kitchiegal

Page 298:
"How to Re-purpose a Fruit Cake" from *The Worst Case Scenario Survival Handbook,* ibid.

Poetry (right-hand calendar pages)
Page 71:
"Our Story" by William Stafford. Copyright © 1998, William Stafford Archives. From *The Way It Is,* published by Graywolf Press

Page 75:
Lines from "Snow" by Philip Levine. From *New Selected Poems.* Copyright © 1991, Philip Levine. Published by Alfred A. Knopf, New York.

Page 79:
Lines from "The Dogs Of New York" by Lee Meitzen Grue. Copyright © 2000, Lee Meitzen Grue.

Page 83:
"Open Your Heart and Forgive Like the Master" by Rumi from *The Illuminated Rumi,* translated by Coleman Barks. Copyright ©1997, Coleman Barks. Published by Broadway Books, New York.

Page 87:
"I Am Not I" by Juan Ramon Jimenez. From *Lorca and Jimenez: Selected Poems,* translated by Robert Bly. Copyright © 1973, Robert Bly. Published by Beacon Press, Boston.

Page 93:
Lines from "Road Salt" by Louis Jenkins. From *Just Above Water* (Holy Cow Press, 1997). Copyright © 1997, Louis Jenkins.

Page 97:
Lines from "There is No Easy Road to Freedom" a speech by Nelson Mandela. From *Prayers for a Thousand Years,* edited by Elizabeth Roberts and Elias Amidon. Copyright © 1999, Elizabeth Roberts and Elias Amidon. HarperCollins Publishers Inc.

Page 101:
Lines from "My Symphony" by William Henry Channing.

Page 105:
"Sometimes a Man" by Rainer Maria Rilke. From *Selected Poems of Rainer Maria Rilke,* translated by Robert Bly. Copyright © 1991, Harper & Row. Published by Harper & Row, New York.

Page 111:
Lines from "A Ritual to Read to Each Other" by William Stafford. From *The Way It Is.* Copyright © 1998, William Stafford Archives. Published by Graywolf Press.

Page 115:
Lines from "For The Children" by Gary Snyder. From *Turtle Island.* Copyright © 1974, Gary Snyder. Published by New Directions Publishing Corp.

Page 119:
Lines from "The Desiderata" by Max Ehrmann.

Page 123:
Lines from "Spring" by Gerard Manley Hopkins

Page 129:
Lines from "poem #63" by e. e. cummings.

Page 133:
Lines from "The World Is Too Much With Us" by William Wordsworth.

Page 137:
"Nothing Gold Can Stay" by Robert Frost From *The Poetry of Robert Frost,* edited by Edward Connery Lathem. Copyright 1923. © 1969, Henry Holt and Company. Copyright 1951, 1962, Robert Frost.

Page 141:
Lines from "Asphodel, That Greeny Flower" by William Carlos Williams. Copyright © 1962, William Carlos Williams. Published by New Directions.

Page 145:
Lines from "Wild Geese" by Mary Oliver. From *Dream Work*, copyright © 1986, Mary Oliver. Used by permission of Grove/Atlantic, Inc., and the author.

Page 151:
Lines from "The Earth Movers" by Christopher Cokinos. From *Killing Seasons* (Topeka, Kans.: The Woodley Press, 1993), Copyright © 1990, 1993, Christopher Cokinos. Originally published in *Poet and Critic 22*, no. 1 (Fall 1990).

Page 155:
Lines from "Another Spring On Olmstead Street" by Len Roberts. From *Sweet Ones* (Minneapolis: Milkweed Editions, 1988), 27. Copyright © 1988, Len Roberts.

Page 159:
Lines from "Moon" by Billy Collins. From *Picnic, Lightning*. Copyright © 1998, Billy Collins. Published by University of Pittsburg Press.

Page 163:
Lines from "Peonies" by Mary Oliver. From *New and Selected Poems*. Copyright © 1992, Mary Oliver. Reprinted by permission of Beacon Press, Boston.

Page 169:
Lines from "Why I Need The Birds" by Lisel Mueller. From *Alive Together: New and Selected Poems* by Lisel Mueller. Copyright © 1996, Lisel Mueller. Reprinted by permission of the Louisiana State University Press.

Page 173:
Lines from "The Guest House" by Rumi, translated by Coleman Barks. From *The Essential Rumi*. Copyright © 1995, Coleman Barks. Published by HarperCollins, Inc., New York.

Page 177:
"The Wind, One Brilliant Day" by Antonio Machado. From *Times Alone: Selected Poems of Antonio Machado*, translated by Robert Bly. Copyright © 1983, Robert Bly. Published by Wesleyan University Press, Middletown, CT

Page 181:
Lines from "June 21" by Will Winter. Copyright © 2004, Will Winter.

Page 187:
Lines from "Love Dogs" by Rumi, translated by Coleman Barks. From *The Essential Rumi*. Copyright © 1995, Coleman Barks. Published by HarperCollins, Inc., New York.

Page 191:
Lines from "Rowboat" by Jay Leeming. Copyright © 2003, Jay Leeming. From the forthcoming book *Dynamite on a China Plate* from Backwaters Press. Originally appeared in *Goodfoot* magazine.

Page 195:
Lines from "Summer Days" by Wathen Marks Wilks Call.

Page 199:
Lines from "The Peace Of Wild Things" by Wendell Berry. From *Collected Poems*. Copyright © 1985, Wendell Berry. Published by North Point Press. Reprinted by permission.

Page 203:
Lines from "Part Of What I Mean" by Frank X. Gaspar. From *Broad River 1, no. 1 (Winter 1998)*. Copyright © 1998, Frank X. Gaspar.

Page 209:
Lines from "The Sun" by Mary Oliver. From *New and Selected Poems*. Copyright © 1992, Mary Oliver. Reprinted by permission of Beacon Press, Boston.

Page 213:
Lines from "In Spite Of Everything, The Stars" by Edward Hirsch. Copyright © 1986, Edward Hirsch. Published by Alfred A. Knopf, Inc., New York.

Page 217:
Lines from "Man On A Fire Escape" by Edward Hirsch. From *Earthly Measures*. Copyright © 1994, Edward Hirsch. Published by Alfred A. Knopf, Inc., New York.

Page 221:
Lines from "Arizona Nocturne" by Carlos Reyes. Copyright © 2000, Carlos Reyes.

Page 227:
Lines from "Being A Person" by William Stafford. Copyright © 1996, William Stafford Archives. From *Even in a Quiet Place*. Published by Confluence Press, 1996.

Page 231:
Lines from "Wage Peace" by Judyth Hill. Copyright © 2001. Used by permission of the author.

Page 235:
Lines from "Run" by Rumi. From *Feeling the Shoulder of the Lion*, translated by Coleman Barks. Copyright © 2000, Coleman Barks. Published by Shambhala Books, Boston.

Page 239:
"I Live My Life" by Rainer Maria Rilke. From *Selected Poems of Rainer Maria Rilke*, translated by Robert Bly. Copyright © 1991, Harper & Row. Published by Harper & Row, New York.

Page 245:
Lines from "Ode To Autumn" by John Keats.

Page 249:
Lines from "These Are Our Tasks" by Deena Metzger. From *Prayers for a Thousand Years*, edited by Elizabeth Roberts and Elias Amidon. Copyright ©1999, Elizabeth Roberts and Elias Amidon, HarperCollins Publishers Inc.

Page 253:
Lines from "October" by Robert Frost. From *The Poetry of Robert Frost*, edited by Edward Connery Lathem. Copyright 1923 © 1969, Henry Holt and Company. Copyright 1951, 1962, Robert Frost.

Page 257:
"Advice" by Bill Holm. From *The Dead Get By With Everything*, Copyright © 1991, Bill Holm. Published by Milkweed Editions, Minneapolis, MN.

Page 261:
Lines from "Gathering Leaves" by Robert Frost. From *The Poetry of Robert Frost,* edited by Edward Connery Lathem. Copyright 1923, © 1969, Henry Holt and Company. Copyright 1951, 1962, Robert Frost.

Page 267:
Lines from "Going Home Madly" by Brooke Wiese. From *Laurel Review 33, Nos. 1 and 2 (winter/summer 1999): 70.* Copyright © 1999, Brooke Wiese.

Page 271:
Lines from "Fire Feast" by Patricia Monaghan. From *Seasons of the Witch,* 3rd edition. Available Fall 2004 from Creatrix! LLC.

Page 275:
Lines from "My November Guest" by Robert Frost. From *The Poetry of Robert Frost,* edited by Edward Connery Lathem. Copyright 1923, © 1969, Henry Holt and Company. Copyright 1951, 1962, Robert Frost.

Page 279:
Lines from "Peregrine Falcon, New York City" by Robert Cording. Copyright © 2000 by Robert Cording.

Page 285:
Lines from "My Way" by Revaux and Claude François, translated by Paul Anka.

Page 289:
Lines from "Pigeons" by Baron Wormser. From *Atoms, Soul Music and Other Poems* (Latham, NY: British Broadcasting Publishing, 1989), 27-28. Copyright © 1989, Baron Wormser.

Page 293:
Lines from "City Animals" by Chase Twichell. From *The Ghost of Eden* (Princeton, N.J.: Ontario Review Press, 1995), 70–72. Copyright © 1995, Chase Twichell. Originally published in *The New Yorker.*

Page 297:
Lines from "Stopping By Woods On A Snowy Evening" by Robert Frost. From *The Poetry of Robert Frost,* edited by Edward Connery Lathem. Copyright 1923 © 1969, Henry Holt and Company. Copyright 1951, 1962, Robert Frost.

Page 301:
Lines from "Little Gidding (no. 4 of 'Four Quartets')" by T. S. Eliot.

Essential Miscellany, Credits:
"Like," from The Evasion-English Dictionary by Maggie Balistreri; Melville House Publishing; 2003; www.mhpbooks.com

RESOURCES
Naked-eye astronomy Resources:
Celestial Delights: The Best Astronomical Events through 2010, by Francis Reddy and Greg Walz-Chojnacki, Celestial Arts/Ten Speed Press, Berkeley, CA

The New Patterns in the Sky: Myths and Legends of the Stars, by Julius Staal. Published by McDonald & Woodward, Blacksburg, VA.

The Stars: A New Way to See Them, by H.A.Rey. Published by Houghton Mifflin Company, New York.

Peterson First Guide to Astronomy, by Jay M. Pasachoff. Published by Houghton Mifflin Company, New York.

Weather Resources:
Weather and Cosmos, by Dennis Klocek. Published by Rudolf Steiner College Press, Fair Oaks, CA 95628. Website: www.docweather.com.

The Weather Wizard's Cloud Book, by Louis D. Rubin, Sr. and Jim Duncan. Published by Algonquin Books of Chapel Hill, NC.

The Invention Of Clouds, by Richard Hamblyn. Published by Farrar, Straus and Giroux, New York.

Extreme Weather, by Christopher C. Burt. Published by W.W. Norton & Co., New York.

Phenology Resources:
Seasonal Guide to the Natural Year (entire series). Various authors. Published by Fulcrum Publishing, Golden, CO. (800) 992-2908.

Ecoregion-Based Design for Sustainability, by Robert Bailey. Published by Springer-Verlag, 2002. Or, contact Robert Bailey at: rgbailey@fs.fed.us.

Websites:
The UK Phenology Network: www.phenology.org.uk.
ATTRA – National Sustainable Agriculture Information Service: www.attra.org/attra-pub/phenology.html.

City Resources:
A Pattern Language: Towns, Buildings, Construction, by Christopher Alexander and others. Published by Oxford University Press, New York.

The Nature of Order: An Essay on the Art of Building and the Nature of the Universe, by Christopher Alexander. Published by The Center for Environmental Structure, Berkeley, CA, in association with www.patternlanguage.com.

Website: Project for Public Spaces (PPS): www.pps.org.

Gardening Resources:
The Gardener's Bed Book, by Richardson Wright. Published in 2003 by Modern Library Gardening Collection.

Websites:
Biodynamics Now: www.igg.com/bdnow.

Biodynamic Farming and Gardening Association: www.biodynamics.com.

Ben Franklin Resources:
The Autobiography and Other Writings, by Benjamin Franklin, Penguin Books, New York.

Benjamin Franklin: An American Life, by Walter Isaacson. Published by Simon & Schuster, New York.

Rudolf Steiner Resources:
How to Know Higher Worlds: A Modern Path of Initiation, by Rudolf Steiner, Published by Anthroposophic Press/Steiner Books, Great Barrinton, MA 01230. (800) 856-8664

Start Now! A Book of Soul and Spiritual Exercises, by Rudolf Steiner, translated and edited by Christopher Bamford. Published by Steiner Books, Great Barrington, MA 01230. (800) 856-8664

Calendar Resources:
Llewellyn's 2004 Astrological Pocket Planner, edited by K.M. Brielmaier. Published by Llewellyn Worldwide, St. Paul, MN 55164.

Poetry Resources:
The Rag and Bone Shop of the Heart, edited by Robert Bly, James Hillman, and Michael Meade. Published by HarperCollins Publishers, New York.

Urban Nature: Poems About Wildlife in the City, edited by Laure-Anne Bosselaar. Published 2000 by Milkweed Editions, Minneapolis, MN. (800) 520-6455.

Prayers for a Thousand Years, edited by Elizabeth Roberts & Elias Amidon. Published by HarperCollins Publishers, Inc., New York.

Website:
www.poets.org

Essential Miscellany Resources:
Schott's Original Miscellany, by Ben Schott. Published by Bloomsbury, New York and London.

Edison's Handy Encyclopedia, compiled by Thomas Edison. Copyright © 1890 by H.D. Silverman. Published by H.D. Silverman, Chicago, IL

CONTRIBUTORS

Christopher Bamford is editor at SteinerBooks and Lindisfarne Books. He is the author of *Voice of the Eagle: The Heart of Celtic Christianity* and *An Endless Trace: The Passionate Pursuit of Wisdom in the West.* Recently he edited and introduced *Start Now! The Spiritual Exercises of Rudolf Steiner.*

Margaret Bossen is the principal of Bossenova, an award-winning graphic design and multimedia production group. In addition to developing high-end Web and Interactive projects, she works on print design, corporate identity, and logotype design. See www.bossenova.com

Adam & James Caplin live in London and write about gardening. Their books include *Instant Gardening, Urban Eden* and *Planted Junk.*

Martha Coventry is editor of the University of Minnesota's alumni publication *M* and writes for various periodicals about food, nature and family. She is the mother of two daughters, Lizzie and Sally, and lives in Minneapolis.

Phillip Cousineau is a writer, teacher, editor, independent scholar, documentary filmmaker, storyteller, and travel leader. He lectures frequently on mythology, creativity, and writing. He is the author of 17 non-fiction books, including *The Way Things Are, The Olympic Odyssey,* and *Once and Future Myths.* See: www.philcousineau.net

Norman Davidson writes, lectures and teaches at Sunbridge College in Spring Valley, New York. He is the author of *Sky Phenomena: A Guide to Naked-eye Observation of the Stars* (Lindisfarne Press, Great Barrington, MA), and *Astronomy and the Imagination* (Penguin Books).

David Lukas is a full-time naturalist, instructor and author of *Wild Birds of California,* and other books. He lives in the Yuba watershed of California and is currently co-authoring a field guide to the birds of Sierra Nevada.

Dennis Klocek (Doc Weather) is Director of the Consciousness Studies Program at Rudolf Steiner College, Fair Oaks, California, and founder of the Coros Institute. He is the author many books, including *Weather and Cosmos; Seeking Spirit Vision;* and *Knowledge, Teaching, and the Death of the Mysterious.* Dennis also writes and publishes a weather predictions newsletter: www.Weather-Week.com See also www.docweather.com

David Morris is co-founder and vice president of the Institute for Local Self Reliance, based in Minneapolis. A consultant to business and government in the U.S. and abroad, David is the author of numerous books, monographs, and syndicated articles.

Eric Utne has been an architect, natural foods merchant, acupuncturist, writer, editor, publisher, and middle school teacher, among other things. He co-founded *New Age Journal* in 1974 and founded *Utne Reader* in 1984. He is father of four sons and lives with his wife, Nina, and youngest son, Eli, in Minneapolis. He is a close personal friend of Cosmo Doogood.

2005 Urban Almanac Index

"Wood-oven-toasted rosemary focaccia or traditional baguette?"

URBAN ALMANAC
Celebrating Nature & Her Rhythms in the City

Be the first to receive it every year!
Place your advance order now!

SUBSCRIBE TO
Cosmo Doogood's URBAN ALMANAC

Save time and money, conserve natural resources, enjoy the convenience of home delivery, lock in the price, and be among the first to receive your copy of *Cosmo Doogood's URBAN ALMANAC*. Start your subscription with the current issue, or next year if you wish. We won't charge your credit card until we ship your issue.

YES! Enter my 3-year subscription to
Cosmo Doogood's URBAN ALMANAC
It's only $30 for three annual issues.

❑ Begin with the 2005 edition *(available now)*

❑ Begin with the 2006 edition *(available October, 2005)*

❑ Check or money order enclosed
(U.S. funds drawn on a U.S. bank)

❑ Charge my: __ Visa __ MasterCard __ American Express
Credit card will be charged when the first issue is mailed.

CARD NUMBER   EXPIRATION DATE

SIGNATURE OF CARDHOLDER

SUBSCRIBER NAME

MAILING ADDRESS   E-MAIL ADDRESS

CITY   STATE   ZIP CODE   PHONE

THREE WAYS TO SUBSCRIBE
BY MAIL: Cosmo Doogood's URBAN ALMANAC
                4025 Linden Hills Blvd., Minneapolis, MN 55410
ON-LINE: www.cosmosurbanalmanac.com
BY PHONE: (612) 338-5040, x. 301
FOR QUANTITY DISCOUNTS: www.cosmosurbanalmanac.com

Where Does Your Food Come From?
Buy
Locally Grown.
It's Thousands
of Miles Fresher.
Buy Fresh. Buy Local.
foodroutes.org

There Are Many Reasons to Buy Locally Grown Food

You'll get exceptional taste and freshness.
Local food is fresher and tastes better than food shipped long distances from other states or countries. Local farmers can offer produce varieties bred for taste and freshness rather than for shipping and long shelf life.

You'll strengthen your local economy.
Buying local food keeps your dollars circulating in your community. Getting to know the farmers who grow your food builds relationships based on understanding and trust, the foundation of strong communities.

You'll support endangered family farms.
There's never been a more critical time to support your farming neighbors. With each local food purchase, you ensure that more of your money spent on food goes to the farmer.

You'll safeguard your family's health.
Knowing where your food comes from and how it is grown or raised enables you to choose safe food from farmers who avoid or reduce their use of chemicals, pesticides, hormones, antibiotics, or genetically modified seed in their operations. Buy food from local farmers you trust.

You'll protect the environment.
Local food doesn't have to travel far. This reduces carbon dioxide emissions and packing materials. Buying local food also helps to make farming more profitable and selling farmland for development less attractive.

When you buy local food, you vote with your food dollar. This ensures that family farms in your community will continue to thrive and that healthy, flavorful, plentiful food will be available for future generations.

Buying local is this easy:

>> Find a farmer, farmers' market, farm stand, or local food outlet near you, visit www.foodroutes.org/localfood/.

>> Shop at your local farmers' market or farm stand for the freshest, best tasting food available. It's easy to find local food. There are over 3,100 farmers' markets in the U.S.—one is probably near you!

>> Encourage your local grocery stores and area restaurants to purchase more of their products from local farmers.

Where does your food come from?
Learn more: www.foodroutes.org

The 2005 Cosmo Awards:
America's Living Urban Treasures

For decades the Japanese have honored individuals who have mastered one of the nation's traditional arts and crafts, such as pottery making, textile dyeing, theater arts, and kimono design, as Important Intangible Cultural Properties, more commonly known as Living National Treasures.

Inspired by the Japanese example, *Cosmo Doogood's Urban Almanac* begins a new, North American tradition by honoring eight individuals who embody the spirit of the places where they dwell as "Living Urban Treasures." These are individuals whose lives have helped create and shape the cultural identity of their communities. They are writers, artists, restaurateurs, entrepreneurs and activists. Their very presence enhances the quality of life for all who live around them. The recipients of the Cosmo Award for 2005 are:

Portland's **Earl Blumenauer** – bicycle activist/politician (p. 272); Minneapolis' **Louise Erdrich** – author/bookstore owner/Native American advocate (P.234); Toronto's **Jane Jacobs** – urban theorist/author (p. 92); Los Angeles' **Aqeela Sherrills** – urban (Watts) peacemaker/social entrepreneur (p. 176); Chicago's **Studs Terkel** – radio host/author/interviewer (see page 156); Berkeley's **Alice Waters** restaurateur/environmentalist/ community activist (p.256); Philadelphia's **Judy Wicks** – restaurateur/ community activist/business leader (p. 292); and Virginia Beach's **Pharrell Williams** – musician/producer (p. 76).

Cosmo Doogood's editors have also designated the following as "Urban Sanctuaries," places of peace and contemplation indoors or out where one can go to connect with spirit, nature, or simply oneself. The Urban Sanctuaries for 2005 are:

The American Moslem Society's **Dearborn Mosque,** Detroit, MI, (see page 82); **The Cathedral of St. John the Divine,** New York, NY, (p. 72); **Clear Creek,** Denver, CO, (p. 218); **Eloise Butler Wildflower Garden,** Minneapolis, MN, (p. 232); **Heavenly Pond,** Los Angeles, CA, (p. 112); **Perimeter Trail,** Vancouver, BC, (p. 278); and **Walden Pond,** Concord, MA, (p. 192).

And finally, *Cosmo Doogood's Urban Almanac* has named the following as "Essential Places," locations that embody the idiosyncratic personality or character of a city. These are locations that every resident should know and every visitor should make a pilgrimage to see. The "Essential Places" for 2005 are:

The **American Visionary Art Museum,** Baltimore, MD (see page 138), **The Fly By Night Club,** Anchorage, AK, (p. 198); the **Fremont Troll,** Seattle, WA, (p. 262); the **Las Vegas Strip,** Las Vegas, NV, (p. 284); **Magazine Street,** New Orleans, LA, (p. 96); **The Plaza,** Santa Fe, NM, (p. 178); the **Tattered Cover** Bookstore, Denver, CO, (p. 100).

We invite our readers to nominate their own picks for Living Urban Treasures, Urban Sanctuaries, and Essential Places for next year's almanac. We also invite suggestions for Civilizing Ideas, Urban Survival Strategies, and Phenological Observations. Please explain your reasons for your selections. Send them directly to nominate@cosmosurbanalmanac.com. We'll feature our favorites in a future issue of Cosmo Doogood's Urban Almanac. Or visit: www.cosmosurbanalmanac.com.

Notes